GERMANY & THE POLITICS OF NUCLEAR WEAPONS

Germany and the Politics of Nuclear Weapons is one of a series of studies sponsored by the Institute of War and Peace Studies of Columbia University. Among those Institute studies also dealing with war, peace, and national security are *Defense and Diplomacy*, by Alfred Vagts; *Man, the State, and War*, by Kenneth N. Waltz; *The Common Defense*, by Samuel P. Huntington; *Changing Patterns of Military Politics*, edited by Samuel P. Huntington; *Strategy, Politics, and Defense Budgets*, by Warner R. Schilling, Paul Y. Hammond, and Glenn H. Snyder; *Stockpiling Strategic Materials*, by Glenn H. Snyder; *The Politics of Military Unification*, by Demetrios Caraley; *NATO and the Range of American Choice*, by William T. R. Fox and Annette Baker Fox; *The Politics of Weapons Innovation: The Thor-Jupiter Controversy*, by Michael H. Armacost; *The Politics of Policy Making in Defense and Foreign Affairs*, by Roger Hilsman; *Inspection for Disarmament*, edited by Seymour Melman; *To Move a Nation*, by Roger Hilsman, jointly sponsored with the Washington Center of Foreign Policy Research, Johns Hopkins University; *Planning, Prediction, and Policy-Making in Foreign Affairs*, by Robert L. Rothstein; *The Origins of Peace*, by Robert F. Randle; *European Security and the Atlantic System*, edited by William T. R. Fox and Warner R. Schilling; *American Arms and a Changing Europe: Dilemmas of Deterrence and Disarmament,* by Warner R. Schilling, William T. R. Fox, Catherine M. Kelleher, and Donald J. Puchala; *The Cold War Begins: Soviet-American Conflict Over Eastern Europe*, by Lynn E. Davis; and *The Crouching Future: International Politics and U.S. Foreign Policy—a Forecast*, by Roger Hilsman.

GERMANY & THE POLITICS OF NUCLEAR WEAPONS

CATHERINE M^cARDLE KELLEHER

Columbia University Press ✠ *New York and London*
1975

Catherine McArdle Kelleher is Associate Professor of Political Science and Faculty Associate of the Center for Political Studies, Institute for Social Research, at the University of Michigan.

LIBRARY OF CONGRESS CATALOGING IN PUBLICATION DATA

Kelleher, Catherine McArdle.
  Germany and the politics of nuclear weapons.

  Includes bibliographical references and index.
  1. Germany (Federal Republic, 1949–   )—
Politics and government.   2. Atomic weapons and
disarmament.   3. North Atlantic Treaty organization—Germany (Federal Republic, 1949–   )
4. Germany (Federal Republic, 1949–   )—Defenses.
I.   Title.
HD9698.G42K44   327.43   75-16168
ISBN   0-231-03960-3

IN MEMORIAM

✠

Catherine Roche McArdle
Francis Xavier McArdle
who believed

FOREWORD

As DIRECTOR of the Institute of War and Peace Studies, I am happy to welcome *Germany and the Politics of Nuclear Wapons* as the latest addition to the list of Institute-sponsored monographs in which questions of politico-military policy are analyzed in the twin contexts of domestic and world politics. In today's world significant decisions affecting alliance patterns and the distribution of nuclear arms are still national decisions made by national governments, and country studies of the politics leading up to those decisions are invaluable. *Germany and the Politics of Nuclear Weapons* completes a trilogy of such country studies for all three of the major defense partners of the United States in the Atlantic Alliance. The first two, Wilfrid L. Kohl's *French Nuclear Diplomacy* (1971) and Andrew M. Pierre's *Nuclear Politics: The British Experience with an Independent Strategic Force, 1939–1970* (1972), deal with the policies of countries which opted to develop a nuclear capability, while Professor Kelleher describes the making of nuclear policy for the only one of Europe's "second-tier" powers that has not developed a nuclear striking force. The three studies all reflect the authors' association with the Columbia group of scholars interested in strategic studies and European security. Catherine M. Kelleher was formerly a Research Associate in the Institute of War and Peace Studies; Dr. Kohl and Dr. Pierre are authors of Columbia dissertations out of which grew their published studies of French and British Policy.

Professor Kelleher had remarkable success in interviewing a broad and representative sample of the most influential contributors to the making of West German nuclear weapons policy. She has given us a monograph which does several different things and does all of them well: (1) she presents an authoritative and detailed account of the development of German policy on nuclear weapons during a critical time period; (2) she relates the development of that policy to major shifts in over-all German foreign policy; (3) she provides an important case study in the history of efforts to control the spread of nuclear weapons; (4) she relates problems in alliance relationships to the internal needs of interest groups, including bureaucratic interests in the Federal Republic; and, finally, (5) she enhances the relevance of her study of German policy in a critical period by tracing its consequences from the mid-1960s to the mid-1970s. The result is both good, solid history and subtle political analysis.

WILLIAM T. R. FOX

ACKNOWLEDGMENTS

ANY BOOK REFLECTS AN AUTHOR'S ODYSSEY—the places of work and rumination, the intellectual debts and financial dependencies incurred. The odyssey underlying this book has been long and varied, even at points arduous. But its principal hallmark has been at every stage the generous assistance and encouraging support of institutions and individuals who here receive quite inadequate due.

The odyssey's origin was a doctoral dissertation prepared in the Department of Political Science at the Massachusetts Institute of Technology. Professor William W. Kaufmann was as wise and patient a chairman as earlier he had been an inspiring guide to the field of national security studies. The thesis experience proved him skilled not only in transatlantic criticism but also in the retranslation of German-ese. Professors Fred Iklé and Gene Skolnikoff were most helpful committee members; Lincoln Bloomfield, Karl Deutsch, Norman Padelford, and Ithiel deSola Pool provided continuing encouragement. Appreciation must also go to the Lerner project group— Professor Daniel Lerner, Dr. Marguerite Kramer, and Dr. Morton Gorden— which provided the rudiments of a "European education" as well as one of the basic stimuli for the study.

Much of the original research was conducted during an eighteen-month stay in Bonn and Paris, supported by a Western European Foreign Area fellowship from the Ford Foundation. The warm interest and generous hospitality of the late Wilhelm Cornides and of Uwe Nerlich made the Forschungsinstitut of the Deutsche Gesellschaft für Auswärtige Politik the principal base for both interviewing and library research. Without this base, and the contacts and unique perspectives it provided, the study would have been measurably less succesful. Special thanks must also go to Dr. Wolfgang Wagner who continued the Cornides tradition of hospitality, to Drs. Helga Haftendorn and Charles Planck of the Institute, to Gesellschaft librarians Gisela Gottwald and Hanna Jahde.

The book itself is far more the product of a long association—first as Research Associate, then as sometime visitor—with the Institute of War and Peace Studies of Columbia University. The generous support and personal interest, as well as the critical judgments and guidance, of both William T.

R. Fox, Institute Director, and of Warner R. Schilling, occasional Acting Director, have been unfailing. Without them, quite simply, the book would not have been completed. A major debt, too, is owed other Institute associates—Annette Baker Fox, Wil Kohl, Andrew Pierre, and Don Puchala—whose comments both on the manuscript itself and in the context of collaboration on the Institute's European security project proved insightful and provocative.

The later stages of manuscript preparation were facilitated by help from two other sources. The German Research Program of Harvard University, under its acting director Guido Goldmann, provided some needed release time as well as an exciting forum for discussion and reconsideration. The Department of Political Science at the University of Illinois at Chicago Circle, under first Richard Johnson and then David Leege, kindly underwrote certain typing and research expenses.

Special thanks must go to the many friends and colleagues who were along for all or part of the journey. David Schoenbaum, Fred Spotts, Ulf Baring, and Bob McGeehan all prodded; Lew Edinger, Ethel Sheffer, and John Yochelson gave needed doses of moral support. Critical comments also came from Peter Katzenstein, Patricia McArdle, Doris Graber, Allen Whiting, Linda Miller, David Stauffer, Morris Janowitz, and Paul Hinniker.

Jane Schilling—as thorough and skilled an editor as ever was—contributed enormously to whatever literary grace the final manuscript possesses. Bernard Gronert and David Diefendorf of Columbia University Press provided insightful suggestions and good counsel. At all stages, the technical preparations were handled brilliantly. Anna Hohri's calm control proved most valuable at several critical junctures. Appreciation, too, must go to Regina McArdle and Dorothy Psomiades, Anita Worthington and Judith Sheehy, Susan Stauffer and Sarah Bird-Peczkowski, and Donna Gotts.

Throughout the journey, James J. Kelleher was always there.

CATHERINE MCARDLE KELLEHER
Ann Arbor, Michigan
May 1975

CONTENTS

✠ Abbreviations, Short Titles, and German Terms

ABC weapons	atomic, biological, chemical weapons
ABM	antiballistic missile
ADM	atomic demolition means
Amt Blank	Blank Office
ANF	Allied Nuclear Force
Bundestag	lower house of the parliament of the Federal Republic of Germany
Bundeswehr	armed forces of the Federal Republic of Germany
CDU	Christian Democratic Union
CSU	Christian Social Union
Die Zeit (NA)	*Die Zeit,* North American edition
EDC	European Defense Community
EEC	European Economic Community
Euratom	European Atomic Energy Community
FAZ	*Frankfurter Allgemeine Zeitung*
FDP	Free Democratic Party
Fraktion	members of a political party in the Bundestag
Führungsstab	Armed Forces Command Staff
Füssvolk	footsoldiers, infantry
GDR	German Democratic Republic
IAEA	International Atomic Energy Agency
ICBM	intercontinental ballistic missile
IRBM	intermediate-range ballistic missile
JCAE	Joint Committee on Atomic Energy
Kanzlerdemokratie	Federal Republic of Germany's constitutional system as modified by Adenauer's personal style
Land	state within the Federal Republic of Germany

MBFR	mutual balanced force reductions
MLF	multilateral nuclear force
MRBM	medium-range ballistic missile
MSB	Military Security Board
NATO	North Atlantic Treaty Organization
NPG	Nuclear Planning Group of NATO
NPT	nuclear nonproliferation treaty
NYT	*New York Times*
NYT (E)	*New York Times,* European edition
NZZ	*Neue Zürcher Zeitung*
Ostpolitik	policy of rapprochement with Eastern Europe
SAC	United States Strategic Air Command
SACEUR	Supreme Allied Commander Europe
SACLANT	Supreme Allied Commander Atlantic
SALT	Strategic Arms Limitation Talks
Schaukelpolitik	policy of playing off East and West against each other
SDZ	*Süddeutsche Zeitung*
SHAPE	Supreme Headquarters Allied Powers Europe
SPD	Social Democratic Party of Germany
WEU	Western European Union

GERMANY & THE POLITICS OF NUCLEAR WEAPONS

INTRODUCTION

✠ THE GERMANS AND NUCLEAR WEAPONS. In the decade before 1966, the conjunction of these words provided a central, continually provocative stimulus in all East-West political discourse. Within the Federal Republic of Germany itself these words were the catchwords of the most bitter of the postwar national debates. For Bonn's allies as well as for its opponents, the words called forth not only fears, past and present, of German militarism or anxieties about an acceptable role within the current European status quo for a rehabilitated, increasingly powerful Germany. The words also provided an effective domestic and international policy tool, allowing manipulation of those fears and ensuring the continuing constraint of Bonn's foreign policy. Indeed, by the mid-1960s some German policy-makers had themselves come to value and exploit this duality. One need note only the most dramatic instances, the invocation of potential German access to nuclear weapons in the campaigns for both the multilateral nuclear force (MLF) and the nuclear nonproliferation treaty (NPT), to recall the intensity and the paradoxical twists of the period's debates.

In the mid-1970s the silence prevailing about German ambitions or technical potential for imminent production of nuclear weapons is all but deafening. The intervening decade, to be sure, has witnessed momentous changes in world politics. Détente among the superpowers, "enemy brothers" in Raymond Aron's words, "who can't make war and can't make peace," seemingly reflects the slowly learned lessons about the limitations of thermonuclear power. In this new era, earlier conceptions of Atlantic partnership, of the North Atlantic Treaty Organization's functions and aims, have lost much of their meaning. And Bonn's Ostpolitik, its determined drive toward accommodation with its now willing Eastern neighbors, signified if nothing else the emergence of a somewhat independent, less cautious German foreign policy.

But even the magnitude of these changes does not fully provide answers to the central question addressed by this study: [1] How could issues concerning control of and access to nuclear weapons seem so central to German politics, to NATO planning, to East-West relations before 1966, but so remote and secondary now? The argument presented here is that key explanatory factors are to be found in the nuclear policy-making experiences of and the lessons learned by the Federal Republic during the period from 1954 to 1966. The insights gained through the analysis of the pattern of Bonn's policy and of the constraints on it, actual or perceived, illuminate both the causes of present German responses to détente and the need for refinements in present estimates regarding future nuclear-policy choices and strategies.

Accordingly, the study's approach is a detailed, chronologically organized reconstruction of the course and nature of German policies toward the use, control, and development of nuclear weapons during this twelve-year span. The study is based on original research begun in 1964 and carried out in the United States and Europe. The aim of the research effort was not to replicate the usual American or German secondary analyses, to update the too frequent free-floating speculations about German motives, or even to impose a logically derived model on past evidence. Rather, it was to find and analyze primary materials from a variety of sources—German and non-German, public and semi-secret—which would allow identification and assessment of the major international and national factors influencing German discussions and decisions.

A major thrust, therefore, was the examination of all available speeches and writings of leading German actors, both those prominent in international discussions and those active only in domestic political bargaining.[2] The purpose, largely fulfilled, was not to discover long explications of strategic rationale, but to identify political positions, recurring themes, and the language of domestic debate. A second task was a careful reading and checking of contemporary press accounts. A sample was drawn from available collections in Bonn and Paris; it included all of the Federal Republic's national newspapers as well as three non-German prestige papers. This allowed coverage of a broad spectrum of opinion and also partially corrected the errors resulting from the author's differential access to specific categories of information or to specific official actors.

The richest and most unusual data source, however, was a group of more than 125 interviews which the author conducted from 1964 to 1966 (with some reinterviews in 1968) with American, British, French, but primarily German officials and knowledgeables. These interviews (described more fully in the appendix) were long (some of them lasting more than three hours) and only loosely structured around a uniform set of questions. The goal was not to develop quantitatively significant results regarding elite opinions; this had already been done to a significant degree by others.[3] It was rather to develop an authoritative account of German nuclear policies and policy-making processes by probing the memories, attitudes, and self-perceptions of persons critically involved in particular developments or decisions.

The value of these interviews to this study is twofold. First, the chronological sequence and the pattern of political influence at every major point have been discussed whenever possible with at least three centrally placed German participants. There were, of course, the usual problems inherent in any process that relies on memory and ex post facto verification. But these personal accounts were systematically compared with contemporary press reports obtained from the press sources listed (along with the abbreviations of newspapers' names used in the notes and data on official German publications used) in the appendix. The data from the interviews and the newspapers were then cross-checked with the account of at least one non-German participant, obtained either from interviews or from available primary materials. Second, particularly telling comments from these interviews have been quoted throughout the text (but, as promised to participants, without direct attribution). This should indicate both the general tenor of the interviews and the range of outlooks captured.

With all this, the study has three significant aspects. First and most importantly, it constitutes a much-needed case study of a central aspect of the making of German foreign policy under Konrad Adenauer and his spiritual and chronological heir, Ludwig Erhard. From almost the first days of rearmament, questions of nuclear weapons use and control came to play special roles as both catalysts and capstones of German foreign policy. This focus, therefore, provides extraordinary insight into the central choices, dilemmas, and limits confronting a nation seeking international rehabilitation, yet formally committed to a triad of basic, purportedly equal and intertwined goals: security against the Soviet Union, equality within the Western alliance, and the eventual unity of the Germany of 1937. Second, the study provides an examination of the effects within and beyond NATO of Bonn's "American connection" on nuclear decision-making; and third, it throws some light on the degree to which aspects of the Adenauerian pattern of nuclear policy-making may be comparable to the experiences of other major nonnuclear states.

In large measure, the special role of nuclear policy in the Adenauer-

Erhard era neither was nor should have been an unexpected development. Any rational decision-making scheme applied to the Federal Republic of 1954–1966 would posit a very special German interest in the details of decisions about the use and control of nuclear weapons, always the cornerstone of the American or Western system within which German security was defined.[4] As the most exposed NATO member, the state on the central front seam, the self-proclaimed guardian of the welfare of the East Germans as well as that of the people of the Federal Republic, Bonn could rightly have viewed decisions on nuclear timing and targeting, for example, as life-and-death matters. Moreover, Adenauer's operational interpretation of the triad of goals, the renowned "policy of strength," placed primary emphasis on the attainment of security. For a Germany striving to reenter the international community, security was not just a present necessity; it was an essential precondition for achieving equality within the Atlantic and European spheres and for eventual national unity and diplomatic advantage in the East.

Indeed, there were many—in Washington and Paris, in the Pentagon and at RAND, as well as in Bonn—who saw grounds to expect the emergence of an independent German nuclear policy, including the acquisition of a national nuclear-weapons capability, within the short-range future. The assumptions underlying these expectations were quite diverse. Many believed that with the progress of rehabilitation, of rearmament, and of time itself, the reemergence of traditional German strategic expertise was predictable—with a perspective almost surely to be at odds with the perspectives of Germany's allies, especially that of the American protector thousands of miles to the rear.[5] Others cited the rapid reconstruction of the German industrial base, which easily would provide the skills and technical capabilities needed for national adaptation of what was really only the most advanced weapons technology.[6] A few even pointed to past experiences with the rehabilitation of defeated major powers. Successful reentry into the international system seemed to necessitate both the regaining of lost influence and the acquisition of those attributes of power deemed crucial by the now-leading power.

However reasonable, such expectations only obscured understanding of the crucial factors underlying all official German policy deliberations and indeed all discoverable serious private discussions on nuclear issues from 1954 to 1966. For the German leadership, as for the wider attentive public, decisions on broad nuclear issues turned only secondarily on such narrowly rational considerations about national security and never followed such "inevitable" logic. The principal cause lay in the very policy constraints, often observed but seemingly often forgotten or underestimated, imposed by Germany's special foreign-policy position. During the first decade of membership in NATO, the Federal Republic did indeed emerge as the Continental state with the largest land forces, an economic giant of ever increasing technological sophistication, the owner of one key to the second largest number of nuclear delivery vehicles in the West, and a persistent claimant to major political status within the Atlantic Alliance. Yet it was also divided, semi-occupied, and, at the beginning, almost an American client state, with a suspect past and a major mortgage on an uncertain political future, bound by a nuclear nonproduction pledge given in 1954 that was as explicit and as solemn as was to be devised until the advent of the nonproliferation treaty.

For Bonn, then, nuclear decision-making necessarily involved broader considerations than those of direct national possession or even strategic military preferences. As with the basic commitment to rearmament itself, the Adenauer-Erhard regimes designed these policies in terms of their goal-instrumental potential—of their serving (1) as continuing clamps on the American commitment to use strategic nuclear weapons, if necessary, to defend Western Europe, a guarantee perceived as providing Germany's only real security, (2) as buttresses for Bonn's full political-military rehabilitation within the West, and (3) as possible limited insurance or bargaining levers for the maintenance of future policy options in the East. Within surprisingly broad limits, the detailed requirements and consequences of specific weapons-system adoptions, of particular military doctrines, even of proposed control-sharing schemes were all potentially acceptable so long as broader foreign-policy goals were well served. Once these were accomplished, the Bonn calculus from 1954 to 1966 posited, Germany would then have secured the future, and the necessary readjustments and specific trade-offs would fall into place.

This Adenauerian strategy for rehabilitation, to an extent, was simply an attempt to make current and future virtue out of necessity—an attempt which was relatively successful in the short run, but quite illusionary. Bonn's continuing formal commitment to an almost all-balls-in-the-air approach—to the equal, simultaneous pursuit of the triad of security, equality, and unity—represented perhaps its only chance for bargaining success, by setting at least the base upon which to trade for current rewards or promise future benefits.

Yet even possible future interest in these goals prescribed guidelines for nuclear defense or for control-sharing formulas which proved contradictory or ambiguous. The continual stress on maintaining future options in nuclear policy as in foreign policy left Bonn open both to suspicion and to continuing, manipulative cross pressures—games played only too well by de Gaulle and by the Russians. Moreover, since final choices between Washington and Paris, between NATO partnership and reassociation in the East were by definition impossible, Bonn's bargaining leverage in any one sphere was never totally credible. And however advantageous the all-balls-in-the-air approach finally proved for the unlikely successors to the Adenauerian mantle—first the Christian Democratic Union (CDU)/Christian Social Union (CSU)–Social Democratic Party (SPD) Grand Coalition, then the Social Democratic Party—Free Democratic Party (FDP) governments—it imposed particularly heavy burdens on a slowly democratizing political system primarily concerned with domestic prosperity.

German policy-making dilemmas were perhaps even clearer in the area that constitutes this study's second focus: the significance of Bonn's American connection within and beyond NATO for nuclear decision-making. On these issues, as on all foreign-policy questions, German deliberations always assumed the primary need for close integration with American policy and American military presence, the principal hostage for German security. Indeed, Bonn's effort to gain a greater nuclear role on whatever level and in whatever sphere was aimed in largest measure at maximizing influence vis-à-vis Washington and thereby obtaining American sanction of German claims to equality and national determination.

Yet the case study shows that the very primacy of this dependence constituted a major limit on it—a special, telling illustration of Richard Neustadt's hypothesis concerning the limits inherent in intra-alliance communication and leadership.[7] The Adenauer and Erhard governments tended to learn their American lessons too well, if at all. German dependence and learning led almost inevitably to a status quo stance and to a hypersensitivity and overreaction to any percieved shift in American preferences or policies. Any change was seen as threatening what Washington had promised and what Bonn had accomplished in nuclear areas, as in rearmament generally, to secure American promises. And such developments only further confirmed Adenauer's fundamental forebodings about the ultimate unreliability of American guarantees and strengthened the determination of some German leaders to preserve all future options, if only against eventual abandonment.

Perhaps more than in Neustadt's Anglo-American case, the German-American alliance admittedly contained substantial propensities for misunderstanding and conflict on nuclear issues as on all matters. Increasingly there were the patently incongruent national goals seemingly characteristic of most postwar alliances between a superpower and middle powers. Bonn's side games on nuclear-control issues with France, and in a different way with the East, in the interest of option maintenance and political insurance, contributed little to the general harmony of the German-American alliance. But a still significant measure of the Bonn-Washington disputes seemed to stem from the very inability (within what would have seemed such an intimate and important relationship) of one set of bureaucrats to appreciate or even feel the need to follow closely the domestic priorities, bargains, and battles of the other, and to comprehend the basic insensitivity of others to their own concerns or even their publicly announced preferences.

The third concern of this study is an expansion of this theme: the degree to which aspects of the Adenauerian nuclear policy-making pattern may be comparable to those of other major nonnuclear states. Put most simply, Bonn's experience suggests the need for critical review of earlier estimates and scenarios concerning the proliferation of nuclear weapons, scenarios which too often merely projected the factors deemed relevant for the British and French national decisions onto all future national considerations.[8] By the mid-1960s Germany met most of the technical and political criteria then specified in predictions about proliferation. It indeed did have the attributes and capabilities which seemingly defined nuclear-threshold status: an advanced industrial and scientific base, considerable political stability, and extraregional foreign-policy interests and ambitions. Moreover, the example and views of Bonn's principal alliance partners made a position of permanent inferiority in questions of nuclear status unthinkable. Continuing voluntary abstinence seemingly implied costly and potentially suicidal policy choices for a state which claimed equal status with England and France in the second tier of the Western hierarchy.

As noted, the crucial factor in the German case was its unique foreign-policy position. Yet its experience as a potential third-generation nuclear power seems in marked contrast to that experienced by Britain or France before 1960 or that hypothesized by proliferation theorists. Long before the NPT and its formal constraints on acquisition and production, any aspirant, whatever its technical capability, faced major barriers to national acquisition that were embedded in the structural hierarchy of the international system. Within their respective spheres, the superpowers increasingly withheld direct nuclear-production assistance or weapons transfers, restricted information flows, and avoided any further weakening of existing physical controls. In the domestic area influential domestic opponents interposed hindrances based on moral or technical or economic considerations from the outset of any deliberations. Most significantly, by at least the third decade of the nuclear era, Adenauerian Bonn, like other capitals, came to learn that the greatest opportunity for influence and bargaining lay not in painful, danger-ous acquisition of national capabilities, but in appearing able to exercise such an option at times and places of momentous national choice or at times when the compensating payoffs were not forthcoming.

This study is at best a partial effort to cover this broad catalogue of issues and hypotheses. The author is only too aware of the dangers inherent in contemporary analysis—of description (to say nothing of hypothesis-test-ing) based on incomplete data in the sensitive areas of ego involvements and the hallowed national-security policies of several states. Many consider-ations have been dealt with far too summarily or left to the reader's specula-tion. Since the principal argument is a developmental one and the mode of analysis is chronological, each of the succeeding chapters can examine in detail only a particular complex. Finally, because the course of events can-not neatly be divided into segments like 1954–1966, there must be a brief nod at the principal developments that spill over these parameters, as well as a broad examination of changes during the years since 1966.

The basic hope, however, is that a beginning has been made toward unraveling the complex interplay of German (and, by linkage, Atlantic) policies, powers, and personalities at stake in the conjunction of the words German and nuclear weapons from 1954 to 1966.

ONE

Prologue:
1945-1954

✠ IN ORDER TO BEGIN (to paraphrase Alice's King of Hearts), it is always best to start at the beginning. The base point for German policies concerning the use and control of nuclear weapons was a pledge, contained in the 1954 London and Paris accords which provided for Germany's accession to NATO, that

The Federal Republic undertakes not to manufacture in its territory any atomic weapons . . . defined as any weapon which contains . . . nuclear fuel . . . and which, by . . . uncontrolled nuclear transformation of the nuclear fuel . . . is capable of mass destruction . . . [or] any part, device, assembly or material especially designed for . . . any [such] weapon.[1]

Since 1954 the character of this pledge has attracted increasing attention, with some observers concluding that it represents something less than its Bonn description, the "first nonproliferation promise." During the discussions surrounding the nuclear nonproliferation treaty in the mid-1960s, for example, the Soviet Union was quick to point out a number of significant "legal" loopholes that, it implied, were deliberate.[2] Germany was not prevented by the pledge from importing nuclear weapons or from achieving effective national control through bilateral or multilateral co-ownership arrangements. Most significantly, Bonn might freely participate in nuclear-weapons development extraterritorially—as, for example, in a nuclear repetition of the Black Reichwehr development in the Ukraine during the 1920s.[3]

Concurrently with the Soviet caveats, German political figures suggested a number of limiting conditions attached to the nonproduction pledge of 1954. Most speakers emphasized the obvious, hardly irrevocable bargain involved: the promise of American protection and of political rehabilitation through full NATO membership in exchange for what Theo Sommer has called "institutionalized foreign control" over German military, particularly nuclear, development.[4] Beginning in 1965, former Chancellor Adenauer was even more emphatic. His pledge, with John Foster Dulles' explicit understanding, had been given only *rebus sic stantibus*—that is, only for as long as Bonn believed the conditions under which it was given still existed.[5]

The central focus of this first chapter will be this narrow "possession" aspect of early German nuclear-control policies. A careful analysis of the origins of the pledge and of the diplomatic circumstances under which it was given will provide little hard evidence about the stakes involved in any retrospective interpretation of past acts or about the probability of future actions regarding this commitment, now subsumed within the broader NPT framework. But it can suggest explanations for what seem at this distance to have been deliberate omissions and ambiguous phrasing. And it will illuminate the earliest of the many instances during 1954–1966 in which Western policies linking Germans and nuclear development had less to do with German aspirations (explicit or expected) than with projections of the lessons of the past and of the present ambitions and fears of allies.

In this early period the most active manipulator of such fears was the Fourth Republic, struggling vainly for both internal stability and a recaptured international domain. The basic dilemma which led France to demand immediate constraints against still-undreamed-of German capabilities was to reappear frequently during 1954–1966, posing great bargaining opportunities but also great hinderances to Adenauerian foreign policy. For Paris (as for a London still far in the background) there had to be maximum effort to counter the certain political, military, and economic challenge a rebuilt Germany would pose to a Western hierarchy defined by cold-war calculus and embedded in NATO's formal organization. And although infrequently perceived or admitted, there was also the fact that France's international ambitions, without the support and the resources of a gradually rehabilitated Germany, would have had to be limited to the role of contributing but not crucial European spear carrier for the United States.

Brief attention is also given in this chapter to the two other aspects of nuclear control that Adenauerian Bonn considered at least as significant: the problematical role of nuclear weapons in Germany's defense and the question of assured access to Washington's nuclear decision-making. Grave concern on the part of Germans at this time was logical, given the strategic context of German rearmament and Bonn's clearly acknowledged dependence on its American connection. For Adenauer, if for only a few others in Bonn, these two aspects set the framework for all of Germany's current and future goals for the full restoration of sovereign equality and eventual unity.

ORIGINS OF THE NUCLEAR NONPRODUCTION PLEDGE

ALLIED DISARMAMENT CONTROLS, 1945–1954

The 1954 pledge can be viewed in many respects as the last in a series of control measures set down by the wartime Allies for a defeated and, subsequently, not-yet-sovereign Germany.[6] From the time the Allies' troops entered Germany, atomic-energy development was made explicitly subject to sweeping prohibitions regarding all goods and installations of "possible value for war purposes." It was not until April of 1946 that a special scientific-research decree permitted—with permission of the zone commander— the conduct of basic research in nuclear physics.[7] But this was to be limited to those activities "directed toward the discovery of new knowledge," was not to involve the use of any forbidden equipment or the development of any specific applications, and was to be subject to the most rigorous accounting and inspection procedures.

These restrictions in large measure merely reflected desires of the Allies to cover every conceivable contingency in their total disarmament-demilitarization program. In Italy and Japan there were similar provisions with the same goal: to provide both a legal basis (usually ex post facto) for current actions and the broadest possible framework for future control. In a period in which the American atomic monopoly was expected, at least in the West, to continue for quite some time, that a defeated and occupied country would make any significant progress in atomic-weapons development in the foreseeable future was scarcely to be surmised.

Nonetheless, these Big Four decrees for all of the German territory— like all immediately postwar considerations of the Allies regarding the German nation and nuclear-weapons questions—seemed more than a little colored by the fears of the past.[8] The 1939–1941 British and American decisions to embark on massive atomic-research programs had been taken largely in the belief that the Third Reich could and would develop military applications for atomic energy, an area of significant German scientific achievement in the prewar period. As the war progressed, intelligence reports concerning the slow progress of the enemy's program were often filtered through the double screen of anxiety and mirror-image projections. If we have been able to progress this far, many scientists and politicians reasoned, how much further must the Germans have come, with their head start in theory and their well-known scientific proficiency?

What the Allies found at the war's end was surprising even to those most optimistic about the Anglo-American wartime lead in weapons development. The German atomic-weapons program had begun in 1939 with the formation of Uran Verein (the Uranium Society) within the prestigious Kaiser Wilhelm Institute for Physics in Berlin. Work had continued there and at other facilities throughout the war, under the aegis of the army, the Ministry for Armament and Munitions, the Ministry of Education, and the research section of the Post Office. By 1944 German scientists still had not succeeded in separating U-235 or in constructing a chain-reacting uranium pile. They had not progressed much further than had the Americans and British in 1941.

There seemed to be many reasons for the German failure, not the least being the effectiveness of the Allies' bombing raids and of sabotage efforts against research facilities and supply centers. A point of some controversy concerns the degree of scientific failure involved. According to many experts, the Germans never grasped the basic idea that a uranium pile could and should be used not as a bomb itself, but rather as a means of producing the necessary fissionable material, plutonium.[9] Moreover, most scientists were convinced that success would be impossible during the war. As Carl Friedrich von Weizsäcker, a young but prominent Verein member, wrote: "We had such a precise knowledge of the difficulties inherent in the production of an atomic bomb and considered them so formidable that it had never occurred to us that America would be in a position to produce atomic bombs during the war." [10]

According to later accounts of several Verein scientists, failure was caused partly by a policy of passive resistance against Hitler.[11] Bureaucratic delays and postponements were welcomed, not resented; promising lines of investigation were ignored or hidden from official view. Some show of effort, some promises to officialdom were necessary, if only to ensure that the development of German atomic research would not be put into other hands. But most members of the Verein had agreed that there were to be no results that would assist in the Nazis' fanatical and senseless attempt at world domination.

For whatever reason, German scientists were spared, in von Weizsäcker's words, "the last hard decision." [12] The Allies, nonetheless, wished to be doubly sure. Scientists and technicians in all fields of possible relevance were captured and questioned. The leaders of the Uran Verein—Heisenberg, von Weizsäcker, Hahn, Gerlach, and five others—were interned in England until the American effort had proven successful at Hiroshima, and then were kept under close surveillance.

These Control Council restrictions on atomic development—like, indeed, most of the demilitarization measures—underwent only gradual formal modification during the subsequent years of deepening East-West conflict and warming German-Atlantic relations. The failure of the Moscow and London conferences in 1947 signaled both the final breakdown of the wartime coalition and the end of all hopes for a quadripartite agreement on the future of the German territories. The Western allies began to take the first steps toward the creation of a separate Western German state: the establishment of a "Bizonia" in 1947, the extension of massive economic assistance, and the limited restoration of certain governmental powers to the Land (state) authorities. The opening shots of the Cold War in 1948—the Czechoslovakian coup, the discussion surrounding the Brussels defense pact, and most dramatically, the Berlin blockade—provided further stimuli. All demonstrated that the principal threat to Western security had become Soviet aggression and that Germany, although perhaps still a source of future danger, had become one of the prizes to be won. Mobilizing of German resources against this threat became a primary consideration in the West; the possibility of rearmament was discussed as early as 1947. In this early period, few Western leaders saw rearmament as a response to acute military requirements. Even after the first Soviet atomic test in 1949, basic Western strategy was deterrence of Soviet military moves by the superior American atomic arsenal and bomber force. An alarming factor was the continuing gap in Europe between the aims and the capabilities for a viable local defense, even one designed to halt the Russians only west of the Rhine or to slow their advance, giving the Strategic Air Command (SAC) time to intervene. The shock of the North Korean invasion made the gap even more perturbing, but hardly modified the widespread conviction of Europeans that it would have to be the German forces, not additions to existing national armies, that would help fill it. And perhaps not even those would be enough, given continuing Soviet conventional-force superiority and approaching American-Soviet strategic parity in the years of "maximum danger," expected by American planners to begin in 1954–1955.[13]

Paradoxically, these developments had only limited consequences for the continuing demilitarization programs pursued by the Western allies. As discussions regarding a German contribution to Western defense began, strict control was still being exercised over the possession, sale, and manufacture of all war matériel, including weapons for police and for hunting. For some time, Marshall Plan programs designed to stimulate German economic recovery did no more than mitigate restrictive control, deconcentration, and extensive dismantling of industries having war potential.

Creation of a western German federal state in 1949 also brought little formal change. Bonn's constitutional document, the Basic Law, contained no provision relating to defense, while in the accompanying Occupation Statute the three Western allies reaffirmed their responsibilities for continuing German disarmament and demilitarization.[14] Even after the signing of the European Defense Community (EDC) treaty in 1952, the now-tripartite Allied Military Security Board (MSB) continued to exercise formal control over all weapons and weapons manufacture and research.

Daily practice, nonetheless, reflected the changed environment and the allies' decreasing interest in specific control. By 1952 the entire complex of demilitarization legislation had acquired a curious political status, being enforced somewhat randomly, if at all. Under the Bonn Conventions—signed in 1952 but in accordance with French demands not to replace the Occupation Statute until the EDC treaty was fully ratified—the allies indeed agreed to the essential restoration of sovereignty for Germany in both internal and external affairs.

The atomic sphere, however, remained one of the most strictly controlled. Any production or research of potential military significance was automatically prohibited; civil development was possible only under the most exacting conditions. The Allied High Commission, through the MSB, regulated "the production, import, export, transport, storage, use, and possession of radioactive materials." No German, for example, could produce "deuterium gas, metallic beryllium, thorium, or uranium" or construct "facilities capable of separating isotopes of uranium with a yield potential in excess of 1 milligram of U-235 per 24 hours." [15] Furthermore, without explicit authorization of the MSB, no one could deal in any way with any article contained in the exhaustive prohibited list.

As the EDC ratification process dragged on through 1953 and 1954, the atomic-energy controls maintained by the allies clearly reflected the tensions and paradoxes inherent in Germany's political limbo. On the one hand, there were continuing concerns on the part of the allies (particularly the French) that any future German industrial development of atomic energy would provide additional inputs for potential economic superiority and would permit uncontrolled diversion for probable military ambitions. On the other hand, there were growing German demands to be free of all vestiges of control and discrimination. The final decision of the allies was to allow considerable latitude to nuclear research efforts, so long as work with U-235, reactors, or specific industrial applications were not involved.

The Germans apparently made little use of these limited freedoms. As one nuclear scientist later explained:

We had the idea that after the war the total area of nuclear science was forbidden to Germany. . . . In the first three meetings of the Research Commission (Arbeitsgemeinschaft für Forschung) of the state of North Rhine Westphalia, we looked into what was then forbidden and what was not. Minister [President] Arnold then sent the results on to the Federal Government. . . . Scarcely anyone believed this and almost no one had done anything about it. . . . The only state in Germany which strove to do intensive work in the areas which were not prohibited was North Rhine Westphalia.[16]

PROPOSED EDC CONTROLS, 1950–1954

The most immediate antecedents of the 1954 nonproduction pledge were the atomic-armament provisions of the ill-fated European Defense Community, an arrangement proposed by France to provide a safe channel for Germany's now-required contribution to western defense. The tortuous and eventually unsuccessful struggle for EDC's creation from 1950 to 1954 needs no recounting. Of interest here are rather the questions of general strategic concept and specific armament restrictions involved in the decision to create a twelve-division, 500,000-man German military establishment that would be integrated within EDC.

The West's formal strategic concept throughout most of these years remained very nearly that of the period immediately following the Korean invasion: principal operational reliance on the American strategic deterrent, but with at least declaratory emphasis on a "respectable" conventional-force capability for local defense in Europe. German rearmament was hailed as the device that made possible the adoption of the ambitious Lisbon force goals of 1952 and the implementation of "forward defense" in depth eastward, eventually to encompass all of the Federal Republic's territory. The West had thereby gained needed bolstering for the approaching time of American-Soviet strategic parity—and, it was sometimes softly added, for that of long-threatened American withdrawal from Europe.

By 1953, however, there was a new de facto strategy, which reflected recent American decisions and had far-reaching significance for the planned twelve German divisions. The Eisenhower administration's intense concern with long-run fiscal responsibility, with budgetary planning for protracted, multifaceted competition with the Soviet bloc had led to a "New Look," particularly in European defense. Given the Communists' manpower edge, the mounting of a conventional-force defense along Lisbon-designed lines would be prohibitively expensive and, in the face of declining contributions from European members of NATO, virtually impossible. The United States, for its own economic well-being, therefore would have to adopt a strategy which exploited to the fullest the advantages that the tactical atomic weapons then under development promised in terms of manpower-firepower trade-offs, and the extension of deterrence, under the massive retaliation doctrine, into the tactical sphere. European conventional forces and especially the planned German contribution, however, would be needed to ensure that any enemy attacks would be concentrated enough to permit the effective targeting of tactical atomic weapons.

Few in the German leadership knew of or appreciated the significance of this shift in American doctrine.[17] Most accepted the Lisbon force goals as the given framework for rearmament and indeed considered war in Europe to be an increasingly remote possibility. The most interest by German civilians perhaps came from within the opposition Social Democratic Party. Under the militant Kurt Schumacher and, later, the more traditionally pacifist Erich Ollenhauer, the party had opposed West-sponsored rearmament at every step, primarily because of its adverse consequences for whatever prospects of reunification remained. Paradoxically, the SPD had also stressed that Western conventional-force goals not only were inadequate to prevent successful Soviet conquest to the Rhine but also were impossible to achieve. The American atomic New Look therefore only strengthened the SPD's con-

viction that Adenauer's planned rearmament under EDC or any other arrangement was simply and knowingly chimerical. There was nothing to be
gained in military or political terms in the Atlantic, European, or all-German
sphere that would not have been forthcoming anyway, and much to be lost,
if measured only in terms of the now-assured atomic destruction of German
territory during a conflict.

There was no official reaction in government circles; the Adenauer
regime continued without change its arguments for rearmament as an essential precondition for Germany's security, political equality with other states,
and eventual reunification with East Germany. Few of the civilian or military personnel within the nascent defense ministry set up under the chancellor, the Amt Blank (Blank Office), seemed to take serious notice of the
American shift.[18] With almost no reliable technical information available,
those who did notice tended to downgrade American hopes for the offsetting
advantages of tactical atomic weapons or to assert the continued primacy of
conventional defense if only Western determination would hold. But most
officials in Amt Blank were totally absorbed in the difficult, almost hopeless
task of finding sufficient barracks, uniforms, and acceptable military traditions to create an army de novo in a fundamentally hostile national and international environment. And there was the even more frustrating task of negotiating and renegotiating the specifics of EDC's implementation.

As dramatically as any other aspect, negotiations concerning German
arms production (including potential atomic armament) revealed the basically incompatible interests of the principal EDC protagonists.[19] France
sought (at a minimum) a controlled German rearmament within a European
framework, a rearmament "sufficient," in the words of a then-popular wit-
ticism, "to awe the Russians but not so strong as to frighten [or compete
with] the French." No matter how tight the controls, any German weapons
production would be distasteful; manufacture in the Federal Republic of armaments capable of striking at France would be intolerable. And the possibility of eventual German military atomic development—at a time when
atomic development by France was only a gleam in certain eyes—was unthinkable.

The principal German theme, then and throughout the following years,
was the demand for "equality," no matter what the sphere of activity. As
Adenauer dramatically declared, there would be no German rearmament
unless German troops received "a fully equal status . . . with respect to

weapons and command.'' [20] The Federal Republic would not simply provide the ''infantry'' (Fussvolk) or the ''battleground.'' It must be an equal partner in every sense; its forces must encompass all three services and possess all weapons, internally or externally produced, necessary to insure the forces' own defense and their equal standing within the Western security system.

The explicit bases for these demands were certain military arguments marshaled as early as 1948 by General Hans Speidel in one of the first German studies of rearmament.[21] Troops whose armament was unequal to that of the forces surrounding them not only would suffer from feelings of inferiority but also would prove a weak link, an attractive target for enemy attack. Given Germany's strategic position, these theoretical principles took on a special significance. Troop morale had to be developed among a population educated to demilitarization as well as to denazification; destruction to the German battlefield had to be minimized. Moreover, commanders of second-class troops from a second-class member state could not expect to exercise more than limited influence over the formulation of the strategic plans they were to execute.

In greatest measure, however, it was Adenauer's basic rearmament strategy that led to the all-pervading emphasis on equality. In his view rearmament could not assure German security directly; its principal purpose was rather to provide the political lever by which the Federal Republic would be raised from the status of an occupied territory to that of a full and sovereign Western partner, to be defended and at least overtly trusted. Given the past and the present, true equality would come only gradually; the question ''Equal to whom?'' could be answered for the present only in vague terms. But current acceptance of any imposed position of inferiority would negate those basic German political goals at stake in the long run.

Throughout the prolonged treaty negotiations Adenauer lost no opportunity to stress the interrelationship of rearmament with the restoration of sovereignty, to gain every possible concession ''on the basis of a contribution of nonexistent German troops to a nonexistent European Army.'' [22] He pointed to the massive domestic opposition to rearmament, to the dangerous SPD policies that stressed the incompatibility of rearmament with the primary goal, reunification. He warned of the growing popular interest in Russian proposals for a reunified, neutralized Germany from which all foreign troops would be withdrawn. All this, the chancellor hinted, declared, and threatened, would come to fruition if the Atlantic allies did not agree to rearmament within the framework of "equitable" political recovery.

Once the principle of equality was established, the chancellor was more than willing to bow to the inevitable and to accept voluntarily significant restrictions on Germany's military capability. The most important form of control would be integration not only of forces but of every phase of military activity, including the design, manufacture, and funding of armaments. An integrated system clearly offered real or potential political benefits for Germany: the limited, equal control of all participant nations and the locking in of Western forces for the defense of the Federal Republic's territory. Its principal value, however, was as a definite counter to allies', particularly French, fears concerning a future German threat to Western security.

For the chancellor and some of his supporters, an integrated European defense structure had another advantage: the protection of Germans against themselves. Adenauer had long been known as a committed "European," an ardent advocate of Franco-German rapprochement, and an opponent of traditional German tendencies toward Schaukelpolitik, the playing off of East and West against each other. His basic approach is dramatically revealed in remarks reportedly made after the EDC's collapse:

I am one hundred percent convinced that the German national army, to which Mendès-France is forcing us, will be a great danger to both Germany and Europe. When I am no longer there, I do not know what will happen to Germany if we have not yet succeeded in creating a united Europe. . . . The French nationalists would rather [have] a Germany with a national army than a united Europe—so long as they can pursue their own policy with the Russians. And the German nationalists think exactly the same way; they are ready to go with the Russians.[23]

De Gaulle reports a similar but even more specific comment made by Adenauer in 1958 during their first discussion of the value of the American security guarantee:

Adenauer set great store by this guarantee because he said, "by providing for the security of the German people and putting them in good company, it diverts them from their obsession with isolation and the worship of power which, to their cost, drove them into Hitler's arms." [24]

An integrated European defense structure, the chancellor told the General, would further encourage the maintenance of this guarantee.

The armament provisions finally included in the EDC treaty represented a somewhat uneasy compromise.[25] All production of weapons (including atomic weapons) was to be subject to the licensing and control of a Board of Commissioners. With respect to the armament of the European Defense Forces (which included all of the German troops but not all of the other participants' military forces), the board was to oversee a system of vertical integration. Weapons were to be financed and contracted for on a common basis, with "due regard" taken of the economic capacities and contributions of the member states. The board was also to develop and implement a common military research program and to ensure the control of civil research that could have military value.

Atomic controls—indeed all the special restrictions on German production—were contained in a second type of armament regulation, the provisions of Article 107, which related to the "strategically exposed areas." French negotiators proposed this stipulation in late 1951, declaring that the Community must be explicitly empowered to forbid significant weapons manufacture in any area subject to certain seizure or destruction in the event of attack. Bonn's protest was immediate. Obviously, only one country was to be designated as strategically exposed; the purpose was to establish de facto discrimination and an unacceptable "legal basis for the continued regulation of Germany." [26]

The controversy continued, without solution, until the Foreign Ministers' Conference in mid-February, 1952.[27] Adenauer decided to accede in principle to French demands, meeting the protests of some of the German delegation with his familiar argument that the current acceptance of restrictions would provide positive demonstration of good faith and would not prejudice revision at a later date. The EDC partners must, however, fulfill two conditions: provision of a formal guarantee of equal arms supplies to German troops, and acceptance of a voluntary German declaration rather than an imposed prohibition regarding these limitations.

Under the final EDC formula, in the strategically exposed areas there could be no German production of six classes of weapons, described by one German commentator as "principally those of an offensive character." [28] There was to be no manufacture of atomic, bacteriological, or chemical weapons or of military aircraft of any type. The prohibitions regarding naval construction and the development of long-range missiles and guided missiles were subject to only minor exceptions. Although the supranational Board of Commissioners was to supervise enforcement, exceptions of any sort could be granted only by unanimous decision of the international Council of Ministers, thus ensuring to France an opportunity to veto.

Perhaps the only detailed evidence of the persistence of past fears about Germany's atomic potential was the rigor of the restrictions regarding German civil atomic-energy development; they were far more severe than those set down for the other five states. For Germany alone, the term "atomic weapon" was defined as including not only all weapons "capable of mass destruction, mass injury, or mass poisoning" and "any part, device, assembly, or material" designed or primarily useful for such weapons but also "any quantity of nuclear fuel produced in one year in excess of 500 grams." Atomic weapons so defined were specifically excluded from the list of weapons for which exemptions for civil production and research could be granted.

During the two years which followed the ministerial conference, the provisions of the EDC treaty were subject to constant debate and some revision. Several changes in the general regulations governing armament production were made. But the provisions regarding the strategically exposed areas were neither discussed nor revised. They were among the few uncontested paragraphs that fell victim to the decisive rejection of the European Defense Community treaty by the French National Assembly in the summer of 1954.

THE PLEDGE AND 1954 LONDON–PARIS NEGOTIATIONS

Simple continuity, then, is the obvious reason for the appearance of a particular formula for German nonproduction of atomic weapons in the 1954 London and Paris accords. In the five tumultuous weeks between EDC's defeat and the final Paris compromises, primary and even secondary attention was on the negotiation of far more significant issues.[29] It was not that the Assembly's action had been unexpected; most observers by at least the early spring of 1954 had been convinced that the Defense Community was doomed. The problem was rather how to find new answers to old questions: the restoration of the Federal Republic's sovereignty and the control of a rearmed Germany within the Western defense system.

The first question was by far the easier to answer. Basic agreement on the return of sovereign powers to the Federal Republic had been reached in

1952; French demands had tied this to a German defense contribution bound within a European framework. The central issue was how and under what controls a rearmed Germany was to be integrated into the Western security system. What relationship should exist between NATO and any new European defense organization? Should Germany be accorded full membership in both? Which if any of the EDC limitations on German forces and armaments should be retained? How were these limitations to be administered?

The EDC lesson learned by the United States, Britain, Germany, and most of the other Continental states was that the only way to secure a German defense contribution and the fullest possible sovereignty for Germany was to grant the Federal Republic direct membership in NATO.

The strategic concept which German forces would help implement was of course no longer that of 1952. In the summer of 1954 NATO was about to adopt a New Look of its own. But whether tactical atomic weapons were to be used in all but the smallest European conflicts or not, twelve German divisions were still an urgent necessity for NATO's shield. And there now seemed even less telling reasons than in 1951 to bow to continuing French fears about the dire consequences of formal German equality within the Atlantic sphere without an intermediary European system of controls and guarantees.

Construction of a new European framework without France seemed unthinkable. For Adenauer, always the European and the battler of bilateral discrimination, the principal value to be served by a European-based defense arrangement was not security but rather the thrust toward an integrated Europe. Yet, with France, any such arrangement—whether on a supranational or international basis—would involve extended negotiations and the possibility of future failure. Clearly, the French would simply have to face the consequences of the Assembly's repudiation of the EDC the French had proposed.

One proposal attracting increasing support advocated European control of German rearmament through a revived and augmented Brussels Treaty Organization. This was a body founded in 1948 by Britain and four Continental countries against potential renewals of German aggression. The new association, to be called the Western European Union (WEU), would serve both as a secondary European guarantee system and as an adjunct to (although legally separate from) NATO, which, as Bonn demanded, would remain an "association of equals."

WEU itself would be concerned with only the political and legal aspects of controlling German rearmament. Within NATO, a strengthened SACEUR (Supreme Allied Commander, Europe) would be responsible for all operational control, including inspection of the German military establishment, all of which (except some Border Police) would be placed under his command.

Despite vigorous French criticism and recrimination, this was essentially the bargain struck. The Federal Republic agreed to participate directly in both NATO and WEU. German forces in all three branches were not to exceed 500,000 men or to include more than a twelve-division army or to have an independent military command structure outside the integrated system responsible to a more powerful SACEUR. Moreover, the chancellor pledged that the Federal Republic would neither use force to bring about reunification or boundary changes nor manufacture on its territory atomic weapons or the other types of major offensive armament specified in the EDC arrangements.

In return—as part of the package, as was stressed then and later—Germany received definite guarantees with respect to its political status and military security. The Federal Republic was afforded "the full authority of a sovereign State." The reserved rights of the Western allies were limited to full responsibility for all matters relating to Berlin, German unity, and a future European settlement (this with Bonn's complete acquiescence); and to paramount "emergency" authority, such authority to be exercised whenever the allies determined that an internal or external threat to their forces in Germany existed (this provision was adopted only after some dispute).

The allies further declared that the Federal Republic was the sole spokesman for the entire German nation in international affairs and that the achievement of a reunited German nation, without prior determination of its allegiance, was an essential and fundamental goal of their policy. Other pledges, not sought solely by Germany, were the conditional British commitment not to withdraw forces from the Continent without prior WEU approval and the American declaration to keep forces in Europe as long as they were "necessary."

Explication of the history of controls over German atomic production requires a closer look at the negotiations and events preceding the final agreements on general German weapons production. From the outset, questions concerning armament production led to protracted and acrimonious debate seemingly because they were not central. Both Germany and France (however grudgingly) realized that the principal issues were all but decided and that political bargaining and delaying maneuvers could be successful only in secondary areas.

In the public press, as well as at the negotiations themselves, France— or more precisely Prime Minister Mendès-France, under intense pressure from his Assembly as a result not only of European issues but also of developments in Indochina and Algeria—called, in essence, for the reestablishment of EDC controls within the Brussels treaty framework.[30] An *autorité centrale* with certain supranational aspects was to control all facets of Continental weapons production except financing, set maximums for NATO-assigned forces, and secure the compliance of member states through "a truly effective control." Germany's social status as a strategically exposed area was to be even more restrictive than under the EDC. Not only was German atomic and heavy armament production to be limited, but the deployment of other weapons and the location of new facilities also were to reflect "the strategic situation." The European defense area was to be divided into three zones, the first or "zone of most danger" covering most of the Federal Republic.

Some of the participant German civil servants interviewed by the author in 1965 and 1966 suggested that for Bonn the issues were somewhat more complex. Throughout the EDC struggle, Adenauer's readiness to agree to restrictions (so long as the general principle of equality was recognized and Germany was allowed to accept the restrictions "voluntarily") had been in sharp contrast to the views of some of his military and political advisors. Under the circumstances of the French rejection and the changed military situation, these views were voiced again and louder this time. Moreover, for several military advisors the prospect of accepting unilateral restrictions within a new Atlantic framework seemed to entail the de facto assumption of second-class membership. Any production prohibitions made necessary by a country's strategic position should be proposed by the NATO command, adopted by the North Atlantic Council, and made applicable to all states in similar situations. Nonetheless, Adenauer, almost from the time of the EDC's defeat, stressed his willingness to accept voluntarily some restrictions which did not impose new "discrimination."

Public or interview sources for the relevant Bonn discussions provide no evidence that a renunciation of atomic weapons production received any more attention than did other production prohibitions, like, for example, prohibitions on manufacture of aircraft or ships. Adenauer, in his memoirs, asserts that the decision to offer the nonproduction pledge was one of his "few personal decisions," made without prior consultation.[31] His principal foreign-policy advisors and the chief Germany negotiators, ambassadors Wilhelm Grewe and Herbert Blankenhorn, have stated subsequently that lack of time precluded anything more than general consideration and provisional drafting.[32] In contrast to restrictions on production of other kinds of armaments, the pledge apparently was considered a self-evident requirement, because of the nature of the weapons themselves (then the exclusive property of three nations) and of the political goals which German renunciation was to serve.

Interview data gathered in 1965–1966 allow the conclusion that some of those involved in these Bonn discussions were aware of the particular interest of the Mendès-France government in atomic development and of the determination of a small group in Paris to preserve the potentiality of French superiority in this area.[33] But interview sources also indicate that most officials in Bonn viewed reports and rumors regarding French aspirations with considerable skepticism. And those who believed the reports tended to believe also that actual development under the immobile and unstable Fourth Republic would be slow, if not virtually impossible. More concrete evidence might have been found by Bonn in some of the revisions of EDC armament provisions that were demanded of Germany by Mendès-France just before the treaty was rejected.[34] He proposed that the definition that an annual nuclear-fuel production in excess of 500 grams constituted war material apply only to strategically exposed areas and that elsewhere such production not be subject to license or control by the Board of Commissioners. A second requirement was that along with other major weapons manufacture atomic production should not be affected by the EDC's distributive stipulations whereby 85 percent of a country's financial contribution was to be expended within its borders. France seemed not only interested in unfettered national atomic development but also eager to have its possible Continental monopoly financed by other member states.

The only certainty, however, is that Adenauer went to the London conference seriously considering, it not committed to, the giving of a pledge forswearing offensive armament production. According to his memoirs, the circumstances of its expression were straightforward. During a second heated session over French demands for production controls, the chancellor rose and restated his familiar theme: the prerequisite for all solutions was the guarantee of a sovereign and equal status for Germany. He then voluntarily offered five concessions, the two most important ones concerning production inspection and limitation. The Federal Republic would favor the creation of a special WEU body to inspect and control armament levels, so long as operational control was retained by SACEUR. And more significantly, Germany was now ready to accept virtually all of the EDC restrictions on heavy armament production and to renounce unilaterally, once again, the manufacture of atomic, biological, and chemical weapons (often referred to as ABC weapons).

It was the scope of this renunciation that was most startling, according to several interview sources. Most of the participants rose and praised the willingness of the Federal Republic to take concrete steps to demonstrate its peaceful intent and to prepare the way for a full and equitable solution of pressing questions. The Dutch and Belgian foreign ministers indicated their readiness to accept similar obligations.[35]

John Foster Dulles seems especially to have welcomed the chancellor's unilateral declaration. According to Adenauer, Dulles rose from his seat, came to Adenauer's side, and said in a voice that all could hear:

Mr. Chancellor, you have just declared that the Federal Republic of Germany renounces the production of ABC weapons on its own soil. You meant this declaration, I assume, to be valid only *rebus sic stantibus*—as all declarations and obligations in international law are! [36]

Acknowledging this reference to the precept that agreements have force only while the conditions under which they were concluded still exist, the chancellor replied in an equally loud voice, ''You have interpreted my declaration correctly.''

Adenauer later depicted this as the move which overcame one of the most serious crises of the conference. Contemporary accounts, however, suggest that it had little effect on Mendès-France. French intransigence was expected to halt negotiations once again. Preventive arms control vis-à-vis Germany, after all, was a central piece of the French negotiating program. It seemed that Adenauer had not gone far enough to please what Mendès-France knew to be a truculent, anxious, and highly volatile National Assembly. Indeed, the only specific mention of atomic weapons in the European press after the session concerned France's own unwillingness to accept any general controls over its future production.[37]

Under the compromise finally worked out, German armament production was to be subject to three sets of controls exercised through the Western European Union.[38] The first was the most general, pertaining to all Continental (but not British) armament industries, regardless of location. A new WEU organ, the Agency for the Control of Armaments, was to supervise the stocks and, to a limited degree, the production of ten conventional-weapons classes ranging from heavy guns and tanks to guided missiles and military aircraft. In light of French objections, the agency was empowered to control all ABC-weapons stocks only after "effective production" was begun on the Continent. The level which any state (except Britain) could achieve was to be determined by simple majority vote of the WEU Council.

The two other controls grew out of the chancellor's declaration, which was noted in and annexed to the protocols themselves. The agency was to ensure the nonproduction of three types of heavy armament (missiles, warships, and strategic bombers) unless modifications were approved by a two-thirds vote of the North Atlantic Council upon a request by the Federal Republic and SACEUR. Control of totally renounced arms (ABC weapons) was to continue throughout the existence of the Western European Union.[39]

In comparison with the EDC provisions, some concessions on what was to constitute atomic production were won by Germany. There was no mention of restrictions on nuclear-fuel output; equipment and material "used for civilian purposes, or for scientific, medical, and industrial research in the fields of pure and applied science" specifically were excluded from control. Full freedom to undertake development of atomic energy for peaceful purposes awaited the replacement of the allies' control measures by German legislation, but the legal independence of the Federal Republic in this area was recognized.

Nevertheless, there was some resistance to the nuclear-fuel provisions, especially French calls for safeguards against possible peaceful-use spillover into the military sector. To meet this concern, Adenauer sent a letter to British Foreign Secretary Anthony Eden (presumably in view of his role as chairman of the London conference) giving certain guarantees for a two-year transitional phase.[40] During this period, the Federal Republic would install only one nuclear reactor, with a maximum capacity of 10,000 kilowatts, and would limit stocks of fissionable materials to 3,500 grams per year.

Significantly, during the ensuing relatively swift ratification of the London and Paris accords, Adenauer's renunciation of atomic-weapons production on German soil received little attention. Most legislatures merely noted the declaration and praised it as an additional safeguard against the rebirth of German militarism and as a demonstration of German solidarity with the West. In Germany itself, the issue of production restrictions in general was scarcely discussed; what mention there was came chiefly from the government in defense of its actions. No question was raised as to the wisdom of the chancellor's declaration.

The matter became important only in France, where according to Leites and de la Malène, the only limitation on German production treated in the Assembly and in the Council of the Republic in considerable detail was the limit on atomic production.[41] The Gaullist, Centrist, and Rightist opponents of the accords raised two major objections: under the accords, Germany was still free to receive nuclear weapons from abroad and, in particular, from the United States; and Germany's right after 1957 to uncontrolled national development of peaceful-use atomic energy programs would constitute, in effect, uncontrolled access to atomic weapons.[42] In a manner characteristic of all French debates of the period (and especially those regarding military and atomic-energy affairs), the Mendès-France government either ignored these charges or merely agreed that they posed important questions.

On May 5, 1955, the Paris accords, together with the protocols providing for the termination of the occupation regime and Germany's accession to NATO, became effective. The Federal Republic thereby gained near-sovereignty, received direct NATO membership, and became the first nation in the West to renounce explicitly and voluntarily the production of atomic weapons.

COMMENTARY

This brief review has sought to make one central point: so far as it existed at all, the problem of German production of nuclear weapons existed almost solely in the perceptions, the fears, and the plans of the wartime Allies. In the array of problems confronting Western countries, it was, without question, neither a major nor a pressing concern. At a time when American-Soviet parity in strategic nuclear weapons had not yet been reached, there was hardly any expectation of a nuclear-armed Germany in the foreseeable future. Efforts of the allies to restrict Germany's capacity for military or civil nuclear production constituted merely a basic measuring stick, a limit (among many) within which the defeated and gradually-to-be-rehabilitated ex-enemy must operate. French fears were perhaps the most specifically future-oriented, but they were only one aspect of a complex, almost convoluted projection of the lessons of the past and of national concerns (or perhaps dreams) of the present.

German efforts in this sphere stemmed from a similar assessment; a limit must be observed, but hopefully as a price (among others) for the mitigation of other restrictions. From both interview accounts and popular legend it seems clear that Adenauer—the "compleat civilian"—had only the most rudimentary understanding of what ABC weapons were. Among his political advisors there was some opposition to the acceptance of any discriminatory status. But whatever secret hopes for the future might have been cherished, all Germans looked upon atomic-weapons production and possession as present subjects for great power aspirations, not for German demands.

Even knowledgeable Germans showed very little interest in or commitment to the retention of German atomic rights. As is discussed more fully in the next chapter, most of the reactivated military leadership, as well as the politicians, still believed in the appropriateness of NATO's Lisbon force goals. When they became available, tactical atomic weapons might be a desirable, but not a mandatory, complement to conventional forces for European defense. Furthermore, the scientific establishment was too small, too busy with recovery tasks, or too disillusioned by wartime experiences to contemplate major civil or military nuclear development programs.

In light of these considerations, the character of the German nonproduction pledge appears fairly clear. There is little evidence to support Soviet claims of the mid-1960s regarding "deliberate loopholes." Given the hectic nature of the pre-London weeks, the more pressing points at issue, and the German love for legal formulas already agreed to, it seems more than probable that the EDC provision—which referred only to production on German soil—was transferred more or less intact. The only change explicitly sought by the Germans concerned restrictions on production of nuclear fuel. From the perspective of 1954, with a firm commitment to total integration of the German military establishment within NATO, why should Bonn worry about production on the territory of others or the possibilities of beg, borrow, or steal? [43]

Whether or not the German pledge was conditional seems, even after extensive research, a somewhat more complex question. Beyond Adenauer's own statements, only secondary accounts of his interchange with Dulles—all published after 1965—exist in the public realm. Interviews with conference participants and involved German civil servants done in 1965 and 1966 indicate only that Dulles did make some remarks "along those lines" and that Adenauer was grateful for his "understanding." [44] No one agreed with Adenauer's later interpretation that the pledge was always understood to be subject to the Federal Republic's exclusive judgment regarding changed conditions.

That Dulles should have made such statements is not inconceivable. Beyond his personal friendship with Adenauer and his gratitude to one who had stood by him in the fight about the EDC, this was the type of "personal diplomacy" and "steadfast friendship" that Dulles relished. Moreover, despite his repeated denunciations of the Soviets' breaches of treaties, Dulles held quite different views on the nature of agreements made by "moral equals." In making this point, Coral Bell has cited two striking assertations by Dulles: [45]

In the absence of any central authority to pass judgment, one cannot consider treaties, as such, to be sacred, nor can we identify treaty observance in the abstract with law and order.

Treaties of alliance and of mutual aid mean little except as they spell out what the people concerned would do anyway.

Dulles' remarks in 1954, furthermore, were not inconsistent with his later views regarding nuclear proliferation in general and nuclear-weapons sharing within the Atlantic alliance in particular.[46] As is discussed below, Dulles' position on these questions was never clear; at times he suggested that the American (and later, the Anglo-American) nuclear-weapons monopoly in the West was to be preserved at all costs. But this secretary of state also repeatedly suggested that some proliferation was inevitable, that the United States must share nuclear weapons with its allies in order to garner any political gain from this wave of the future.

Confirming evidence might also be found in Dulles' similarly ambivalent position about the division of labor between Europe and America within the alliance. In most of his public statements, Dulles took great care to stress the primacy and the uniqueness of the European defense mission, the need for a continuing American presence as well as major efforts by the European states, and the need for particular exceptions in Europe to the principles of massive retaliation. Yet at times he seemed to admit the inevitability of withdrawal of American troops from Europe and consequent sole reliance on strategic deterrence; and he repeatedly referred to the many "undeniable" budgetary constraints that threatened even existing American troop levels in Europe. Whichever his true opinions, why should he allow the Federal Republic to make an excessively binding commitment that would only complicate a future American effort to Europeanize European defense?

But the only hard evidence for these arguments stems from later periods, making it unwise to attribute to these London statements too much meaning in terms of American or German 1954 policies. Insofar as Dulles had any concrete conceptions at all in mind, his frame of reference must have been related to developments in the distant future. No evidence suggests (and a geat deal denies) general American willingness at any point to foresee a nuclear-armed Germany, through either a revision of the unilateral renunciation or any other method not explicitly forbidden. If France's atomic ambitions were to be discouraged, surely no superior treatment for the enemy of yesteryear could be expected.

To Adenauer at that time, Dulles' remarks probably merely signified agreement with the basic tenets of his policy on restrictions. Restated in political terms, *rebus sic stantibus* meant: agree to what is necessary for political benefit in the present, the future will take care of itself. In this sense Adenauer's offer can be seen as a preemptive move; he knew from the outset that France would not agree to any solution that did not provide for major restrictions on German rearmament. By freely offering some of the limitations France sought, Adenauer not only demonstrated his good will but substantially improved his bargaining position with respect to other more vital German interests: immediate restoration of essential sovereignty and direct entrance into NATO.

At work, therefore, in the restrospective Adenauerian interpretations of the 1954 pledge and its meaning, first offered in the mid-1960s, would seem to be a much later policy, namely, Bonn's conscious manipulation of Western (and occasionally Eastern) fears about German nuclear development by means of strong emphasis on a still-open national "option." [47] From the late 1950s onward, Adenauer—and much more explicitly, his bombastic defense minister, Franz Josef Strauss—had as their aims far shorter-term, more realistic international political gains than a potential national nuclear-production capability: gains such as progress on a NATO nuclear force, more status for Franco-German defense cooperation, or the undermining of a discriminatory Soviet-American non-proliferation agreement. The circumstances, the nuances, the expectations of 1954 had largely been forgotten or swept aside. Why not use in one's political campaigns or efforts to rewrite history a veiled threat of proven usefulness vis-à-vis Germany's allies?

In the somewhat exaggerated words, delivered in 1965, of one long-time Bonn political pundit:

We undoubtedly have much more to gain from being "persuaded" not to build the bomb than we would have once we actually started. It would probably take us a while, thereby destroying everyone else's faith in our scientific genius. There'd be very little we could or would do with it—we've always folded in crises. . . .

But the threat that "we just might do it yet" has proved quite a bargaining card—in the West, but of course, not [for] the Adenauer dream for the East.[48]

But this political strategy clearly was not the dynamic at work in 1954. At that time the equality and the substantial freedom from fear of a Soviet attack that was needed for such a strategy had still to be achieved.

✠ TWO

The Transition: 1955-1956

✠ ON MAY 9, 1955, the Federal Republic of Germany formally became the fifteenth member of the North Atlantic Treaty Organization. From the viewpoint of most Western observers, the major problems surrounding a German contribution to Western defense had now been resolved. There still was some popular German opposition to rearmament, focused primarily on the moral issues involved and the consequences for future reunification. But the results of the 1953 elections had vindicated the chancellor's decision to rearm and had given him the parliamentary strength needed to proceed. It now seemed only a question of time until the long-sought and long-promised 500,000-man German forces were ready.

It was not to be that easy. Two years passed before more than a handful of German soldiers were in uniform, and that handful was raised under a radically changed strategic concept with a substantially reduced schedule for rearmament. These developments partly were the result of factors that had plagued rearmament planning from the beginning, such as: continuing underestimation of the economic, technical, and personnel problems inherent in the attempt to raise 500,000 men in a rebuilding economy; difficulties, caused by shifting governmental coalitions, in meeting legislative requirements; and not the least, unabating popular opposition to remilitarization.

But in largest measure the causes were to be found in Bonn's increasing recognition of the consequences of its dependence on others' nuclear weapons, of the significance of what have been broadly defined here as nuclear-control issues for all its foreign-policy goals. With the American and NATO New Look decisions, Western strategy now emphasized the doctrine of massive retaliation and the role of tactical nuclear weapons in offsetting failures of the allies to meet the Lisbon force goals. What now would be the military or, more important, the political value of a German defense contribution, designed and raised according to the requirements of 1950–1952? What bargaining leverage would German achievement in the form of twelve conventionally armed divisions win in either East or West?

These were questions few Germans were willing, prepared, or able to answer. This proved true whether the questions were posed in political or military terms, whether discussions took place within the government or in the public sphere, whether the issues were debated by supporters or opposers of rearmament.

Yet the pressure of developments within NATO and most especially in Washington forced consideration and finally resolution of these basic issues. Above all, two crises, the first induced by NATO's Carte Blanche exercise in 1955 and the second by America's Radford Plan in 1956, impelled examination of two problems: the new role of nuclear weapons in Western defense and specifically the relationship between conventional and nuclear forces in Europe; and the preconditions for access to Washington decision-making about nuclear weapons. The policy decisions that ensued marked not only the transformation of German conceptions about Western defense generally but also Germany's transition from a "prenuclear" state to a full-fledged partner in New Look policies.

Viewed from a more analytic perspective, these two crises dramatically illuminated basic conflicts of interest with which German decision makers would have to cope in different degrees throughout the next decade. On perhaps the simplest levels there were the tensions between a government committed to rearmament and NATO membership and a population largely uninterested in military affairs, yet deeply frightened by even the remote prospect of warfare, not to mention nuclear warfare, in Central Europe. How, for example, were the costs and requirements of rearmament to be met without disturbing public confidence in an untroubled future or without disrupting the search for domestic prosperity, an essential condition for political stability?

On another level was the tension within the government between those who were much more interested in the international benefits of rearmament than in its narrow military significance and those who were eager for a military program that would give Germany the best possible chance of survival should war occur. Throughout the decade this split roughly paralleled the division between political and military authority and even the lines of older interservice rivalries. Yet at stake, too, was the definition of basic German foreign-policy goals, of the kind of security to which any middle power could aspire in a nuclear age. Stated quite specifically, what were the requirements for securing the American guarantee for German security and how adequate would that guarantee prove to be? Given American strategic strength, however it might be challenged by increasing Russian efforts, were there any payoffs to be gained through extensive preparations for a defense at the Elbe?

Finally, and of greatest interest in this chapter, there were the tensions arising from Germany's self-defined role as America's faithful ally. Washington was demanding achievement of promised force levels, yet all the while brandishing the political weight of its tactical nuclear weapons as both the basis for its leadership claims and its excuse for not increasing its own conventional-force levels in Europe. How was Bonn to operate, when its extreme vulnerability to what Richard Neustadt has called an alliance's "false sense of intimacy" was dramatically exposed? What were the limits of Bonn's bargaining power vis-à-vis its ally; what was the nature of the compromises to be sought?

THE CARTE BLANCHE CRISIS

From June 20 through June 28, 1955, NATO held its first major combat exercise of that year, the air maneuver Carte Blanche. Held over the Low Countries, northeastern France, and the Federal Republic, the maneuver was designed to explore problems of air offense and defense in the event of a Soviet attack with tactical nuclear weapons against Western military targets. Three thousand planes and numerous military personnel from eleven NATO states participated; more than 335 simulated bombs were dropped in the battle zones.[1]

There were two reasons for the nature and timing of the exercise. First, NATO, following the lead of the United States and Britain, had recently adopted the New Look strategy. By a decision of the North Atlantic Council made the preceding December, the Western European defense system was to be based on two premises: the major threat to European security was a massive Soviet invasion; and such an invasion could only be countered by the early employment of tactical nuclear weapons both in Europe and by the SAC.

The precise implications of this council decision for alliance operations and force requirements were not yet clear. Despite continuing problems in getting specific information from Washington, plans for conversion of the alliance's tactical air forces to the new strategy were perhaps the most advanced. Officers at SHAPE (military headquarters of NATO's European command) were eager to subject the new concepts to a major testing that would provide education to, and operational evaluation by, member states as soon as possible.

Of greater political importance was a second reason: the date of the Geneva summit meeting. Many of the often cited requirements of the West's negotiation-from-strength posture seemingly had been met in mid-1955. A rearming Germany was now in NATO; Western superiority in strategic nuclear weapons and the concomitant massive-retaliation policy were unassailable. A major air maneuver, particularly one emphasizing the recently acquired capability in tactical nuclear weapons, not only would serve as a demonstration of NATO's strength but also would highlight the great risks inherent in further postponement of an equitable European settlement.

Whatever the effect on the Soviet Union, Carte Blanche produced widespread unrest and agitation within the Federal Republic. During the first days after the exercise's conclusion, all the principal press organs carried sensational reports stressing the maneuver's simulated results: more than 300 atomic bombs dropped on more than 100 targets between Hamburg and Munich, with 1.7 million Germans killed, 3.5 million wounded, and incalculable additional casualties resulting from fallout.

The general population reacted with shock and fear. There were public meetings; pacifist groups (including an ad hoc group of eighteen German Nobel Prize winners) [2] issued dire warnings of an apocalyptic future. For most Germans it was their first real introduction to the postwar revolution in weapons. If a repetition of the last terrible days of World War II was unconfrontable, this new horror to which their government had exposed them was inconceivable.

A substantial majority of the electorate had been supporters, however reluctant and passive, of Adenauer's plan to rearm within EDC, within NATO. But support had been founded on the premise that war on German soil would thereby be avoided. As the chancellor himself (true to his nickname, the Great Simplifier) had assured the Bundestag in February, 1955: "So long as we do not belong to NATO, we are, in the case of a hot war between Soviet Russia and the United States, the European theater of war, and if we are in the North Atlantic Pact Organization, then we will no longer be the battlefield. . . .'' [3]

Press commentaries on the lessons of Carte Blanche for future German security were only somewhat less emotional, following the lines set down by Adelbert Weinstein, the prestigious military commentator of the *Frankfurter Allgemeine Zeitung*.[4] Carte Blanche, Weinstein argued, was simply the latest, most striking proof that all previous theories of defense—and indeed the very concept of security—were inapplicable in an era of atomic warfare. Both West and East were preparing to fight a "classical atomic war" in Europe, in which all of the Federal Republic's territory automatically would become the "primary combat zone" and its people the first victims of annihilation by atomic weapons.

Under these new conditions, Weinstein concluded, there was no point in Germany's fulfilling the conventional-forces rearmament program designed in 1952 and reapproved in 1954, namely, a 400,000-man army, an 80,000-man air force, and a 10,000-man navy. For even if these forces and the other tactical forces in NATO were trained and organized for conditions of atomic warfare, they could not mount an effective defense of the Federal Republic's territory. The only true security for its people, he said, lay in the immediate establishment of an extensive system of passive civil defense.

The Adenauer government quickly gathered its forces to combat not only these reactions but also the growing attacks by leaders of the opposition SPD. A series of somewhat unrelated events significantly increased the sphere of discussion and the government's difficulties. In May, 1955, as the Geneva summit meeting neared and talk of détente and coexistence in Europe increased, Adenauer had become increasingly concerned about Germany's bargaining position vis-à-vis its new allies. He had pressed all Western leaders for reassurances that any solution reached regarding the unification of the German nation would involve full recognition of the sovereign, equal rights of the German people in respect to both international and domestic affairs. But to make doubly sure of the Federal Republic's bargaining leverage, he ordered swift introduction of the first enabling legislation for military forces. This would serve both to demonstrate Germany's good faith and allegiance to the West and to face the allies and the Soviet Union with a fait accompli, the creation of military forces by a sovereign state.

The SPD immediately seized upon the third reading of this Volunteers Bill to focus on Carte Blanche and its implications for the long-disputed rearmament program. Resulting discussions of the role of nuclear weapons were neither detailed nor completely accurate; statements by both opposition and government spokesmen were highly emotional in tone and surprisingly general in character. Yet in contrast with earlier public considerations, these statements contained the first emphasis on strategic issues and the first public delineation of German policies regarding the use and control of nuclear weapons.

Primary themes of the somewhat confused attack by the SPD were the "obvious" consequences of NATO's recent "atomic revolution." [5] The opposition, its spokesmen stressed, had always believed the previous strategic concept—deterrence and defense by SAC with supporting European conventional forces—to be unworkable. But now with East and West planning the massive employment of tactical atomic weapons in Europe, the probability of any European conflict ending in "collective suicide" was even greater than before. Neither the American strategic nuclear capability nor NATO forces in Europe—whatever their size, training, armament, or organization—would protect the Federal Republic or its population against nuclear annihilation.

Of equal importance in the SPD's attack was a second and somewhat contradictory theme. The Adenauer administration, SPD spokesmen said, had never understood that rearmament would hinder if not preclude acceptance by the Russians of future reunification of the German nation. But even in terms of its own goals the government had acted irresponsibly. It had not only failed to inform the population about the threat of and the consequences of atomic warfare in Europe, but in its official planning it had also totally ignored developments in nuclear weaponry and military doctrine. Its programs reflected the theories of World War II and the currently outdated plans and conceptions of the EDC period.

The government's rebuttal of these points largely recapitulated the general political-military arguments of earlier rearmament debates. [6] A contribution to Western defense would mark Germany's full reacceptance into the Western community and secure greater consideration of German interests, including reunification, by both East and West. Substantial European forces—and therefore substantial German troops—were needed to reinforce the primary deterrent (the power of SAC), to counterbalance Soviet superiority in conventional forces, and to discourage or defeat Korea-like challenges by the Soviet Union or its satellites. Moreover, almost every speaker hinted at but left unsaid a suggestion that Germany's principal objective was not defense but deterrence, and, in the case of war, the immediate activation of the American nuclear guarantee.

With respect to the specific lessons of Carte Blanche, the government again rested its case on familiar arguments. From an official standpoint it was not yet clear what specific role or value tactical atomic weapons would have, particularly with respect to European defense. Given the most revolutionary developments conceivable, these weapons apparently would never obviate the need for substantial conventional forces. It was even possible that conventional forces would be of primary importance in the future, since the United States and the Soviet Union were rapidly approaching a point of mutual deterrence in the area of strategic nuclear forces. Under these circumstances, a substantial Western conventional-force capability would not only prevent easy Soviet ground gains but would improve chances for negotiated disarmament of nuclear weapons.

Perhaps the most interesting speech from the government side was the rather differentiated stance taken by Franz Josef Strauss, cabinet minister without portfolio and acknowledged, ambitious defense expert of the Christian Social Union, the Bavarian sister party of Adenauer's Christian Democratic Union and its perpetual partner in the governing coalition. Discussing the meaning of a German defense contribution in light of the Carte Blanche lesson, he declared:

There is no doubt that the development of weapons of mass destruction and the capacity to produce them in ever larger numbers have, on the one hand, raised the possibility of bringing them, with manned or unmanned guided missiles, into every territory, and on the other hand, have not only raised the deterrence factor for the aggressor but also called forth a strategic revolution. There is no doubt that ground forces no longer have their original meaning, that from a military absolute they have become a relative quantity.[7]

Strauss, however, hastened to add that these conclusions did not apply to German forces that were to have no "independent strategic meaning." Thus, "the twelve German divisions, conforming in organization, equipment, and training to the age of atomic war . . . are exactly what they should be—an extension and strengthening of NATO."

These Bundestag statements, however, only faintly reflected the impacts of Carte Blanche on intragovernmental relationships, one of the most significant being a shift in influence among the experts on strategy within the political leadership. In previous months, Minister-without-portfolio Strauss and his CSU supporters had repeatedly (though privately) attacked Defense Minister Theodor Blank—a former labor leader and faithful Adenauer lieutenant—for his inability to give meaningful direction in military affairs. Carte Blanche provided the opportunity both to mount renewed attacks and to establish, before a national audience, Strauss's prestige as a modern military expert, familiar with the latest military technology, strategic doctrine, and American developments. Despite Adenauer's continued defense of Blank, Strauss's supporters were successful in pushing for a broader division of defense responsibilities in the form of a national Defense Council. This special cabinet committee, finally established in October, 1955, served to publicly embarrass Blank in his position as defense minister and to secure a prominent position for Strauss, the council's executive vice-president.

It was among officers in the newly formed Defense Ministry that Carte Blanche had its greatest impact, however. As Hans Speier has well detailed, military thinking within Amt Blank on nuclear developments had been limited and unsophisticated.[8] Under the press of massive technical difficulties, within the determined subordination by both civilian and military officials of their personal preferences to the dictates of the postwar political leadership, it was hardly unexpected that Amt Blank generally regarded the collective framework and the NATO strategic concept as unquestionable givens. A further contributing factor was the military's virtually unshaken confidence in their expertise, gained from being the only Westerners who had ever fought against contemporary Russians. That experience had led to the firm conviction that only large, well-armed troops could force termination of warfare in Central Europe. Interview accounts suggest that although Amt Blank did have ongoing discussions about the role of nuclear weapons, the general pattern of German military thought was one of substantial resistance to change and of what one military respondent in 1965 called the "deification of the eastern-front experience." Whenever internal critics went beyond the accepted limits of discussion or asked the wider official or public spheres to consider alternative concepts, they were either silenced through honorific exile to an overseas post or forced out of office.

In public the reaction of the military to Carte Blanche was cool and offhand: the results of the maneuver revealed, after all, nothing revolutionary, just evidence of new levels of destructive power. In timing, however, the exercise coincided with the first examination of NATO documents and plans permitted to the German military, as well as to much of the political leadership. Carte Blanche served as a dramatic illustration of developments in NATO strategy that had been intermittently observable, but not fully known or discussed.

The majority view among defense ministry officials—most of whom were army officers—was that Carte Blanche reflected only too well the limited combat experience and American predilection for airpower that had fostered NATO's ill-advised decision of December 1954. In the officials' view, the major threat to European security was the possibility of a large-scale Soviet invasion—most probably a massive tank assault—in the central region, which would clearly signal the beginning of World War III. Broadly resembling the outline of World War II, this future conflict would be characterized by wide geographic engagement, extensive involvement of all service arms, major destruction of population and industrial targets (particularly in the Soviet Union), and the eventual triumph of the West.

Nuclear weapons would not play the decisive role in such a conflict; their primary significance would be in the strategic sphere, especially in retaliatory attacks directed against the Soviet homeland. The new tactical nuclear weapons—about which very little was known—might provide increased strength once problems of radiation effects, reliability, and logistics could be solved. But as Army Inspector General Adolf Heusinger had summed up:

It also seems clear to me that, in the future as well, we can under no circumstances do without ground forces. In my opinion the thought that in a future war . . . one could perhaps put everything on the air-force ticket is wrong. This judgment is particularly applicable to us in Germany and to our situation. Our geographic position and, in particular, the immense strength of the ground forces on the Soviet side forces us not to neglect the ground forces on our side. It is self-evident that the organization of these units must in an atomic age be held flexible. . . . Our planning has as its object the creation of an organizational pattern from which we can, without difficulty, take every further development of atomic weapons into account.[9]

There were a few military members of the Defense Ministry—because of traditional interservice rivalry, chiefly air-force officers, but also a few young army men—who were prepared to go further in their assessments.[10] To them it was clear that in all but the smallest European conflicts the use of tactical nuclear weapons at an early stage was now inevitable. The reason would be not only the eventual existence of extensive capabilities on both sides but also the major advantages and economics involved. Tactical air forces and ground atomic armament would therefore assume not *a* primary but *the* primary role in the execution and termination of conflict. Few, however, had any specific conceptions of how employment of tactical atomic weapons would be coordinated with existing ground defense or what significance these plans for employment would have for the size or character of the planned German contribution.

For all groups within the military as well as the political leadership, two other major questions remained unsettled. It was not yet clear how many tactical atomic weapons would be available for European defense or how soon. A more basic issue was that of the respective European and American roles, which soon would be defined. Although there had been some indications that European NATO states might eventually receive some form of atomic armament, other factors pointed to continuation of American control or establishment of exclusive competence among special Anglo-American units. Earlier difficulties and restrictions in transfers of information from Washington did not suggest an easy future, however common tactical atomic weapons might become.[11]

By the fall of 1955, in a pattern which was to recur throughout the decade, these intraministry discussions—like almost all the echoes of the Carte Blanche crisis—had become less frequent and less important. For the public, Carte Blanche had become at most an uneasy memory; press commentaries on nuclear warfare or general strategic issues were few. Most of the government—on both the leadership and staff levels—had returned to the pressing problems of getting the remaining rearmament legislation passed and preparing for the induction of the first German soldiers.

There were certain broad hints of future change, nonetheless, signifying the continuing saliency of broadly defined nuclear-control issues. Specific information surfaced late in December, 1955, in two press reports (purportedly based on "information from the Defense Ministry and Atlantic headquarters in Paris"), which the Adenauer government uncharacteristically did not deny.[12] The first reported new plans for the organization of the twelve German divisions, to be designed as "the most modern fighting units in the world." As in the American pentomic scheme, each division was to be relatively small and divided into several highly mobile battalions or "building blocks." Each unit was to be capable of "independent" or "joint" action. Further, ground divisions were to have not only increased tactical air support but also increased fire power of their own, including "atomic artillery."

The focus of the second article was present and future planning for the German air force. Under the EDC planning still in force, the Federal Republic was to create, within four years, twenty-one air wings, with 1,300 jet fighters, fighter bombers, and reconnaissance and transport craft. German air-force officers had come to favor a greater investment in jet fighters, since these would permit "needed" speed and range, as well as the possibility of "bombing" and "modification" for "light" atomic bombs.[13] In the quoted opinion of the acting head of the air force, Werner Panitzki, the long-range goal was equipment with supersonic fighters outfitted with "modern rockets" and having, perhaps, a vertical takeoff capability.

Despite these indications, final decisions about the structure of the German forces and their role in Western Europe's defense, given the tactical nuclear-weapons revolution, apparently had not yet been made. These had to await the second crisis, which occurred during the summer of 1956.

THE RADFORD CRISIS

The months of July through October in 1956 saw a series of major upheavals and changes in German strategic thought and planning that are known in the Federal Republic as the Radford crisis. The opening shot was a *New York Times* story of July 13, entitled "Radford Seeking an 800,000 Man Cut." [14] The article reported that the Chairman of the Joint Chiefs of Staff, Admiral Arthur Radford, had called for achievement by mid-1960 of major changes in American strategic planning, changes required by both economic necessity and revolutionary technological developments. In a logical extension of the New Look approach primary attention was to be devoted to attaining a demonstrable American superiority in strategic retaliatory means. All other forces were to be progressively reduced in size; the Army, in particular, was to lose 450,000 men, the majority to be withdrawn from overseas assignments.[15] The *New York Times* report concluded that although a decision had been postponed until after the national election in November, Radford's proposal had already received significant administration support.

According to subsequent accounts, the majority of the Joint Chiefs— with strong army opposition—had agreed on two basic strategic principles. First, the probability of a conventional war with direct American and Soviet involvement was almost nonexistent; that of a limited war on the Korean model was minimal. Second, and more important, the United States could not or should not afford the cost of conventional-weapons programs adequate to meet these contingencies.

The most obvious application of these principles was to Western European defense and the American contribution to it. Since any conflict in the NATO area would immediately involve both the United States and the Soviet Union and would result in a general nuclear war, there was no longer a need, in Radford's view, for substantial numbers of American ground forces in Europe. Small American "atomic task forces," supporting those ground and air forces which the other allies were already committed to providing, would be sufficient. They would pose the threat of immediate nuclear escalation and demonstrate NATO's willingness to implement that threat, even in response to attack with conventional weapons.

Despite immediate denials by Radford and other administration leaders, the press reports called forth sharp criticism in Washington, in capitals of all the other allies, but most extensively in Bonn. Telling foreign journalists that he considered the Radford Plan a "mistake" and "extremely questionable . . . for all humanity," Adenauer immediately activated the full German political-military apparatus.[16] Ambassadors to NATO states were instructed to gather information and express German opposition to any such revisions or withdrawals; the German ambassador in Washington held lengthy interviews at both the Pentagon and the State Department. Within a week, four leading diplomats were dramatically called home for consultation. A long, unusual meeting of all major cabinet officers at Adenauer's vacation home followed.

The chancellor also moved quickly to head off the domestic repercussions of the report on the Radford Plan. His task required not only allaying popular fears about immediate American "abandonment" and the prospects of "automatic" nuclear war in Europe but also meeting numerous intense challenges launched by the opposition, the press, and some members of the governing coalition itself. The charges were the same as those made during the Carte Blanche aftermath: all previous German defense planning, if not the value or significance of any German defense contributions, had now been invalidated; given such an American posture, the Apocalypse would be at hand, should war come.

A complicating factor was another coincidental interweaving of internal debates and external developments. Only one week before the *New York Times* report, Adenauer, after considerable American criticism about his "unreasonable delay" in fulfilling his pledges, had finally secured the Bundestag's approval for a 500,000-man Bundeswehr.[17] The struggle had lasted from February until July. In the end, to ensure disciplined support within its own ranks the government had been forced to postpone consideration of its proposed eighteen-month term of service for all conscripts.

The principal public challenges had come from the SPD opposition, which had called for a 200,000- to 250,000-man Bundeswehr, made up of long-term professional volunteers.[18] What function this smaller force might perform was not clear; SPD justifications ran from "a balance to East German and/or satellite forces" to "a major step towards a global relaxation of tensions." Despite continuing stress on the horrors of nuclear war, the July remarks of Fritz Erler, the party's military expert, had suggested a "predetermined" role in nuclear defense:

The strategy of NATO leaves no room for doubting that an armed conflict in Europe—even with 500,000 German soldiers—will not remain a conventional conflict. The NATO plans are based upon immediate and direct employment of atomic weapons. . . . An official resolution to that effect was passed in December, 1954. . . . It is correct that General Gruenther said, first, in order to meet his plans . . . 500,000 soldiers are needed. Second, he also said that these 500,000 forces are needed in order to force the Soviet Union in the event of imminent attack so to concentrate its forces as to create the possibility of the Western use of atomic weapons.[19]

Of far greater political significance had been the two-pronged attack mounted by the CSU and the business community (long a CDU power base), which threatened the government, or more precisely Adenauer's CDU, from within. One issue was the eighteen-month term of service which, Amt Blank had declared, was necessary to raise 500,000 men by 1959, but which opponents considered a burden on the strained domestic labor market. A second concern was Amt Blank's purportedly outmoded and economically unrealistic planning for the new forces; it called for "quantity before quality" and for an "inflationary" $16-billion annual defense budget.

With the CSU stressing his recognized expertise and superior knowledge of alliance planning, Strauss (now serving as minister for atomic affairs) had made the theme "quality before quantity" his own.[20] This, Strauss argued, meant not only that "just for the sake of a goal, forces should not be raised which do not meet modern requirements" but also that German forces must be equal in "armament" and "position" to those of the "major" NATO powers. He had hedged on a final figure, but had hinted that a 300,000-man professional Bundeswehr created over a longer period might take fuller advantage of technological (i.e., nuclear) developments.

In its rebuttals the government had added two accents to its arguments of 1955; both stemmed from changed Defense Ministry appraisals. First, although NATO planning did envisage the possible use of tactical atomic weapons, such use implied only a reorganization, not a reduction, of planned conventional forces. Furthermore, there were a number of conceivable instances in which the use of these weapons could not or should not be automatic—a Soviet attack with conventional forces under conditions of increasing American–Soviet strategic parity, a low-level incident, a proxy attack by a satellite state, or a "civil war" fomented by East Germany. A strong conventional-force capability—and 500,000 German troops—would help the West maintain a choice other than capitulation or immediate escalation to the use of nuclear weapons, tactical or strategic.

Finally, government spokesmen had added, all this discussion of an upcoming drastic change in American strategic thinking was rather irresponsible. American officials and NATO authorities, as well as German military advisors, had stressed the absolute necessity for a 500,000-man force with an eighteen-month minimum service period. In Adenauer's words in early July,

> Where colleague Erler got his information about a revolution in the policy of the United States of America fully mystifies me. Besides, I was in the USA just a short while ago, and I can assure you that the present government of the United States and public opinion there (which, after all, I have also gotten to know) think exactly the same as I.[21]

The government's efforts to hold to this basic strategy during the first days of the Radford crisis were quickly undermined by further American developments. Questioned about Radford's proposal at his July 18 press conference, John Foster Dulles expressed general agreement with the "growing feeling throughout the world that recent developments call for greater emphasis on modern weapons . . . and perhaps less weight on manpower." [22] The secretary declared (somewhat weakly) that the planned German goals should be met, but added the qualification "unless and until there is some change by the joint action of NATO."

> If there is an agreement in the NATO Council upon lower force levels, there would be no particular reason that I can think of from a political standpoint why we should urge something higher than the force goals the military people thought were important.

There was also the "me too" which the House of Commons's foreign-policy debate of late July seemed to sound. Presenting Britain's version of the New Look argument once again, Prime Minister Anthony Eden declared that the principal Soviet threat was political and economic, not military, that defense planning must now be geared to the "long haul" and the "most modern armament," that conventional warfare in Central Europe was now "impossible." [23] Foreshadowing the thrust of the 1957 Defense White Paper, he announced that pressing economic problems would necessitate further reductions in all British forces and maximum reliance on the benefits of the new technology.

Adenauer's response was to redouble his efforts to present and dramatize German opposition to the planned British and American force reductions and strategic shifts. Perhaps the most unusual move by Adenauer was the repeated publication in Germany of an article, signed by the chancellor himself, that set forth the reasons for his opposition to the recent moves. In simple but bitter words he wrote:

Since, in my opinion, atomic weapons truly constitute the greatest danger for all humanity, I therefore consider it right to push now for controlled disarmament. All energy should be used to make nuclear war impossible. In my view, it is particularly important to localize possible smaller conflicts. And for that we need divisions with conventional weapons. Their number must be sufficient to prevent a small spark from igniting a rocket war between continents. In their planned numbers, the German divisions could contribute much to this. . . . As resolutely as I support all which can serve controlled disarmament, I unequivocally declare my opposition to any conversion [Umrüstung] to atomic weapons. Too, if the West reduces its ground forces, the land army of the Russian colossus will gain importance with respect to Europe.[24]

August and early September saw little further public discussion but many indications of transatlantic reassurances and heated intragovernmental debate. Members of all political parties began unofficially to challenge or question previous planning; the CSU again approached Adenauer on the immediate necessity of cutting the national and international political costs that Blank's "ineptitude" had produced. The chancellor proved less than receptive, telling Strauss: "Your criticism is unjustified and if you think that as a result of it I am ever going to make you defense minister, you are mistaken. You will never become defense minister in a cabinet of mine." [25]

By mid-September the die was cast. On September 18 the CSU Fraktion (party members holding Bundestag seats) formally asked the government in which it was participating to draw up defense programs which "should take into consideration the scientific and strategic factors." After a full cabinet meeting and a heated CDU/CSU caucus, the government on September 27 announced that it would ask for only a twelve-month term of service for all conscripts. In justifying this action, the official release stated:

An 18-month term of service was originally considered. When plans for a sharp reduction of the American armed forces became known through press reports, the Chancellor authorized deferral of such a proposal . . . *in the conviction that by this time,* an agreement to the 18-month service period by the Bundestag *was no longer obtainable.*[26]

Although not explicitly stated, this decision was clearly part of a larger decision to stretch out and reduce the German force-development program. The Defense Ministry had not obtained, and seemingly had little hope of obtaining, enough long-term volunteer enlistments to offset the cut in conscripts' service periods. More important, the conscription pattern to be followed was the introduction of annual classes, e.g., all males born in 1938. As the government itself had argued during the spring, the low birth rate during the war years meant that a twelve-month conscription period for the war-years classes would not result in sufficient forces to meet the 500,000-man goal by 1959.[27]

Other predictable announcements came in rapid succession. On October 16 it was made known that Franz Josef Strauss was immediately to replace Blank as defense minister. His first task would be to inform the allies that the Federal Republic had "gone too far" in its manpower pledges to NATO, that it would not be able to raise 500,000 men by 1959, and that it was forced to reconsider its total planning.

Days later, the public transition to a New Look strategy was complete. First Strauss in a London interview and then Adenauer in a foreign-press conference in Bonn declared their government's intention to seek atomic armament for the Bundeswehr.[28] Not only must German forces have armament equal to that of the other major NATO contingents; exploitation of "modern technological developments" also would allow the Federal Republic, despite manpower deficiencies, to create a Bundeswehr smaller in size but equal in strength to the promised 500,000-man force.

Strauss was more direct. He pointed out that the Federal Republic had renounced and would continue to renounce atomic-weapons production under the Paris accords. NATO, however, could and should put atomic weapons from the production of other allies at the disposal of German forces.

COMMENTARY

As noted in the introduction to this chapter, these crises viewed together constitute a dramatic introduction to the substance and pattern of German decision-making on issues involving the control of nuclear weapons. This commentary discusses first and primarily the complex intertwining of these issues with the nature and limits of Germany's American connection. The focus then shifts to two "process" elements of the decision-making pattern that were essentially domestic in character and were even more persistent over the 1954–1966 period: the relation of policy-making on nuclear matters to trends in domestic opinion, and the differential roles of officials in Bonn who were interested, respectively, in what might be categorized broadly as deterrence and defense.

NUCLEAR-CONTROL ISSUES AND THE AMERICAN CONNECTION

What were the reasons for the sudden German reversal from determined opposition to the Radford concept to seeming acceptance and even imitation of its basic aspects? Many scholars—for example, Hans Speier and Gerald Freund—have argued that the reversal was a simple case of "political opportunism." [29] The Radford crisis was not really a crisis in German decision-making but rather an attempt to make the United States the whipping boy for revisions that the Adenauer government would have been obliged, or had already planned, to implement in any case. This cover permitted a cessation of domestic debate well before the 1957 national elections, a more acceptable justification to the allies for major cutbacks, and an easier transition to the "modern" (i.e., nuclear-armed) posture from which the Federal Republic feared it might otherwise be excluded.

There seems to be a little question that, even without the report on the Radford Plan, domestic pressures ranging from business-community lobbying to military frustrations with procurement delays would have forced some stretchout and cutback of German rearmament in the near future. It cannot definitely be stated whether in early July Adenauer really hoped to withstand these pressures—whether, in postponing decision on the eighteen-month term, he had not already accepted the inevitability of some delays and reductions. His public stance (like the later account in his memoirs) suggests a definite yes; his record as a practical politician renowned for his abilities to "catch the wind" suggests the opposite. Certainly the fight for rearmament had been a long and bitter one; compromise on one "technical" aspect would not totally undo the accomplishments of the previous six years. The only barrier was Adenauer's own constant interpretation of the rearmament bargain: the need to meet allies' demands for the complete redemption of Germany's pledges regarding force levels in order to gain security and equality within the West.

The impact on Adenauer's position of the reports of the Radford Plan and of Dulles' remarks undermined any remaining chances for success. The news from America not only revived the basic issues concerning Germany's defense contribution and the popular fears of an apocalyptic future, but it also effectively destroyed the credibility of Adenauer's six-year stance and visibly embarrassed him in his command of the Bundestag. To a degree the chancellor's efforts to sustain an atmosphere of crisis and alarm were gestures to the public gallery, the moves of an adroit politician preparing for retreat and interested (as always) in the longest possible period of preelection harmony within the coalition and of cloture on debate. Yet remarks made in many interviews in 1965–1966 suggest that his actions also reflected feelings of acute dismay and a sense of betrayal by Washington—betrayal into the hands of the East, of the other allies, and most unforgivable, of his domestic enemies.

From this perspective, the Radford crisis constitues a special case of what Richard Neustadt has called the crisis-making propensities inherent in an alliance's "false sense of intimacy." [30] To an objective and especially postdictive or retrospective observer the components of the dispute, perhaps even of the crisis, had been present for some time. Yet for most officials in Washington as in Bonn the intensity of the crisis, indeed the crisis itself, came as a shock. On the German side particularly, its course followed rather closely what Neustadt found to be the classic pattern: muddled perceptions of the goals and concerns of the alliance partner, limited or stifled communication about changing plans or priorities, disappointed expectations about particular actions, and finally, somewhat paranoid reactions (How could they do that to me? Are they never satisfied?). All efforts at resolution, for a period at least, were to no avail.

With the Neustadt argument reduced to its simplest lines, the crisis can be seen as the inevitable result, first, of the priority accorded by all factions within the Federal Republic to the imperatives of domestic bureaucratic and electoral politics, and second, of the convenient assumptions on each side, American and German, about the interests, expectations, and national constraints of the alliance partner.[31] Evidence indicates that the "Washington game" that was centered on the Radford proposal (essentially just one skirmish in the continuing debate within the Eisenhower administration about money and doctrine) contained two quite different sets of convenient, optimistic assumptions about German stakes and reactions. Those army and State Department officers who leaked the report on the Radford Plan to the *New York Times* presumably hoped to generate enough national and transnational pressure to force public discussion and a negative decision on the Radford scheme before the November elections. With a need for drama and surprise, they had to maintain as much preleak silence as possible, even vis-à-vis such potential allies as the Bonn leadership.

However, once their goal was reached—once the American commitment to an effective army and an effective local European defense had been reinstituted and the furor had died down—this group expected the Adenauer government to carry on with its planned force contribution. The promised German troops were, after all, a key element in Western Europe's defense, and as one State Department participant said nearly a decade later, "It was the defense of their country, wasn't it?" Adenauer might have to weather some public furor and the usual attacks by the SPD, but in the end, as always, he would prevail.

The assumptions of the Radford Plan's supporters were similar in character, if not in substance. They assumed: that the Germans in the end would have to understand the American position and accept an essentially equivalent but different form of the American guarantee; that Bonn then would want to continue or perhaps even expand its efforts on behalf of its own national security; and that Adenauer, despite interminable delays, had all but completed the basic rearmament program. Again, secrecy was crucial (to a degree, even after the *New York Times* story), given the potential explosiveness of such issues during an election year in the United States, the still pending budgetary debates to be fought out within the Pentagon, and the unsecured flank in the State Department. Adenauer's game, after all, was thought to be much simpler, with real and perceived constraints on any serious anti-American policy; he could and would make the necessary adjustments.

Enough has been said about the priorities and convenient projections at play in Bonn's domestic game. The major point is that the events of the crisis only heightened Adenauer's convictions concerning the incalculable vagaries of the American political process and confirmed his worst suspicions that abandonment or at least withdrawal was possible at any time, almost irrespective of German achievement. Bonn's main concern must therefore not be with the truth or falseness of the reports on the Radford Plan but with the signal they conveyed concerning future changes. And if all this were true, why should the chancellor invest any more precious domestic capital in saving someone else's economic or electoral stakes—in doing more than was minimally necessary to secure the continued American guarantee?

It is in this sense that Adenauer's eloquent plea for strength in conventional forces substituted "good reasons for real reasons" in terms of his international and domestic constituencies.[32] As Neustadt persuasively argues, much of the time it does not matter that political leaders and bureaucrats, particularly those in Washington, do not appreciate the internal stakes of alliance partners or the effects on allies of fallout from their internal bargaining moves and calculations. Distance alone usually ensures that there will be intervening and therefore moderating circumstances; the realities of power generally assure at least minimal compliance by allies with American preferences. Moreover, to expect accurate perceptions from busy men would constitute not only an unnatural but perhaps even a counterproductive diversion of attention, in terms of ultimate domestic accountability and desirable freedom of maneuver.

Clearly, too, misperception had a far smaller impact on Bonn-Washington relations than on Neustadt's London-Washington interactions, because both Bonn and Washington recognized and always proceeded on the basis of the fundamental inequality involved in this partnership. Not only basic German compliance but even a degree of surface conformity with American preferences was assured, in all but the most discriminatory cases, by the passage of time alone. So long as minimum measures against fundamental uncertainty were taken within this framework, Bonn's tolerance for continuing contradiction and ambiguity was impressive. And all this was for reasons which made "appropriate" bargaining handles or even prolonged direct interventions largely irrelevant.

Nevertheless, the findings in this study suggest several major corollaries to the Neustadt false-intimacy theses that would better account for the majority of alliance relationships, which do not conform to the stable, enduring, purportedly equal, postwar Anglo-American connection. Over the long run, there may be higher risks involved in continuing gross misperceptions of stakes and idealized projections of one's own game and rules in all situations of dominance (like Washington's role vis-à-vis Bonn in nuclear-control matters throughout 1954–1966) or in explicit dependence relationships (as in German reliance on the American guarantee). The tendencies toward convenient assumptions about outcomes, about the comfortable intimacy and the incentives of others, would seem much stronger and the chance of adverse influence (unknowing and knowing) on crucial issues much greater. In the German case, as in most other conceivable instances, the lesser partner could expect on any specific issue to be the one to adapt or pay. Yet over the decade both sides bore substantial costs in the form of recurring tension and crisis, the storing up of manipulable grievances, and the cumulative, debilitating impact of communication breakdowns on credibility and future expectations.

Such conclusions, however, do not explain the Radford Plan's catalytic effect on German discussions regarding the acquisition of tactical nuclear weapons for the Bundeswehr. Clearly, by July, 1956, the most influential German military men considered these weapons an integral, necessary component of the Western defense system. They had become better informed about the nature and possibilities of these arms; selected officers were being trained in their use at American centers. Statements made in 1956 by President Eisenhower and Defense Secretary Wilson indicated that at some future date all alliance forces would possess some type of tactical atomic-weapons capability.

But the evidence presented here as elsewhere suggests that these changes had not been accompanied by any basic revision of German criticisms and fears concerning excessive reliance on nuclear defense in Europe.[33] The military leadership still regarded tactical atomic weapons as powerful supplements to conventional-force strength, allowing, for example, greater effectiveness in rear-area air strikes or in the canalization of the enemy's tank action. Tactical atomic weapons were not automatically to be utilized in every conflict nor to be considered, to any major degree, replacements for planned manpower levels. Either use not only would negate the principles of NATO's forward strategy but also would virtually assure the total destruction of the Federal Republic (and East Germany) in the event of a Soviet invasion. And under such conditions there was a further equally terrible possibility: no American response at all.

The impact of the Radford Plan lay in the fundamental military-political questions which any apparent change in American nuclear strategy raised regarding all the gains for which rearmament had been undertaken: the future security of Europe, the nature of the European-American relationship, and the position of Germany within the Atlantic alliance. Most fundamentally, a "peripheral strategy" meant the massive withdrawal of American forces (i.e., hostages) that were believed to be Germany's only direct guarantee of American willingness to use all means to defend German territory. Even if Radford's proposal specified the maintenance of some American troops, with more effective weapons, there was no reliable assurance that further withdrawals would not be made or that these weapons would ever be used. The basic military purpose of German rearmament had been to secure a continued American presence—not to permit or hasten the withdrawal of American troops.

There were also the ominous implications for the future division of labor within the alliance of increasing American emphasis on the primacy of nuclear weapons. Carried to its logical conclusion, Radford's proposal (and Eden's contemporaneous remarks) seemed to imply division of NATO functions between "sword" states and "shield" states. The principal agent of Western security, strategic nuclear capability (sword), was to remain the chief function and exclusive domain of the United States and Britain. The Continental allies were to bear the burden of providing almost all the shield forces that would be necessary at the onset of war to secure maximum opportunity for immediate retaliation.

It was for this reason that Germany (and the other Continental states) raised major opposition to the Radford type of thinking in alliance forums.[34] First, Western Europe should not and would not play the role of NATO's "infantry." If maintenance of a conventional capability was proving too great an economic burden for the alliance's leader, the smaller states could not be expected to be equal to the task. And, it was added sotto voce (then as in the later MLF experience), had not the United States demonstrated that there was indeed a "nuclear way" around the onerous and increasingly expensive task of raising conventional forces in an indifferent environment?

Of greater significance (although not equally emphasized in discussions) was the question of the European allies' future influence—in peace-time as well as in the event of war—over decisions concerning their own security. The existing American monopoly in weapons and decisions, spokesmen argued, was no longer acceptable, because of growing Soviet capabilities and increasing European self-confidence. Tactical atomic armament not only would be a more effective, less expensive means; it also would physically guarantee some form of European participation in the Western deterrent system, a physical counter against possible abandonment by the United States.

Most far-reaching of all were the consequences of Radfordian thinking for Germany's political position within the alliance. It was not that the Federal Republic was uninterested in eventually obtaining a tactical delivery capability; even Adenauer's words, viewed in context, were not a demand for a wholly conventional strategy.[35] It was rather that the Federal Republic was faced with a difficult choice, one which involved the possibility of major political costs, whatever its final decision.

Without question, any German attempt to acquire a dual capability would meet with significant political opposition. The domestic foes of rearmament would certainly increase in number. More important was the resistance to be expected within the alliance, even though American spokesmen had promised that all interested Continental allies would be included in NATO weapons-sharing programs.[36] NATO discussions during 1956 had revealed significant French and British opposition to German acquisition of nuclear-capable weapons. Moreover, French policies and tactics during the Euratom negotiations (discussed below) clearly were designed to prevent any German threat to French domination of the Continental atomic energy sphere, civil or military.

Yet the calculations which had led to the initial decision to rearm were still decisive. The German military effort, whatever its size or character, had as its fundamental purpose assurance of a full, equal German participation in Western affairs, both in political decision-making and in the deterrent system. Should the Federal Republic submit to further restrictions on the armament of its forces, accept a position of de facto inferiority, or persist in independent action at variance with prevailing American doctrine, the basic political position—and the fundamental security it provided—would be jeopardized, if not lost.

Whatever German political and military reservations concerning the role of tactical atomic armament existed, political status and necessity were at stake in the final analysis. And as CDU/CSU politicians stated in interview comments made in 1965, the basic argument was but one step away from that used by Strauss (here paraphrased) in the stormy Fraktion caucus held before the government's announcement of September 1956:

Power today is military power.
Military power today is atomic power.
Without atomic armament Germans will supply only the bakers and the kitchen-boys for the forces of the other allies.
And with such a role, the future of Germany is decided.

PROCESS ELEMENTS IN NUCLEAR DECISION-MAKING

One of the principal parameters in German consideration of nuclear-control issues throughout this period was both the cause of and a political legacy of the Carte Blanche and Radford Plan crises, namely, volatile popular sensitivity to any indication that a war might be fought in Central Europe. Both episodes produced massive unrest and extensive efforts by the government to calm and reassure. The flurry was soon stilled, with popular and press consideration dwindling to an almost negligible point, only to flare up with renewed intensity at the next crisis point.

This volatility was in part a direct result of the way in which public opinion with respect to all foreign-policy issues was handled by the Kanzler-demokratie—that curious blend of Adenauer's personal style with the Federal Republic's constitutional system.[37] Adenauer seemingly never felt obliged to consider extensively the views of, or to educate, the populace. Complex or unpleasant choices were always reduced to the simplest terms: alliance with the West or chaos; my policy or chaos. Moreover, the government most often delayed explaining or even indicating the nature of specific decisions until forced to do so, either by an electoral contest or by developments outside Germany.

In following this strategy Adenauer revealed not only his adherence to an older German tradition but also a shrewd understanding of the postwar mentality regarding defense. For most Germans the defeat in World War II had brought more than enough horror, more than enough education in warfare for one lifetime. Except when strongly pressured to do so (and as the SPD discovered, often not even then), most Germans would not or could not contemplate a new, more terrible war. The majority preference was to concentrate on personal affairs, not to question too deeply into these matters of national security—in short, to trust the government and increasingly NATO to make the necessary and appropriate decisions. War probably would not come; if it did, all would be lost, almost irrespective of what Germany had done or decided.

In manipulating these popular sentiments in a crisis, however, the Adenauer government faced a twofold difficulty. Its usual aim was to administer as soon as possible the necessary and desired reassurance. Simplicity and speed—especially in this early period—would not, however, prevent the recurrence of the same questions with the same intensity in the next crisis. Moreover, there were instances when the government might wish so to use or redirect popular agitation as to strengthen or underline its bargaining position vis-à-vis its allies. But in such cases it must keep this unrest within tolerable limits and be able to restore the status quo ante should its external efforts prove unsuccessful.

A related problem was the degree to which nuclear and in fact all defense questions were the concern only of a small elite, and then only upon occasion and in the broadest political terms. A similar situation prevailed (and would continue to prevail) in most NATO countries, even in the United States. Yet the particular nature of the German postwar experience made this narrowing of the scope of the attentive public an even more difficult and potentially dangerous development for the Federal Republic.

For most of the German elite, both within and outside the formal political structures, rearmament and all that it entailed were simply the prices to be paid for the restoration of political sovereignty and the promise of American protection.[38] Sharing popular views on both the improbability of and the Armageddon character of a future war, few knew or sought to know the details of German or NATO defense planning. Except when defense policies clearly affected their domestic or economic interests, members of the elite took positions on the basis of general political preferences and were willing to leave all military assessments and discussions to experts.

As both crises showed, the problem, however, was "Experts in what?" Neither the interests nor the talents of the responsible political leadership lay in continuing detailed consideration of strategic questions. Theodor Blank had been appointed defense minister, at least in part, for that very reason. As a liberal trade union leader he was so obviously outside the military tradition that his presence reassured both the wary allies and the uneasy German populace. As a loyal CDU lieutenant he was sincerely committed to Adenauer's basic goal: fulfillment, with the fewest interruptions and questions possible, of the goals set by the allies. Developments in nuclear weaponry or grand strategy and resulting possible changes in German planning were not, nor were they expected to be, among his major concerns.

Of all the Bundestag leaders perhaps only five—Fritz Erler (SPD), Richard Jaeger (CSU), Kurt Georg Kiesinger (CDU), Erich Mende (FDP), and Franz Josef Strauss (CSU)—had special competence or continuing interest in strategic issues. All five had been involved somewhat in the EDC discussions and planning; all had made study trips to Washington, London, or Paris.[39] Yet with the exception of Strauss no one was considered more than a defense expert for his party, devoting substantial but not complete attention to this area. Moreover, on nuclear questions as on other topics their particular views were subordinate to their parties' stands on the political benefits of rearmament.

There were no extragovernmental sources which could have—or more important, would have—been asked for advice or evaluation. Quite apart from the traditional German separation between the official and university spheres, the number of intellectuals interested in contemporary developments, let alone strategic issues, was limited. These few were either already committed to an antirearmament position or had joined the handful of political anslysts writing in the national press.[40] Either attribute reinforced the government's predisposition to discount and disregard their views; the opposition merely added them to the chorus.

What was left was the most obvious source of expertise—the military, including both the leading officers within Amt Blank and a small group of influential consultants, chiefly retired military officers, now willingly or unwillingly in civilian life.[41] As discussed above, their ability to assess or even follow the newest strategic developments was limited by inadequate staffing, limited information, and all-consuming physical preparations for rearmament. Under these circumstances, it is hardly surprising that at this point their conceptions regarding nuclear strategy and deployment were only slightly revised versions of the conventional-force doctrines used by Germany in World War II.

Both crises also highlighted a more general factor: the definite political limits within which the military, whatever its specific conceptions, had to operate.[42] In essence, military officers were free to plan, to direct, to revise the rearmament program only so long as three conditions were met. There was to be no move which would threaten in any way the government's hard-won domestic consensus, or significantly conflict with alliance plans or expectations, or most important of all, give particular strategic considerations priority over the political aims of rearmament.

Acceptance of these constraints was partly the result of the changed position of the military leadership itself—the loss of much of its traditional prestige and independent authority. During most of the postwar period, military ideas and influence had had to be exercised through, and therefore at the discretion of, the chancellor's office.[43] Any attempt to circumvent an Adenauer dictate by arousing popular support contradicted the terms not only of German military tradition but also of political reality.

But a further fundamental factor was the overwhelming military support for the chancellor's alliance strategy: pay the necessary price now for the political benefits that will assure a more favorable future. In terms of alliance doctrines on use and control of tactical atomic weapons, it would prove to be an ambiguous guide.

THREE

Germany Goes Nuclear: 1957-1960

✠ THE PERIOD 1957–1960 without question constitutes the most formative phase in the development of German policies on issues broadly defined here as issues concerning the Federal Republic's access to nuclear weapons. These years witnessed not only the increasing emergence of a German position in NATO discussions and planning on nuclear questions. They also saw within the national sphere the impact of these issues on the definition of broad national-security goals and on the adoption of basic military programs, all with far-reaching consequences for the future.

The factors prompting these developments were both internal and external. The shock produced by the Radford Plan had forced many in the political leadership to consider seriously for the first time the relationship between the details of Western nuclear strategy and the role the Federal Republic hoped to play within the Atlantic alliance. The appointment of a new, politically ambitious defense minister, vitally interested in the consequences of the continuing nuclear revolution for Germany, meant further attention to these issues. Whatever his interest in ministerial autonomy, Franz Josef Strauss consistently called the attention of the leadership—and in a different manner, the attention of the German public—to the role and the needs of the German defense structure in a nuclear age.

The gradual maturation of that military structure also created significant pressures for decisions on nuclear policy. The primary questions became less "How do you build up forces from point zero?" and more "What role do and/or should these forces play in Western defense?'' There was also the need to obtain further legislation for and popular acceptance of the changes in force development and equipment that were dictated by adherence to the New Look. To be sure, given the domestic political context discussed in chapter 2, most often the Adenauer government successfully strove to gain general toleration of such changes while avoiding specific discussion of their significance for German foreign-policy choices.

Yet the combined pressure of growing budgetary requirements and a continuing, well-informed, vocal SPD opposition led to recurring debate. Despite restricted information, major confusion, and at times extreme emotionalism, argument managed to focus on the central issue: the details and implications of the Germans' full participation in a system based on (1) the early use of tactical nuclear weapons on their own territory and (2) on the sufficiency of American strategic nuclear forces to ensure deterrence of enemy attack and guarantee of German security, at a time when the advent of Soviet-American strategic parity was foreseen.

The most significant factor, however, was Germany's increasing participation in NATO and the resulting requirements for a specifically German view of issues confronting NATO. The period 1957–1960 saw a striking transformation in the Federal Republic's power position within the alliance. In 1957 Germany was still the new boy, barely knowledgeable about or accepted in political and military discussions, possessing no more than a handful of troops. By December 1960, the Federal Republic was rapidly replacing withdrawing Gaullist France as the largest conventionally armed power on the Continent and the principal Continental audience for and sounding board of the United States within NATO.

What emerged from the debate was not a series of discrete national decisions reflecting narrowly rational or independently derived national preferences and perspectives. It was rather a German accent to prevailing doctrine, planning, and political dogma within NATO, or more accurately, SHAPE. Implementation once again fell far behind outward political adaptation; there were still major doubts, notably among the military, about tactical nuclear doctrine. But the overwhelming tenor of Bonn's deliberations during 1957–1960 was that of constant reaction to policies defined elsewhere and of determined dependence and adaptation.

This reflected, to a degree, merely the Federal Republic's particular developmental stage in military affairs. SHAPE was the NATO body in which

Bonn participated most fully and directly; a major role for Germans either in NATO's top military executive committee, the Standing Group, or in the European command had yet to pass years of French and particularly British opposition. The Germans, moreover, still were conspicuously underdeveloped in a technical sense; most of the leadership was only beginning to understand even the broadest consequences of the nuclear revolution for both East and West. Increasing knowledge indeed tended to heighten Germany's unwillingness to consider rigorously the requirements of national defense. Personally and politically, Germans found it easier to adopt a downpayment perspective on the military program, to transfer responsibility for the details and the hard choices to NATO, and to trust in the operation of deterrence while concentrating on domestic priorities.

As in the outcome of the Radford crisis the most important factor was the faithful-ally stance. If there ever had been any question, the events of 1956 demonstrated that broader rationality lay in the nurturing of the American connection. At a minimum, NATO was to be viewed as the most acceptable framework for the tightening and interweaving of this bilateral bond, of assuring access to if not explicit participation in crucial decisions on nuclear policy. SHAPE and its SACEUR thus had a dual significance: on the one hand, as the interpreters and embodiment of continuing American commitment and policies; on the other, as an effective intermediary channel for the expression and support of German-cum-European interests vis-à-vis Washington.

As before, this did not mean that the Federal Republic was simply to accept what SHAPE determined or Washington deemed appropriate. The Federal Republic must constantly emphasize its rejection of any less-than-equal status, its right as a major partner to a meaningful role in the alliance, its expectation of future recognition and future inclusion in all crucial decisions and instances. But there was no international, much less domestic, political advantage to be gained from being conspicuously efficient or independent. Too many demands too soon, too extensive a development of national planning and command structures, too great a distance from, or even too great a questioning of, existing doctrine—all these would undermine if not destroy the political benefits so carefully sought since 1949.

Yet even the decision to "go NATO" on nuclear issues did not ensure a coherent or stable policy for the Federal Republic. The alliance itself was neither unified nor certain with respect to the general question of nuclear-weapons use and control. The period 1957–1960 witnessed rapid change in weapons and doctrine and much debate within and among NATO states. There were ongoing disputes regarding the use of tactical nuclear weapons, the possibility of limited war in Europe, the actual threat posed by the Soviets' medium-range ballistic missiles (MRBMs), and the present and future limits of the American nuclear guarantee. Most NATO decisions of the period were either stopgap measures, subject to later revision, or plans bearing little relation to existing capabilities or political realities.

For the short run at least, these uncertainties and problems did not significantly deter the course of Germany's adaptation or education. To the extent that leaders were aware of these issues at all, most (with the conspicuous exception of Strauss) believed them to be matters for decision by NATO and the Americans. Indeed, this period saw the first hard evidence of perhaps the central fact and success of the NATO experience: for Germany as for the United States (and as for virtually no other member state), NATO was at the center of national preoccupation, whatever the particular details or circumstance. The issues of NATO and of nuclear control, broadly defined, were not simply interrelated; they were virtually synonomous, then and into the 1960s.

Accordingly, the German accent on publicly advanced nuclear questions placed primary emphasis on the scope of German participation in NATO. The key themes, nationally and internationally, were the goals of "equality" and "integration." The first goal was simple in concept: to insure German participation in all phases of NATO's functions—armament, planning, decision-making—as a partner, not merely as a troop supplier or satellite. The second goal was more complex. Integration of German forces with as many NATO and especially American forces as possible would mean material advantages for those developing German forces, would allay fear about German adventurism, and would further bind Western forces to the defense of Germany. Beyond this, it would in a relatively short time lead necessarily to the de facto revision of the alliance's power structure, would prompt inauguration of new bodies and new contingencies in which Germany's growing role must be recognized.

The object of this and the following two chapters is to explore systematically the three major dimensions of Germany's adaptation on nuclear-control issues that German membership in NATO brought about. This chapter focuses on the Germans' interpretation of nuclear dependence within the

general alliance debate about the future defense of Europe. Chapters 4 and
5 deal with several aspects of the related issues of access to Washington
decision-making and of physical control, namely, (1) the specifics of Germany's adaptation in armaments and force development and the opposition
this adaptation engendered at home and abroad, and (2) Germany's role in
the alliance's search for control-sharing mechanisms and formulas.

STRAUSS: HIS ROLE AND POLICIES

That any meaningful examination of 1957–1960 policies must be preceded
by a discussion of the character, role, and policies of Franz Josef Strauss
tells much about the pattern of Germany's policy-making on nuclear matters. This defense minister was one of the central actors in European affairs;
his speeches and writings on security issues while in office and afterward
reached a volume unequaled in the postwar German experience. He was certainly the most visible figure; for both his national and international audience
he increasingly became the public personification of the Bundeswehr.

In this case there is considerable congruence between public image and
political reality: many of Germany's 1957–1962 policies on nuclear-control
issues can be attributed as much to Strauss as to Adenauer. Objective analysis at this range is difficult, of course, particularly since Strauss was and still
is a subject of controversy.[1] But evidence supports the argument that the
politics if not the broad course of Bonn's adaptation to membership in
NATO would have proceeded quite differently without Strauss. Moreover,
his consuming interest in the forms of access to and sharing of nuclear
decision-making, and his quick grasp of the political aspects of the latest
military developments, were unmatched among any of the CDU/CSU leadership except for the aging chancellor. As Klaus Epstein once noted:

He is the first defense minister in Germany (if one excludes Hitler) who made civilian supremacy a fact rather than a theory; his ruthless personnel policies—however
unfair in individual cases—succeeded in making even stiff-necked generals realize
who was boss. . . . Strauss's technical achievement of building up the Bundeswehr
is generally recognized. . . . There is no gainsaying the great achievement of building up, in the short period of seven years, an army of 420,000 men which has
become the backbone of the conventional forces of NATO.[2]

Until the formation of the CDU/CSU-SPD Grand Coalition in the mid-
1960s, Strauss was perhaps the best-publicized figure of Germany's postwar

political generation. The son of a Munich butcher, he, to paraphrase one commentator, had the good fortune to be too young during the Nazi era.[3] Strauss was neither a sympathizer with Nazis nor an emigré from them; some evidence suggests that he was not very politically conscious or concerned. He spent the pre-1945 years compiling an impressive academic record and serving a totally undistinguished, compulsory term of military service.

His political career began at the war's end under the aegis of the American military government; he served first as a translator, then as an appointed provincial official. Strauss early became involved in the founding of the Christian Social Union, a new interconfessional party that was essentially the Bavarian equivalent of Adenauer's CDU. In rapid succession Strauss became an elected provincial official, general secretary of the CSU, a Bundestag deputy, and finally, when only thirty-three years old, chairman of the CSU Fraktion.

Until the *Spiegel* crisis in 1962 forced his retreat, Strauss's years in Bonn were marked by increasing prominence and power. Appointed minister without portfolio in 1953 by a somewhat reluctant Adenauer, Strauss soon elbowed his way to a position of jack-of-all-trades in the areas of defense policy and foreign policy. To the fullest extent possible he capitalized on his considerable rhetorical prowess and his wide-ranging experience and good personal relations with political and military leaders in France and especially in the United States. In October, 1955, Strauss, somewhat disgruntled, took the top job at the newly-created Ministry of Atomic Affairs; by October, 1956, he had achieved his stated interim goal, the Defense Ministry, which he headed for the next six years.

Strauss's unmistakable drive to the chancellorship was halted when events in 1962 revealed his willingness to use the antisubversion powers of his office to suppress *Der Spiegel*, a newsmagazine determinedly hostile to him. The resulting public furor (discussed further in chapter 6), since such suppression evoked the reminder of similar behavior by Nazis, led to his resignation from the government but not his removal from the CSU leadership or from the small group of Bonn's influentials and rivals under Erhard. In 1966 he reemerged as an architect of the CDU/CSU-SPD Grand Coalition and became not only finance minister but ideological leader of the anti-NPT forces. At present he remains ascendant if not dominant within the opposition parties.

Throughout his career Strauss's political style has remained the same. In every respect he is a curious combination of an intelligent, shrewd tactician and a rolled-shirt-sleeves, free-swinging Bavarian "pol." Whatever the task, he throws himself into it—a leader who is dynamic, intelligent, bombastic, but often brutally aggressive and always bitterly hostile toward any criticism or interference in his domain. In some respects he is the ultimate politician; he has a quick, intuitive sense for power and for short-run political advantages to be gained from current developments. Yet particularly before 1962 Strauss seemed repeatedly to misperceive (if not to ignore) political limits, to miscalculate totally what was politically acceptable or feasible, domestically or internationally.

His term as defense minister must be seen as a special phase of his career, if only because of the ruthless determination with which he sought the position. Strauss's motive seems obvious; at a very early point he recognized the potential for personal power that was inherent in the office of defense minister.[4] Whatever risks to popularity existed—the fact of German rearmament, the nature of the East-West confrontation, and the direction of the nuclear revolution in warfare—they would give a shrewd minister a national and international position only slightly second to that of the chancellor. And the most damaging brickbats probably would be aimed at the first defense minister, Theodor Blank, not at his successor.

Beyond Strauss's own statements and popular conceptions fostered by a succession of devoted press officers, little public evidence concerning his operational role as defense minister exists. What is perhaps the most widespread belief concerning Strauss's role stresses his rapid assumption of total control within the ministry. Observers point to his successful reorganization plan of 1957, to his popularity among the military because of his professional attitude, and to his successful take-charge approach to the civilian administrative structure. Some enthusiasts even compare Strauss's impact on the ministry during 1957–1960 with respect to augmenting and assuring civilian control to that of Secretary of Defense Robert McNamara on the Pentagon during 1961–1963.

Closer examination of Strauss's record as defense minister does reveal some limiting conditions. When appointed, Strauss had several general conceptions regarding the organizational reform of Blank's chaotic legacy. But from the beginning his was a personal, almost charismatic, style of leadership, based on personal relationships and subject to rapid shifts. Apparently he neither had nor could ever develop any comprehensive, long-term plan for rationalizing ministry operations.[5]

Strauss's principal administrative achievements were measures which reinforced the primacy of the minister and to a limited degree modernized the organization of the military services. He came alone to a ministerial post that had no substantial professional staff attached to it and continually bemoaned the lack of a responsible and imaginative brain trust. He had made certain contacts during the anti-Blank campaign, particularly among air-force officers, and soon gathered a considerable number of devoted followers. Yet throughout his term he had difficulty attracting and keeping personal advisors within or outside the ministry who were competent and responsible as well as loyal. Furthermore, in a number of cases Strauss chose the wrong man or put too much trust in a subordinate's capacity for independent judgment.[6]

Quite apart from these difficulties and the general problems inherent in mastering any modern bureaucracy, Strauss faced powerful potential rivals within the ministry itself. Two, in particular, had served in the defense establishment for a considerable period and enjoyed personal access to the chancellor and to other major political leaders. The first was State Secretary Josef Rust, Strauss's second-in-command until 1959; the second was General Heusinger. Although never publicized, disagreements with what was in effect the Defense Ministry's operational leadership proved embarrassing to the minister, particularly when cabinet approval was involved. Several political and military figures interviewed in 1966 suggested that Strauss was forced to make "a number of major compromises" and to act always within, not against, the hierarchical commands and administrative structures.

A final limiting factor was Strauss's personal relations with high-ranking military officers. During his first years in the ministry, a considerable degree of mutual respect existed. Strauss's academic achievements were widely known and admired;[7] his dynamism and knowledge of military affairs contrasted sharply with Blank's record. Strauss, moreover, seemed to accord the military a position of honor and importance generally denied to them in the postwar political system.

Yet there remained reservoirs of criticism and suspicion. To the more conservative officers Strauss's personal behavior (his purported drinking bouts, noisy activities in Bonn's night life, and amorous escapades at international conferences) seemed scandalous, erratic, and "typical for a butcher's son." However they might feel about his views on defense issues, officers objected to Strauss's tendency to introduce military questions into the political arena. Internal discussions often were exploited for the minister's personal political advantage; on more than one occasion the viewpoints and reputations of military leaders were used to bolster Strauss's position in a personal battle within the party.

Perhaps the best-known incident was the one that grew out of the "Generals' Memorandum" of August 1960. An article, "Requirement for Effective Defense," was issued as a special supplement to the official military publication, *Information für die Truppe,* and immediately reprinted in the official *Bulletin.* Apparently Strauss intended to use this vaguely worded paraphrase of a recent speech by Inspector-General of the Armed Forces Heusinger as a way to combat the "pernicious" efforts of the SPD to develop contacts within the Bundeswehr. The speech, however, also contained considerable (but for the period, not unusual) stress on the need for tactical nuclear weapons. The article countered the SPD's antinuclear stand, but it had the more important effect of touching off an international controversy about the "nuclear demands" of the "German generals." [8]

Similar limits must be put on the image of Strauss as the *eminence grise,* directing without challenge all defense decisions of the Adenauer government. Without question, Strauss played the central and most dynamic role in discussions of all national-security questions within the cabinet and its subgroup, the Defense Council. His position under the German concept of ministerial responsibility was heightened by his status as a technical expert. Among colleagues who had little understanding of strategic affairs, he was the man with the facts and the figures, the man who through personal contacts knew what the Americans would do next.

Moreover, Strauss's relationship with Adenauer was a good one on balance. In what he considered to be technical matters the chancellor was willing to grant the minister considerable freedom and to be attentive to his estimates and proposals. Also, Strauss was valuable as Adenauer's "ramrod for delicate affairs"; his willingness to act as a trial ballooner, to be the focus of public controversy, allowed the chancellor to have a certain political flexibility without the costs of public involvement.

Nevertheless, Strauss's dynamism encountered numerous obstacles in the cabinet. His propensity for intrigue, his thinly veiled political ambitions, and his flamboyant personal behavior were the targets of continuing criticism. A point particularly disputed was Strauss's tendency to act as if he were both defense minister and a second foreign minister. The relationship between Foreign Minister Heinrich von Brentano and Strauss usually was cool; the Foreign Office not only had no permanent liaison with the Defense Ministry at the bureaucratic level but also as a whole tended to view any action by Strauss as "ill-advised," "sensational," and "inconsistent." On several occasions Adenauer joined von Brentano in privately criticizing ventures of Strauss that appeared to be attempts to independently shape foreign-policy choices.[9]

Strauss's efforts to dramatize the primary role and requirements of the Defense Ministry also encountered repeated resistance from Economics Minister Ludwig Erhard and Finance Ministers Fritz Schäffer and Franz Etzel. Every defense project which appeared to endanger, by its financial or manpower demands, the continued growth of the domestic economy was closely scrutinized and exhaustively debated. Strauss's more ambitious proposals regularly suffered major revisions; several were consistently and successfully opposed.[10]

Strauss's ambitions also were seriously constrained by the chancellor's thoroughgoing distrust of prospective heirs and their empire building. The defense minister's supporters—the CSU and some CDU members—made no secret of their conviction that he eventually should assume Adenauer's mantle or of their disappointment that Adenauer did not clear the way for Strauss's later accession by accepting the presidency of the Federal Republic in 1959. After this episode the chancellor was extremely chary of expressing support for Strauss and tried, somewhat unsuccessfully, to limit the growth of his ministerial power and national popularity.

Strauss's role in discussions about strategy is the most difficult to evaluate. Although clearly the product of ambition, Strauss's interest and capability in broad military questions cannot be underestimated. Unquestionably he was (and to a limited degree still is among) the most qualified within the CDU/CSU. Once his interest was aroused, his considerable intellectual abilities and voracious curiosity led to a quick, wide-ranging command of the general area. The intensity of his approach was described by one commentator in these terms: "Technology fascinates him; he has a horror of slipping behind and being caught unawares by tomorrow's new plane when most people are still learning the name of today's already obsolete one." [11]

Strauss's expertise was not simply the result of private reading and research; he also proved an eager pupil. Beginning in 1952 when he assumed the chairmanship of the unofficial Defense Committee, Strauss sought contact with foreign, particularly American, officials and civilian strategists. His interest and enthusiasm were warmly welcomed by those in Washington anxious to hasten Germany's contribution to the alliance and to educate "reasonable, responsible" Europeans in American thinking about defense matters.

The same pattern on a somewhat higher level continued during Strauss's years as minister. Each of his numerous official and unofficial visits to the United States featured a wide-ranging round of discussions and inspections, in the Pentagon, at military installations, and at production facilities. He and his staff maintained frequent, friendly contacts with American military officials both at SHAPE and with the Seventh Army in Germany. As several American interview respondents remarked, during 1957–1960 Strauss, in contrast to many of his Continental counterparts, was "a man with whom you could really talk."

Interview comments, both critical and approving and from both military men and politicians, attested to Strauss's continuing interest and influence in discussions about strategy within the ministry. Beyond formulating general policy guidelines, he took a major part in the definition of problems for internal study and in the preparation of German position papers for NATO meetings. Almost all those interviewed mentioned his ability to assess quickly the political-military consequences for Germany of a given development, whether it concerned technical capability, force structure, or military deployment.

Several of the respondents who had served in the Defense Ministry contended, however, that Strauss occasionally placed far too much faith in his own expertise. Confronted with a new problem at a NATO meeting or in the United States, the minister reportedly would make an immediate statement about the German position on that problem. He would then turn over the problem to the responsible Bonn group for more extensive study as to why his assessment was correct. The controversy thus generated did not matter to him; the divergent views or overridden responsibilities of his subordinates were of even less importance.

With the data available and the controversy that still surrounds Strauss, a final judgment is impossible. Clearly he played a major role in and significantly influenced the direction of German thinking about strategy. But the weight of the factors discussed above suggests that a busy politician could not continually assume the major role in even the final stages of policy formulation. Strauss had to rely substantially on the views of advisors; he had to accept the judgments of persons involved in defense matters on a full-time basis. Moreover, the existence of major international constraints, formal and informal, on German military developments must have required devoting considerable time to allaying allies' fears, if not to reacting to their initiatives.

The only published materials of relevance are Strauss's numerous speeches and writings—evidence of his thinking, if not of his actual role.[12] Here, too, any judgment must be a partial one, based on incomplete data. Neither the general national or international background nor the Adenauer government's political style was conducive to major public exposés of strategic thought. But there is enough material to allow an impressionistic comparison of Strauss with his counterparts in other Western countries and a drawing of some general assessments.

The first conclusion is that searching through documents to discover a detailed, systematic, peculiarly Straussian concept that encompasses all security issues is useless. Most of his statements were liberally sprinkled with Latin quotations, historical allusions, expert jargon, and little else. Shifts in emphasis from one broad strategic theme to another reveal primarily an extreme political sensitivity to events of the moment—a new Soviet offensive, an upcoming NATO meeting, an American call for troop reduction, and most especially, day-to-day political developments in Bonn. As one respected Bonn journalist remarked in an interview echoing Neustadt's observations about the importance of domestic political calculations for foreign-policy positions:

You can almost never accept Strauss's public statements at face value. The basic themes—such as they are—remain the same. But to really understand them, you have to know what was in the wind at the moment. What was the SPD doing? Was there a state election coming up? Did Strauss need to stress how valuable he was as defense minister to ward off the criticism in another arena? Was he trying to force the cabinet's hand? What was going on in the ministry?

Only a few of Strauss's statements during 1957–1960 deal with basic national-security or nuclear-control issues in any detail. Most were made during the latter part of this period, after parliamentary approval in 1958 of the last rearmament issue, nuclear-capable armament of the Bundeswehr. Moreover, a number of statements were made to, or with consideration of, the alliance or some other international audience. They principally seem to be steps in Strauss's attempt, beginning in 1959, to establish himself as the leading statesman of the post-Adenauer era.

Even in this latter period Strauss's presentations rarely contained new or revolutionary themes. Most of them differed only in minor respects from arguments previously advanced by alliance spokesmen, most notably by General Lauris Norstad (SACEUR from 1956 to 1963), and demonstrated only a limited degree of analytic sophistication. To state the obvious, perhaps, Strauss was first a politician and only second a defense minister and a strategist. In essence, his approach was merely a more sophisticated, expert version of that taken by Adenauer. Defense policy was principally a means to enhance the political role of the Federal Republic (and that of Strauss). Means might vary with daily circumstances; goals did not.

What Strauss saw as Germany's proper role was grounded in four convictions. The first was that at least for purposes of present policy making, Germany's past must be considered a closed issue. Assisted by those countries directly responsible for its creation, the Federal Republic persistently and unashamedly must seek its rightful place and furtherance of the rightful interests of the German people. Bonn's basic attitude should be that once allegedly displayed by Strauss in an aside to an anxious von Brentano during a difficult North Atlantic Council session, "Don't apologize for being here; we were invited." [13]

Strauss's second conviction was that the existing division between East and West allowed, at least for the foreseeable future, little choice for Bonn. Whatever the present tactics of Communists, the fundamental, unchanging cast of communism permitted no hope for accommodation or even partial agreement on any German goals and certainly not on reunification. A neutralist pan-German or nationalist course would be inefficient as well as dangerous. Given its threatened position and its limited international political potential, Germany's only conceivable hope lay in complete alliance, principally with the United States and secondarily with the other Western countries. A united European framework might be the ideal solution; but for the Strauss of this period it was too distant a possibility.

Third, Strauss believed that since formal alliance alone would not assure a full voice for it, the Federal Republic had to be willing to make major national efforts, particularly in the vital area of defense, to gain political advantage. As Strauss once forcefully formulated his own policy of strength:

For such negotiations [concerning reunification] the Federal Republic must see its task in creating for itself the necessary background, the necessary "weight," in order to be able to participate with any sense of success at all. Germany must be so indispensable for its Western friends, and for its potential enemy so deserving of respect, that both sides lay worth on its participation in negotiations. . . . Without the possession of potential power within the North Atlantic alliance Germany will never have a chance to be heard.[14]

Fourth, Strauss was convinced that German military efforts would be of value only if they truly commanded respect. Within the limits of the possible the Straussian yardstick was the effort of the major powers, again principally the United States. Only the most modern armament possible and only participation in major defense missions and decisions would be enough to ensure for Germany full, equal status within the Atlantic framework.

The greater portion of Strauss's actions during 1957–1960 can be viewed as the exploration and adoption of means to these ends. His course was not always clear or consistent, behavior to be expected of a man described with some accuracy as an "opportunistic pragmatist." [15] But his basic operational principles remained the same: test the limits of the possible; keep all possible options open; and try to anticipate if not shape the future.

Strauss's attitude toward nuclear weapons during this period exemplifies a special instance of this basic pattern.[16] There is little question that even before Strauss became defense minister he was convinced that atomic weapons were the key to military and political power. Within Germany Strauss's conviction was unique in terms of the speed with which it was reached and the frequent public emphasis given to it. But this was hardly proof of what so often has been described as Strauss's Machiavellianism or nuclear madness. It was a conclusion shared by other Continental leaders—most urgently by the French—who drew it from the example, rather than from the hortatory nonproliferation policy, of the United States and Britain.

Strauss seemed equally aware that the course finally chosen by France, national production of nuclear weapons, could not be followed by Germany in the near future. The nature of his efforts, as well as remarks purportedly made in private conversation, evidenced his conviction that under existing circumstances any direct independent effort to acquire nuclear weapons would have brought decisive Western, if not Eastern, retaliation. He did not like this situation; he probably did have hopes for the future; but for him national production was not a feasible present alternative.

Thus the German relationship to nuclear weapons dictated by Strauss's basic political strategy was to be sought in some other way. In the 1957–1960 environment there were a number of options: transfer of warheads from producer states; indirect participation through SACEUR in decisions regarding use of nuclear weapons; direct involvement in an alliance pooling of warheads and forces; and possibly even participation in the creation of a European nuclear force. These options again were not a uniquely German concern; they were topics of discussion within the alliance and within the United States itself.

Strauss's unmistakable aim throughout the period was to maximize the options open to Germany within this atmosphere of indecision. He constantly tested the limits of the often ambivalent American position on sharing of nuclear weapons, explored the relative possibilities and advantages of Atlantic and European arrangements, and tried to shape future developments. In these efforts, he used the total array of means open to him: diplomacy, speech-making, off-the-record remarks, veiled hints, bluffs, intrigues, press leaks, and—almost solely among the German leadership—pointed references to those possibilities not explicitly prohibited by Adenauer's 1954 pledge that Germany would not produce nuclear weapons. But however threatening or questionable his tone, his goal was only to ensure that whatever solution was finally accepted or tolerated, the Federal Republic would be a primary, equal participant.

GERMAN STRATEGIC THOUGHT, 1957–1960

The development during 1957–1960 of German thinking on matters of strategy constitutes one of the most basic, yet complex, aspects of Germany's adaptation to membership in NATO. By the end of 1960 the political and military leadership had been educated in the alliance's strategic concepts. There still were some points of peculiarly German emphasis—the reflection of earlier considerations—but the basic pattern was one of reliance not just on NATO decisions but on the particular plans and perspectives developed at SHAPE.

What made this development complex was the selectivity of the reliance, in an atmosphere of protracted uncertainty and of debate specifically centered on the role of nuclear weapons in the defense of Europe. As has often been discussed, at issue for NATO were the consequences to be drawn from the increasing vulnerability of the United States to strikes by the Soviets' strategic nuclear forces.[17] How was the defense of Europe now to be assured against both direct attack and indirect pressure and blackmail? Was limited war in Europe—fought with nuclear or even conventional weapons—now more likely to occur? How indeed was conflict in Europe to be limited? What types and levels of forces and armaments were necessary or desirable? Was there still a credible, significant mission for conventionally armed forces?

By the end of 1960 most of these questions still were largely unclarified and unresolved. The official American doctrine of "massive retaliations plus European land defense" had undergone few significant modifications. American military and civilian proponents of limited or conventional-force response had been extremely vocal, but had evoked little agreement in Washington or among the concerned but passive European allies. The only official initiatives had come from SACEUR (General Norstad) and from his headquarters (SHAPE), principally in the form of a tentative, ambiguous exposition of the "pause" concept.

In broad outline the German position in this debate resembled that of the other Western European states. The primary mission of the alliance was deterrence, based on the threat of general nuclear war should Western Europe be attacked. The probability of direct attack by the Russians was low, but it would remain low only if American nuclear capabilities—strategic and tactical—were inextricably involved in the defense of Europe. Public acceptance by Europeans of the concept of a limited war fought in Europe with nuclear or conventional forces that were somehow separated from the strategic retaliatory power of the United States would not only undermine the deterrence system, it would also admit the unconfrontable: repetition of World War II.

Several peculiarly German factors did tend to pose the issues of the debate more sharply. First, the Federal Republic's exposed position brought demands for the effective forward defense of all its territory. Second, in contrast to its allies Germany was building up sizable military forces. The pace was slower and the target-goal lower than originally foreseen, but the requirements of being a good ally and of creating a German weight within the alliance forced buildup efforts and expenditures to go forward. Third, within Germany, military controversy regarding nuclear warfare—controversy rooted in the discussions which had preceded the Radford crisis—continued.

These special concerns, however, led to little independent consideration or formulation of doctrine. Throughout the four years, the German leadership—politicians and to a lesser degree the military—was more than willing in matters pertaining to military doctrine to place its trust in NATO or, increasingly, in SACEUR. There were points of difference; there was perceptible German influence in some discussions at SHAPE. But in the final analysis it was SHAPE that provided the concepts—however tentative, ambiguous, or ambivalent.

Germany's adaptation to NATO doctrine began somewhat uneasily in the aftermath of the Radford crisis. Speaking for the political leadership as a whole, Strauss repeatedly advocated primary reliance on the superior, ever increasing strategic retaliatory capability of the United States. Although admitting that the possibility of calculated military aggression by the Soviets was limited, he declared: "The most important aim, politically and militarily, is the prevention of general war, of total atomic war. The plans we have to make must in the first instance be for defense in the event of general war." [18] The defense system, after all, must take account of "possibilities, not hypotheses."

Under questioning, the new defense minister stated that other types of aggression also were possible and should not be forgotten. There were cases in which a more limited response was desirable: "You don't use a big stick when you want to dislodge a fly." But the fly at most would be an "armed border incident" which, "common sense" would indicate, was not prompted by "the political will to aggression." [19]

Official German views regarding the necessary conventional-nuclear balance in Europe again reflected accepted thinking in NATO. Although existing force levels should be met "as soon as possible," nuclear-capable equipment would provide both a strengthening of the deterrent and the means for "effective defense." Conventional weapons provided a less important but nonetheless needed residual capability, given the requirements of local defense and given that "even in an atomic conflict, it will not be possible to use tactical atomic weapons everywhere . . . but only at the decisive points on the battlefield." [20]

There occasionally was evidence of somewhat different assessments regarding the value of conventional forces. The most explicit calls for strong forces came from Strauss, Adenauer, and Foreign Minister von Brentano, all striving to prevent any reduction of the allies' presence or of the existing physical commitment to the immediate defense of all the Federal Republic's territory. Continuing withdrawal of French troops to Algeria occasioned private rebukes and demands for future fidelity to the concept of forward defense. British force reductions in the wake of the 1957 Defence White Paper prompted forceful warnings that "grave consequences" for Western defense would result from overoptimistic estimates of possible trade-offs of manpower for firepower.

Of far greater strategic significance was the continuing dissatisfaction of the military, particularly prominent army officers, with what still was considered the allies' infatuation with tactical nuclear weapons. This group now fully acknowledged the need for tactical nuclear weapons as the only counter to Soviet superiority in conventional forces and the requisite balance to the growing Soviet strategic nuclear capability. Nevertheless, in their view these weapons primarily were supplements to, not replacements for, conventionally armed forces, whatever the nature of current or expected developments in nuclear technology.

Like their counterparts in the American army, these critics focused, first, on the widely though not officially accepted concept of the short war. They questioned whether a future conflict would be waged almost exclusively in the air, whether strategic retaliation or, in Europe, tactical air strikes would be the only decisive elements. They repeatedly challenged the adequacy of this "American" doctrine, given the nature of the Soviet threat. As one then high-ranking military man explained in a 1965 interview, "They—the Americans—had no idea what a Russian tank assault was really like. It wouldn't make any difference if you dropped atomic bombs behind them. If they were primed, they would roll to the Rhine and then to the Atlantic."

What was needed was not an "unreal" primacy for the air force that would cause loss of the air support needed for ground forces, nor merely sufficient troops to act as a tripwire, as British doctrine advocated. There must be at least thirty strong divisions, capable of mounting an effective, mobile defense with both tactical nuclear and modern conventional weapons.

A second concern of these critics was the need to preserve some form of conventional "insurance policy" for threats greater than an incident but short of all-out war. As in the pre-Radford crisis phase, their reasons were conditioned both by past experience and by continuing fears about the escalatory effects of the use of tactical nuclear weapons. But as yet they had little conception as to how or with what forms this insurance could be achieved.

A statement by a member of this group, published later, suggests some of the tenor and ambiguities of their argument:

We are on the front line. . . . We do not want to have to rely on atomic weapons to halt an aggressor. So we must have enough conventional forces to deter an aggressor or, if it comes to war, halt him as far to the east as possible. Our forces need not be big enough to defeat the enemy but they must be strong enough to halt an attack and restore the status quo within two or three days.[21]

These criticisms, however, were only positions in intraministry debates, rarely echoed in public discussions or in the press. They would have remained so, had it not been for two developments in 1957—a lengthy SHAPE study concerned with European defense requirements in an era of approaching equilibrium in the American-Soviet strategic balance; and the launching of Sputnik—both of which broadened and highlighted German discussions about strategy.

The SHAPE review—the first major planning exercise in which Germans fully participated—dealt primarily with the future nature and structure of NATO's shield, those allied, integrated forces in central Europe bearing primary responsibility for the direct defense of Western Europe. As formulated in SACEUR's report and the final, well-publicized MC-70 plan,[22] the goal set was thirty full-strength divisions in the central region. These were to be essentially nuclear forces, armed and trained with the "most modern" (i.e., nuclear-capable) weapons, but having a "residual" conventional capability. The need for reserves and for the buildup of supplies sufficient for ninety combat days did receive some attention. But the highest priority was accorded to the requirements of "modernization" (that is, conversion to nuclear capability in the air and on the ground) and "immediate combat readiness."

Conversion to nuclear weapons of shield air forces was to be more complete. Tactical air forces were to be "substantially modernized"; their principal missions were to be counterair and interdiction strikes in the enemy's rear. Other ground-support functions were accorded a far lower priority; missiles were to assume a major role in air defense.

The proposed force structures were largely the elaboration both of earlier NATO decisions (in 1954 and 1956) and of proposals made by General Alfred Gruenther (SACEUR from 1953 to 1956) and General Norstad. What was new was the rather ambiguous suggestion, growing out of protracted SHAPE discussions, of a possible limited-war function for the shield forces. In his initial statement regarding his report,[23] Norstad mentioned two primary missions: the shield's contribution to the peacetime deterrent, and its role, if attacked, in the defense of Western Europe. He then added a third: provision of a means "to meet less-than-ultimate threats with a decisive, but less-than-ultimate, response." This would result in greater political and military flexibility, with a limited but significant option between strategic retaliation and capitulation.

This advocacy of an intermediate response category represented an uneasy middle ground in the continuing debate about strategy within the alliance, particularly among Americans. It differed significantly from the Eisenhower administration's repeated assertion that all but the most limited attack on Western Europe would mean general war. Yet it explicitly denied the possibility or necessity of preparation for limited war in Europe, a preparation advocated by United States Army officials (notably General Maxwell Taylor) and, by 1957, by many civilian strategists (notably those at RAND). Such wars, in Norstad's words, were "most unlikely to the point of being impossible" in the area under his command. The primary concern still was the deterrence of general war; this new mission would require neither more forces nor special preparations.

Although echoes of this SHAPE initiative were to be heard in post-Sputnik discussions throughout the countries comprising the alliance, the German reaction was among the most direct and most rapid. In a series of interviews and articles Strauss tried a cautious testing of several new straws while carefully reiterating old beliefs.[24]

First, while condemning the Western "missile psychosis" and "emotional" reaction to Sputnik, Strauss declared that these developments would have major consequences for NATO's total defense system and particularly for the political and military position of the United States. There would have to be a significant "expansion" of the Western deterrent. There might even be, paradoxically, an increase in the value of conventional weapons, because "missile technology, advanced into the apocalyptic, into the superdimensional, makes global war an impossibility." [25]

Strauss's second point concerned the possibility of limited war under the new circumstances. Echoing contemporary statements by American officials, he declared:

It is even more necessary not to attempt war prevention through dependence on the pure deterrent factor of ultimate great weapons but rather to keep in view the possibility of meeting more limited conflicts with more limited weapons, most especially situations in the non-European sphere.[26]

It would, however, be "military madness" to try to defend Western Europe or Germany without strategic nuclear weapons.

Public statements over the next few months were buried by the bitter internal debate over plans to equip the Bundeswehr with nuclear-capable armament (discussed in chapter 4). Given the German context, the specific strategic issues involved not surprisingly were of little significance. For the SPD all issues were resolved into the "Campaign against Atomic Death," a blanket repudiation of all things nuclear. For the government, the overwhelming fact was that without equal armament Germany would have neither significance nor importance and would "automatically leave NATO."

Nonetheless, in the last debate phases the government was forced to engage in somewhat more specific discussion. The principal stimulus was a public statement by an air-force officer then heading the Führungsstab (Armed Forces Command Staff), General Werner Panitzki, concerning the "benefits" of tactical nuclear armament.[27] Use of these weapons, Panitzki argued, would cause immediate escalation to general nuclear war. Their incorporation into the NATO shield would therefore deter aggression at lower levels and ensure that the Western defense line in central Europe was independently capable of absolute retaliation.

Panitzki's remarks prompted a sharp retort by Strauss that verged on support for a doctrine of limited nuclear war.[28] A "limited reaction" with tactical atomic means, Strauss declared, would allow a considerable chance of battlefield success against a "local attack." But the principal consideration, he quickly added, was that such a reaction would prevent an attack from occurring at all.

Tactical nuclear weapons were but one aspect of what Strauss called a system of "graduated deterrence." In terms similar to those already used in the Washington debate and by Norstad himself, the defense minister declared that the West must not in every situation face "the terrible alternative of total atomic war with all its horrors or step-by-step capitulation." Tactical nuclear armament of the shield was the first step toward a capability for response to enemy actions "in a graduated manner, according to their nature and their size." The primary consequence of course would be to demonstrate to the aggressor that even if he explicitly set a "partial goal," he could not hope to "underrun deterrence."

In tactical terms the armament of all shield forces with nuclear-capable weapons was necessary because

if the attacker knows he faces a defense armed only with conventional weapons, he can mass his troops for a breakthrough since he knows he has no atomic strike to fear. The defense, on the other hand, must disperse its force—in a form suitable for defense against conventional attacks—because it cannot be at all sure that the attacker will not use tactical atomic weapons. The conventional breakthrough of the atomically armed invader will thus be favored. . . . A temptation to aggression . . . thus will result.[29]

If the attacker could not mass his forces, the decision to undertake aggression would be "considerably more difficult" and in fact "highly improbable."

Strauss also echoed Norstad in stressing the need for flexibility and choice in the event of less-than-ultimate attack. There must be a sufficient number of tactical nuclear weapons readily available at all times. But if the West was prepared, the use of these weapons need not always be "automatic" nor an unfortunate "matter of course" that bore no relation to the existing situation.[30]

Like Norstad, Strauss refused to discuss the most probable or desirable choice of means. The major goal must be to avoid any "one-sided" approach in planning, armament, or organization. Such an emphasis, whether nuclear or conventional, would provide an invitation to aggression and reduce the West's chances for political maneuver.

Interview comments suggest that these same themes were of even greater significance for internal discussion during 1958–1959. The framework was the nine-month general review initiated within the Defense Ministry after German approval of the initial MC-70 plan. In the words of one long-term civil servant interviewed in 1965, the review was the first postwar attempt at formal planning and study in terms of both the long view and the implications of technological developments. More important for most German military men, it constituted their first systematic introduction to a substantial complex of NATO doctrine and planning concerning tactical nuclear weapons.

The limited information about this review gleaned from interviews with past and present Defense Ministry officials suggests that it was at most only relatively systematic.[31] The difficulties that had beset earlier discussions continued: the basic assumption that existing NATO plans should be perpetuated; the lack of sufficient information and expertise; the reluctance to initiate a full-scale national reappraisal in the face of both particularly intense external scrutiny and continuing domestic political uproar centered on nuclear issues (both discussed in chapter 4). The primary element was the continuing controversy between the air force and the army—a debate phrased in terms of strategy but embedded in the postwar competition for prestige, in traditional rivalries, and in the now even more intense fights over respective shares of the military budget.

Along several dimensions it was the German air force which had profited the most from the changes and slowdowns inherent in German adaptation to NATO planning. Under Strauss, as under Blank, the air force still would have only 100,000 men, but these now would be organized in 28 rather than 44 squadrons and would be assigned a nuclear mission.[32] Indeed, the two questions in the review of most interest to the air force were what value and role were to be assigned to manned aircraft in the approaching missile age, and what was the priority of the new tactical counterair mission in comparison with the other traditional functions of ground support?

As mentioned above, these questions had first been raised during Blank's ministry. Influenced by American developments and the evolving of NATO planning, German air-force officials had repeatedly criticized the planned force concept centered around tactical ground support and active air defense as "appropriate for World War II." Given developments in aircraft and missile technology, active air defense confined to the national borders or the immediate war area was no longer possible. Command of the air and swift destruction of the enemy's rear-area supplies and forces required modern supersonic aircraft, equipped to permit the early and effective use of tactical atomic weapons.

In 1958 these demands were raised with renewed fervor, and they caused even more bitter ministerial infighting. One group within the ministry, reportedly those air-force officers with the greatest exposure to their American counterparts, did not believe the planning goals were modern enough; in their view the future of defense against the enemy's airpower lay solely in defensive missiles. The most significant opposition, of course, came from members of the army, who (like their American colleagues) waged an intense continuing battle against the air force's concentration on a single model of combat—a short, air-dominant conflict, with little or no ground-force involvement or conventional defense of any sort. There was no attempt, they complained, to provide flexibility or selectivity in deployment of nuclear weapons: there was no recognition of the necessary interrelationship of air and ground operations. As one central army figure retrospectively remarked, the views of some air-force officials bordered on "irresponsibility or even adventurism."

Again echoing the contemporary American debate, army criticism focused on two specific propositions. The first was the decision to assign to the air force all air defense functions, especially those performed by defensive missiles. This, in the army view, would not ensure the necessary coordination with ground operations, nor would it fulfill NATO guidelines. The second was the proposal to purchase the American Starfighter (F-104). This seemingly involved a decision to provide minimal if any ground support. The air force would have no substantial funds remaining for the purchase of support aircraft; the Starfighter itself was primarily suited to, and thus had been selected for, a nuclear-strike mission. There were even hints that the army might have to develop its own support force.

In almost all respects the budgetary and assignment decisions finally reached were victories for the air force and for the airpower concept espoused by its head, General Kammhuber.[33] More than seven hundred Starfighters were to be procured and configured both as fighter-bombers and interceptors. The defensive missiles obtained, the Nikes and the Hawks, were classified as an "air defense component" and remained under air-force control. The only apparent compromise was the purchase of the Italian Fiat G-91 light strike plane, but this was more a result of NATO planning and political factors than of persuasion by the army.

To state the army's positions more broadly, the basis of deterrence was a "spectrum of weapons," nuclear and conventional. As described in the first army command manual, *Truppenführung 1959,* only these weapons in combination would delay automatic strategic retaliation, "if not prevent it altogether." [34] There must be "all-around flexibility in military planning and leadership."

Of particular interest were the more specific propositions that were advanced by army officers concerning the use of tactical nuclear weapons. Given the Soviet advantage in conventional forces and the potential for destruction involved, these weapons were now a sine qua non for most defense contingencies. Ground operations, whether large or more restricted in size, would require these weapons—particularly the long-awaited "battlefield" nuclear weapons, limited in range, payload, and hopefully radioactivity. A benefit to the defender, they would allow forces to halt a Soviet tank assault and to implement a system of zonal defense against infiltration and regional breakthroughs.

The army was beginning a basic reorganization of all present and planned units to lessen the gap between the capability planned by Blank and this new doctrine. Given the surviving goal of twelve divisions, but drawn now from 200,000 rather than 350,000 men, the aim would be to adapt at the division level to the increased need for conventional and, especially, tactical nuclear firepower. Special nuclear support groups for missiles and advanced artillery were being formed; training programs and exercises in modern warfare in Germany and the United States were proceeding apace.

The army nonetheless argued that the use of these weapons in all defense missions was to be determined according to two traditional military dicta: "no one weapon is decisive" and "man must rule materiel." Contrary to the declarations of the air force, the British, and some American army officials, tactical nuclear weapons could not be used over the long term as manpower substitutes or as all-purpose weapons. Employment in particular must always be on a *selective* basis, in view of the neighboring population and property and the need to allow for political flexibility.

Moreover, there was a small number of contingencies in which the West would be unwilling or unable to initiate use of nuclear weapons. Even before the Berlin crisis that began in November, 1958, German army commanders quoted in a WEU report of that year stressed situations arising out of "political tensions in East Germany and Central Europe." [35] Their concern reportedly was less for a massive Korean type of action than for a popular revolt like the East German uprising of 1953 or for massive border crossings with Eastern forces in pursuit. But whatever the cause, to counter these "limited conflicts" the West must retain a "sufficient" and "independent" conventional capability.

In all these discussions of the requirements for flexibility one factor remained constant: the demand for true forward defense of all of the Federal Republic's territory. Despite their public statements neither the defense minister nor the military believed that such a defense could be completely implemented, given contemporary force levels. But at all costs this was to remain a principal goal of NATO, in terms of both strategic planning and tactical doctrine. There could be no formal or final adoption of a defensive line at the Rhine or anywhere short of the zonal border, no acceptance of operational guidelines that would prevent or prejudice "the most resistance necessary as close to the border as possible." [36]

Throughout 1958 and 1959 the need for graduated deterrence remained the dominant, unchanging theme in Germans' discussions of strategy. It received little further clarification and seemed at times colored by German attempts to emphasize the continuing value of their force contributions to NATO and by the uneasy interim resolution of the doctrinal and budgetary differences among the services. Its relation to the other allies' discussions of strategy, which were brought to the surface by Khrushchev's ultimatum on Berlin of November 1958, apparently was minimal.

By far the most extreme—and for the Germans least acceptable—arguments were advanced by the American and British civilian proponents of what was now termed a flexible-response strategy. The range of threats to Berlin, these critics argued, dramatically underlined the need for both a limited-war capability in Europe and a choice between nuclear and conventional responses in such conflicts. Shield forces must be able not only to force quick resolutions of attacks resulting from accidents, miscalculations, or probing maneuvers but also to delay as long as possible the precipitous escalation inherent in any crossing of the conventional-nuclear threshold.

In his numerous public statements General Norstad still stressed the need for "immediate response," but now used somewhat different and highly ambiguous words: the need to compel a pause.[37] In response to a conventional attack, the West should not immediately resort to strategic nuclear retaliation, but rather attempt to make the aggressor aware that failure to restore the status quo ante would result in general (all-out) war. Norstad declared, however, that the pause would not constitute a limited war; fighting during the pause might be of long duration or more probably a matter of hours.

Although the will to use all necessary means was the only guard against repeated "salami tactics," Norstad argued, the general principle in any one case must be to resist aggression with no more force than was necessary. Conventional means were to be used if possible; this would require the organization of conventional defense. Tactical nuclear weapons, which were equally essential, would be used "as early as necessary." The buildup of strong conventional forces would allow NATO to raise the threshold at which nuclear weapons would be used, a threshold which should be "as high as possible."

Norstad's position (perhaps deliberately) left a number of fundamental questions unanswered and critical ambiguities unresolved for Washington as well as for Bonn. He refused continually to calculate the probability of escalation once tactical nuclear weapons were introduced; it would depend on circumstances, he said. His insistence on a primary nuclear-strike mission for the tactical air forces seemed to contradict his calls for a buildup in conventional arms, for raising the threshold, or for a pause of any duration before resort to nuclear warfare. He declared repeatedly that the force levels and structures designed for the general-war mission also would be appropriate for enforcing a pause.

Some evidence from interviews suggests that both Strauss and Adenauer differed with Norstad on several key points concerning contingency planning for Berlin 1959–1960. In several forums they and other German representatives stressed the primary need for deterrence and diplomatic cohesiveness among the Western allies and their fears about the early use of any significant force to preserve the status of Berlin or its autobahn link with the West.[38] In private conversations Strauss reportedly echoed earlier European concerns about the judgment and reliability of Americans, about Americans' uncritical willingness to use tactical nuclear weapons in the territory of East Germany or the Federal Republic in defense of a symbol. If there was a decisive move by the Soviets or East Germans, he argued, the only response left to the West was a defensive position imposed not so much by terrain as by its inferiority in conventional arms. Even if at that point the use of the Federal Republic's forces on East German soil was politically acceptable, they hardly would be able to fill the yawning gap.

Despite these exchanges, not until early 1960 did German leaders publicly discuss these questions—and then, characteristically, only in terms not related to Berlin. In a speech to the WEU, for example, Stauss called for a "weighted system" of forces which would "allow countermeasures of equal weight" and prevent the blunting of the weapons used for strategic deterrence.[39] Echoing the pause phraseology, he declared:

There can be no room whatever for speculation that a limited military action can lead to the success of surprise, a situation from which an aggressor can then offer peace and couple the refusal of his peace terms with the threat of intercontinental-missile war. We must be in a position to immediately restore the military departure point and to make clear to every possible aggressor . . . that any further step will carry the risk of his own annihilation.

Strauss's remarks, however, made clear his view that this capability was one element, but not the most important element, of the total graduated deterrent. Nuclear weapons, whether strategic or tactical, were still the primary factors in deterrence. And although an improved conventional capability might be valuable in certain limited situations, at least equal attention must be given to the long-planned and (by Washington) long-delayed buildups in tactical nuclear weapons, particularly for the forces of the European allies.

Most of the military leaders, of whom an overwhelming majority were army officers, adopted a similar stance, but with many more privately expressed reservations.[40] Expansion of the alliance's conventional capability had been a continuing concern of the Germans; some respected authorities believed that with sufficient efforts by the allies reliance indeed could be placed primarily on an initial conventional-force counter to the Russians. But the prospects for such efforts were slim. By the end of 1960 the NATO shield would have at most a combat strength of sixteen divisions, eight of them raw, undermanned German forces rated as being of only "limited combat effectiveness," the lowest NATO rating. On the whole, they would most probably be without the arms, training, or organization necessary for effective conventional defense.

In compelling a pause—as in all actions—the West therefore would be forced toward immediate use of tactical nuclear weapons. Quite apart from the resulting danger of escalation, only the American forces and to a lesser degree the British forces possessed the necessary equipment and support facilities. Other allies' forces were still awaiting completion of equipment deliveries and training procedures. And there was no assurance of the Americans' unfailing willingness to release the necessary warheads in the face of any, let alone a conventional, attack.

Most important, what would be the relation of a pause or conventional mission to the requirements of forward defense? Even if the initial conquest of some of the Federal Republic's territory was almost inevitable, there must be no unnecessary sacrifice of ground or German lives, then or in the future. Any response must begin as close as possible to the demarcation line, with as little threat and damage as possible to East German population centers and as much damage as possible to Soviet forces and supply lines. And the defense of Berlin still posed some special and unconfrontable problems.

Thus the situation stood in late 1960, with the Germans somewhat questioning but basically supporting Norstad's lead in the debate about doctrine. From all indications leaders in Bonn were only vaguely aware of the conflicts or discrepancies between SACEUR's position and either the position still proclaimed by the Eisenhower administration or that espoused by its many critics, especially the associates of the incoming Kennedy administration. Within the first months of 1961 German leaders would become, from their perspective, rapidly aware of these differences.

FOUR

Adaptation & Controversy: 1956-1960

✠ THE MOST CONTROVERSIAL ELEMENTS in Bonn's adaptation to NATO during 1957–1960 did not turn primarily on debates about strategic doctrine. During these years a series of hard, unambiguous decisions by NATO for the thoroughgoing equipping of shield forces with armament capable of utilizing nuclear warheads established a military posture totally dependent on early use of nuclear weapons, strategic and tactical. By any standard the Federal Republic and its slowly building military forces became fully engaged in this equipment revolution. Increasingly large portions of the defense budget were devoted to nuclear-capable equipment, to what Adenauer soothingly called "the most modern weapons"—primarily nuclear-strike aircraft, short-range nuclear artillery, and intermediate-range missiles. By 1960 operational adaptation was far from complete; actual weapons deployment had only just begun. But the Adenauer government, the military leadership, and particularly Defense Minister Strauss already had significant material and psychic stakes in the acquisition of what was eventually to be the second largest capability for delivering nuclear warheads in the West.

One possible explanation, of course, is that these actions indicated Germany's determination to gain access to nuclear weapons through the back door, since direct development was denied to it. Procurement logically suggests purpose and high expectation of future use or value. Why else would Bonn make such purchases, relatively meaningless alone and highly inefficient for use with conventional warheads, unless it had assurances of timely delivery on German terms of nuclear warheads or even of nuclear warheads subject to its own control? And was not the primary priority Bonn accorded to the acquisition of nuclear-capable weapons during this period in itself objective evidence of the kind of defense posture that Germany believed to be of the greatest military and political value?

This chapter argues that while intuitively appealing, such explanations impose simplistic rationality on both the context of these specific decisions and the general process always involved in balancing Germany's three foreign-policy goals. To make only a first cut, a substantial part of the explanation for these procurement patterns may be found in Adenauer's constant concern not to fall too far behind emerging American and British defense examples (and become isolated). Strategic rational and doctrinal rhetoric aside, the Federal Republic had to strive for full nuclearization to maximize the political value of its contribution to NATO—to become a respected, highly valued equal. Without question, this would entail not only major revisions in previous planning but also expenditures far exceeding those foreseen for conventional equipment. But these were the terms in which equality was now defined and under which a return to object status, within the West or between East and West, would be avoided.

The usual explanation for American weapons procurement of the period—that economic considerations determined it—contributes only marginal insight into Bonn's decision-making on this issue.[1] Given the additional expense involved and the widespread concern of elites and the general public for ensured economic prosperity, the Germans' enthusiasm for "more bang for the buck" seems paradoxical. Yet for most of the German political leadership and business community the logic of the New Look seemed irrefutable. The cost of each nuclear-capable weapon might indeed be higher, but American doctrine indicated that increasingly fewer arms would be required to reach a specific level of effectiveness. Other promised benefits included the need to withdraw far fewer men from the domestic manpower pool, already overtaxed by a booming economy, and the probability of technological spillover into the civilian sphere.

For a few leaders in Bonn, including Strauss, this last benefit was the crucial one. The Federal Republic essentially was at point zero in the defense area, with neither an existing military establishment nor entrenched defense industries. Why not adopt whatever measures seemed most efficient in creating "the most modern forces possible"? Substantial purchases from

abroad of high-technology equipment would allow Germany swiftly to re-
coup a ten-year lag in military preparedness and to reassure others of continuing control over German reattainment of military competence. The
amounts involved in such purchases surely would cushion residual political
discomforts that governments of the allies might suffer.

For most Germans, however, the argument again turned on the dictates
imposed by the American connection. Whatever the impact on military posture or expectations of war, modernization of German arms would constitute
still another binding payment on the American security guarantee, and
would provide further evidence of the Federal Republic's status as a good
and true ally. Germany's major delivery systems would be purchased from
the United States, as Washington unmistakably wished, in accordance with
NATO war scenarios and equipment plans both of which were determined
principally by American leaders. This would ensure greater integration of
German forces with allies' forces and greater equality as well as significant
standardization of armament and interchangeability of equipment. Further, it
would help offset those Washington forces that were urging the reduction of
burdensome deployments in Europe since at least one ally would be seen to
be doing its "fair share." Although Bonn's costs would be high, there
would no longer be an easy justification—within the United States or in dia-
logues with Bonn—for threatening withdrawals of troops.

Despite all these advantages, Bonn constantly was confronted with the
high costs entailed in any such German adaptation to allies' desires; the
costs were political far more than military and were imposed internationally
even more than domestically. That most of the other allies were acquiring
the same, essentially national, nuclear delivery systems seemed of little consequence.[2] Questions constantly were raised about Bonn's—and only
Bonn's—expectations about availability of warheads, the nature and security
of the control procedures involved, and the probable conditions of eventual
use originating from German soil. This in turn brought queries from friends
and manipulative critics alike about the relationship of this capability to Germany's present or prospective international role. And these queries, as well
as outright suspicions of renewed German ambitions for military power, led
to a multiplicity of efforts to block such armament or to limit the consequences of German ascendance, actual or potential.

Adenauer's response was constant and determined, if not always con-
vincing to his opponents. The principal counterarguments emphasized the

fulfillment—no more, no less—of NATO directives. In the domestic arena the government stressed NATO demands for conversion to nuclear-capable armament and succeeded, in effect, in mobilizing its allies against itself to gain the necessary Bundestag authorization and appropriations for such equipment. Internationally, Bonn stressed its rights and responsibilities as an equal, sovereign member of the alliance and its unwillingness to encounter further discrimination without adequate political compensation. On balance, however, these were costs which the Adenauer government believed it was necessary and possible to bear. The stakes were high, the risks reducible at least.

At the simplest level, therefore, this chapter provides insights into some convenient fallacies about Germany's attitude toward nuclear weapons, fallacies such as the acquisition of hardware providing unquestionable evidence of interest in a backdoor or shortcut approach to national nuclear development. Of greater analytic interest will be the examination of three critical aspects of Germany's decision-making patterns: the vague, essentially reactive character of Adenauer's public statements whenever policies concerning access to or control of nuclear weapons were challenged; the constant interaction of Bonn's domestic and international environments whenever nuclear-control issues were at stake; and the degree to which not only Bonn but its allies and opponents continually made these issues the test of the necessary interrelation of security, equality, and eventual unity. This analysis will deal first with the process through which nuclear-capable equipment was acquired and secondly with the domestic and international opposition encountered. Consideration of specific access and sharing formulas and German expectations about those formulas within the Atlantic alliance or on a bilateral basis is postponed to chapter 5.

NUCLEAR-CAPABLE ARMAMENT AND THE STRUGGLE FOR EQUALITY

THE DEMANDS

During the first years of the 1957–1960 period the most constant and intensely developed aspect of German pronouncements about defense matters was the demand for "tactical nuclear armament" of all the Bundeswehr. Making almost no distinction in public between delivery systems and warheads, government spokesmen repeatedly declared such armament to be an absolute requirement for Western and German security. One reason was the force of technological development; in Adenauer's simplistic but seemingly sincere formulation, "Today, atomic armament is in flood tide. The Germans must adapt themselves to the new circumstances. In practical terms, tactical atomic weapons are a further development of modern artillery." [3]

Strauss, as always, was more direct. A newspaper's paraphrase of a speech had him reviewing recent technological advances and declaring that he was of the firm opinion that "atomic armament would come in all European armies, independent of whether the Americans were for or against it. . . . The Bundeswehr must also adapt itself to this apocalyptic military future." [4]

A second and more common theme was the need to maximize Germany's military effectiveness within the Atlantic framework. NATO had decided that tactical nuclear weapons were needed to counter an opponent possessing both superiority in conventional forces and a growing capability in tactical nuclear weapons. To fulfill its mission the Bundeswehr also must have these weapons because, in the words of Foreign Minister von Brentano, "either one has effective armament or one could renounce armament altogether." [5]

A third line of argument was familiar from past rearmament debates: German forces must possess armament equal to that of the other NATO shield forces. Adenauer's formulation was perhaps the most simplistic:

How is it conceivable that the German troops in NATO are to be less well-armed than the Americans; that the Americans, the Italians, the French, the Belgians, the Dutch have small atomic weapons and the German troops do not have them? That means, in other words, the unravelling of the entire Western defensive belt against the Soviet Union.[6]

A German "weak link" would contribute little to Western defense and would raise Soviet hopes of successful aggression.

Equality was also indispensable, given the Federal Republic's responsibility to its Bundeswehr. Time and time again, government leaders referred to the bad consequences which inferior armament would have for troop morale. Moreover, "armament inferior to what the Americans have" would mean that in event of war a Soviet attack would be directed primarily against the German divisions in the shield.

The fourth and perhaps most telling argument concerned the political and military consequences that Germany's failure to adopt nuclear-capable armament would bring. As Adenauer dramatically declared in the final debate in the Bundestag on this issue:

I want as many Germans as possible to hear this. If an important part of NATO doesn't possess weapons as strong as those of its potential opponents . . . then it has neither significance nor importance. If the strategic planning of NATO—and we must naturally and will naturally test this—desires that we too, the Federal Republic, make use of this development, and if we hesitate to do so, then we automatically leave NATO (and are left at the mercy of the Soviet Union).[7]

Despite the intensity and the apparently nationalistic appeal of these arguments, such demands were neither a uniquely German phenomenon nor totally unheralded. Since 1955 officials of the other allies had repeatedly urged tactical nuclear armament of all shield forces, including those of the Federal Republic.[8] Lord Ismay, the retiring Secretary General of NATO, asserted in May 1957, for example, that although no alliance-wide decision had yet been reached, the refusal of Germany or any other large country to introduce the latest equipment "would have the most dangerous consequences for strategy, would harm the Alliance, and force the organization to review its military posture." [9]

A more dramatic expression of encouragement by the other allies was General Norstad's statement in February 1958, during an interview on German television.[10] Asked his estimate of the future prospects for a German role in European defense in light of continuing popular opposition to tactical nuclear armament for the Bundeswehr, SACEUR replied:

So long as the overall situation does not change, defensive atomic weapons are absolutely indispensable for the strengthening of the defensive power of the Bundeswehr. . . . Now, however, from the German standpoint, it is wholly unthinkable that these forces should be condemned to a secondary role, to a second class function in which they would be practically useless in defense.

With this degree of official NATO support, the question of the necessity for any particularly German demands arises. Analysis shows that such German statements in late 1956, 1957, and early 1958 were part of a general effort by European members of the alliance to secure tactical delivery vehicles from the United States. Past years had seen both the evolution of an American strategy based on use of tactical nuclear weapons and repeated expressions by American officials of willingness to make these weapons available to the alliance and the allies. But, paradoxically, there had been no formal American commitment on deliveries and no decision as to how these weapons were to be integrated into the shield or how access to warheads was to be arranged.

Interest among the Western Europeans had been further stirred by the events of the summer and fall of 1956. British and French initiatives at Suez reportedly had caused more hesitation in the United States about prospective nuclear arrangements.[11] The Radford crisis itself both had demonstrated American insistence on independence in its own national security decision-making and had raised the specter of a nuclear-armed Fortress America. Coming so shortly thereafter, the American response to the Suez crisis—and for some militant anti-Communists in Germany, to the Hungarian uprising as well—made many Europeans even more doubtful about the willingness of the United States to use any means in defense of its allies.

These concerns clearly emerged at the North Atlantic Council meeting in December 1956, when Germany together with the Continental states and Britain urged a greater tactical nuclear buildup within the shield. National forces should receive nuclear-capable weapons directly, rather than be dependent on special American nuclear-armed support groups.[12] The United States also should assure its allies that the necessary warheads would be available in time of war—either by direct transfer (asked for by France) or through some stockpile arrangement (the request of the Netherlands, Germany, and Turkey).

Full American agreement with these requests had to await the council meeting of December 1957, and adoption of the MC-70 plan in April 1958.[13] Each member state that expressed interest was assured delivery ''as soon as possible'' of a specified range of ground and air weapons with both nuclear and conventional capability. Although the requisite warheads would remain under exclusive American control in peacetime, these would be stockpiled in Europe and released in wartime on the recommendation of NATO authorities.

OPERATIONAL ADAPTATION

Long before final action by the alliance on nuclear-capable armament and before approval at home had been won, German military planners had begun to consider the what and the how of the Bundeswehr's modernization. Their views on specific types and arrangements of weapons primarily were conditioned by developments in American thinking and continuing discussions at SHAPE. But the general guidelines had been set soon after Strauss's appointment as defense minister.

In his first remarks Strauss asserted that two principles would govern both the general buildup of the Bundeswehr and armament planning.[14] The first was his familiar slogan, "quality before quantity." The Federal Republic would no longer follow former Defense Minister Blank's scheme of making major armament purchases immediately for later use as forces were established. Strauss declared, "Particularly in an age of technical evolution, of rethinking and reevaluation, one must proceed step by step and defer questions of total planning for the sake of such development."

In operational terms this meant that no major decisions were to be taken until the alliance had reached agreement on the specifics of nuclear-capable armament for the allies. In the interim, Strauss said, there must be a kind of holding action, allowing for both a stretch-out and some limited activity:

If one sets 1960 as year X, the beginning of a fully new armament epoch, up until that point one still has to arm and equip the Bundeswehr. Thus production and planning must be so plotted that up to year X, combat-ready units are created but . . . are not "unmodern." [15]

Moreover, the primary consideration in weapons purchases must be to secure "the most modern weapons available." Strauss declared somewhat bombastically that although economic and diplomatic considerations still were important they "no longer would be decisive." The inference was clear; the Federal Republic would use its purchasing power to seek the best, rather than consider—as Blank had done—only that which the former occupation powers offered under grant-aid or at bargain prices.

What was to be sought was rarely discussed, in part because of continuing uncertainty about details but mostly because of Adenauer's usual strategy of vagueness in the public discussion of unpleasant topics or military matters. Government spokesmen referred only to "tactical nuclear armament" or "modern weapons." Strauss's answer to a press-conference question was perhaps the most specific: "One should rather speak of atomic weapons for tactical purposes. There is no universal definition for these weapons. The tactical use of these weapons could extend to the rear lines, the enemy's supply and support, and thus reach into the broad depths." [16] As of yet, he continued, there were no small-caliber atomic weapons; on the other hand, there were atomic bombs for fighter aircraft and also missiles for tactical use.

The first public presentation of the government's modern-armaments program came in November 1957. The timing of these statements seemed determined in part by the submission of the NATO Military Committee's armament recommendations for 1958–1963, recommendations eventually adopted as NATO plan MC-70. The timing seemed to reflect also the government's desire to respond—quickly and negatively—to Washington's decision, spurred by Sputnik, to offer intermediate-range ballistic missiles (IRBMs) to the allies for joint deployment in Europe.[17]

At a press conference the defense minister declared that since the alliance had assigned German forces a "fundamentally tactical mission," the only types of modern equipment sought by Germany were "tactical weapons." Specifically these were anti-tank rockets, surface-to-surface tactical missiles, guided missiles for air defense, and missiles which would replace tactical bombers and long-range artillery, that is, with a range of under 1,250 miles.[18] Strauss blandly commented that all of these could be used with conventional as well as nuclear explosives, but that the final choices would be made according to alliance decisions.

With final Bundestag authorization in March 1958, and NATO's approval of the MC-70 plan the following month, the Federal Republic formally initiated its armament modernization program. Over the next three fiscal years more than 25 percent of the defense budget—which in Germany includes expenditures for civil defense and troop-offset costs—was spent on weapons procurement. And as table 1 illustrates, almost half of the total 5,693.9 million DM ($1,423.5 million) went for acquisition of aircraft and missiles.

A closer look at the types of modern armament purchased or planned during 1957–1960 (table 2) provides little hard evidence regarding intense German interest in the backdoor acquisition of a domestic nuclear-weapons capability.[19] Clearly, much of the armament procured was specified for Germany under NATO's MC-70 plan and was congruent with the mission assigned to German forces under the strategy of massive retaliation plus. The numbers were substantial, but so was Germany's share of the overall NATO force establishment and, under both objective and punitive standards of burden-sharing within the alliance, so was its capacity to pay.

Yet interview comments in the 1960s emphasized that whenever there

TABLE 1
**Procurement Expenditures for Weapons and Weapons Systems and
Total Net Expenditures for the Bundeswehr, 1956–1965
(millions of marks)**

Year	Combat vehicles and other ordnance materials	Aircraft and missiles	Ships	Total net expenditures for military forces *
1956	997.4	401.1	95.9	3,404.4
1957	1,226.0	432.8	188.4	5,395.4
1958	738.3	888.5	498.9	7,714.2
1959	681.0	972.8	394.4	8,397.2
1960	471.4	710.8	336.5	7,333.6 †
1961	535.8	1,190.2	401.0	11,574.3
1962	832.0	1,739.0	481.8	15,508.1
1963	1,087.4	2,479.3	391.3	17,856.7
1964	1,103.7	1,492.8	532.4	17,207.8
1965 ‡	970.0	1,216.0	490.0	18,389.2

SOURCE: Gerhard Brandt, *Rüstung und Wirtschaft in der Bundesrepublik* (Witten/Berlin: Eckart, 1966), 237, 269.

* Excludes veterans pensions; includes expenditures for civil defense and payments to allies to offset cost of allies' troops in Germany.

† Reflects shortened fiscal year (April 1–December 31) caused by change in Federal Republic's accounting system to conform to NATO standards.

‡ Budgeted figures.

was room for choice Bonn attempted to obtain the most advanced weaponry available, which in 1957–1960 was also that with the most sophisticated capacity for delivery of nuclear warheads. Contemporary press reports indicate that German persistence in this regard did not go unnoticed or unopposed. One ranking American officer reportedly declared, "By 1962–1963, West Germany is going to have the most modern army, navy, and air force in Europe." [20] British military and political leaders were particularly critical of German motives and the drawn-out procurement process being used. Noting in June 1958 that the Federal Republic still had not selected a fighter-bomber, one British official half in earnest declared: "Maybe he [Strauss] intends to wait until manned aircraft are obsolete and then move Germany directly into the missile age." [21]

Some American officials joined this criticism, declaring that Strauss's ambitions with respect to advanced weaponry far exceeded his grasp in terms of support and training.[22] The defense minister's desire to make

TABLE 2
Modern Delivery-Vehicle Procurement for the Bundeswehr, 1956–1960

Type	Function	Capability	Range *	Source *	Outcome by 1960 *
Air-defense missiles					
Nike-Hercules	surface-to-air	dual	75 miles	purchase from US	authorized
Hawk	surface-to-air	conventional	15 miles	pool production under US license	authorized
Sidewinder	air-to-air	conventional	2 miles	pool production under US license	authorized
Seacat	sea-to-air	conventional	limited	purchase from Britain	authorized
Short-range vehicles					
203mm howitzer	surface-to-surface	dual	under 10 miles	purchase from US	authorized
Honest John missile	surface-to-surface	dual	12–15 miles	purchase from US	authorized
Sergeant missile	surface-to-surface	dual	75 miles	purchase from US	authorized
Davy Crockett cannon	surface-to-surface	dual	under 5 miles	purchase from US	planned
Long-range vehicles					
Mace missile	surface-to-surface	dual	700 + miles	purchase from US	authorized
Pershing missile	surface-to-surface	dual	300 + miles	purchase from US	planned
Polaris missile	sea-to-surface	dual	500 + miles	purchase from US	under consideration
Starfighter airplane	fighter; strike	dual	400 + miles (radius)	purchase from US and pool production under US license	authorized
Fiat G-91 airplane	light strike; reconnaissance	potentially dual	limited	pool production	authorized

* Information possessed by German military authorities during 1956–60.

American forces his model meant that he considered most off-the-shelf equipment unsuitable for the still-building German forces. His remarks during his many buying tours in the United States indicated, in the words of one long-time Pentagon official interviewed in 1965, that "he always wanted to be at least one jump ahead."

A factor often cited by those suspicious of German backdoor efforts was indeed just this "jump": Bonn's extensive use of its considerable purchasing power to acquire the newest sophisticated foreign arms or technology for later application at home. From 1955 through mid-1958 the government followed a "balanced" purchasing program, which meant that it relied on national suppliers for most munitions, some conventional vehicles, and some light equipment, and on foreign suppliers for all technologically advanced arms and supplies (tables 3 and 4).[23] Such a program, Strauss and Adenauer argued, allowed for economies of scale and minimized the burden on the mushrooming national economy while reassuring Germany's former victims of peaceful intent. Purchases primarily from the United States also would permit a more rapid buildup and a continuation of the supply arrangements begun under initial American armament grants through the Military Assistance Program (grants which totaled $900 million throughout the 1950s).

All available evidence suggests that the primary motive for foreign purchases was a far simpler and more exploitative one than backdoor access to a domestic nuclear capability. Germany was faced with the complex problem of reimbursing its allies for the costs of their troops stationed in Germany.[24] Despite American and British pressures, the Adenauer government after 1954 increasingly opposed continuing the direct payments for the costs of foreign troops required under the occupation regime ($52.4 billion was paid). After many recriminations Bonn agreed with both governments to take British and American troop costs into account in its military expenditures overseas, that is, to buy as much as possible from the United States and Britain. This policy occasioned little controversy and seemed then (if not later) a clever strategy to maximize Bonn's political gains in an area of inevitable concession by Germany but of at least potential mutual benefit to Germany and its allies.

Pressures from Washington for such purchases were the most insistent, and they measurably increased as the American balance-of-payments situation worsened in the late 1950s. Where military interest, aggressive sales-

TABLE 3
Sources and Volume of Materiel for the Bundeswehr, 1955–1967

Materiel	1955–60	1961–67	1955–67
		(percentage of total volume)	
Sources			
Domestic	51	64	60
Foreign	49	36	40
		(billions of marks)	
Total volume	17.0	52.6	69.6

SOURCE: Horst Mendershausen, *Troop Stationing in Germany: Value and Cost*, RM-5881-PR (Santa Monica: RAND, 1968), 89.

manship, informal contacts, and appeals to congruent political interests once had sufficed, there now were official demands and protracted negotiations about what later would be called offset agreements. The culmination was the Anderson mission of November 1960, which set forth an annual target figure of approximately $650 million to be offset, as the virtual price for the continued presence of American troops in Germany. Although not agreeing

TABLE 4
Foreign Procurement for the Bundeswehr by Weapon Category, 1955–1964

Category	Estimated foreign purchases (millions of dollars)		Approximate percentage of total procurement
	Minimum	Maximum	
Aircraft	1,625	2,000	50–60
Shipbuilding	13	25	1–3
Electronics	300	450	50–75
Tanks and vehicles	1,125	1,438	40–50
Ordnance and munitions	875	1,500	40–65
Total foreign purchases	3,938	5,413	35–52

SOURCE: C. J. E. Harlow, "National Procurement Policies," 44, part 2, *The European Armaments Base: a Survey*, vol. 2, Institute for Strategic Studies, *Defence, Technology and the Western Alliance* (6 vols., London, 1967).

to the figure or even to the concept of offset payments, Bonn during the next few years did actually make military purchases in the United States amounting to the target figure (table 5).

There was still considerable if relatively unsuccessful competition by the British and French for German contracts (see table 5). Perhaps the best example involved acquisition by Germany of a supersonic airplane designed to fulfill a number of missions, but principally nuclear counterair strikes.[25] By the end of 1957, much to the disappointment of the British, the choice essentially had been narrowed down to the American F-104 Starfighter and the French Mirage III. After extensive discussion and open lobbying by the contestants, the Defense Ministry in October 1958 announced that it had selected the Starfighter and would purchase some (96 in all) from the American manufacturer and produce others (554 in all) under license.

It is clear from later disclosures that a number of factors influenced the final decision. Technologically the Starfighter was judged superior. In terms of speed, range, and rate of climb, for example, several German officers considered it "the dream of every pilot." One version of the Starfighter was

TABLE 5
Foreign and Domestic Bundeswehr Expenditures for Materiel Purchases, Maintenance and Improvement, Research and Development, 1956–1967
(millions of marks)

| Year | Domestic | Foreign | | | | | Total * |
		US	UK	France	Italy	Other	
1956	1,425	528	—	55	—	76	2,083
1957	1,113	1,264	108	92	24	397	2,999
1958	2,225	1,161	39	133	9	76	3,643
1959	1,794	1,638	118	325	118	383	4,375
1960	2,118	617	72	311	76	725	3,918
1961	3,635	950	77	254	158	470	5,543
1962	5,000	1,469	199	329	159	710	7,866
1963	5,113	2,271	380	535	139	875	9,312
1964	4,793	2,122	76	687	204	667	8,548
1965	4,390	1,720	93	522	90	480	7,294
1966	4,647	626	155	423	89	263	6,203
1967	5,905	887	148	492	54	328	7,813

SOURCE: Horst Mendershausen, *Troop Stationing in Germany: Value and Cost*, RM-5881-PR (Santa Monica: RAND, 1968), 132.

* Discrepancies in figures are due to rounding.

already in use in the United States, making delivery and further support services far easier to obtain. Only eight Mirages had at that point been produced. Further, the Starfighter seemed to allow greater freedom in making the major technical additions required by European conditions and German desires.

More important than these considerations, however, were the political factors involved. Interview comments by career diplomats and politicians indicate that the United States and France used every possible channel to emphasize their demands for the contract. Embassies, military personnel, and informal social networks were pressed into service. With increasingly less subtlety and greater bitterness each nation played the cards of prior political commitments: the French invoked commitments to the development of Western Europe and an independent European technology; the United States, commitments to the need for fostering closer German-American interdependence and a continued American presence in Germany.

Although unmistakably shaded by subsequent scandals surrounding the poor performance of the Starfighter, interviews conducted in the mid-1960s suggest that it was both American pressure and Defense Ministry prescriptions which in the end weighed most heavily. A decision in favor of the Starfighter would mean large procurement figures; a conservative estimate later was some $500–$600 million in all. Moreover, it would ensure de facto equality in modern weapons, continued presence of American forces, and considerable gratitude in Washington.

Some civil-servant respondents, somewhat knowledgeable about policy-making in that period, indicated that various Americans who were pushing the Starfighter did more than hint at a relationship between purchases of armaments and later supply of the nuclear explosives needed for their maximum use. Hard evidence to support these assertions can be found only in the known position of some of the leadership of the military: they favored provision to major European allies of both delivery systems and warheads under bilateral control arrangements similar to the double-key arrangements with Britain after 1957. It also is quite plausible that such explicit hints were offered, given the endemically fluid, unreliable character of communications within the Washington-SHAPE-Bonn triangle, the multiplicity of authoritative actors involved, and the more directly observable occurrences during the subsequent arguments regarding establishment of an MLF. But that these suggestions were taken as official policy, in light of the consistent opposition of the State Department (discussed below), or accepted in the face of the preferences of Adenauer and others for broader, more integrated control arrangements within NATO (discussed in chapter 5) seems doubtful.

What the Starfighter decision did make possible was direct German participation in sophisticated technological production—a type of national armament development, albeit within an integrated European framework. Strauss's public argument was that the Federal Republic, because of its ten-year abstinence from all military affairs, must give priority to weapons production under license (chiefly American) and to joint projects with other European states.[26] Only thus could Germany maintain a "connection with the most modern scientific level of the rest of the world" and accelerate its fledgling research and development efforts.

From 1957 onward, the defense minister relentlessly pursued such arrangements. His first accomplishment was F-I-G, a quasiformal agreement between the French, Italians, and Germans with the ostensible purpose of developing and producing in common certain "modern" light weapons presumably nuclear as well as conventional.[27] As chapter 5 discusses in greater detail, F-I-G also included relatively secret attempts to arrange German and Italian financial support for the still-developing French nuclear program in return for "technical advantage, some of which could have military applications." [28] But once in power, de Gaulle moved almost immediately to halt this threat to the national character of the eventual nuclear force; not surprisingly, the cooperative conventional ventures then never materialized.

Within the Atlantic framework Strauss's interest in license-production agreements proved more productive in the short run. Germany was one of the primary contractors (even in some instances to the point of absorbing larger item costs than any other national participant) in the European consortia organized and licensed to produce the Hawk and Sidewinder missiles and the Fiat G-91 conventional aircraft. In December 1959, Strauss joined other European leaders in pressing the not unwilling Secretary of Defense Thomas Gates for a jointly produced "European MRBM," perhaps a version of the Polaris missile.

Even when the arrangements did not touch so directly on sensitive interests as did F-I-G, Strauss's push for joint production arrangements came under considerable attack. Western press commentators—joined in private by foreign-office officials in Britain, France, and the United States—again interpreted these moves as first steps toward the establishment of German "self-sufficiency" in "nuclear production." [29] Strauss's pet projects already had required changes in the WEU restrictions on aircraft, ships, and submarine construction. It would be only a matter of time, critics (particularly in Britain) claimed, before all prohibitions including the ban on production of nuclear weapons would become too "restrictive" or "irrelevant."

Strauss's major domestic critics included Economics Minister Ludwig Erhard, Finance Minister Fritz Etzel, and Foreign Minister Heinrich von Brentano. They repeatedly asserted, in public as well as in the cabinet, that Strauss and his supporters among the German industrialists were wrong; these investments would not result in major technological payoffs or provide a long-term stimulant to the then-slowing rate of German economic growth. The huge sums involved would be better spent on consumer industries. Such expenditures not only would be more effective economically but also would not result in foreign distrust or "military rule of the economy."

In response, the defense minister repeatedly denied that he believed an autarkic armaments industry to be possible or desirable for Germany. He did not wish to change the general-purchases ratio from its division of 50 percent domestic and 50 percent foreign. He fully agreed with his cabinet colleagues that as a general principle no new facilities should be created if sufficient capacity existed abroad, especially in the United States.

There must be certain critical exceptions, however, to this rule, namely, the motor-vehicle, shipbuilding, and aircraft industries.[30] Here, Strauss was successfully arguing by 1959, there was a need for major investment to stimulate and modernize production, and through modernization, to ensure the Federal Republic a role in the areas of modern aircraft and outer-space travel. Moreover, he added privately within the Defense Ministry, Germany could not accept so basic a dependence on a source of supply 3,500 miles away.

The only public evidence for the explicit coupling of weapons purchase and access to warheads—the coupling that critics alleging backdoor methods have found so clear-cut—appears, perhaps, in German-American interactions over the question of MRBMs in late 1959 and early 1960.[31] Presumably stimulated both by Norstad's long-standing arguments about the need for MRBMs in the European theater and by balance-of-payment pressures, Secretary of Defense Gates talked somewhat informally at the North Atlantic

Council meeting in December 1959 about the imminent provision of missiles from present or planned American inventories for quick-reaction launch from barges or flatcars. Some type of joint control of warheads was to be established. American army representatives in Paris reportedly lobbied on behalf of the planned Minuteman missile; the navy supported a version of the Polaris missile; the air force championed what became known as Missile X. By the council meeting of April 1960, Gates had modified his proposal to an offer of an arrangement for joint European production of a Polaris type of missile, again with two-key control implied by its proposed mobile deployment. His proposal included a lure oriented to the French of allowing any residual launcher production (after NATO requirements were met) to revert to national control.

According to contemporary reports (but not to all interview accounts gathered in the mid-1960s) the Germans'—or more precisely Strauss's—interest in such a scheme was high. The first public indication, perhaps, was a statement by Strauss in June 1959 that the Federal Republic looked forward to joint production of MRBMs in the 1960s as a means of replacing obsolete fighter-bombers.[32] His forecast was followed by active German participation in the submission of an unsuccessful proposal for European MRBM production to the North Atlantic Council in December 1959, and by an enthusiastic response to Gates's proposal in April 1960.[33]

Official pronouncements outside NATO forums still projected only cautious interest. During a two-week visit to Polaris development facilities in June 1960, Strauss repeatedly denied that he was seeking a national purchase or production-under-license program.[34] He stated that the Federal Republic had not changed its decision not to accept MRBMs on German soil and that any further considerations would follow a NATO decision on this matter.

Interviews conducted in Washington and Bonn in 1964–1965 suggest that Secretary of the Army Wilbur Brucker was somewhat more accurate when in a Bonn press conference in July 1960 he stated, "We know that Herr Strauss is interested in acquiring medium range ballistic missiles. We have no objection at all to their acquiring weapons with a strategic range." [35] After Strauss protested, Brucker issued a clarification. At issue was not the minister's personal interest in weapons for the Bundeswehr, but rather the German position on a known NATO proposal.

The degree of enthusiasm aside, this cannot be said to have been a uniquely German position or even a fully developed, cabinet-approved policy of the Federal Republic. A major factor in all of these NATO developments had been the three-stage plan (discussed further in chapter 5), proposed by General Norstad and SHAPE, for the mounting of European counterweight to the Soviets' 700 MRBMs targeted on European cities. The first stage had been the post-Sputnik deployment of Thor and Jupiter missiles in Italy, Turkey, and Britain. European production of a Polaris missile with deployment under SACEUR's control would thus constitute a second state, serving both to put into operation the concept of burden sharing and to provide a training or probationary period toward eventual meaningful intra-alliance sharing of control over nuclear weapons. This, Norstad argued in Europe and in Washington, both would offset the political glamour of the incipient French national effort, and would sooth the fears of critics within Congress about European irresponsibility.[36]

A third phase, not clearly spelled out by SHAPE but again of interest to Strauss, foresaw this European production consortium taking a leading role in the design and manufacture of all succeeding nuclear-capable delivery systems necessary for European defense. French demands that at least a portion of any such production be reserved for exclusive national use would not be met; all weapons manufactured would be placed at NATO's disposal. Left unexplored was the implicit assumption that such a controlled dissemination of delivery-system technology most probably would involve substantial insights for the consortium into warhead technology as well.

SHAPE planners studied a number of possible missile configurations that might assure implementation, and by 1959 they had formulated plans for a mobile, primarily land-based, Polaris system configured to assure rapid firing from almost any geographic location. Their scheme covered two of the three phases, with the possibility of some European production after initial purchases of the original Polaris missile from the United States and the eventual exercise of control over firing by SACEUR under authorization of the president of the United States and the North Atlantic Council.[37]

However, Bonn did not follow Britain's lead into active negotiations for the proposed purchases of the Polaris.[38] The explanation lay in part in the doubts Adenauer's closest foreign-policy advisors had about the seriousness of the American proposals. As one prominent lawyer and civil servant commented in 1965, "With both a summit meeting and an election in the offing, Gates's tentative proposals certainly did not preclude still

another American volte-face and more 'Congressional objections.' We'd
been through that once before.''

The question of German interest became relatively academic as the alliance sank into the dead stillness imposed, during this period, by any American election campaign. Delay would have been imposed in any case, by the
course of American bureaucratic infighting on this issue, specifically the
eventually successful challenge to Gates's proposal mounted by the Department of State and its Policy Planning Staff, which is discussed in chapter
5.[39]

Indeed, by 1960 the crucial policy variable in all aspects of German
defense planning was the commitment to dual-capable equipment rather than
the slow process of acquisition itself. Strauss's administration clearly had
rejected Blank's plan to raise a 500,000-man, principally conventionally-
armed force in three years or indeed over.[40] The goal was now a seven- or
even eight-year buildup to a peacetime level of 350,000 men, equipped and
organized according to the modern principles demonstrated by the American
conversion to nuclear weapons. Interim readiness of even those forces was
of secondary importance; what counted was the chance for full exploitation
of the new technology in the interests of progress, economy, and political
equality.

The material as well as the psychic investment is demonstrated in table
6. The force reorganization announced in 1958 fully recognized the air
force's claims, both budgetary and doctrinal, to be the most modern of the
three services. Although the final manpower goal of 100,000 remained
fixed, the new air-force profile called for 28 (rather than 44) squadrons
designed principally for a major role in NATO's nuclear interdiction and
counterair missions.[41] A share in active air-defense missiles as well as
planes was a second priority; tactical air support ran a poor third.

The army's bowing to the nuclear revolution was only slightly less
striking, albeit in the face of widespread, continuing internal opposition and
a manpower loss of 30 percent under the new organizational scheme.[42]
There were still to be divisions, but drawn now from 200,000 rather than
350,000 men. The organization, the training, and even the method of establishment of these divisions explicitly were made contingent on the principles central to American pentomic divisions and British nuclear brigades.
And given the many lessons to be learned, Strauss's plans foresaw a fairly
long period during which German forces could be expected to bear NATO's
lowest effectiveness rating, that of ''limited combat readiness.'' [43]

TABLE 6
Total Weapons Procurement Costs for the Bundeswehr by Service Category, 1957–1969
(millions of marks)

Year	Army	Navy	Air Force	Other	Total
1957/58	1539.8	262.3	553.1	39.9	2395.1
1958/59	601.8	599.8	1097.3	46.2	2345.1
1959/60	1042.3	462.9	702.8	46.0	2254.0
1960 *	745.9	386.2	901.6	33.9	2067.6
1961	987.1	464.3	1414.8	73.7	2939.9
1962	1473.7	634.1	2075.5	85.8	4269.1
1963	1559.3	593.4	2630.5	83.6	4866.8
1964	1475.9	885.7	1572.6	78.4	4012.6
1965	1325.1	691.7	1158.5	64.7	3240.0
1966	1271.7	550.1	739.5	122.1	2683.4
1967	1652.1	742.7	1107.5	73.5	3575.8
1968	1177.1	589.0	1236.5	46.7	3049.3
1969 †	1477.1	456.7	1575.1	72.9	3581.8
Subtotals	16328.9	7318.9	16765.3	867.4	41280.5

SOURCE: Bundes Presse- und Informationsamt, *Weissbuch 1970: Zur Sicherheit der Bundesrepublik Deutschland und zur lage der Bundeswehr* (Bonn, 1970), 197–98.
* Reflects shortened fiscal year (April 1–December 31).
† Estimated costs.

In sum, by the end of 1960 the German stake in full if not yet immediate operational adaptation to a nuclear-capable posture was considerable. Such a posture represented the converging interests of influential and not always compatible groups. For example, it suited simultaneously those who wanted to minimize the budgetary and manpower drain of rearmament and those who wanted to exploit rearmament expenditure for the maximum possible technological payoff to the civilian sector; it also suited both those who saw no point in extensive military efforts once the immediate political vis-à-vis Washington had been gained and those who felt dual-capable equipment was one vital and necessary step toward the only essential capability. Strauss himself had made nuclear conversion his hallmark, at least in his image making, if not through his actions.

There still were many opposed (as is analyzed below) on grounds of doctrinal adequacy, of expense, of impact on relations with other countries, of impact on whatever options for reunification might still remain. But by 1960 the opponents largely had been overcome, defeated in debate or simply refugees in silence in view of the Germans' seemingly united front on the role the Federal Republic should play in NATO defense. And all this had happened despite the arrival of only a few major weapons systems and the extension of some promises of delivery.

THE OPPOSITION

A nuclear-capable Bundeswehr, in the minds of many critics, was one real or at least politically manipulable step too close to an independent German nuclear capability. The outpouring of criticism and fervid opposition at home and abroad found an Adenauer government steadfastly maintaining not only that its claims were right and just but that such steps indeed were required and desirable. Its efforts, however, were marked by a curious (although characteristic) blend of vagueness and insistence, by a clear desire to avoid unnecessary or premature public controversy while at the same time demanding full acknowledgment of its rights.

The most frequent outcome, not surprisingly, was continued charges and increased suspicion. What specters Strauss's bombastic claims had not already raised about Bonn's longing for a national nuclear capability Adenauer supplied through his constant, simplified insistence that German denuclearization was acceptable only in direct exchange for reunification. For the logical next question had to be "and after that exchange, what then. . . ?" or more frighteningly, "if that exchange was not completed or seemed in question, then. . . ?"

From the outset, therefore, the question of nuclear-capable armament was inextricably and dramatically intertwined with that of reunification. This stemmed not from public or elite concern for the logical consequences of these decisions; that these weapons most probably would be used against targets in or close to East Germany, for example, was never publicly mentioned. It was rather that this was seen as the last of the rearmament battles and, in some ways, the most bitter phase of the rearmament-versus-reunification conflict that had characterized the Kanzlerdemokratie from its inception. For the chancellor, if not for all of his CDU/CSU associates, this "transarmament" represented only a logical extension of the decision to enter NATO—to reachieve the unity of the German nation through Western negotiation from strength and the Federal Republic's indispensable share in that posture. The slogan of the 1957 federal election campaign, "No experiments," meant just that. Nothing had changed in either East or West which made necessary a reconsideration either of the bargain struck in 1950 or in 1955 or of the inevitable (but only eventual) interrelationship of the three German foreign-policy goals.

Adenauer's opponents and critics agreed only on one broad point: in terms of political appearances at least, an irrevocable choice had not yet been made or perhaps even seriously considered.[44] Beyond this there was enormous variation in interests, motives, and specific conceptions of what was indeed at stake. The effort here will be to develop briefly only the major strands of argument in the two principal, interacting arenas of debate, the domestic opposition and the disengagement or denuclearization movement.

Consequently, one basic question—the degree of freedom with which the Adenauer government could even seriously consider the choices posed— is answered here by assertion. The assumption here is that at least until Khrushchev's Berlin ultimatum of 1958, the convergence of German and American interests in opposing any denuclearization proposal was more a function of dominant American policy than of Adenauer's basic political calculus.[45] Quite apart from the reinforcement provided by the chancellor's frequent pleas and remonstrances, the Washington of Eisenhower and Dulles neither could nor would allow any change in the European status quo that lessened or obviated a German role in NATO and the West. And however provocative the opportunity—whether dangled by Moscow, London, or quite incredibly by the SPD—this was the crucial variable.

THE INTERNAL OPPOSITION

In many respects Adenauer had an easier time with his critics at home, trapped as they were by the very specificity of their concerns about the acquisition of dual-purpose weapons. Their arguments were not always logical by military or even philosophical standards. Their conclusions were related more to Adenauer's lack of progress toward reunification than to the particular consequence of any particular decision for German defense or the general deterrence posture of the West. Nevertheless, their intensity and perseverance resulted in what unquestionably can be counted among the most bitter public debates ever to occur in the Federal Republic.

The most pointed and technical critique came very early in the debate, too soon to serve as more than a limited, frightening catalyst. The source was not a political party but a group of eighteen leading German atomic scientists, most of whom had been engaged in nuclear research under the

Nazis.[46] The occasion was Adenauer's "modern artillery" metaphor, which galvanized their long-felt private disquiet about the direction of German rearmament policy. Their Göttingen Appeal of April 1957 set forth their belief that

today a small country like the Federal Republic will best protect itself and do the most to advance world peace by expressly and voluntarily rejecting the possession of atomic weapons of any kind. In any case, none of the undersigned would be prepared *to take any part* in the production, testing, or use of atomic weapons.[47]

The resulting diatribes of the government were focused explicitly on the scientists' "unwarranted intrusion in foreign-policy matters," but more significantly, the implicit aim was to avert any adverse impact on the national elections scheduled for September 1957. In the face of the blanketing, simultaneous assertion of governmental authority and assurance, the scientists in effect retired from active debate, albeit with their pledge still firm. However, the opposition parties—principally the SPD—immediately seized on the issue, making "atomic armament" the principal focus and watchword of all foreign-policy debates during the next eighteen months.

The opposition's action stemmed in part from what seemed an unquestionable advantage in popular appeal, an advantage that could be mobilized in the struggle for an ever elusive electoral victory for the SPD.[48] In largest measure this action was simply the logical extension of earlier pro-reunification, anti-rearmament positions to which the "old Socialist" leadership under Erich Ollenhauer still was ideologically committed.[49] The SPD, however, soon found itself in its usual dilemma: it was unable either to make political capital out of the choices implied in technical armament decisions or to make the existence of an acceptable reunification option seem credible, imminent, or even desirable. The SPD's only major support in this second task was the stream of Russian disengagement proposals (discussed below), hardly political assets from either an ideological or a pragmatic perspective.

The Bundestag debates in the spring and the election campaign later in 1957 therefore were characterized by highly emotional but rather primitive and ineffective arguments by the opposition.[50] SPD leaders inquired vainly as to the government's plans regarding atomic armament and simultaneously issued a blanket repudiation of any and all arrangements. In their electoral appeals they limited themselves to such slogans as "Atomic energy for the food of mankind—an end to the policy of atomic bombs." Their parliamentary demands were only somewhat more detailed: unilateral renunciation of atomic weapons by the Federal Republic and withdrawal of all such arms from German soil as steps toward both the halting of nuclear-weapons proliferation and the reopening of reunification negotiations.

Their efforts, therefore, were extremely vulnerable to the well-practiced tactics of governmental evasion and dismissal. Strauss and Adenauer responded, if at all, by justifying atomic armament as an absolute requirement of NATO which Germany must fulfill.[51] Before any such step was taken, CDU/CSU leaders asserted, and before such weapons were available (at least a two-year period), a number of changes might occur—for example, a wide-ranging disarmament agreement. A unilateral renunciation by Germany at this time would only weaken the position of the West in such negotiations, as well as reduce the stakes for future bargaining for reunification "from strength." Neither German security nor eventual unity would be served by denying German forces or allies' troops on German soil the vaguely defined "necessary nuclear means."

In March 1958, the issue seemed finally joined in a long Bundestag debate marked by unparalleled personal invective and acrimony. The initiative came from the now-exclusively CDU/CSU government, flush from its resounding electoral victory and eager, in the face of popular post-Sputnik worries and continuing American pressures, to end debate on an approved policy of the Atlantic alliance. Accordingly, the outcome was approval of the government's responsibility to undertake not only atomic armament but indeed all measures necessary to avoid "disrupting" or "leaving" NATO. As expressed, the sense of the Bundestag was that

In accordance with the requirements of this defensive system (the North Atlantic defense community) and in light of the armament of the possible opponent, the armed forces of the Federal Republic must be so equipped with the *most modern weapons* that they are able to fulfill the obligations assumed by the Federal Republic within the NATO framework, and to make, in an effective manner, the necessary contribution to the securing of peace.[52]

In a maneuver that was extraordinary and in one sense extralegal, the SPD continued the fight outside the legislative arena. The result was the five-month "Campaign Against Atomic Death" (Kampf dem Atomtod), with its innumerable emotional speeches, rallies, protest demonstrations, attempts to institute popular referenda that were expressly prohibited by the Basic Law, and mountains of antiatomic propaganda.[53] What was perhaps the only effort to present an alternative policy was made in May 1958 at an SPD party congress, which called for a small professional army that would be "in proper relation to that of its immediate neighbors, particularly the German military force on the other side of the demarcation line . . . [and] not equipped with instruments which are designed only to destroy, not protect: atomic weapons and missiles." [54] Such a defense force, it was argued, at least would not seal the division of the German nation.

The government's response was to launch a countercampaign, with government spokesmen for the first time strongly emphasizing that the question at issue was that of dual-capable weapons with the warheads to be held under constant American control, not of actual atomic armament.[55] Strauss and others ridiculed the SPD's easy assumption of the "red or dead" argument and stressed the need for a strong NATO front against Moscow's continuing attempts to "isolate" Germany. The principal ploy, however, was to ignore the specific issue and simply ask whether Adenauer's policy of secruity, resistance to communism, and no experiments should continue—a ploy that was very effective among the general population.

Both campaigns had a decisive impact on the extragovernmental elite. Debates raged in all areas—among businessmen as well as within churches, among journalists as well as among university professors. As one seasoned political commentator described it in 1966, for many it was

a real battle and the most difficult period in postwar Germany. There was total division, a total tearing apart that revealed all the old wounds. There seemed no basis for consensus; it was impossible even to talk—you were either for or against and that was that. Nobody would ever want to go through something like that again.

The de facto end of the Atomtod campaign came with the results of the test state elections in North Rhine Westphalia, with the "atomic" CDU winning its first absolute majority in that important state since 1949. Protests and demonstrations did continue, along with the publication of numerous antiatomic tracts and limited debate within the intellectual community. But for both major political parties the direct issue was now settled; the last of the rearmament battles had been fought.

The terms of this settlement were of profound significance for the future development of both the SPD and the domestic debate about strategy. This second crushing electoral defeat of the SPD ensured the intraparty triumph of the right-wing reformists—Willy Brandt, Fritz Erler, Carlo Schmid, and Herbert Wehner—who had long dissented from the party's previous militant, ideological, quasi-pacifist stand. The SPD henceforth was to be a Volkspartei (mass party) with a broad pragmatic program rather than a limited-membership, ideological union clinging to an outdated Marxist orientation. It would become a party which would be not only capable but also credible, nationally and internationally, as a replacement for the CDU/CSU.

In defense policy, as in all other aspects of foreign policy, the SPD reformists propounded policies only moderately different from those of the government. In rapid succession party conferences (the first and most famous at Bad Godesberg in 1959) approved declarations ranging from approval of "the defense of the country" to promises of present and future allegiance to the Atlantic alliance. There were moves clearly prompted both by domestic electoral considerations and by final (though still implicit) admission by the SPD that reunification on acceptable terms was improbable in the foreseeable future.

There was still another factor, set forth in Fritz Erler's long-pressed arguments.[56] Given the accomplished fact of rearmament, the SPD's proper role was to act as a defense critic "from within." As in the British Labour Party tradition, the party now must accept (though not necessarily support) the existing framework set by the government and attempt only to influence subsequent decisions about armament and strategy. There was no purpose to be served—for the party, the defense of the country, or the creation of a stable democracy—in continuing attempts to deny history or to radicalize all discussion of defense matters. There was no way now to change history, nor was any profit left in recriminations about "lost opportunities" for reunification.

The SPD's position on nuclear matters clearly revealed the tensions involved in such a course. The SPD, party leaders repeatedly declared, had not given up its opposition to the Bundeswehr's acquisition of nuclear-capable delivery vehicles or to the adoption of strategy predicated only on never-failing deterrence. Given the grave risks of escalation and the overwhelming destruction that the Federal Republic would experience in even a limited war, efforts must be made to achieve a real forward defense of its territory and advance the security of all the German people, in Berlin and the East, just as in the West. Moreover, the SPD still believed unilateral renunciation of nuclear weapons or perhaps creation of a Central European nuclear-free zone to be a necessary and acceptable precondition for any serious future negotiations toward reunification.

Yet the Federal Republic already possessed a minimal delivery capability, party spokesmen were quick to add, and such weapons were considered an integral part of NATO's defensive posture. The SPD must direct its current efforts toward limiting Germany's dependence on nuclear weapons. It must oppose further purchases of equipment that was "exclusively nuclear" and demand a substantial strengthening of nonnuclear capabilities. It should support demands for an equal German voice in all alliance arrangements for control of nuclear weapons but not any role which sought to "make politics with nukes" or which weakened the basic American-alliance guarantee of German security.

Thus by 1960 militant domestic opposition on nuclear issues had all but ceased. The tacit agreement of the major parties not to argue vigorously in public was tentative; major differences on substantive issues still existed and would be partially re-aired during 1961–1962. Yet a basic truce, however uneasy, had been struck; it would prevail until 1964. And the SPD now had acquired NATO and nuclear dilemmas of its own.

THE EXTERNAL OPPOSITION

Opposition in both East and West to Adenauer's search for equality in nuclear-capable weapons was considerably less specific but far more tenacious and unswervable than the domestic criticism.[57] The primary forums were the ever present discussions about the broad political and military postwar settlements in Central Europe—discussions, that is, about "the German question." But there also were numerous direct attacks upon Germany's "nuclear obsessions" and its determination to achieve "national nuclear control." Bonn's response to all criticisms was uncompromising rejection of any discriminatory political-military settlement and frequent reiteration of the Federal Republic's right to and need for equal participation in NATO's nuclear strategy. And the Adenauer government expected, indeed shrilly demanded, that its allies adopt the same stance.

Far more than the domestic turmoil, therefore, this international interaction constituted a major explicit assault on Adenauer's Eastern policy and its relation to ultimate reunification. If Bonn was truly concerned about the restoration of unity, the argument ran, then almost a decade of building toward negotiation from strength had yielded few results. Given this evidence, let alone the onset of East-West strategic nuclear parity, what value was to be gained through yet another rearmament step, particularly one which represented a quantum step in destructive potential? And if the road to reunification really did go through Moscow, what benefits would dual-capable armament bring in view of either Moscow's well-founded fears about German intentions or the overall balance of forces in Europe?

The spate of schemes for disengagement raised other questions, even among Adenauer's CDU colleagues, concerning more pragmatic interpretations of Adenauer's goals.[58] In 1950 or even 1955 it had seemed beneficial to seek political advantage (in return for a contribution of arms) in the West while warding off both any recognition of the status quo in Central Europe (e.g., the legitimation of the German Democratic Republic [GDR]) and any change which would not meet all of Bonn's objectives or trade-off formulas. But in respect to both political and military considerations, that time was past; advantage currently must be sought at least equally in relations with the East. The possibility of a Schaukelpolitik, that playing off of East and West in the manner of Stresseman and the post-World War I era, perhaps was no longer relevant. But what interest did Germans have in a Central Europe filled with opposing foreign forces deployed eye-to-eye across a rigid demarcation line and increasingly equipped with nuclear weapons to be used on a two-Germany battlefield? Was not more to be gained through minimally amicable relations with Moscow that might allow not only for the undermining of the status of East Germany's Ulbricht but also for the assertion of Bonn's influence in Eastern Europe, a traditional sphere of German influence?

Seen from this perspective, the discussion of European disengagement and attendant denuclearization substituted good and potentially manipulable questions for the real questions. So long as Adenauer held to the priority of reunification (even with the qualification of "in peace and freedom") and to his policy of minimal, primarily defensive Ostpolitik, he was vulnerable to continuing attack, to blackmail by his allies as well as his opponents. He could neither achieve any of his goals nor profitably renounce them. And there were (and are) many who saw this as the greatest failure of an otherwise extraordinary record in diplomacy.

Perhaps the chancellor's major historical vindication, however, can be seen not only in the similar fixation of American policies under Dulles but also in the vacillating policies of the Russian leadership under Khrushchev.[59] Without question, Moscow was the principal instigator and manipulator of the disengagement-denuclearization concept, with the Atlantic alliance affiliation and nuclear potential of Germany the principal targets. Until the finality of their ultimatum of November 1958 concerning Berlin (but really directed at the Federal Republic), the Soviets pursued two inherently contradictory objectives vis-à-vis the West: greater influence and security through the detachment or isolation of Bonn from the West, and consolidation and legitimation of the Stalinist heritage in Eastern Europe through achievement of détente with the United States. It was a double-edged policy requiring far more skill and consensual support within the Russian and Eastern European elites, it seems in retrospect, than a Khrushchev could muster.

None of this, however, was immediately apparent in Eastern or Western proposals for European disarmament or security arrangements; all proposals now focused solidly on new dangers attendant on the introduction of nuclear-capable weapons. In the disengagement formulas or other indirect means of attack it was stressed that Central Europe had become, suddenly, a tinderbox, a constant ominous threat to global peace and security. A freeze, a phased reduction, or a total withdrawal of all foreign troops and nuclear arms, particularly from German soil, would reduce tensions and open the way to a lasting arrangement for Central Europe, including the rapprochement (if not the reunification) of the two Germanys.

It was proposals emanating from the Soviet bloc that focused most clearly on the tactical-armament plans of 1956–1958. In the Gromyko Plan of 1956 and more fully in the two Rapacki proposals (1957 and 1958) the aim was to prevent any nuclear weapons-sharing, whether through the stationing of jointly controlled American missiles or the European allies' acquisition of dual-capable equipment. The basic Eastern position was set down in detail in the second Rapacki memorandum (February 14, 1958):

The proposed zones should include the territory of Poland, Czechoslovakia, German Democratic Republic and German Federal Republic. . . . [They] would undertake not to manufacture, maintain, or import for their own use; nor permit the location on their territories of nuclear weapons of any type, as well as not installing or admitting to their territories installations and equipment designed for the use of nuclear weapons including missile launching platforms.[60]

The formal campaign of the Eastern countries was reinforced by massive, skillfully differentiated propaganda efforts. Toward the Federal Republic itself, Soviet-bloc agencies directed diplomatic notes, radio programs, and press reports that attempted, with some success, to stimulate popular fears about nuclear warfare. The Federal Republic purportedly was "playing with fire" for the sake of the Americans; it was foregoing chances for eventual reunification in order to become "one big graveyard" in a nuclear war.

It would be those European states that accepted American weapons, not the United States, that would be the first victims of war by design, accident, or the insubordination of mad generals.

For the NATO allies and the European neutrals the Eastern tactic was to raise the specter of a "revanchist, nuclear-mad" Germany. The "Nazi generals" in Bonn wanted such weapons for conquest in the East; even the tightest system of controls could not hinder designs for diverting or capturing the weapons. Unless the allies wished to risk their existence to help German aggrandizement, they must prevent any German finger from ever reaching a nuclear trigger.

A second and almost equally important objective in all Eastern moves was the de facto if not the de jure recognition of the GDR. Whatever armament remained on its territory, the Federal Republic for the foreseeable future was to remain allied to the West and separated from the other part of the German nation. Reunification, so far as it was possible at all, was to depend on the course of relations and negotiations between the two Germanys, with minimal involvement of the other Atlantic allies, especially the United States.

Proposals advanced in the West, particularly those of George Kennan and the British Labour Party leadership, were more expressly concerned with the "intolerable," inherently unstable status quo in Central Europe. Disengagement and détente not only would reduce military tensions, the argument ran; they also would necessitate long-postponed political agreements. A conventionally armed, eventually neutral and reunified Germany as well as a "normalized" Eastern Europe would be the most probable and most desirable result.

Some politicians in the West and especially in Britain found this method of dealing with the Germans' "nuclear obsession" most attractive.[61] Any hint in the press regarding possible Franco-German cooperation in production of nuclear weapons (discussed below) or suggesting too great a German role in NATO nuclear-weapon arrangements was enough to arouse large segments of the Labour membership, particularly those in the left wing. United with them in spirit were a number of Conservatives, always somewhat anti-German in general orientation and ever protective of Britain's special standing in nuclear matters within NATO and vis-à-vis the United States.

The response of the Adenauer government to all of these proposals was to reiterate unceasingly the basic stand Bonn had taken during the Geneva discussions of 1955, which because of the "unchanging character of atheistic Communism" still pertained.[62] There must be no agreement on disarmament or détente in Europe without a simultaneous overcoming of the "central source of tension," the division of the German people. Any measure was unacceptable which even in its initial stages tolerated or perpetuated that division or limited the freedom of the German people united by free elections to shape their own foreign policy and defense policy. In the interim, neither the Federal Republic nor its allies would or could brook any interference in the fulfillment of its "legitimate security needs."

On the renunciation of nuclear-capable armament or the stationing of nuclear weapons on German soil, the Adenauer government echoed the strategy arguments of the Eisenhower administration.[63] Such arrangements were now part of the accepted NATO posture; renunciation would result in a weakening of the alliance's strength and in a "dangerous" imbalance of conventional forces in Central Europe. There would be no guarantee against clandestine deployments in the East or against a sudden move to replace weapons that had been withdrawn (relatively easy given the geographic situation). In an era of long-range missiles and aircraft, moreover, such regional security arrangements had lost all meaning.

More central in Bonn's argument was the political discrimination involved, seen as yet another move toward the constant Soviet goal of isolating the Federal Republic from its Western allies.[64] Denuclearization would impose upon Germany a political and military status radically different from that of the other alliance members, a status which had not been imposed by its voluntary 1954 nonproduction pledge. The withdrawal of tactical nuclear weapons probably would necessitate the drawing back of American troops from the front line. The Federal Republic's territory also would be subject to constant and probably "provocative" inspection by the East, which thus would have a de facto veto over any changes in existing defense postures.

The basic theme, however, was the forced surrender, without compensation, of a major German counter for future negotiations on a European settlement and reunification. The armament restrictions undertaken in 1954 had been a gift to the Federal Republic's allies in return for definite pledges of protection and support. Unless there was a real prospect of obtaining reunification, no German government would consider further restrictions and certainly not nonparticipation in common NATO arrangements.

This remained the official German position until Khrushchev's Berlin ultimatum effectively ended all talk of disengagement and forced the reopening of East-West talks on the central question of the unity of the German nation. Despite major initial disagreements, the joint proposal of the Western states to the Foreign Ministers Conference held in Geneva in May 1959 only made the interrelation of unity, European security, and disarmament problems more explicit. Commonly known as the "Herter Plan," the proposal foresaw three phases of tightly interwoven political and military measures, culminating in free elections (after two and one-half years and after the creation of a Mixed Germany Committee). The Federal Republic's security and status before unity was to be safeguarded by the permitting of only limited changes in existing force deployments and by extension (during the second phase) of its ABC-weapons nonproduction pledge to the GDR and other Eastern European states.

The Federal Republic supported the Herter plan, but made clear its view that this proposal represented the maximum tolerable concessions the West could make to Soviet demands.[65] Even the most limited forms of disengagement, denuclearization, or détente were acceptable only within a fixed framework that had reunification as its assured goal. No other formula, however partial, was to be considered. This was the legalistic, determined stance that was maintained with great effort well into the 1960s in the face of German popular sentiment and allies' policy shifts.

FIVE

The Search for Control-Sharing: 1957-1960

✠ FROM 1957 TO 1960 Germany's principal choices with respect to nuclear-weapons policies turned on questions about sharing of control over nuclear weapons. As in questions of strategy and equipment, Bonn's interests were hardly unique. At issue in the growing debate within the alliance was a general Western European challenge to the American monopoly in decision-making about nuclear weapons. Public arguments were couched in terms of the changing strategic environment: the declining credibility of the American nuclear guarantee under the post-Sputnik balance of terror, the improbability of risking New York to save Berlin, the yawning missile gap. Only barely concealed, however, was the questioning of the basic European-American bargains embedded in NATO, a questioning reflected in the strident calls for more national "independence," for a "more appropriate" division of labor within NATO, for a "more equitable" European-American relationship.

The European challengers were themselves divided about the specific factors required for a solution. Would it be sufficient to participate only in the alliance's planning or contingent decision-making, and if so, with respect to which weapons and functions? Would some form of NATO control be feasible and desirable, or was actual physical control the only assured safeguard of national interests? Would this be achieved through weapons transfers from the United States, or was independent production on either a national or multilateral basis a political necessity?

The crucial variable for all the allies was the behavior of the United States. In its actions, if not in its declaratory policy, Washington had carefully educated its allies in the advantages of a nuclear defense posture. How far was it now willing to go in realizing the political consequences? What degree of participation or independence would it (or could it) permit now or in the future? How would the various nuclear options—actual, proposed, or conceivable—affect the nature of the American presence in Europe or the nature of the power relationships within the alliance? The answers offered throughout these years even by the same American actors were neither clear nor unchanging.

The Federal Republic's position in this debate was a very special one. From one perspective the Germans' range of choice among policies was very limited. Given the 1954 nonproduction pledge and the certain opposition of both ally and enemy, Germany could not follow France's example and pursue—or even effectively threaten—national development of nuclear weapons in the near future. Too, whatever Bonn's interest or wishes, a European nuclear consortium was not a realistic option, if only because of the problems a German role would pose. Most important, Germany's primary dependence on the United States both for its security and its political future limited its explicit demands to those at least superficially congruent with American control-sharing policy.

Yet for these same reasons the Federal Republic by 1960 viewed the nuclear-control issue with a degree of concern surpassing that of any other ally. To the most exposed NATO member the minute-by-minute decisions of the United States in war or deterrence situations could mean existence or annihilation. Moreover, in accordance with the American model all of Germany's still-building forces were being organized and equipped for nuclear warfare. Without arrangements to assure direct, timely release of warheads, these forces not only would be valueless in war but also would constitute a hollow basis for claims by Germany for equal partnership within the Western deterrent system.

In political terms the Federal Republic had even more to lose if it did not gain full participation in a new nuclear-control scheme. As the 1958–1959 Berlin crisis clearly underlined, German hopes for present status and significant influence in a future European settlement were totally dependent on the constant equal exercise of influence over American decisions, that is, equal at least to the influence of any other European NATO partner.

Such a role would be secured only if control arrangements gave particular recognition to Germany's nonnuclear but integrated status within NATO and thus lessened the rewards which national nuclear independence promised Britain, as well as France. And as the basic Adenauer policy of strength dictated, this recognition of Germany's stake also had to be unmistakably clear to the Soviet Union.

The position Bonn adopted and pressed increasingly was, not surprisingly, advocacy of the exercise of greater control by the North Atlantic Council and its agent, SACEUR. This position quite simply made political virtue of Bonn's foreign-policy necessities. An Atlantic framework meant continuous, relatively harmonious American involvement in European defense, full German participation in the new control arrangements, and a de facto downgrading of the British and incipient French nuclear forces as long as they remained outside NATO. And for the few who worried or cared, the option did not absolutely foreclose any future options or eventualities—Atlantic, European, bilateral, or national.

The way to this let-NATO-do-it decision, however, was considerably less unidirectional than the route involved in questions of strategy and equipment. This analysis therefore includes a somewhat artificial separation of the debate along the lines of Bonn's two principal bargaining perspectives. The first part, considerably richer in chronological detail, treats the special German variant of the European allies' dialogue with the United States. The other focuses on Bonn's second-order dealings with its major potential competitors within the alliance hierarchy, Britain and France. The commentary then tries to weave the two strands together.

THE GERMAN-AMERICAN DEBATE

OPENING SKIRMISHES, 1956–1958

Like most other Continental capitals, Bonn in the months from December 1956 through June 1958 became ever more involved in the search for a more equitable sharing of control over nuclear weapons.[1] The earlier vague, sporadic musings about future possibilities sharpened rapidly under the impact of three developments: growing operational dependence on a nuclear defense, the British decision and the French ambition to pursue national nuclear independence, and Sputnik and the growing number of Soviet MRBMs targeted on European cities. The debate within the alliance was confused and confusing; the alternatives proposed by Bonn and others were tentative, partial, and often impracticable. But the basic strategy of the Adenauer government did emerge: an artful mixture of calls for Atlantic integration, German-American solidarity, European independence, Franco-German convergence and SACEUR's transformation.

The first testing of the strategy came during the extended discussions held in the wake of the Suez crisis at the North Atlantic Council meeting in December 1956. Bonn joined those states which under French leadership demanded that Washington immediately permit a wider distribution of its tactical nuclear weapons. It was no longer simply a question of implementing the 1954 nuclear-response decisions of the alliance by equipping all national forces (not just the American and British units) with nuclear-capable armament. There must also—at the very least—be a binding American assurance that in a conflict nuclear warheads would be available when and where they were needed and that all allies would have some say in their use.

Proposals by the European allies on the operational form that such an assurance should take were few and far from detailed. However strong their desires, most other European allies, like Bonn, viewed the possibility of direct transfer of warheads to be a question for the future. Given the constraints of American atomic-control legislation embodied in the (to Europeans) infamous McMahon Act of 1946, all that now could be hoped for was some form of alliance control over the size of and conditions under which warhead stockpiles would be used. One suggestion—associated particularly with NATO Secretary General Paul Henri Spaak but reportedly favored by many leaders, including Adenauer—called for independent control by SACEUR over release of warheads subject to guidelines established by the North Atlantic Council.[2]

Bonn clearly distanced itself from the farthest-reaching demands— those calls for direct sharing of information about weapons and missile production that were pressed by France.[3] This German stance was rooted in estimates that Bonn's primary interest lay in securing equal nuclear-capable armament for its forces without undue disturbance in either the national or international arena. There might be latitude for some demands in the name of "equality" or "national interest." But neither the basic principles of Adenauerian foreign policy nor German dependence on the American security guarantee would permit the appearance of an explicit national initiative.

Moreover, even at that point both Adenauer and Defense Minister

Strauss seemed to believe that broader control-sharing within the alliance was inevitable. The defense minister perhaps was more optimistic, sharing the convictions of a number of Continental leaders that an American transfer of warheads or authorization of direct European access to them was only a question of time.[4] He reportedly based his view on "informed" estimates of the debate taking place in America as well as on the "inescapable" thrust of technology. Several prominent American military and political leaders had already supported a gradual evolution in control-sharing arrangements; most probably, Strauss argued in Defense Ministry circles, only the shock of Suez and Congress's resulting suspicions had delayed wider public discussion.

There also might come a time, Strauss hinted darkly, when the United States no longer would be so concerned with European defense. Development of intercontinental ballistic missiles (ICBMs) soon would remove the need for European bases; then the principal battle routes between the United States and the Soviet Union no longer would need to go over Europe.[5]

More salient for the chancellor was his belief in the necessary evolution of a different European-American balance within the alliance. Adenauer throughout his career was quite ambivalent about the direct role that America should play in European affairs. As a political realist he knew that without major American involvement there would be no effective security for Europe or substantial support for Germany's special political and military interests.[6] Even if Adenauer's hopes for a united Western Europe, with an achieved European defense community, were realized, Western Europe would for a considerable time have neither the financial nor the scientific resources to allow it to catch up with the Soviet and American nuclear programs. For Adenauer in this period, therefore, any Western Europe, however united and determined to provide its own defense, could at most be an Atlantic partner, one which would change the West-East balance from 1:1 to 2:1.[7]

The chancellor, however, always was extremely pessimistic about fulfillment of the American share of the Atlantic bargain.[8] As shown most dramatically in such lapses as the Radford crisis, few in Washington understood the primary importance of Europe, not Asia, for American security or the necessity of constantly adapting the alliance's military and political relations to changing conditions.

Whatever the particular strategic rationale of the moment, Adenauer's approach to the nuclear-control problem flowed from these general guidelines. Given Europe's increasing dependence on nuclear deterrence and defense and the unpredictability of American behavior, the Europeans must seek some insurance.[9] There must be a form of control that guaranteed nuclear-weapon release before the Federal Republic's territory had been overrun and, more important, that would convince the Soviets of Western European if not American determination to use nuclear weapons. The Continental allies must circumvent any Anglo-American efforts to make possession of nuclear weapons the sole criterion for political influence within the alliance. The political framework for this European effort need not involve for the moment supranationality or indeed anything more than intensive bilateral negotiations. It must be a joint effort, since no single Continental state (especially not a vulnerable Germany) had sufficient credibility and influence for this maneuver vis-à-vis Washington or Moscow.

But as the chancellor repeatedly warned the French, all this must not be undertaken in direct opposition to the United States.[10] Western Europe clearly could not be defended, if only because of financial constraints, without some American involvement. In the months before Sputnik this position of Adenauer's took on even greater significance in light of a set of continuing discussions with French leaders on a potential European defense organization and opportunities for joint production of modern weapons. As is detailed later in this chapter, these talks produced few results and involved extensive reservations and tactical calculations by both states. At a minimum, however, they represented a mutual interest in holding open a European-defense option both for the future and for present bargaining advantage vis-à-vis Washington.

American nuclear-control policy itself seemed to be undergoing wide-ranging discussion and possible major revision. For Adenauer and Strauss one less hopeful sign was another qualitative expansion of the special Anglo-American relationship in nuclear matters through the Bermuda accords.[11] More encouraging were the remarks of Eisenhower and Dulles about reform of NATO in general and stockpile-sharing in particular. At a press conference in July, although mentioning the problems involved in revision of the McMahon Act, Dulles declared that

now . . . we do not ourselves want to be in a position where our allies are wholly dependent upon us. We don't think that is a healthy relationship. Therefore we are studying ways whereby, through perhaps a NATO stockpile of that sort, there can be assurances to our allies that if they are attacked, if war comes, that they will not then be in the position of supplicants, as far as we are concerned, for the use of atomic weapons.[12]

Eisenhower on the following day echoed Dulles's statement that the proposed stockpile "would be an act of confidence which would strengthen the fellowship of the North Atlantic Community."

The promises implicit in these remarks were reinforced by reports that some American leaders were willing to go further in sharing. General Gruenther, a former SACEUR, already had suggested that one means to ensure Western defensive superiority in Europe would be to transfer (after legislative approval) nuclear warheads directly to the various allies. It also was rumored that the majority of the then-secret Gaither Committee, appointed by Eisenhower to undertake a major review of foreign policy, had favored creation of a European nuclear missile force. Purportedly, in the words of one member, this would involve "direct and significant European participation." [13]

Strauss and a few other European leaders believed that the nucleus of such a force might come through a proposal, then being privately circulated to the capitals of NATO members, by the SACEUR, General Norstad. Based on the broad review SHAPE had conducted in early 1957, Norstad's recommendation called for the establishment not only of extensive nuclear stockpiles but also of a NATO MRBM force, both of which were to be under SACEUR's direct control. Such a force was a "military requirement," first, to provide a "theater balance" to developing Soviet missile forces, and second, to "modernize" SACEUR's obsolescing tactical air interdiction forces. Although the precise missile system to be used was still open, Norstad urged that it be land based and amenable to "direct" control by the alliance (i.e., by SACEUR). Norstad's proposal reportedly was a deliberate effort to distance himself from the plan then being suggested by Washington to place IRBMs (functionally indistinguishable from Norstad's MRBMs) in all European NATO countries under direct bilateral arrangements.[14]

The Federal Republic's leadership found Norstad's proposal even more absorbing in the confused discussions among allies which followed the advent of Sputnik in October 1957. For Germany as for the other restive European allies the successful Soviet launch primarily meant that the long-predicted balance of terror now was a reality, and the long-questioned

American guarantee now was manifestly not credible. Of greater significance was the failure of American technological leadership that Sputnik had revealed. Not only would the West now have to find new cooperative means to ensure the reattainment and maintenance of technological preeminence, but also there was more justification (and opportunity) than before for European demands that America share its nuclear-production monopoly. It was no longer natural for the United States to assume the role of nuclear producer for the West; the often heard claims of economy, efficiency, and experience were no longer valid.

Still further impetus for intensified Continental demands for control-sharing were the persistent rumors of a post-Sputnik, Anglo-American agreement on a new division of responsibilities within NATO. According to one report, the United States and Britain, under a revised McMahon Act, were to produce strategic and tactical nuclear weapons that then would be placed at the disposal of the alliance "under certain conditions." [15] France and Germany would be encouraged to produce modern tactical weapons, including short-range rockets. However, neither they nor any other European NATO members would have the right to American or British assistance for national nuclear production or to a voice in nuclear decision-making.

All these factors were reflected, if only between the lines, in the public proposals presented for action by the Continental allies at a meeting of NATO states' heads of government held in Paris in December 1957. As summarized by Secretary General Spaak, the Continental agenda called for thoroughgoing discussion of existence of stockpiles of tactical atomic warheads in Europe; transfer of control over such stockpiles to SACEUR; organizations and methods involved in decisions regarding use of tactical atomic weapons; equitable division of labor in modern armament research and production. [16]

The American position presented at Paris was somewhat responsive. [17] There would be adequate nuclear-warhead stockpiles in SACEUR's domain as soon as possible; the previously proposed IRBM force similarly would be placed at SACEUR's disposal rather than, as originally suggested, under a series of bilateral agreements between the United States and each Continental ally. Dulles also offered substantial new concessions toward developing European production capacity. Under a to-be-revised McMahon Act, Washington would make available information on the use and design of IRBMs and nuclear-submarine propulsion plants; it would gladly accept joint European efforts for modern armament production in the IRBM field as in others.

On three basic issues, however, there was to be no compromise at that time. The United States would continue to be the sole producer of warheads—in Dulles's words, "as a matter of simple efficiency and economy . . . for a considerable time." [18] Predetermined control guidelines presented unacceptable disadvantages, as indeed did any required alliance-wide consultations on aspects of this area. And whatever the intervening arrangements, the United States reserved to its president (and then to his generals) the final decision to fire any nuclear weapon.

The official German position at least superficially was completely congruent with this American stance. [19] In accordance with NATO decisions the Federal Republic wished to ensure the continuous availability of the most modern weapons for its forces. Germany therefore endorsed the stockpile and IRBM-force concepts, although it had "not yet" reached a decision about stationing of IRBMs on German soil. Joint weapons research and development in Europe were one but not the only area of European interest and concern about increasing the common control of vital alliance activities. Unless specifically invited to do so, of course, Bonn would not seek a lifting of any of the 1954 prohibitions on production of weapons.

The tone of the intragovernmental considerations behind this formal statement, however, was considerably less congruent and moderate; it was a clear indicator of growing German anxiety and uncertainty. Mounting frustration with the evolving structure of the alliance and the role of its Continental members was reinforced, yet also tempered by fears about future American policies and Adenauer's commitment to inextricable American involvement in European defense. The desire of most politicians and civil servants to delay decision, to exercise reserve to prevent international distrust were countered by fears—most explicitly expressed by Strauss and his circle—of "being left behind," of losing out at this critical juncture in the alliance's political development.

Perhaps least controversial were the decisions adopted regarding the American IRBM proposal. The Adenauer government was convinced of the need for European-based IRBMs, the conviction being a product of Strauss's early enthusiasm and the educational campaign mounted by SHAPE and Norstad. Yet there was a total reluctance to accept Thors or Jupiters on German soil. The basic military argument was that set forth in a special Führungsstab study: permanently emplaced, liquid-fuel missiles should not be situated in the "foremost trench." [20] They would be primary targets for the enemy's strategic forces as well as extremely vulnerable prizes for enemy ground offensives. Given the strategic position, the limited geographic area, and the popular temper of the Federal Republic, these missiles, in contrast to supersonic aircraft capable of the same missions would prove extremely cumbersome, expensive, and a source of constant domestic agitation. Most important, they might come to constitute a "fixed line" of defense, which would justify withdrawals of ground forces and abandonment of the forward defense of the Federal Republic's territory.

Political arguments against acceptance of IRBMs were less detailed but equally compelling. The ones that prevailed, according to interview reports in 1965–66, were those contained in an unpublicized Foreign Office study, namely that deployment and eventual joint production of IRBMs might lead to charges that the Federal Republic was developing an "offensive" military posture and that a confidential French report that the Continental allies were not to be offered the preferential control arrangements accorded to the British was probably well founded.

A small minority of CDU liberals, most notably Kurt Georg Kiesinger and Eugen Gerstenmaier, were more persuaded by a third factor: the recent receipt of a relatively conciliatory letter from Soviet President Nikolai Bulganin. It suggested, in new, somewhat credible forms, a trade-off of progress on reunification or a nonaggression declaration for a German decision rejecting deployment of IRBMs or nuclear-capable weapons. Adenauer himself was at one point in late 1957 persuaded that further probing on this suggestion with Moscow was in order.[21]

Substantial political and military debate surrounded the final decision to urge wider-ranging powers for SACEUR to control warhead stockpiles and release procedures. In reviewing the possible operational forms this control might take, military and political leaders were able to agree only on a general, essentially negative statement, according to interview reports. There must be enough warheads under a form of control-sharing to ensure combat effectiveness and national influence over their use, but not enough to raise the risks of American displeasure or withdrawal, "undue" or "debilitating" national dependence on these weapons if war threatened, and damaging delay in critical American decision-making, especially regarding the use or threatened use of SAC's forces.

Direct transfer of warheads under either bilateral or alliance control clearly was the simplest and most efficient method. As Adenauer repeatedly pointed out, the path to revision of the McMahon Act was difficult, however, and despite American promises, as yet unprepared.[22] A majority of the Adenauer-von Brentano faction believed, moreover, that an alliance-wide sharing formula was undesirable. It would increase the dangers of unauthorized use and blur the political significance of major force contributions, Bonn's principal bargaining lever.

The final decision not surprisingly followed the basic Adenauer strategy discussed earlier. For the moment, the most practical course would be again to seek a substantial increase in SACEUR's autonomous control powers, leaving Norstad to fight the operational arrangements through the American government and to clarify through negotiation the fuzzy areas of the American legislation.[23] Bonn should press discretely for the establishment of council-approved nuclear-weapons guidelines and ask for influence over both the conditions of release (simultaneously to spur and to brake American planning) and the projected targets (to insure selective, discriminating use with respect to the populations and territories of both Germanys).

On the questions involved in production-sharing proposals, the final decisions were more tortuous. Against some opposition the broad plans for Bundeswehr modernization and for close cooperation in production with the French and other European countries had general cabinet approval.[24] Some members, reportedly including Foreign Minister von Brentano, had even spoken of a return to the joint production and financing arrangement foreseen under the EDC—arrangements which someday even a reluctant Britain could join.[25] But as Strauss's private conversations in Paris and Adenauer's November talks with Undersecretary for Foreign Affairs Edgar Faure had shown, the French interpreted joint production to include a sharing in nuclear production in or by Europe as a collectivity.[26] A minority in the cabinet opposed this on ethical grounds; others, centered around Strauss (and basically supported by Adenauer), saw the threat of a Continental nuclear bloc as both an effective instrument of pressure vis-à-vis the United States and an insurance policy for the future, whether through joint or national production.

The final decision was in essence a holding policy; Bonn should take no direct action until the American position was totally clarified.[27] It was not in Germany's interest to aid in furthering French claims for equal national status with America and Britain or in enhancing French chances to exercise leadership in whatever kind of Europe finally emerged.

Above all other considerations, the Adenauer government must avoid appearing to seek a wholesale lifting of the EDC or 1954 production restrictions; suggestion of their abrogation would be political dynamite at home and abroad.[28] As Adenauer told Faure, "anything on the research level" would not require revision of the 1954 restrictions on production of nuclear weapons; and Bonn could more easily ask for other changes once a NATO-approved basis for argument existed. As always, a policy of reserve, a strategy of stressing only the faithful implementation of NATO directives would prevent present and future distrust.

The uncertainty and anxiety of the Germans about how to broaden nuclear-control arrangements were masked, of course, in the ringing declarations of alliance members that closed the December meetings. They re-emerged publicly in early 1958 in the wake of developments in American nuclear-control policy portending increasing restrictions. The first was announcement of a "separate" (meaning double-veto) Anglo-American control arrangement over the use of IRBMs based in Britain.[29] The second was the trend toward discrimination being shown in congressional deliberations on revision of the McMahon Act.[30] The statements of both administration and congressional leaders proved that Britain's status as the most favored nation in nuclear affairs would be extended indefinitely. Weapons information and weapons components were to be transferred only to nations where they would "improve" preexisting nuclear capabilities (the administration's formulation) or to nations that had "made substantial progress in the development of atomic weapons" (the stricter congressional amendment). These formulas seemed merely legalistic descriptions of an Anglo-American nuclear trusteeship within the alliance.

Further, the watering down of the administration's request in response to congressional pressure made implementation of Dulles's previous encouragement of joint European production extremely questionable. The principal aim with respect to the continental allies was merely to share data needed for maximum military efficiency. As Dulles eventually put it, the necessary data was only that "required to enable them to share in the planning of a nuclear defense and to make them capable of using nuclear weapons received from us if hostilities occur." [31] The administration's original request for authority to transmit information on nuclear-ship propulsion and IRBM design, as well as actual nuclear fuels for the reactors to propel ships, vanished completely from Congress's considerations.

Even more disturbing for those few in the Federal Republic's leadership who followed these deliberations was the sharpening commitment to a total nonproliferation strategy that was underscored by hearings held by the Joint Committee on Atomic Energy (JCAE). Dulles in his testimony, for example, reiterated his beliefs that significant, discriminating nuclear weapons-sharing was the best means to lessen the incentives in Europe toward either national nuclear development or policies of neutrality toward or nonparticipation in NATO.[32] Yet he repeatedly assured the committee that the administration would not depart from a "tight security" information program or proceed with previous or private understandings. Moreover, he (and virtually every administration witness) promised that there would be no surrendering of exclusive American control over present or planned nuclear components within the NATO defense system. SACEUR would have control only in his twin position as commander in chief of the American forces in Europe, and sharing of planning within the alliance was not foreseen as having any direct operational component.

Any remaining German hopes for joint Franco-German production efforts with American approval underwent indefinite postponement upon de Gaulle's assumption of power in June 1958. His demands to Dulles about nuclear-propulsion information and national control over stockpiles or IRBMs on French soil marked the first specific (and disillusioning) testing of the limits of the newly revised McMahon Act. Moreover, Bonn—with Adenauer in the lead—viewed the General's pronouncements, past and present, as reassertions of nationalistic goals with respect to Europe as well as to the Atlantic alliance. What Adenauer later characterized as an important start towards European cooperation in the atomic sphere thus ground to a complete halt.[33]

THE DEBATE CONTINUED, 1958–1959

In the months following de Gaulle's investiture, the Federal Republic's formal consideration of the problems of nuclear control drifted and waned. De Gaulle's proposal for a tripartite global directorate produced a brief flurry of discussion and opposition in Bonn, but was soon lost in the shadow of Khrushchev's Berlin ultimatum. For more than a year Germany and the rest of the West primarily were absorbed in hammering out a common response to the Soviet challenge and in closing the rifts it had revealed and intensified within the alliance.

Bonn's anxiety about control, however, hardly lessened in this atmosphere or in light of several related developments that seemed to undermine further the credibility of the nuclear guarantee. The trend toward a Fortress America seemed to accelerate steadily. In the midst of constant reiterations of America's willingness to risk total war for the defense of Western Europe, rumors and unofficial recommendations of major withdrawals of American troops persisted.[34] Constant German demands for reassurance met with bland statements of general support and ambiguous assertions about "no such present plans." Moreover, even before initial emplacements of Thors and Jupiters had been completed, Washington announced that the original IRBM program was being "reappraised" and then cancelled because of rapid developments in ICBM technology.[35] Most officials in Bonn had feared the lightning-rod effects of the original proposals; they now were at least equally discomforted by the prospect of America's withdrawing across the Atlantic and barricading itself behind its ICBMs.

Most disturbing were the questions raised by American policy concerning the defense of Berlin.[36] To most of the allies, primary reliance on threats of strategic nuclear retaliation to defend it presented the prospect of unnecessary, irresponsible risk. In the view of most allies, Berlin was not worth the risk of destroying any nation except perhaps the Germans, however small that risk might be. It was not just that some solution other than military confrontation had to be found. At issue was whether such life-and-death decisions should remain the exclusive province of the United States.

On the other hand, not only the Germans feared the possibility of American weakness and failure. Without the nuclear threat Berlin was deterrentless as well as defenseless. Moreover, the Berlin offensive seemed but the first step in Soviet "salami tactics," rooted in Russian estimates of American irresoluteness. If the United States was not willing to accept maximum risks to deter an attack against Berlin, where would the line be drawn?

And both Adenauer and de Gaulle asked: Even if the military threat abated, what of America's irresolution as evidenced by its willingness, under British pressure, to negotiate about Berlin?

Beyond these substantive fears was the German feeling of helplessness. Germany's influence vis-à-vis the United States declined perceptibly; American responses to German requests for reassurance were tinged by hints about the "German rigidity" publicly emphasized by the British. Too, although Dulles and Adenauer always had differed more than was generally believed, the secretary's progressing illness and subsequent death seemingly closed what had been Adenauer's most effective channel into Washington decision-making.

More immediately alarming, however, was the trend toward Soviet-American rapprochement.[37] Despite Eisenhower's reassurances, Adenauer saw the meetings with Khrushchev at Camp David as the first step toward long-feared superpower agreement on Europe's division, toward acceptance of the primacy of the common Soviet and American interest in hegemony. The argument long used by the chancellor vis-à-vis his public and, later, de Gaulle—that Washington would remain bound at least in the short run to the defense needs of a Europe that bore its fair share of defense costs—appeared measurably less credible.

The cumulative impact of these developments greatly heightened German desires for a new system of nuclear control-sharing. The immediate channeling and precise formulation of this desire, however, were largely shaped by an outside factor—the contemporary control-sharing proposals and doctrine of SHAPE and General Norstad.

During his years as SACEUR Norstad had assiduously cultivated a "European" stature in Bonn as in the other Continental capitals. At first, the reception given him was cool, especially among military leaders suspicious of his embodiment of the "American Air Force" and "nuclear tendencies." However, his obvious concern with all aspects of European defense, his desire to be truly SACEUR and not just another American commander, and his willingness to judge according to present achievements rather than past guilt soon won him considerable prestige and many cordial contacts within the Bonn leadership. Particularly for Adenauer, he rapidly became "the man to whom one could go," the American who understood Europeans' anxieties about the changing strategic environment and whose interest in the Europeans' having more control over nuclear matters within the alliance was congruent with Bonn's own interests.[38]

Crucial for control-sharing issues was Norstad's emerging role as NATO's de facto Supreme Military Advisor, with access to members' governments virtually unhampered by domestic restraints (such as the JCAE).[39] With the Eisenhower administration's tacit blessing Norstad and SHAPE increasingly became the driving forces in the search for liberalized control arrangements. The motives of this SACEUR were undoubtedly mixed, with at least a measure being the competitive drives of a theater commander and a skillful soldier-politician. But a large component was Norstad's own analysis of the consequences for the 1960s of the changing strategic balance, of

the need to use military requirements to anticipate foreseeable political demands of the allies. As he later phrased it,

How do we meet a growing but still somewhat confused and conflicting desire
among our European allies for a broader sharing in the control of nuclear weapons?
How can the alliance as a whole be assured that such weapons will be available for
their defense, the defense of Europe? [40]

Norstad's principal instrument in this search was his assigned responsibility to put into operation the North Atlantic Council decisions of 1957.[41]
His first target was the IRBM force promised his command, which according to the operational blueprints put forward in SHAPE studies involved
three rather new components. Thors and Jupiters were indeed to be placed in
Italy, Turkey, and Britain as arranged. But because of their relative obsolescence and extreme vulnerability, they were to be replaced by 1960–1965
with 300 to 600 more modern, more versatile missiles, which would fulfill
SACEUR's MRBM requirement.

Of greater interest to the Germans was Norstad's suggestion for sharing
the blueprints of these second-generation missiles with a new, NATO-controlled production consortium composed of the major allies. This sharing
would be understood as a training or probationary period toward eventual alliance control, a step which would both offset the glamour of incipient national efforts and soothe the fears of critics within Congress about European
irresponsibility.[42] Still open, however, would be the question of an eventual
sharing formula and of the least dangerous location for such missiles within
the densely populated central front.[43]

Norstad's second and related concept was that NATO itself should
become the "fourth nuclear power." [44] The SACEUR's somewhat tenuous
basis for this concept was the "NATO atomic stockpile" arrangement
agreed to in 1957. His military requirement again was the need to ensure
both the close geographic proximity and the rapid though controlled release
of necessary warheads to delivery vehicles held by allies. Although some
progress had been made, technical factors, delivery problems, and delays in
the negotiation of stockpile agreements had contributed to slowed implementation of stockpiling goals. Moreover, Norstad argued, alliance plans for the
further expansion and dispersal of dual-capable equipment—in the case of
the Davy Crockett cannon, perhaps even to the company level—raised technical doubts about the future feasibility of exclusive, assured American control over stockpiles.

Norstad's political aims were twofold. The initial purpose of NATO's becoming a nuclear power was to meet continuing European concerns not only for influence over use of stockpiled weapons but also for data concerning what kind of weapons in what quantities were in fact being stockpiled. Reportedly, as Strauss later was fond of repeating, the Continental allies officially did not know "whether they had potatoes or warheads stored on their territory." Of waxing interest to Norstad and Bonn, however, was the political value such a concept would have in blunting òr offsetting France's drive toward acquiring its own nuclear force.[45] Whether France participated or not, those European states that gained a real share of control would be less interested in following the expensive and risky French example and less susceptible to calls for a third-force Europe that would be based on France's possession of a nuclear force.

Official German statements did not touch on this second proposal of Norstad, not going far beyond general refutations of French demands for national control or expressions of the need for maximum integration of nuclear weapons within the alliance.[46] A review of Strauss's statement during this period, for example, revealed only three types of generally related comments. The first, frequently made, was a demand for greater German representation in a reformed, more powerful NATO command structure.[47] A second typical remark was occasioned by persistent rumors about German aid to the French nuclear program and German desires and schemes for similar independence in strategic nuclear weapons. In one instance the defense minister repeated earlier denials and then declared that for Germany such a course would be militarily superfluous, politically wrong, and economically infeasible."[48]

A third and very frequent theme of Strauss was the need to develop a rational division of labor within the alliance. Although the Adenauer government believed that only the United States and Britain should bear the responsibility for the sword mission, the Federal Republic must have a voice in the control of all weapons, whether strategic or tactical, on which questions of German existence turned. In one interview Strauss introduced a term, *Mitbestimmungsrecht* (literally, the right to also have a say), which was to reverberate throughout the discussions of the 1960s. He declared,

But this concept includes [the caveat] that as a result of their accomplishments, so essential for the strategic armament of America and Great Britain, the German and French bearers on nonstrategic armament have a right to codetermination (*Mitbes-*

timmungsrecht) in the employment of strategic armament if it should be used for their own protection.[49]

THE ISSUE JOINED, 1960

Bonn's reserve soon changed, when in early 1960, in the wake of a lessening Berlin crisis, control of nuclear weapons once again became the major focus of public debate among the allies. One of the initial catalysts of discussion was the first public presentation of Norstad's proposal that NATO become the fourth nuclear power.[50] His terms were tentative: "for thinking purposes only" and "if politically feasible" and "in complete accordance with required control procedures." But in his speeches and even in testimony before the JCAE he left no doubt that he considered adoption of his plan to be an important task, of the utmost urgency as perhaps the last chance to divert the now-successful French nuclear program or to prevent a shift of Germany to nuclear nationalism.

More startling was a statment by President Eisenhower that seemed to signal resumption of the earlier campaign to liberalize sharing arrangements. Questioned by a reporter about possible changes, the president said,

Well, from the very beginning, from what I knew about allied cooperation and so on, I have always been of the belief that we should not deny to our allies what the enemies, what your potential enemy already has. We do want allies to be treated as partners and allies, and not as junior members of a firm who are to be seen but not heard. So I would think that it would be better, for the interest of the United States, to make our law more liberal as long as . . . we are confident . . . they would stand by us in times of trouble.[51]

Congressional alarm and massive JCAE blackmail, however, caused another administration retreat, as did Khrushchev's thinly-veiled threat that any new weapons-sharing scheme might have dangerous implications both for the summit meeting planned for May 1960 and for current Warsaw Pact arrangements for control of nuclear weapons. Norstad, with his carefully tailored mix of military requirements and political strategies, was once again, with Eisenhower's obvious approval, in command of the public discussion of nuclear-control sharing within the alliance.

A further cause for German optimism was reports, fragmentary and somewhat inaccurate, of a semisecret State Department initiative on sharing similar to that proposed by Norstad. According to the information when available to Bonn, a study done by Professor Robert Bowie had urgently recommended not only an increase in NATO's lagging conventional buildup but also the establishment of a NATO-controlled MRBM (actually strategic) force.[52] To alleviate European fears the force was to be sea-based; SACEUR was to be given a significant number of Polaris submarines (perhaps as many as a dozen). European demands for sharing control were to be met in two ways: through cooperation with the United States in decisions affecting the force and, later, through direct physical involvement in a system of mixed manning. Physical multinational participation, Bowie felt, not only would ensure against uncoordinated or unauthorized use by Western Europe as a whole or by individual nations; it also would lessen the incentives toward further proliferation along the lines being pursued by the French.

Apparently ignored or discounted by Bonn and the other Continental proponents of control-sharing were the signs of continuing if not stiffening resistance to any such changes. These signs included the withdrawal of the Gates proposal because of European (notably French) demands for a national share from any joint production of missiles and Washington's failure in the face of congressional resistance to meet a Dutch (and reportedly also a French) request for the information about nuclear-submarine propulsion offered in December 1957.[53]

Of even more specific import for Germany was the sharp, horrified reaction of members of the JCAE when they discovered in the course of a European inspection tour German aircraft loaded with armed American nuclear weapons and routinely stationed on runways guarded by only a handful of American soldiers.[54] Over the next months they pressed their demands for tighter custodial arrangements with increasing success and even to the White House itself. By 1961 all nuclear weapons in Europe—even those needed for planes and launchers on NATO high-alert status—were to be made responsive only to a presidential firing order, by means of installation of permissive action links or other electronic locks.

The German position was a special variation on the somewhat hopeful European theme. In private discussions in Washington and at SHAPE, remarks by German officials left little doubt about the Adenauer government's demand for changes, its basic support for Norstad's proposals for an "atomic NATO," and its considerable interest in other, rumored possibilities.[55] Perhaps the only major statement of the German position came in Strauss's speech to the WEU Assembly in May 1960. Adopting the vocabulary of current American discussion, the defense minister declared,

[The Atlantic alliance] must be based on two pillars. It must have two functioning reliable components, the North American component and the Western European component. . . . It is not only a question of the division of military tasks; it is primarily
a question of political insight, that of the recognition of reciprocal dependence.[56]

The last months of 1960, however, witnessed a quite different German
approach—more determined, detailed, and with some hints of stridency. According to Adenauer's memoirs and to the accounts of a number of the
then-leading political and military figures interviewed in the mid-1960s, the
catalytic event was de Gaulle's uncompromising statement of France's opposition to integration made during his meeting in July with the chancellor.[57] Despite the references to Atlantic allegiance in the final communiqué,
the General forcefully told Adenauer that the alliance neither could nor
should remain an integrated organization with an Atlantic-wide scope.
France would not under any circumstances submit to the dictates of others;
through its own national military efforts it would both secure its destiny and
restore the essential feeling of national responsibility for its defense.
Adenauer returned to Germany apparently deeply disturbed and repeatedly
told his staff that now, more than ever, French national ambitions would
force America's withdrawal and effective dissolution of the alliance.[58]

A partial solution, however, seemed to emerge from a meeting on Lake
Como in early September 1960, at which Adenauer, together with Spaak
and Dutch Foreign Minister Dirk Stikker, listened with "great interest" to
Norstad's newest formulation of the atomic-NATO proposal.[59] Foreseen
was the creation of a NATO atomic stockpile under SACEUR's direct control, comprised of the land, sea, and air missiles necessary for all missions
concerned with European defense and the requisite warheads which were to
be used by SACEUR only according to whatever guidelines were established
by unanimous vote of the North Atlantic Council. Assured by Norstad of at
least Eisenhower's approval and cooperation, the chancellor set about gaining France's toleration, if not support, for this project. A crucial meeting
with Prime Minister Michel Debré ended with Debré's agreeing to convey
Adenauer's arguments to Paris, but he forcibly expressed both his grave
doubts that a proposal to Congress by Eisenhower was of even low probability and his own views on the political and military liabilities for France in
continued integration of kind within the alliance.[60]

A little more than a week later, Strauss publicly expressed official German support for a fourth-nuclear-power NATO.[61] In an interview with Adel-

bert Weinstein in the *Frankfurter Allgemeine Zeitung*, the defense minister
discussed two "suggestions": Norstad's concept of a *force de frappe* on
land, sea, and air, and a reported upcoming proposal from Secretary of State
Christian Herter for a "maritime version." Strauss expressed no personal
preference between the two proposals, declaring that the most important
point was their common basic assumption that the alliance should exercise
meaningful control over a nuclear capability. The chancellor took a more
definite stance, welcoming the upcoming discussion of integration and calling for the immediate creation of a "common organ . . . which would feel
itself responsible for all the people who face a heavily armed nuclear
enemy." [62] At all costs the frightening prospect of further nuclear proliferation must be excluded in the interest of the quest for nuclear disarmament
and of future unity in the West.

It was noteworthy but not surprising that in all these statements made
prior to the December meeting of the North Atlantic Council there was no
mention of Germany's preference for any specific formula for SACEUR's
control; there were only general calls for greater control and more participation by European allies. Of course, there already had been lengthy discussions of several proposals in the Defense Ministry, as at SHAPE itself. [63]
The omission appeared to result from customary reserve and from desires to
await specific American proposals.

Secretary Herter's final presentation to the council's ministerial meeting
of December 1960 was not a proposal but rather a new, tentative "concept," significantly mixing—to Norstad's obvious distress—elements of the
SHAPE and the Bowie proposals. Herter raised the possibility that if
Congress approved, the United States before the end of 1963 would "assign" to the NATO command five Polaris submarines, with each carrying its
full complement of sixteen nuclear-capable missiles. There would be two
preconditions: an acceptable agreement among the allies on an effective system of multilateral control of the force, and willingness of the European
allies to purchase in the United States an additional 100 MRBMs that would
be deployed on "other kinds of vehicles" (presumably land or sea
launchers, but never actually specified) also under direct NATO control. [64]
No mention, however, was made of any transfer of the required warheads to
NATO or to national authorities.

The general response of the European allies was one of cautious enthusiasm. In both the political and economic sphere this vaguely defined, uncertain mating of the Bowie and Norstad concepts clearly raised more problems

and questions than it resolved. Further, although the newly elected President Kennedy had acquiesced to presentation of the concept, his statements and those of members of his incoming administration indicated a disinclination to be bound by any former commitments. It therefore seemed far better and wiser to postpone formal considerations and to reserve the question for study by the council's permanent representatives.

The German delegation—in particular, Strauss—was willing to go somewhat further. In a forceful speech the defense minister discussed at length the momentous questions involved, but repeatedly stressed the great urgency of the issue for all concerned.[65] A definite timetable for consideration—perhaps less than a year—must be established; NATO's authorities should be instructed to develop a "comprehensible and trustworthy formula" for discussion at a "NATO summit" meeting in the spring.

The German position found some echoes, but it did not affect the final outcome. Herter declared that he could take no step which would commit the new Kennedy administration to particular discussions or actions. Like all the other European allies, the Federal Republic therefore had to be content with agreement in principle on the creation of an alliance system and with its hopes for the future. In the stiff phrases of the final communiqué,

The United States Government suggested the concept of a MRBM multilateral force for consideration by the Alliance. The Council took note of the United States' suggestion with great interest, and suggested [that] the permanent representatives . . . study the suggestion and related matters in detail.[66]

THE SIDE GAMES

Bonn's search for nuclear control-sharing also involved a number of secondary games—negotiation, disputes, and even intrigues—with its two major European allies, London and Paris. For all three states the stake in the nuclear-control debate was not just the shape of future European-American relations but also the future status hierarchy within Europe. Accordingly, respective bilateral relations always involved varying mixtures of competition and cooperation and were assessed in the context of current bonds to the United States.

THE BRITISH GAME

Of the two relationships, the Anglo-German bargaining process was the more constant and unidirectional. Postwar relations between Bonn and London were (and have generally remained) rather cool and distant, the product in considerable measure of traditional antipathies, painful wartime memories, and some unfortunate experiences during the occupation.[67] The fundamental factor, however, was the relative power status of the two countries in the 1950s: the Federal Republic, only part of the German nation and militarily vulnerable, was in the midst of booming prosperity and rapid political rehabilitation, in contrast to Britain, victorious and the third nuclear power, yet in straitened economic circumstances and undertaking a painful withdrawal from its global commitments and influence. For both, the Washington link was their principal hedge against present political adversity, the sine qua non for attaining future goals.

This antagonism was further exacerbated by the strictures of cooperation within the alliance. From Bonn's vantage point, Britain's membership on the tripartite Standing Group, its yearly demands for reimbursement of troop-support costs equal to that paid to the United States,[68] and its unwillingness to bind itself more closely to the Continent's defense seemed relics of the wartime experience, supported only by the special Anglo-American tie. Withdrawals of British forces were always either in process or being threatened, and according to several apocryphal but suggestive stories that German military officers were telling in 1965–1966, the British Army of the Rhine soldier's first instruction in event of war was "report to London."

British counterarguments were no less negative. Bonn pursued total economic prosperity while others paid for Germany's defense; Bonn found anti-German discrimination in every alliance program; it constantly demanded unquestioning support from the allies for its unrealistic policies on reunification and Berlin. Moreover, as discussed in chapter 4, most of the British leadership and populace viewed any increase in German military power or nuclear-capable capacity with suspicion, if not substantial alarm.

The nuclear-control debate brought all of these attitudes to fullest measure, with the most obvious aspect being Britain's determination to preserve at almost any cost the unique nuclear relationship with Washington that it had assiduously cultivated throughout the 1950s. London lost few opportunities to remind the Continental states of its special status. To Adenauer's obvious disgust this was the principal reason the Eden government gave for not joining the European allies in development of nuclear power for peaceful uses through Euratom in 1956.[69] More threatening were the unrelenting (and quite successful) British claims of "special nuclear responsibilities" as justification for withdrawing troops or for pressing for preferential modifications in American nuclear-control policies.[70]

According to several officials from the Foreign Office and the Chancellor's Office who were interviewed in the mid-1960s, Britain also began as early as 1957 to oppose actively any wider nuclear sharing under alliance or bilateral agreements. Examination of press reports of North Atlantic Council meetings show that once its own agreements with the United States were secured, Britain rarely supported Continental requests for wider dissemination of information and production capacity or for broader control powers for SACEUR. As with the later MLF, London reportedly raised serious doubts about the dangers inherent in any specific proposals (for example, the Herter concept) and set numerous preconditions for placing any of its nuclear forces under alliance-wide control.[71]

A further point was Britain's extreme sensitivity to signs or hints of the Continental allies' cooperation in nuclear matters. On at least two occasions—the discussion of a military component for Euratom in 1956 and the formation of a French-Italian-German weapons consortium in 1958—the British government attempted diversionary tactics, offering "cooperation possibilities" and "information exchange." [72] These probes were later withdrawn, simultaneously with British press drumbeats about the beginnings of a "German nuclear threat." To the German leadership and particularly to Adenauer, this was merely a "nuclear updating" of Britain's traditional policies concerning the Continental balance of power.

A more specifically anti-German thrust was perceived in British advocacy of disengagement and denuclearization in Central Europe. Particularly in the last years of the 1950s Adenauer viewed the Macmillan government as being quite willing to seek détente at the expense of both reunification and German security, to trade Berlin's freedom for the possibility of a broad (and unacceptable) European settlement with the Russians.[73] Even if one discounts the chancellor's usual pessimism and anti-British bias, his view was not totally unrealistic. Denuclearization of Germany—then as later—was an easy price for London to pay.

The Federal Republic's basic strategy toward Britain in respect to nuclear sharing was far simpler. First, Bonn effectively used the rubric of integration to protest every instance of pro-British discrimination in control arrangements. The Defence White Paper of 1957, for example, prompted sharp comments by the chancellor to Washington and to Norstad concerning the "unforeseeable consequences" of the British example for alliance cohesion and implicit threats about further nuclear developments, especially Franco-German cooperation.[74] On more than one visit to America, Strauss reportedly also challenged the preferential custodial system accorded to the British and openly asked how much longer Germany and the other members of the Continental alliance would have to bear the cost of "British nuclear drama."

Germany's second tactic was to do little or nothing to improve the poor state of Anglo-German ties. There were recurring disputes about paying the costs of the British Army of the Rhine, disputes which were not eased by constant German recriminations about the withdrawal of British troops to pay for Britain's nuclear deterrent. And Bonn was not spontaneously inclined to make up the deficits through armament or other military expenditures.[75]

A final, less frequent German maneuver was to stress the need to provide even a reluctant Britain with a European defense home. Adenauer, but particularly Foreign Minister von Brentano, from time to time revived discussion of a possible nuclear "EDC plus Britain" or a functioning integrated WEU possessing its own deterrent forces, an organization to be in partnership with the United States. Further, one of the many attractions of both the Norstad and Bowie proposals for Bonn was that a collective deterrent force would possibly capture the British force and thus effectively level the "artificial distinctions" among the European members of the alliance.

In the final analysis the problem of nuclear control-sharing was not the central focus of either British or German concerns about the policies of the other state, nor was it the only subject of continuing Anglo-German discord. But the debate on this issue served both to highlight and to reinforce the basic political differences between Bonn and London.

THE FRENCH GAME

In contrast, nuclear sharing was a significant, recurring focus in Franco-German relations from 1956 to 1960. Obscured at times by the crumbling structure of the Fourth Republic and the ambiguous advent of de Gaulle, the pertinent issues involved the patterns of potential cooperation or conflict between not only Paris and Bonn but those capitals and Washington and even London as well. Although historically the choices were relatively predetermined, a rueful Adenauer would still later argue that much might and should have been done differently.[76]

As in all its postwar relations with Germany, France sought—and therefore suffered—quite conflicting goals in its nuclear sharing policies. On the one hand, Paris sought to control German access to all nuclear weapons, much as it had sought to control German access to any kind of weapon during the early 1950s. French preeminence in nuclear matters must be assured, first and traditionally, to deter a direct (although hardly credible) attack by Germany or an intolerable expansionist threat and, second, to dictate the terms under which the inevitable German claims for full equality would be considered. American or even Anglo-American control would be neither sufficient nor tolerable; France must exercise its own responsibility as one of the Western Big Three.

Perhaps the clearest example of these French ambitions was Paris's strategy during the Euratom discussions in 1956.[77] From the issuing of the first proposals, controversy and debate had surrounded Euratom's possible responsibility for the military applications of atomic energy. All of the initial statements (such as the Benelux proposal and the Monnet Action Committee declaration) posited a Euratom with exclusive control over nuclear materials and dedicated to the development of atomic energy for peaceful uses. National military programs were seen to conflict with that goal and with the process of integration; at most, armament production was to be a common responsibility.

Throughout the discussions of 1956 the French vehemently opposed permitting Euratom to develop any military competence. Despite earlier assurances to the contrary, French representatives repeatedly demanded that military production plans, facilities, and materials be exempted from any form of supranational control, since France would tolerate no interference in its national defense effort. Moreover, Paris believed that there must also be certain safeguards in the community's nonmilitary controls to allow both the protection and the expansion of national military programs.

From the Germans' viewpoint, the net effect of the provisions demanded by France would have been to ensure European and particularly German subordination to French national ends. In the military field the problem was not simply that of a national nuclear force; given the instability of the Fourth Republic, such a force then seemed a question for the distant future. The problem was rather that despite the wishes of the other five members, Euratom was to be used as a source of both financial and research support and as a political shield for France alone. A prime example was the French demand for a common isotope-separation plant, which would be costly, politically risky (given mounting American opposition), and of limited value for current development for nonmilitary purposes.

Moreover, there also would be careful control of any progress by Germany, present or future. The materials monopoly that Paris demanded for the community would ensure that any German initiative—in basic research as well as in the industrial sector—would be subject to a possible French veto. American assistance, including the transfer of low-cost enriched fuels, would be dependent on similar regulation. France thus would remain in sole control of any military accomplishments and would become the arbiter of the community's relations with the United States as well as of Germany's (and other European countries') national development programs. Not surprisingly, Bonn strenuously objected and, when in part overridden, contributed to Euratom's almost immediate ineffectiveness.

Simultaneously, France, even under the Fourth Republic, had to recognize the utility of a strong Germany for the attainment of French "great power" ambitions in the nuclear area as in all European affairs. Bonn would be a convenient source of political support as well as of financial and intellectual resources., For bargaining purposes alone, close Franco-German cooperation would make the threat of a French-led European bloc more credible. Furthermore, rapprochement would prevent both the emergence of a united Western Europe on terms unacceptable to the French and excessive concessions to Bonn in the interests of continued Anglo-American hegemony. The final goal for Western Europe, especially as articulated under de Gaulle, was not to be egalitarian integration but rather a more limited, differentiated partnership of mutual benefit. Above all, there must be no back-door possibilities for an independent German nuclear program.

In this respect the interests of Adenauer's Germany nearly coincided with those of France. Although formalized control and discrimination were to be avoided, a de facto junior partnership for Germany in nuclear affairs—as in the construction of a united Western Europe or the meander towards reunification—was inevitable in the short run. Bonn also needed a strong European ally to support its interests in the ongoing transatlantic bargaining and in the eventual lessening of the American commitment to Europe or growing Soviet-American agreement based on the partitioning of the German nation. Too, Adenauer's own career was premised on a lasting European reconciliation, rooted not only in the overcoming of past hatreds but also in the emergence of a stable, democratic (or at least noncommunist) French ally.

The limits of cooperation for Bonn, however, were set by the present requirements of the American link and of future equality. No French effort could (or should) in the foreseeable future effectively reduce or provide a replacement for Bonn's primary dependence on America for its security. Moreover, a nuclear France not bound by Atlantic integration or a European organization was even more threatening to Germany's political ambitions than was a nuclear Britain. However remote the prospect of French success, the Federal Republic must not provide the key contributions for a purely national French nuclear program.

These complex Franco-German interests took on specific form in a somewhat inconclusive series of bilateral conversations on nuclear-weapons problems in 1957.[78] For example, Strauss visited Paris and the Sahara missile-development stations in January and concluded a ministerial agreement providing for further cooperation in the development and production of modern weapons.[79] This gave rise to numerous rumors of planned atomic coproduction, which Strauss and his opposite number, Maurice Bourgès-Maunoury, only intermittently disclaimed. On more than one occasion the German defense minister declared that such a project was not "excluded" from the Franco-German program [80] and added, with a bow to Britain, "none of [these] three countries can afford the luxury of parallel and separate defense research." [81]

As recounted previously, these discussions took a more serious turn in the wake of Sputnik and the tightening Anglo-American duopoly within NATO. In his memoirs Adenauer cites a particularly intense conversation of November 1957 in which France's Undersecretary for Foreign Affairs Edgar Faure declared the immediate creation of a Continental nuclear production capacity to be an absolute necessity for the continued political existence of the Continental allies.[82] With such a capacity Europe could either force American assistance (in Faure's phrasing, "God helps those who help themselves") or effectively refute Anglo-American arguments for a "two-class" NATO. Adenauer and von Brentano agreed in principle, but suggested only general coordination and research cooperation until the American position was clarified.

Follow-up conversations between Strauss and Defense Minister Jacques Chaban-Delmas led, apparently with Dulles's direct blessing, to the creation in early 1958 of F-I-G, a consortium, which included the Italians, to produce modern weapons.[83] The first meeting resulted in public agreements only on joint production of conventional weapons, with short-range antitank and antiaircraft missiles, ground vehicles, and tanks receiving priority. Joint efforts in the military applications of nuclear energy were not specifically excluded, however, and actually figured in the somewhat vague, future-oriented remarks of several of the major participants.

Without question, the prospects for cooperation within at least the letter of what the 1954 prohibitions permitted were exhaustively explored. Commenting on the F-I-G proposal, Premier Felix Gaillard, for example, stated that NATO decisions on sharing would be crucial, but ''the three countries are ready to pool their efforts to a certain extent on the research and manufacture of arms so that they can benfit from a position of equality in NATO.'' In his view, Germany's special status would not necessarily hinder nuclear cooperation: ''Germany can contribute scientific cooperation or certain manufactures not in themselves nuclear but which enter into the construction of atomic missiles.'' [84]

Strauss's statements, on the other hand, were more equivocal. Initially he stressed the primary F-I-G interest in ''armament standardization'' and declared that true to the 1954 pledge, German officials had engaged in no discussion of common atomic production on German soil.[85] Several subsequent statements, however, struck a somewhat different note. First, there was Strauss's remark, as paraphrased in a newspaper, that although there had been no request for or offer of German participation, ''we are indeed interested in the use of atomic energy as a power source—but it must first be determined whether warships or planes propelled by atomic energy might not be too expensive. Without question, we are also interested in learning whether France wishes to become a third Western atomic power.'' [86] And second, there was his observation to an admittedly hostile British Labour leader: ''I can guarantee that for three, four, or even five years there will be no German nuclear weapons. After that, however, if other states, especially France, produce their own atomic bombs, Germany could also be dragged in.'' [87]

Obviously, however, these discussions did not progress very far. The proposed German contribution reportedly was sketched only in broad outline; the Federal Republic was to provide an unspecified amount of financial assistance as well as cooperate in basic research on warhead production and in the development of delivery missiles. In return, Germany would receive assured access, presumably to French-held common stockpiles, in time of emergency.

This vagueness was the result of major uncertainties in both the French and the German positions. Although Gaillard and Chaban-Delmas had in fact taken the first steps, their further moves in this most sensitive area were governed by the dictates of prudence and by political calculations. Furthermore, the French political leadership as a whole still had hopes for substantial American assistance. Definite agreement with the Germans at this point might provide one more reason for the withholding of American aid and possibly might prove unnecessary, if major transfers of American information or even weapons themselves were forthcoming.

The roots of Germany's reluctance have already been touched upon. First and foremost, neither the German political leadership nor Strauss himself was ready to make any final choice against the wishes of the United States. The prospects of French success were at least questionable; hopes for rapid future equality in a Franco-German partnership, on the basis of past experience, were somewhat illusory. Direct American sharing or even the highly improbable prospect of direct American assistance would ensure more effective results and fewer major political liabilities in the future. Strauss himself believed such assistance to be inevitable, and reportedly his American contacts, particularly during an American trip in the spring of 1958, did little to dissuade him.[88]

Whatever progress was attained came to a halt in the weeks after de Gaulle's return to power. The General lost little time, particularly in his June discussions with Secretary of State Dulles, in stressing the acceleration of the French national program and in demanding effective national control over all nuclear weapons stationed on French soil. When routinely consulted about continuing the F-I-G discussions in general and about European nuclear cooperation in particular, de Gaulle answered, to the surprise of some advisors, with a flat "no." During Strauss's interviews in July with the General, as well as with Army Minister Guillaumat, this message was explicitly conveyed.[89]

Nuclear issues reportedly assumed far less significance in the months of gradual Franco-German rapprochement which followed. After a reserved and somewhat distrustful beginning, the de Gaulle-Adenauer meetings were marked by growing cordiality and mutual respect.[90] By the time of the third dialogue in early 1959, de Gaulle's deference towards Adenauer and his wholehearted support of the long-sought Franco-German friendship reportedly had completely changed the chancellor's earlier suspicions of "the man on horseback.'' In the view of some observers it was a spell which continued as long as the relationship.

Their greatest bond was de Gaulle's support for the German position on a settlement for Berlin or for Central Europe. The French president had repeatedly opposed moves toward negotiation, whether at the summit or on the personal level, whether concerned with Berlin, disengagement, or the general question of the two Germanys. Moreover, despite his indirect call for recognition of the Oder-Neisse line, de Gaulle, of all the allies, continually gave the strongest pledges concerning the appropriate goals and means of reunification.

If mentioned at all, problems of nuclear control and production were raised only in the context of the well-known Gaullist criticism of integration and the American nuclear monopoly. De Gaulle repeatedly emphasized the need to consider the future, the time of a withdrawing America following a ''peripheral strategy,'' of growing agreement between the superpowers of a Western Europe without the means to control its own destiny. Adenauer's memoirs also mention several occasions on which some of de Gaulle's closest advisors suggested the resulting need for the closest possible Franco-German cooperation (if not indeed union) in European defense.

In all discussions Adenauer signified that he shared these fears concerning the present Atlantic relationship as well as fears about all future forms. But increasingly—particularly after de Gaulle's dramatic assertion of French nuclear independence in his Ecole Militaire speech in November 1959—the chancellor and his advisors made clear that in their view de Gaulle's policies were the surest means of bringing these feared events to pass. As already mentioned, the principal rubric for argumentation became integration—German commitment and French failures, the present and future benefits of locking in the American guarantee, the advantages and limits of similar European arrangements for the future. The results by 1960 were still inconclusive.

For both Paris and Bonn nuclear issues increasingly became the touchstone of their relations, the sticking place of often simultaneous trends toward conflict and cooperation, toward an Atlantic or a European framework. The basic French strategy was (and indeed would remain) one of preemption: a denying of German resources and political support to American-prescribed alliance arrangements or even to the future ambitions of German nationalist leaders. Germany's basic tactic was to keep open the option of bilateral cooperation while making no firm choices, as a hedge against the future and to enhance Bonn's current bargaining situation from Washington. The interplay of strategies and circumstances from 1956 to 1960 was such that at least for the short run the orientations of both countries were successful. But Franco-German interaction was to prove an increasingly difficult balancing act.

COMMENTARY

To tie this rather wide-ranging examination together, a number of basic findings need restatement. Some relate to Germany's policy regarding nuclear weapons as a special case of the general attitudes of the other European allies; others relate to specifically German characteristics and calculations.

Viewed from one perspective, the major changes in Germany's policy from 1956 to 1960 occurred not in Bonn's decisions or stance but rather in the general shape of the control-sharing debate within the alliance. Bonn and the other allies clearly had few specific conceptions about possible sharing arrangements. A growing sense of urgency was accompanied by the evolution of very few criteria for judgment beyond either those suggested by the United States or those derived from crude measures of the distance from physical possession or the degree of American disapproval. This uncertainty resulted in part from the complexity of the problems involved. A Strauss or a Spaak could define or attempt to structure at least some of the options available for the present or perhaps only for the future. But most European leaders had neither the information nor the commitment to push independent suggestions; they were quite content to make their demands and entrust the formulation or alternatives to Washington and others.

American policy consistently proved to be a guide of minimal value. The ambivalent, rapidly changing American position only further stimulated European desires and anxieties. Washington's earlier concessions to Britain raised both hopes for similar treatment and fears of possible exclusion. The repeated introduction of new technological possibilities only increased confusion and engendered false hopes destined for disappointment. Halfway measures, such as the offer of MRBMs with some degree of control or of assistance (of unspecified type) in the area of nuclear propulsion, could be interpreted either as first steps toward greater sharing or as evidence of intractable American shamming.

Furthermore, particularly after 1958 no definite agreement within the American government as to what could or should be offered seemed to exist. The Eisenhower administration's short-run goal was clear: to stop or deflect the French nuclear program while holding out the prospect of some type of compensatory reward to the other allies. But how this was to be done or what relation any efforts would bear to basic policy goals or future hopes for the American-European or American-Soviet axis was the subject of long and fruitless debate within the government. The field of specific initiative, therefore, was left to General Norstad, whose selling of the atomic-NATO concept encouraged and channeled European demands in ways neither foreseen by the Eisenhower administration nor welcomed by the incoming Kennedy administration.

It is hardly surprising that throughout these discussions Germany's position was phrased in terms of alliance control and the development of common responsibility. As discussed above, the basic tenets of German foreign policy allowed no other focus. German leaders neither were desirous of nor felt themselves capable of exploring specific alternatives on a national basis. Strauss's discussions with French officials during 1957–1958 were the only exceptions; they perhaps were dramatic departures from some declaratory policy, but were more in the nature of probes or a flirtation. If the emergence of de Gaulle and the nature of Strauss's immediate goals are disregarded, imagining a final agreement that would have satisfied both French and German interests in the nuclear sphere is difficult. It is even more difficult to conceive of continued participation by Germany under Adenauer in the face of an intense American opposition that was sweetened by promises of more favorable alliance arrangements in the future.

German advocacy, particularly after 1958, of direct NATO control was an attempt to maximize the political advantages to be gained from the possible. The calculation of interests, the determination to make this policy serve several major goals, involved the familiar German triangulation. To summarize once again, an integrated alliance system would: permit American involvement on terms supposedly acceptable both to the United States and to most Europeans; provide the most effective means of redressing the existing structure, frozen into place in 1952 and reinforced by the de facto division between nuclear and nonnuclear countries; minimize the impact of the French nuclear program and perhaps eventually provide the means of capturing the not-yet-operational *force de frappe;* and prevent the Soviets from brandishing the threat of German "nuclear revanchism" within their bloc and from making denuclearization of Germany an easy precondition for Big Four agreement.

Thus for the German political leadership a role in a NATO control system was the most possible and therefore the most advantageous means to several ends. Primary concern was with the tactical sphere, i.e., control over decisions in Europe; the concept of an alliance strategic force was a new and for most Germans an essentially complementary solution. But the precise nature and components of the system were secondary matters, certainly of less immediate importance than the approval and implementation of the basic principle of integration.

Left unanswered was a fundamental question, a variant within the alliance framework of the N + 1 country problem. In the nuclear sphere just as in other areas, the Federal Republic wanted general recognition of equality. Only in this way could Germany be safeguarded against overt discrimination or the imposition of further restrictions. But for both military and political reasons Germany opposed the full, equal participation of all NATO members in all phases of nuclear control. Fifteen fingers on the nuclear trigger would undermine the effectiveness of the deterrent and would lessen the possibilities of immediate concerted action. And that even Italy would view the seizure of Hamburg as sufficient cause to risk total escalation through nuclear response was not at all certain.

More important, operational equality would have precluded recognition of the political status Germany had earned by virtue of its military contribution. The Federal Republic's basic aim was a de facto expansion of the original Standing Group concept: explicit or implicit equality with Britain and France vis-à-vis the United States.

What was involved was a difficult if not impossible task of balancing. A direct German demand would engender opposition from Britain and France and from the other NATO countries. Recognition of Germany's prominence, moreover, surely would lead to an Italian demand for equality, to be followed perhaps by a procession of others. The formation of an "executive agency" under American aegis seemed one answer, but even then, the limits of the allies' agreement and possible influence were by no means certain.

And so the matter stood in late 1960. The basic Atlantic course had been charted; only the all-important details remained for the future.

SIX

Discord
over Strategy:
1961-1962

✠ THE PERIOD 1961–1962 is in many respects the most interesting in the development of Adenauer's nuclear-control policies. The steady,
often daily outpouring of official statements on the "German position" and
the detailed calculus of German interests thus revealed marked the major
changes in German status that had occurred since 1955. The increase in Germans' self-consciousness about national purpose and position was almost inevitable as the economic miracle continued unabated, as military strength
and experience within the alliance accumulated. Bonn's need to soothe or
dissemble before domestic critics was no longer salient; the basic aspects of
force structure and armament already had been thoroughly debated and accepted. Moreover, with the continuing Berlin crisis and the growing French
nuclear program the Federal Republic had greater reason than before to
define and defend its military and political stakes in the alliance.

The primary stimulus, however, again was external: the challenge to
those stakes posed by new American policies concerning use and control of
nuclear weapons. The almost totally unanticipated initiatives of the new
Kennedy administration toward greater emphasis on a conventional-force
response in Europe, toward assured centralization of control over nuclear
weapons, toward safeguards against further national nuclear development—all forcibly called into question Adenauer's basic foreign-policy
choices. These initiatives marked the first public unsticking of the rearmament bargain that had been struck in 1954 to gain for Germany security

and American political support. And the negative implications for Germany's bargaining power in the Atlantic context scarcely improved prospects for its other cherished options—equality in the European and unity in the all-German spheres.

The resulting German-American discord pervaded every dimension of nuclear-control policy. In the short run the lines were most sharply drawn on questions of nuclear use, on the limits of McNamara's flexible-response and conventional-weapons emphasis for deterrence and defense in Europe. Not only was this the issue most specifically developed by Washington, it also was the issue perceived by Bonn as threatening the cornerstone of its existence, the American nuclear guarantee. Pragmatically, too, the consequences of this shift in American policy were the most immediate: the need to revise and restructure buildup of military forces, to meet demands for further conventional-force efforts, to consider new Berlin scenarios.

Less structured and less intense but of greater long-term significance was German-American conflict over the intertwined issues of access to nuclear decision-making and physical control-sharing. The degree of disinclination if not direct unwillingness of Kennedy's Washington to proceed seriously with earlier American initiatives or vague new proposals was more than equalled by the intensity of Bonn's belief that the imperatives toward control-sharing were now stronger than ever. Specific German proposals or demands were still somewhat muted, still designed for timely approaches to Washington, and they still bore a conspicuous accent on cooperation within the alliance. But every quarrel about strategy, however minor or theoretical, only intensified Bonn's interest. And every Soviet or American initiative regarding a Berlin or European settlement only heightened the need felt by most of the German leadership for an equal, assured voice in an Atlantic or European nuclear force.

Accordingly, analysis of this period deals with these two aspects in sequence: in this chapter, with the discords over questions of strategy and with some attention to the chronology of the dispute; and in the following chapter, with discords relating to access to and sharing of physical control over nuclear weapons. In both, as in the concluding commentary, there also is further development of earlier themes: the still largely reactive nature of German policy, the recurring problem of "strategic lag" in alliance debates and disagreements, the continuing inconsistencies between doctrine and policies for force development and equipment.

The central focus of course will be on the nature and dynamics of the German-American relationship revealed by this discordant period. The commentary particularly will focus on the limits on influence imposed by the very character of this connection—further evidence of the constraints set by Neustadt's false intimacy and by the structural barriers inherent in any dialogue between a superpower and a second-tier state, as well as by the very different political and strategic perceptions of a front-line state and an alliance leader.

THE MONTHS BEFORE THE BERLIN CRISIS

For Germany and the other anxious European allies the inauguration of John F. Kennedy in January 1961 marked a step into the unknown. There was little hard evidence concerning the new president's plans for future American-Euopean relations, for in its public statements, preliminary preparations, and private discussions the new administration had dedicated itself only to two interrelated global goals.[1] The first was to intensify Eisenhower's faint attempts to develop a new relationship with the Soviet Union—specifically, to seek stabilization of the increasingly unstable arms race through greater communication, exploration of areas of common interest, and perhaps conclusion of limited arms control agreements. The second was to correct the dangerous failings, weaknesses, and indecision of the Eisenhower administration's defense posture—to rationalize the relationship of ends and means in the new era of perceived Soviet-American parity in nuclear weapons. American military strength, based on reliable conventional and nuclear capabilities, must be maintained and expanded to permit deliberate choices in an array of possible situations and to permit the constant exercise of careful, discriminating political control.

Among the European allies the Germans were particularly anxious, not only because they had a greater stake in the American connection, but also because Kennedy's election had come as a considerable shock. Bonn's expectation had been for Nixon's victory; Adenauer in particular had made no secret of his hopes for a continuation of Republican support for German interests. The new president was virtually unknown. His campaign statements had revealed almost no interest in European problems; his advisors seemed a group of untried or unsympathetic men.

Questions about strategy attained some prominence in Bonn's efforts to determine and anticipate probable administration policies. Several interview respondents then close to Defense Minister Strauss asserted that this emphasis resulted from garbled information received from Washington and SHAPE about Kennedy's purported interest in a "more conventional, less tactical nuclear" thrust for the defense of Western Europe and in particular for the role assigned to German forces. Germans' multiple soundings at the NATO meetings of December 1960, and a quick reconnaisance trip by Strauss to the United States in January lent credibility to a widely dispersed press leak that Secretary of State Dean Rusk had proposed that only a conventional-force response be mounted against a conventional-force attack of any size on Europe.[2]

The result was a limited replay of the Radford crisis of 1956, with its waves of reaction and speculation, of transatlantic rumors and denials. The Federal Republic again was in the forefront of those allies asking for immediate clarification and information. Despite repeated denials by Washington, Adenauer approached Norstad for confirmation, expressing his fears of an imminent withdrawal not only of American nuclear weapons but also of numerous American troops. As in 1956, the Bundestag staged a major debate designed more to reach the ears of the American leadership than those of the German electorate.[3] The SPD once again adopted American strategic arguments, charging Adenauer's government with failure either to comprehend the changing strategic situation and its requirements or to consider the implications for German security and German forces of the changes in American strategic doctrine.

This time, however, the rejoinders by government spokesmen—Strauss and Bundestag Deputy Georg Kliesing—were detailed and emphatic, a striking mixture of reassurances and demands regarding relations with the United States. Both officials declared that no definite decisions had been reached and that the Federal Republic legitimately could expect and would request "consultation behind closed doors" before any final steps were taken.[4] But Strauss's dramatic summation raised two pointed arguments that were to be used repeatedly in the debates of the coming months.[5] First, a major conventional capability, mobile and modernized, clearly was necessary for the limitation of brush-fire wars—like the conflicts in Laos, the Congo, or Cuba—where political instability led to miscalculation or accident. But, he said, "wars in Europe do not break out by accident, like an earthquake or a conflagration or an avalanche. Behind them lies a political intention to use force.'' Any weakening of defense readiness or of the willingness to use nuclear firepower would only encourage such "intentions" and make combat "a political means," as it had been in World War II.

Second, if the West was not prepared to use all means of deterrence, an aggressor—with a free choice of place, time, and means—would be tempted to try a surprise attack toward a limited goal. He could then offer peace on the basis of the fait accompli, an offer which the West, if only on psychological grounds, might not be able to refuse. As Strauss declared,

Does anyone believe that if a dividing line between atomic and conventional weapons is allowed, the democracies will then say "If you don't go back and surrender [your] booty, then tomorrow at six o'clock, total atomic war begins with which we will drive you back." [6]

And Strauss dramatically emphasized that the last condition, a chain reaction of successful limited attacks, would be worse than the first.

The next weeks witnessed even greater speculation and suspicion within not only the political leadership but also the Defense Ministry. Attempts to gain information and guidance through the usual channels, SHAPE and American military leaders in Europe, only increased the confusion and doubt. These sources knew only the broad outlines of Washington discussions and like Norstad himself were generally opposed to what they perceived to be the new direction of American policy. Within the ministry itself data from the United States were disseminated only sporadically and often were first filtered (reportedly not always with the greatest objectivity) through Strauss's office. [7] Discussion, even on the basis of limited information, tended to follow familiar lines. Air Force Inspector Kammhuber and his associates viewed American developments with at least as much critical suspicion as Strauss himself did, while army leaders welcomed the new emphasis on a conventional-force capability and insisted that there be no change in either the provision or forward deployment of tactical nuclear weapons. [8]

Kennedy's first major statement on these issues took the form of an address in April to NATO's Military Committee. [9] The speech in essence reflected only the preliminary conclusions of his administration, particularly those of Secretary of Defense Robert McNamara and former Secretary of State Dean Acheson, who was now studying NATO problems for the White House. These views were the subject of continuing debate in Washington, of criticism from those (particularly Pentagon military officers) who felt that the views represented too great a departure from the past, and from those around the president who believed that they did not go far enough in terms of the future. Yet the interruption of the Berlin crisis caused Kennedy's address to be the principal statement of administration aims until almost the end of 1961.

As Kennedy expressed it, to meet the challenges of the 1960s NATO was in need not of a new strategy but of a vigorous implementation of past goals in the nuclear and especially in the long-neglected conventional sphere. Strengthened nonnuclear forces were necessary not only to enhance the strategic deterrence but to permit the often discussed intermediate option. "NATO needs to be able to respond to any conventional attack with conventional resistance which will be effective at least long enough, in General Norstad's phrase, to force a pause." A final comment, however, seemed to set rather narrow limits for future discussions:

In our studies, we have found a serious need for a sensitive and flexible control of all arms and especially over nuclear weapons. We propose to see to it, for our part, that our military forces operate at all times under continuous, responsible command and control from the highest authorities all the way downward . . .[control] exercised before, during, and after any initiation of hostilities . . . and at any level of escalation. We believe in maintaining effective deterrent strength, but we believe also in making it do what we wish, neither more nor less.

In the midst of speculation touched off by this speech Adenauer paid his first visit to the Kennedy administration. Beyond the expected consultations on Berlin the chancellor and his advisors raised—reportedly in a very restrained manner—their concerns about changing American strategy. The president personally assured Adenauer that no major changes were planned, that the American pledge to use all necessary means including nuclear weapons for the defense of Western Europe remained unaltered.[10] The current emphasis on conventional forces reflected only America's desire to secure implementation of the vital but long-neglected MC-70 plan levels, goals which even Germany only partially had met. Moreover, the new electronic control devices soon to be installed on tactical nuclear weapons designated for use by Germans (and other Europeans) would neither prevent nor delay the weapons' timely release in war.

Adenauer returned home quite disturbed, a mood attested to both by later interview comments and by the rather ambivalent tone of his report to the Bundestag about his visit. His barely concealed belief that Kennedy did not or would not "understand" was echoed in increased public criticism of purported American goals for the denuclearization of German forces. One such flare-up focused on the announcement in April that Washington had cancelled Germany's 1957 order for longer-range (and never produced) Mace missiles (700 + miles) and had suggested the substitution of shorter-range Pershings (300 + miles), to be delivered in late 1963. Strauss, backed up publicly by Norstad, denied that this switch reflected any change in American policy.[11] The solid-fuel Pershings were superior; the difference in range was not a significant factor; German forces would continue to be supplied and treated on "an equal footing."

Strauss's public and private positions on such issues clearly did not coincide. In conversations with the American ambassador and other officials Strauss reportedly expressed his dissatisfaction with existing delivery rates on nuclear-capable equipment. Whatever the need for increased conventional strength, these orders must be met before the mounting American pressure for greater German armament purchases to offset American troop-maintenance costs would be accommodated. Moreover, any real or apparent delivery stoppage in the tactical nuclear-weapons sphere and any attempt to deny the necessary warheads would have disastrous consequences both for Bundeswehr morale and for the political fortunes of the Adenauer government.[12]

As the German national election campaign moved forward, both Adenauer and Strauss made nuclear issues the focus of repeated public statements. Comments by the increasingly frail chancellor were limited to election rallies; his repeated albeit vague demands for "atomic armament for the Bundeswehr" prompted frequent headlines, criticisms by the opposition, and considerable clarification on the part of his advisors and the Defense Ministry.[13] All available evidence indicates, however, that the Great Simplifier was merely restating the NATO-as-fourth-atomic-power concept. Strauss's more detailed but equally emphatic declarations were only more explicit versions of his earlier calls for the putting aside of "the weekly clever plans" and for an unspecified redefinition and strengthening of the basic deterrence concept of NATO.[14]

THE BERLIN CRISIS AND ITS STRATEGIC LESSONS

June 4 marked the end of the Kennedy-Khrushchev meeting in Vienna and the beginning of the Berlin crisis of 1961. Given the hints and pronouncements of earlier months and the steadily increasing flow of refugees from East Germany, Khrushchev's bellicose demands and threats hardly were unexpected. Yet the grim intensity of his arguments and his refusal to discuss or acknowledge interests of the Atlantic allies convinced more statesmen than just Kennedy of the need to close ranks, to demonstrate a common determination. In Germany public criticism regarding nuclear strategy and control no longer seemed appropriate or relevant in the face of such threats.

Behind the public front, however, and even after the Berlin Wall was built, the discussion continued. For the most part it focused on the strategic questions involved in the defense of Berlin, questions which in 1961 differed little from those of 1958 or even 1948. Given Western determination to remain in Berlin, any armed incident within the city, any direct attack upon it, or any interference with the Allies' access routes would require a military response. The initial level of the response might vary: a showing of the flag, institution of an airlift, a probe along the autobahn, or a full-scale attempt to relieve the allies' Berlin garrison. Whatever the case, the primary danger was the possibility—and given the West's weakness in conventional forces, perhaps the inevitability—of rapid escalation, perhaps to total war.

The position of the Federal Republic with respect to the defense of Berlin was an anomalous one. All official documents issued by the Federal Republic referred to Berlin as the capital of the German nation; informally, Berlin's three western sectors were by 1961 fully associated with the Federal Republic in all aspects but that of the electoral process. Yet on the basis of political calculations and treaty agreements the Federal Republic steadfastly proclaimed the principle of three-power responsibility; the involvement of German forces or military officials was neither legally possible nor desirable. Berlin and its defense were the responsibility of the wartime allies as of all other NATO states. All indications from both public sources and detailed interview probes in 1965–1966 suggest that the Defense Ministry neither sought nor expected information which was not available to the other NATO allies.

To the extent that they existed at all, German conceptions in early 1961 of the defense of Berlin reflected the position of 1958–1959. As Strauss expressed it, the changed strategic environment only emphasized the impossibility of the major Western tank probe or conventional campaign that had been contemplated in 1948–1949.[15] It was not only that NATO possessed insufficient conventional strength to undertake such a mission while maintaining a forward defense at the border. Given the existence of tactical nuclear weapons and approaching East-West parity in strength over the entire weapons spectrum, any extended Western action also necessarily must involve the risk of escalation and the outbreak of total war. It was this threat alone that would prevent Soviet action, that would influence Khrushchev's calculations, whether about a direct move against Berlin, a supposedly spontaneous civil disturbance, or proxy actions by the East Germans on the autobahn.

This almost total reliance on nuclear deterrence was at sharp variance with the evolving Berlin policies of the Kennedy administration. From the outset the president and Secretary McNamara had been concerned with what they saw as the inflexibility of Eisenhower's reliance on the nuclear threat, with his failure to provide for or recognize any options between the most limited conventional probe and the resort to rapidly escalating nuclear warfare. Not only had this strategy seemingly proven frightening and incredible to the allies and especially, Kennedy thought, to the Germans, but it also prescribed an essentially automatic response, not amenable to sure further control and direction. Both Acheson and certain Pentagon advisors were urged to evaluate alternatives open to the West and forces available or required for such missions.

The somber outcome of the June Vienna talks served as the last and most dramatic stimulus to the ongoing Berlin studies.[16] By the end of July a final presidential decision had been announced, first to the National Security Council, then to a nation-wide audience in Kennedy's television address of July 25, leaving little grounds for a miscalculation of the West's military intentions.[17] All necessary means including the full panoply of nuclear weapons were to be used to defend the allies' rights and commitments in West Berlin. To provide those means the president did not proclaim a national emergency, as Acheson had suggested, but requested a number of specific measures designed primarily to strengthen and increase Western nonnuclear forces. The general aim, Kennedy said, was "to make clear our determination and our ability to defend our rights at all costs, and to meet all levels of aggressor pressure with whatever levels of force are required. We intend to have a wider choice than humiliation or all-out nuclear action." [18]

The final decision on the sequence of military actions to be followed was more limited. As William Kaufmann notes, McNamara and Kennedy thought that since available nonnuclear strength was not sufficient for any major conventional action, the West would be forced to adopt a strategy of escalation.[19] The initial response to any Soviet action would be an application of conventional force to up the ante and thereby make Western commitment clear and irrevocable but allow sufficient time for reconsideration and negotiation by the aggressor. If the Soviets persisted, the West would attempt—although the prospects for achievement were not certain—a careful, discriminating, graduated use of nuclear force, perhaps first on the tactical level and finally in the strategic range.

Germany's public position on these American decisions was one of complete, unconditional support.[20] In private, however, apparently almost all of the German political and military leaders questioned the need for and consequences of the American push for improved conventional capabilities. In NATO as in the Four Power Ambassadorial Working Group, Bonn's basic position remained that of Norstad, namely, any nonnuclear military phase would of necessity be limited in scope and duration. Of what value would a nonnuclear response be if a convoy's start toward Berlin met a firm, substantial Soviet trap, or at several points precipitated popular uprisings of the size that had occurred in 1953, or set off a rush of East Germans toward the major crossings into the Federal Republic? Moreover, despite the president's firm words, a major conventional effort still would suggest irresolution regarding early use of nuclear weapons, the basis of any threat of escalation.

Strauss's criticisms and those of the leading military commanders were focused more specifically on the nature and aims of American planning, as a lengthy exposé by Strauss in the August issue of *Aussenpolitik* dramatically revealed.[21] First, in their search for all-purpose theory Americans wanted to develop "something like a catalogue for the use of atomic weapons . . . [to] make it known . . . in an edition of a million copies."

A similar interest was shown by their emphasis on such concepts as "pause," "threshold," and "flexible response," which in Strauss's words were "conceptual aids for the precalculation of the inconceivable and incalculable nature of the specific." To take just one such concept,

What is a pause? A standstill—*drôle de guerre* or static warfare? A limited cease-fire about which no one knows how it shall come to pass? In both these cases, the attacker will have made territorial gains—more or less. Should he then be forced back by the ultimate threat of nuclear use? Or . . . should the attacker be thrown back to his starting point . . . whereupon there is a pause before nuclear conflict continues? In this respect, there is neither a clear conception nor a usable definition.

The erection of the Berlin Wall forcefully interrupted discussions and debates. The first reaction on the part of all the allies was shock; the second, at least for the Americans and most Germans, was a decision to take no military action that would precipitate a further crisis or raise the dangers of an uncontrollable civil revolt in East Germany. Strauss reportedly told German military and political leaders who privately urged immediate action against the wall itself that this would risk World War III; it was a risk neither he nor any responsible Western official would run for such a gain.[22] Germany's only course was to support the American position of an increased military buildup to prevent further action and a delayed show of force once the tension had lessened.

As contingency discussions continued in Washington and then in Paris, however, the German-American strategic debate resumed its old shape, only slightly hampered by Adenauer's embarrassing inability to form a new government for two months after the September elections. The lesson of Berlin, if it had done anything, had further sharpened the differences between the two countries. American leaders were now painfully aware of the political, military, and financial costs of anything less than a conventional-force buildup that would be maintained well into the future. Accordingly, they turned with renewed emphasis to questions of future planning and programming with NATO.

As Secretary McNamara argued, to meet the wide range of threats faced by the West there must be multiple balanced capabilities, each at a high level of effectiveness and subject to careful, continuing control.[23] Nuclear strike power—sufficient, protected, and reliable—clearly was the first requirement. Its essential complememt, however, was conventional force, perhaps strong enough "to engage in large-scale nonnuclear warfare." To prevail, especially against an all-out Soviet conventional attack, use of nuclear weapons still might be necessary. But an effective conventional force would permit greater flexibility and choice, allow a more credible posture, and forestall automatic escalation.

For military and economic, but above all political, reasons the realization of this concept required full European participation and support by the European allies, which was to be obtained through a tripartite American campaign. The first goal was to secure substantial implementation of all aspects of the MC-70 goals through what was essentially an American-European trade-off. Beyond further strengthening its own conventional forces, the United States within certain limits would step up its delivery of promised dual-capable equipment and its stockpiling of controlled warheads in Europe. The number would not be as high as that still being sought by the Joint Chiefs of Staff, but it would go a considerable way toward meeting European demands. In return, the European allies would be expected to make a significant start toward providing the promised number of active divisions, at or near full strength and backed up by lower-strength reserve units.

The continuing deficiencies and ambiguities in the total defense structure were to be treated within a second framework: alliance planning for the 1964–1969 period. In September, 1961, the administration submitted its first proposal for the MC-96 planning document, a draft which in effect cancelled a plan presented by the Eisenhower administration in late 1960 as a successor to MC-70. Not only were specific armaments (like battlefield nuclear weapons) deleted, conventional forces and logistics were to be raised to the full MC-70 level, if not higher. Existing force structures—ground and air—must undergo major revision to permit an effective, extended nonnuclear response, perhaps through segregation of tactical nuclear weapons in special units. The United States already had begun its buildup and reorganization; its allies must now follow.

Compliance by the Europeans, the argument of the administration ran, could only be secured if an aggressive program was mounted to explain the technical basis for these recommendations and for the new Kennedy-McNamara strategy as a whole. Europeans' continuing fears about the relative status of American strategic forces must be answered; the results of contemporary studies regarding comparative Eastern-Western strengths on all levels must be shared as soon as these were available. More important, the Europeans must be given the data and shown the strategic calculus that underlay the adoption of flexible response—especially current views on the requirements of deterrence and the possible consequences of miscalculation or unnecessary escalation. This clearly would help to minimize if not eliminate real or proclaimed European fears, misunderstandings, and criticisms.

The final goal was to bring the major Western European states, once they had been "educated," into more direct association with nuclear decision-making. However, as is discussed below, the administration was divided on specific means of implementation.[24] Some, particularly in the State Department, supported a multilateral solution like that embodied in the Herter concept, arguing that only physical involvement would eradicate European fears and lessen the temptations of the French example before it was too late. Others, particularly in the International Security Affairs office of the Defense Department urged a gradual disassociation from the "common hardware" approach and the insoluble problems of common control. They also urged the substitution of a major push for multinational arrangements for information-sharing and consultation.

Perhaps the first evidence of this tripartite campaign was McNamara's data-rich presentation to the North Atlantic Council meeting in December 1961,[25] to which the German reaction (among others) was quite negative, reflecting the very different assessments made in the weeks after the Berlin crisis. Measured by actions, the German response to American demands for military buildup had indeed surpassed that of any other ally.[26] German conscripts' term of service was raised from twelve to eighteen months; more recruits and reservists were called up; the force goal for all services was returned to the original 500,000-man mark. Strauss had not only recommended increased expenditures for fiscal 1962, he had also signed a long-sought agreement with Deputy Defense Secretary Roswell Gilpatric providing for purchases of $600 million worth of American equipment and for integration of the two countries' logistic systems. The defense minister, too, repeatedly had called for greater European efforts to provide conventional forces, for the creation indeed of thirty full-strength divisions. It had been past failings, he alleged, which had "encouraged Khrushchev's Berlin adventure."

Publicly and privately, however, German spokesmen still declared the primacy of total deterrence, unmistakably rooted in constant Western readiness and willingness to use nuclear weapons. Conventional forces were indeed necessary to counter "aggressive incidents" and to take "first steps." But their value was neither "primary" nor "independent" of use of nuclear weapons. Furthermore, as the military commentator of the *Frankfurter Allgemeine Zeitung* reported Strauss's words, "One could not . . . mathematically calculate the military and political importance of classical divisions and atomic bombs. For the Communists . . . there was no such military difference in questions of armament . . . they were expansionistic in peace and war." [27]

Far more compelling grounds for German action was the need to deflect increasing American pressures for strategic changes that were occurring within the context of NATO's MC-96 planning discussions. In the draft of September 1961, which was considered at early-January sessions of both the Military Committee and the Council's permanent representatives, the Kennedy administration had requested major revisions in the size and organization of all European forces. The Germans now were to bring their divisions up to full strength, to raise at least six additional covering brigades, to intensify their efforts in support and logistic areas, to boost and modernize the long-neglected territorial defense and reserve units. Moreover, there was to be a marked deemphasis of nuclear-capable armament. The not-yet-completed program of nuclear air armament, for example, was to be delayed in favor of developing effective conventional ground-support capabilities.

Although the formal response from Germany had been conditional acceptance of this program as a "planning basis," Bonn sources reportedly raised immediate sharp public criticism (mostly conveyed through indirect channels) that focused on two new arguments. First, the strategy of flexible response was based on the assumption of "spiritual partnership" with the enemy, on the hypothesis that even in conflict his calculations and actions would mirror "the new American model." This concept disregarded not only the nature of warfare but also the basic character of revolutionary expansionistic Communism and the lessons of past conflict with the Russians. As one then high-ranking military leader remarked in 1965, still with considerable feeling, "I kept telling them if there were other people in Moscow, the idea might be sound. But we got to know the Russians only too well . . . and you simply can't count on them being like us."

Secondly, continued American insistence on possible large-scale conventional warfare confined to Europe would merely establish the military and psychological preconditions for Communist success. As the argument ran, particularly among higher civil servants, it was not just that the resulting destruction would make the distinctions between conventional or nuclear annihilation merely of academic interest for the Federal Republic. A more immediate and important result would be the gradual destruction of the populace's morale, even without any hostilities. Why should the Germans continue to sacrifice to provide a defense capability, to remain true to the West, if they were to be abandoned in any case?

Interviews conducted even as late as 1966 suggested that those criticisms were but pale reflections of privately reflected views. Perhaps the most dramatic glimpse into these criticisms, pressed especially by Strauss and the air force leadership, was contained in a major newspaper article entitled "The Transformation of the Apocalypse" and written by Colonel Gerd Schmückle, Defense Ministry Press Secretary and long a Strauss supporter. Writing in what might be categorized most charitably as purple prose, Schmückle offered a sweeping review of the tenets and failings of flexible response. His basic conclusion was that given the existence on both sides of nuclear weapons which inevitably would be used and used against the "maximum" urban targets, the "idea of a conventional war in Europe was military alchemy."

A second indication, in the form of assertions purportedly made by certain air-force leaders in the first major nationally initiated strategic planning exercises, undertaken in December 1961, was more secret. One of the scenarios considered was a full Soviet nuclear air strike against Western Europe; the general estimate reached was that at least 75 percent of Germany's "national substance" immediately would be destroyed. Given this estimate, a limited-circulation memorandum of January 1962 concluded, a preemptive nuclear strike would be the only means of reducing losses even to the 50 percent level.[28] Retaining a "sufficient" nuclear air-missile capability and securing a direct national firing trigger that would induce nearly simultaneous American action had become imperative.

The army leadership rejected these propositions and consistently called for full buildup of conventional forces at the expense of "nonessential" missiles and destroyers. Some of the studies prepared by the special Army Command Staff and supporting memorandums from German officers holding high posts at NATO argued (as did General Speidel and General Heusinger) that increased conventional forces would constitute major components of deterrence, that they alone would permit a true forward defense, that employment of thirty-six to thirty-eight NATO divisions would prevent decisive loss of ground or nuclear exchange.[29] Others placed more stress on political factors: accession to American demands would strengthen Germany's political position, heighten consideration of German interests, and reaffirm the vital American nuclear guarantee. Even if the existing American commitment did not fulfill all German demands, there was no benefit in reducing the chances for agreement still further by unthinking obstructionism and insistence on "all or nothing."

Neither group, however, maintained that the tactical nuclear weapons currently available or foreseen could or should be limited or withdrawn. Their value as deterrents was unquestionable. Just as in the American army, leaders viewed these arms as essential complements to, or in the not-yet-deployed lower kiloton ranges, as components of, what they viewed as conventional defense.[30] The weapons were most necessary because, as one respected army general wrote,

there is always the Damocles sword of atomic warheads hanging over the battlefield. . . . As to where, how long, and under what conditions [conventional forces will be used] . . . I offer no opinion. . . . This seems conceivable only at the beginning of a war, for a limited time, or as a side action. As soon as one side wishes a decision, it will turn to nuclear weapons.[31]

Just what the consequences of their use would be was a subject of debate. Some officers subscribed to the common American assertion that the course of escalation would be uncertain and probably uncontrollable. Others, in the majority, declared that escalation need not be automatic or total, that at lower levels it well might follow a step-like sequence amenable to some control. Yet their arguments did not go much beyond the statement of general propositions, nor did they, as Uwe Nerlich notes, resolve "the dilemma that one cannot have controlled escalation without the possibility of limited war—not even by pointing to the presence of strong American troop contingents on the territory of the Federal Republic." [32]

And there was still the unavoidable factor of cost. According to calculations worked out by both the Führungsstab of the Bundeswehr and the Army Command Staff, a military establishment of approximately 750,000 men would be needed to meet the new goals for conventional forces together with the old goals for nuclear-capable equipment.[33] The cost of fulfilling the American demands, together with new expenditures for nuclear missiles and for naval equipment, would reach at least thirty billion DM. Given the fixed budget ceiling of 20 million DM imposed by the Finance Ministry and the equally clear if more informal limits set by public demands for unabated growth of the domestic economy, major reductions in (if not a choice between) the conventional and nuclear programs would have to be made.

And there positions stood for the next several months, as far as the public view was concerned. Both within and outside the Defense Ministry the strategic debate became submerged in the intense controversy and condemnation surrounding the publication of the Schmückle article and its presumed reflection of Strauss's views. Officials neither at SHAPE nor at the

White House made any effort to suppress their displeasure with Strauss and his associates, who in Norstad's reported words were remnants of the "dangerous" 1956–1957 strategic tradition. Adenauer publicly called on Strauss for a full explanation and simultaneously remarked that the minister's colonels wrote too much for his taste.[34]

Strauss, never a stranger to public attack, suddenly found himself besieged on all sides: by a parliamentary inquiry sponsored by the SPD, by ad hominem broadsides issuing from the news magazine *Der Spiegel,* and by a plethora of personal, party, and political troubles. Under these pressures, Strauss the defense minister, quick to seize and frame the latest turn of the alliance's strategic debate, had to give way to Strauss the complete politician, striving to retain his political power and his influence over nominations for the chancellorship, now certain to be vacated by 1963.

THE PEAKING OF DISCORD

The spring of 1962 indeed saw some public and private cooling and directional change in the German-American strategic debate. In part it was due to displacement of Strauss's attention and personality to other concerns, but the major cause was the now full-scale effort of the United States to educate its allies in strategic matters. The cornerstone was Secretary McNamara's speech to the North Atlantic Council ministers' meeting at Athens in May, in which he set forth in unprecedented detail the basic tenets and modes of American strategic thought.[35] His first concern was with the problems of general nuclear war: the clear superiority of American strategic forces; the need to consider the improbable but possible failure of deterrence; the dangers of attack through miscalculation or accident or calculated irrationality; the significant gains in damage limitation that adherence to a discriminating counterforce strategy and maintenance of constant, centralized control probably would ensure. But he devoted almost equal attention to European-defense issues, arguing that although tactical nuclear capabilities had to be maintained, the primary need was to strengthen and improve the Alliance's nonnuclear forces to the level of ninety-day readiness against a "superior" but not "overwhelming" opponent. As the later Ann Arbor formulation put it, "These achievements will complement our deterrent strength. With improvements in Alliance ground force strength and staying power, improved nonnuclear air capabilities, and better equipped and trained reserve forces, we can be assured that no deficiency exists . . . and that no aggression, small or large, can succeed." [36]

McNamara's presentation was supplemented by a wide range of programs, bilateral and utilizing SHAPE, to provide information and explanations to America's allies. As with the other major allies, there were detailed presentations to high-ranking German military and political figures (both those in Bonn and those serving in NATO posts) and varied efforts (e.g., study trips, embassy contacts, personal briefings) to transmit background data not previously available. The obvious aim was to eliminate or shorten the strategy time-lag, the seemingly inevitable gap of eighteen or even twenty-four months between Washington decisions and allies' understanding or acceptance.

In the short run, at least, the specific results were disappointing to the Kennedy administration. Few in the German leadership were enthusiastic about the thrust of the Athens presentation; Adenauer, now increasingly identified with a small, self-styled Gaullist group within the CDU, was in private bitterly critical of both its tone and content. Strauss was somewhat more approving, but he declared that considerable further study must precede any definite changes in strategy or force structure. Strong conventional forces were a necessary component, but as he publicly had warned at Athens, no further German contribution in this area could be expected. Under present conditions, he asserted, these forces were anything but simple and cheap.

One concrete technical example. There are American battlefield weapons of very short range and limited effect. A single shot from one of these weapons is equivalent in effect to forty to fifty salvos from the entire artillery of a division. When one considers the munitions requirement and all the problems related to it—supply, depot storage . . . the number of personnel, etc.—then naturally, there is a limit to our capabilities in the area of conventional armament. [37]

Interview comments made four years later indicate that American briefings and presentations fared even less well. To many American officials it appeared that the German political as well as military leadership refused to understand or deliberately misunderstood their arguments. Presentations met with a polite hearing and a low-keyed statement of German criticisms but within days there followed sweeping misstatements from Bonn of the very positions the Americans had tried to explain in detail. For the Germans these sessions seemed to provide further evidence of the Americans' determination to impose, not to discuss, changes in the common strategy, changes that would benefit the United States. The decisions already had been made and publicized; German counterarguments were obstacles to be overcome, not legitimate points worthy of further consideration.

Direct American approaches to high-ranking German military men proved only relatively more productive. One difficulty was that explanations almost always were pitched at too high a level. Few German officers had the basic knowledge necessary to follow the lines of American arguments in full detail; none had previous access to the detailed studies on which the arguments were based. Quite apart from the problems that American tight-security policies on information dissemination still posed for NATO planning as a whole, the primary channels for any available American information were SHAPE and the defense minister's office, in this instance hardly neutral sources. Moreover, as the court proceedings in the *Spiegel* case later dramatically established, the Defense Ministry's collection of publications dealing with military affairs was neither as comprehensive nor as current as that held by the news magazine.

In most cases the reaction was one of confusion and bafflement, expression of which was hampered by the legendary pride of the German military. In the words of one ranking interview respondent recounting his participation (actual or imaginary) in one briefing: "They were so 'expert' you could hardly understand them. I told them they should just once stop proclaiming their figures and assumptions and listen to those who had actually fought the Russians."

Given all these factors, the fact that the greatest short-run successes of American efforts to provide information and education were achieved with German officers stationed in Washington is not surprising. Obviously, this group did not constitute a clear-cut counterexample; a number of them indeed had received these posts of honorific exile because of previous opposition to Bonn's prevailing views on strategic matters. Moreover, their general position by the end of 1962 did not even approach total acceptance of or agreement with the American stance. Yet the existence of a relatively favorable environment, of relatively free access to information, of direct professional contacts, seemed to make specific discussion and appreciation of the American position considerably easier. Some officers reported in 1965–1966 interviews that when they returned to Bonn they had "no one with whom they could talk," or worse, no one who wanted to talk to them.

Yet in the judgment of both the German and American participants subsequently interviewed, the long-run prospects for agreement (or at least less acrimonious, more informed debate) would have been favorable had it not been for an even further deterioration of general German-American relations throughout the spring. The chief source of contention remained the nature of the West's negotiating position on a Berlin settlement; when it was discussed again at Athens, German objections had been constant and strenuous. To Bonn the Kennedy administration still seemed more than willing to sacrifice not only Germany's political rights but also significant numbers of its security requirements in return for guarantees of minimal security and stability for Berlin and a definite agreement with the Soviet Union. Washington, on the other hand, was increasingly irritated by the Germans' "inflexible negativism," constant references to the hallowed days of Dulles, and Adenauer's leakage of confidential negotiation points whenever he was unable to gain from Washington a hearing for his "obstructionism." [38]

The proximate cause for the peaking of the public part of the strategic debate was the curt announcement by Washington in July of Norstad's imminent and reportedly forced retirement. Replacement of SACEUR without extensive prior consultation would have brought protests from the allies in any case; the peremptory replacement of Norstad as a result (the European allies purported to believe) of his disagreements with Washington's new line signalled "the end of an era." [39] Norstad had been an alliance commander, a strong advocate of a European MRBM force, of greater control-sharing, of strong nuclear and conventional forces. His successor, General Lyman Lemnitzer, and the new chairman of the Joint Chiefs, General Maxwell Taylor, were considered "McNamara men" and were not known to be sensitive to special European interests or requirements.

Bonn's severe and overly dramatic reaction reflected not only Adenauer's rage at the arrogant style of Washington's choosing a SACEUR but also the strong policy and friendship bonds he felt with Norstad. Even after the domestic rationale for the American shift was explained confidentially, thinly veiled official criticism continued, reinforced by widespread "inspired" rumors about impending American shifts to a complete peripheral defense. In these accounts Norstad's dismissal signalled the start of American nuclear disengagement: the withdrawal of SAC's protection and of already deployed weapons. In ringing tones sources in Bonn pointed out that Taylor himself had written that a strategic nuclear response should be confined to cases of "atomic attack on the continental United States, or the discovery of indisputable evidence that such an attack was about to take place." [40] Even a large-scale attack on Europe clearly was of secondary importance, not worth the risk of American cities' destruction.

Kennedy's testy denials and Taylor's public repudiation of his 1959 statements blunted but did not halt the spread of these rumors.[41] German reaction again went further than that of any other NATO ally. Strauss—reportedly with Adenauer's blessing—indeed used the dynamics of the crisis to launch his most dramatic and far-reaching attacks on the tenets of flexible response.[42]

Although most of his presentations contained only intense restatements of earlier themes, Strauss on one occasion argued with a bitterness and a specificity rarely (if ever) present in the public part of the German-American strategic debate. The defense minister declared that a definition of NATO strategy must be reached not by fiat but through continuing discussions. Although they shared the same views, Germany could not adopt the tactics of France, which were simply to ignore American concepts. "Our historic past, the geographic position of the Federal Republic, and the political situation of Berlin make similar German action unthinkable. Moreover, we have pledged ourselves under treaty not to produce any ABC weapons."

There were three basic points on which German-American differences must be resolved, Strauss said. First, American theory called for a counterforce strategy that disregarded the very nature of strategic nuclear weapons. These were area-coverage (flächendeckende) weapons, with which one could inspire popular fears of bombardment and thus gain political pressure to deter war. As the Russians well understood, the actual use of strategic weapons would negate any military advantage a country possessed; therefore, any theorizing about their use "shook deterrence."

Despite American calculations, Strauss next argued, it was not necessarily true that the use of even the smallest atomic weapon would set off total escalation. The new battlefield weapons, such as the dual-capable Davy Crockett cannon, had value both as political deterrents and military instruments. Moreover, under current manpower shortages only divisions equipped with such weapons could ensure a true forward defense.

Finally, if the debatable American concept that only conventional divisions would prevent the most likely conflicts was true, the defense of Western Europe would require not thirty but sixty to one hundred divisions. It was not only the limitations of political willingness and available European space which made so large a force unthinkable. Of equal importance were the facts that it "would increase the tendency to use military means to achieve political ends [and] . . . would provoke an atomic strike by the adversary, since no one wishes to be defeated."

Public pronouncements by Strauss and to a degree Adenauer continued in this vein until October 1962. The chain of events which came to be known as the *Spiegel* affair forced Strauss's dismissal and the eventual fall of the fourth Adenauer government. The first link in this chain did indeed relate to the German-American strategic debate, the proximate cause being publication of an account of the latest NATO maneuver, Fallex 62, in *Der Spiegel,* the Hamburg weekly perhaps best described as blending the traditions of *Time* and *Ramparts.*[43] The principal aim of the article was disclosure of the air force's still-secret "preemptive strike" memorandum of January 1962 (which had been brought to *Der Spiegel*'s attention by a troubled Command Staff officer, Colonel Alfred Martin), for which the Fallex results would provide an interesting updating lead-in. More important, for the past several years *Der Spiegel* had carried on an increasingly bitter campaign against Franz Josef Strauss, with attacks on Strauss the man, Strauss the politician, and Strauss the administrator. The memorandum plus the results of Fallex 62 would provide the stuff with which to discredit his still-sacrosanct standing as defense minister.

To an outside observer it seems ironic but somehow typical that the resulting scandal bore almost no relationship to the specific content of the *Spiegel* article or to its damning assessment of the inadequate if not unrealistic character of all German defense efforts of the previous seven years. At issue was rather the behavior of the federal government once the possibility of "treasonable disclosures" by *Der Spiegel* had been raised. Had or had not the government been justified in the immediate arrest of *Der Spiegel* editors and informants? What end justified the irregular request to Interpol for the arrest of the *Spiegel*'s defense editor vacationing in Spain? Who sanctioned the seizure at night of *Der Spiegel*'s offices, files, and forthcoming publications? Was it the role of a defense minister to intervene directly in an arrest, to withhold (and urge others to withhold) relevant information from the minister of justice, the constitutionally responsible cabinet minister? How could Strauss deny his actions or knowledge publicly and, more important, before the parliament itself?

Strategic issues played a totally secondary role and then only as tragi-comic elements. Colonel Martin had come forward because of his basic (though unstructured) opposition to the strategy proposed, as well as his fears about Strauss's irresponsibility. He had hoped a *Spiegel* report would mar-shal national discussion and bring swift action by a seemingly uninformed Adenauer in concert with Washington and other NATO allies. He had nei-ther seen the memo itself, however, nor participated in the subsequent dis-cussions. He also was not aware that it was little more than a restatement of a strategic concept based on nuclear airpower propounded by Air Force Inspector Kammhuber in 1956.[44]

Certain of Strauss's flailing attempts at self-defense constituted perhaps a more extreme example of irrelevant discussion of strategy. In numerous private conversations Strauss stressed *Der Spiegel's* reflection of American strategic arguments, the willingness with which a member of the Gehlen Or-ganization (the German intelligence agency acknowledged to have close American ties and sponsorship) had voluntarily supplied information to *Der Spiegel* editors, and *Der Spiegel*'s known contacts with many foreign in-telligence services.[45] It was highly probable, he reportedly convinced an in-creasingly bitter and removed Adenauer, that the CIA was behind the whole affair. He, Strauss, had posed too many problems for the Americans' plans to shape NATO strategy for their own benefit, so they had decided to be rid of him, using *Der Spiegel* as a willing instrument.

This represents the most paranoid of the many notes of sound and fury which accompanied the inevitable denouement of the *Spiegel* affair. In mid-December Strauss's forced departure from the Defense Ministry (accom-panied nonetheless by full military honors) brought to an end the most turbulent period of German-American disagreement on the strategy and con-trol of nuclear forces.

SEVEN

The Debate about Control-Sharing: 1961-1962

✠ WITHOUT QUESTION, the most salient fact concerning German-American disagreements about sharing of control over nuclear weapons is the degree to which these disagreements were inexorably intertwined with the debate about strategy. All the basic characteristics of the two debates were the same: waves of intense interest, then dormancy; repeated discontinuities in transatlantic communications and expectations; growing mutual frustration, spontaneous and manipulated. The same techniques of disagreement abounded: harsh public words and even harsher private judgments; continuing press leaks; the use of all possible channels of influence, often to little avail. And there was of course the same political context: an Adenauer failing and facing a painful final retreat; a Strauss deeply engaged, yet under intense political pressure in other areas; a new Washington team committed to sweeping foreign-policy changes in all spheres, including those pro-German mistakes of the past; a Berlin crisis which served as a flash point illuminating and intensifying all the basic issues and contradictions.

Yet there were some significant differences crucial to the somewhat cooler tone of the debate about control-sharing, crucial to its less hostile development. At the simplest level there was a reversal of roles, with Bonn insistently pushing for new decisions and structural changes and Washington resisting in the name of further deliberation on all the significant factors. Necessarily, therefore, the pressure and discord were less pervasive and less specifically focused. Not only was the second-tier Federal Republic in the always weaker position of claimant, demanding changes that in a strict sense required the assent of fourteen partners, not just one; it also was forced to consider seriously any approach which promised assured, nondiscriminatory access to decisions about its military and political security, in peace even more than in war.

This pragmatism also was made possible by the very fluidity of Kennedy's general control-sharing policy, which never solidified behind or against any particular proposal. Whatever the specific motivation at any one point, the formal approach remained largely that enunciated by the new president in his Ottawa speech of May 1961. His administration would continue to work with the allies toward "suitable" control-sharing arrangements, perhaps even the eventual establishment of "a NATO sea-borne missile force . . . truly multilateral in ownership and control." [1] But the initiative toward putting the force into operation would have to come from the Europeans; they would have to draw up command-and-control proposals to meet the twin requirements of close control and assured credibility in crisis. If no country was interested, American forces still were adequate to the task of strategic deterrence, and even more effort could then be devoted to the first priority task of building up the alliance's conventional forces.

THE AMERICAN DEBATE

Perhaps the most telling evidence of fluidity was the obviously unresolved debate on control-sharing within the American political elite itself. [2] More often than not, the immediate question concerned policies toward the developing French nuclear force. But given the model of nuclear proliferation then in highest vogue—that proliferation was inevitable—and Germany's insistent interventions through NATO and especially through bilateral channels, the expectation of imminent German claims for a direct share in nuclear-weapons control was omipresent.

The differences among American policy-making institutions, noted earlier, indeed gave rise to the three quite different control-sharing approaches, all of which competed for support and ascendancy at home and abroad and all of which claimed (with some truth) presidential approval. The first and most familiar was the joint hardware–joint control scheme, eventually to be transmuted into the MLF, which would embody both the promise of the Herter concept and the newer doctrine of "Atlantic partnership." As designed by Robert Bowie, supported principally by Europeanists in the State Department and vaguely outlined in presidential statements in 1961 and 1962, this approach saw a common strategic nuclear force (but not Norstad's land-based MRBMs scheme) as the way to cap the political (but not strategic) reality of transatlantic interdependence. The major allies thus would gain a significant share in decision-making, although America's continuing veto power would at most be lifted gradually and then only in the interest of a workable, integrated decision-making system involving all of the European allies.

Bowie's justifications, then as later, probably embodied the elements of the inevitable proliferation model most closely, focused as they were on the special problems a rehabilitated Federal Republic posed for both Atlantic and European unity. As he later formulated it, any effort short of an integrated force would lead in the long term to German national nuclear development, because "the German leaders have repeatedly stated that the Federal Republic cannot indefinitely accept a second class status or discrimination. . . . Over the long pull, the 1954 WEU limitation can hardly keep Germany from demanding equal nuclear status with the United Kingdom and France." [3] And similarly, "Half-way measures will hardly satisfy a German aspiration for equality. Germany and other European nations would certainly not be content with merely taking part in a 'control group' for French and British national forces. . . . The Germans would be led to press for their own national force whether by removal of the United States joint control of nuclear warheads, by French assistance or some other way." [4]

The second approach was the almost diametrically opposed "software" approach advocated by Secretary of Defense McNamara, most civilian Pentagon strategists, and some close presidential advisors. These placed at the center of their calculations centralized, discriminating presidential control over all nuclear weapons. Insofar as joint or national forces diluted this principle, they were dangerous and therefore not worth even the somewhat improbable political gains cited by their advocates. And as McNamara expressed it at Athens and Ann Arbor in 1962, such forces also were not only "expensive, prone to obsolescence, and lacking in credibility" but also unnecessary, given the now-certain American stragegic superiority.

The American presentation to the Athens meeting indeed spelled out in greatest detail the consequences of this approach for the European allies' nuclear "education and involvement." [5] First, there was to be a NATO

"Nuclear Committee," which would serve to lead the Europeans through the kind of analysis that had convinced McNamara and his associates. It also would serve as a channel for greater sharing of such information as the size and condition of NATO nuclear-warhead stockpiles on each ally's territory and as a forum for some "predecision" consultation regarding current planning and capabilities for tactical and strategic nuclear warfare. Second, there were to be continuing American pledges and demonstrations that strong American nuclear and conventional forces would remain in Europe "so long as they are necessary, whenever they are necessary."

Finally, there was to be formal recognition of European allies' rights to gradually expanding roles in nuclear decision-making. As explained in a newspaper interview with Strauss, the initial American definition that was approved specified only three broad cases: "If it should come to a large enemy attack comprising all weapons and means, the participation of different states in the decision to use atomic weapons was naturally out of the question. With respect to an attack conducted with stronger [sic] weapons but limited in scope, consultation was questionable but under [certain] circumstances possible. With respect to smaller attacks, consultations were always thinkable." [6]

But even in his Athens assignment of the long-promised Polaris submarines to NATO or in his toleration of the later MLF, McNamara made it clear that he construed rather narrowly the limits of a European role and of sharing. He and his staff met questions about the allies' interest in physical sharing by essentially denying not only their validity but also their existence. For example, in a later formulation of his position on sharing McNamara stated:

So far as I can recall, no political leader, as I say, has asked that the United States go beyond assuring effective participation regarding use and actually grant the right of use to a single nation or group of nations excluding the U.S., or taking away from the U.S. the right of veto. Now as I say no single political leader has asked that, to my knowledge, and no leader of the Federal Republic has asked for that. [7]

His overall judgment reflected his position that "giving NATO an artificial strategic capability makes no sense."

In the sanitized version of the Athens speech that he delivered at Ann Arbor in June 1962, Secretary McNamara made his famous attack on small independent nuclear forces and emphasized the need for centralized command and control.

At the same time, the general strategy I have summarized magnifies the importance of unity of planning, concentration of executive authority, and central direction. There must not be competing and conflicting strategies to meet the contingency of nuclear war. We are convinced that a general war target system is indivisible and if, despite all our efforts, nuclear war should occur, our best hope lies in conducting a centrally controlled campaign against all of the enemy's vital nuclear capabilities, while retaining reserve forces, all centrally controlled.

He did not acknowledge any need for sharing control over strategic weapons.

The third Washington approach—variously identified as the "multinational" or "nuclear aid to deserving allies"—was markedly less coherent, less visible, and less institutionally based than the other two. Essentially it stemmed from the renewal of old Eisenhower administration themes by high-ranking military men in the Pentagon and SHAPE (but not Norstad), some persons in the State Department, and some in the executive branch, especially those concerned with worsening balance-of-payments problems. Their arguments ran variously: the multinational approach would be the only way to bring Gaullist France back to full NATO participation; coordination of existing national nuclear forces would be the most that Britain and France would ever agree to; or this approach at least would buy time (or allow full revelation of the costs of French folly) for the allies' education in the calculus of discriminating, flexible response.

There also was little consensus on what by the spring of 1962 already was being categorized as the German problem. Some officials like the Defense Department's Roswell Gilpatric and Paul Nitze, argued in early 1962 that a probable German claim for equality in nuclear matters would simply have to be handled apart from the reality of current French developments.[8] Others concluded with the McNamara group that the Germans would just have to learn that nuclear proliferation was not inevitable and therefore they would have to be content with whatever other status compensations could be arranged. A few, mostly military men, foresaw no need, once a few more years had passed, to exclude any eventual German nuclear forces.

THE DEFINITION OF GERMAN POLICY

German policy in the face of these different concepts, all now subsumed under the rubric of the Atlantic option, essentially followed the lines set down during the later years of the 1956–1960 debate. Above all else, German policy supported integrated NATO arrangements—those which neither would further sanction British or French independence nor would devalue Germany's special claims based on size, exposure, and its position as the alliance's nuclear storehouse. There most probably should be common forces as well as improved consultation and information-sharing, particularly in view of the slow and generally unsatisfactory progress after Athens. And as Norstad had long argued, the forces must have a European character in order to provide the required theater defense against the Soviet MRBMs targeted on European cities, provide for effective "partnership," and act as an acceptable magnet to eventual French participation.[9]

What was new was the greater clarity, urgency, and enterprise with which this policy was pursued. Strauss in particular left no doubt that Bonn sought change almost immediately, that it totally rejected Washington's precondition of substantial nonnuclear buildup by the Western Europeans. These two years saw on Bonn's part a steady stream of insistent demands, proposals, and Washington visits, the only exception being the first, testing months of the Kennedy administration and the times of sharpest disagreement about strategy.

Whether concerned with new strategic forces or tactical nuclear-weapons control in Europe, the central focus of all of Bonn's proposals was the restructuring, or even reduction, of exclusive American veto power. During his first visit to Kennedy's Washington, for example, Adenauer presented the so-called Strauss plan, which was concerned with maximizing the impact on deterrence of control-sharing.[10] In the event the United States had not yet decided on a nuclear response, the plan proposed, the joint recommendation of SACEUR and the country attacked might bring about at least initial use of nuclear weapons in that country. The American response to the plan reportedly was cool, even after the chancellor suggested that SACEUR would clearly be bound by previous presidential directives.

The months after the Berlin crisis saw the mounting of a major campaign by Germany for more sharing of control—directly the reverse of McNamara's analytic educational effort. In part the campaign took the form of renewed emphasis on general NATO control over all tactical weapons in Europe. In Adenauer's dramatic but simplified and rather confused formulation,

We must arrange within NATO so that a decision can be taken to use atomic weapons even before the President is heard from . . . for it may be that an immediate decision has to be taken when the fate of all could be decided in one hour and the President . . . cannot be reached.[11]

It was the possible creation of a new NATO strategic force, however, that became the focus of particularly intensive German efforts before the December meetings of the North Atlantic Council—a development not uninfluenced by the growing competition among the three Washington approaches. In its inaugural statement the new Adenauer government (finally formed as a coalition of the CDU/CSU and FDP) called for establishment of the new force "as soon as possible," in order that NATO forces be raised "to the same technical level" as that enjoyed by the adversary.[12] Public statements defined only three broad system requirements: a procedure for a quick-firing decision without the involvement of fifteen fingers, a guarantee for ultimate approval of firing by the American president, and recognition of Germany's special need for consultation and access to decision-making.

Contemporary press reports suggest that in view of the not inactive German role in continuing SHAPE discussion on control formulas throughout 1961, Bonn privately had made more specific suggestions.[13] Among the alternative formulas considered within the Defense Ministry and cabinet's Defense Council were creation of a five-member Executive Group (to be composed of the United States, Britain, France, Germany and a rotating Mediterranean state); establishment of regional decision-making bodies for central Europe (the United States, Britain, France, Germany, and a Benelux state); and institution of a system of weighted voting that probably would have guaranteed to the United States and Britain a majority vote. Clearly there had been an official ordering of these proposals, but no public indication had been given as to what internally was the preferred formula.

Perhaps the most unusual proposal—a suggestion for an eventual Atlantic Union—came from Strauss himself, during a well-publicized (although reportedly hastily prepared) Washington speech.[14] He began with the assertion that in the postwar world not even the United States could survive any longer without surrendering certain major national prerogatives to the requirements of "nuclear alliance." The future of the West could only be secured through common efforts and "equal" sacrifices in all spheres: "The way which history and fate demand of us proceeds from cooperation and coordination to confederation and from there to a partial federation." [15]

The major stumbling block to this process, in Strauss's view, was the uncertain question of nuclear control; the possession or right to use nuclear

weapons was becoming the new "symbol" of sovereignty. Some system of
guarantees must be found, he politely threatened, which would prevent further proliferation and give the consciousness of partnership, a feeling absolutely required for continued alliance "since the nonmembers of the so-
called nuclear club are practically defenseless if the deterrent effects of these
new weapons are not at their disposal."

The high point of the German campaign for more control was Strauss's
speech to the North Atlantic Council meeting of December 1961: the speech
was (with foreknowledge, some respondents claimed) the direct antithesis of
McNamara's education presentation.[16] It might indeed be true, the defense
minister said, that American forces at the moment could adequately cover
the Russian MRBM targets, but what would be the situation in two
or three years when the Soviets reached parity in ICBMs? If the European
states did not then have an adequate countermeasure at their disposal in
Europe, they would bear the constant risk of exclusive blackmail by the Soviets, of threats which offered sanctuary to the United States in return for
nonintervention. If NATO could not unite on the Norstad fourth-atomic-
power plan or some acceptable substitute, not only would the future of the
Western security system be uncertain, but the examples of Britain and
France "could easily find followers." [17]

Lest anyone miss the point of the inevitable proliferation analogy, German statements throughout the subsequent winter gave new emphasis to
Bonn's position as the major storehouse of NATO nuclear weapons—a role
rejected by Gaullist France on grounds of lack of control sharing. Even
statements designed to soothe—like Strauss's remarks in the Bundestag in
April 1962 in answer to an SPD attack against his "nuclear obsession"—
referred to the rights and status these stockpiles should and must allow the
Federal Republic.[18] The "minimum" requirements of nuclear partnership,
Strauss argued, were three: sufficient information, a guarantee against arbitrary American withdrawal of forces and armament, and a certain measure
of codetermination (*Mitspracherecht*) with respect to all weapons stored on
German soil. The form of this equal participation must be further specified
in joint talks, but it basically must assure a "positive" and a "negative"
voice for Germany while safeguarding the president's "ultimate right of
decision."

In light of this, McNamara's speech and the American control-sharing
proposals at Athens met with limited response.[19] What optimism there was

in Bonn was tempered by the slow if not imperceptible progress toward implementation of the Athens decisions. Political and military leaders complained that they still officially did not know how many and what types of weapons were stored on German soil, not to mention how and when these might be used. The decision to designate the permanent representatives of the North Atlantic Council as the Nuclear Committee offered little hope of new, more extensive, or more detailed consultation. The limited participation of German officers in SHAPE's targeting and planning clearly was to remain as before. Moreover, the American attitude during even the preliminary preparations seemed to indicate little willingness to engage in anything but a more extended exposition of American concepts.

A second source of dispute was the Americans' continuing disregard of Norstad's (and by now Strauss's) European-MRBMs requirement. Few military or political leaders were willing to accept Strauss's counsel of "tactical delay"; for them the growing Soviet MRBM threat required immediate action to ensure a theater balance—the "atomic defense of Europe from Europe." Yet the United States had now assigned the long-promised Polaris submarine to SACLANT (Supreme Allied Commander Atlantic), not to the integrated, European SACEUR. Further, McNamara's speeches at Athens and Ann Arbor and Rusk's comments during his June visit to Bonn had emphasized that existing American forces were more than adequate for defense against the Russian MRBM's and that the requirement of centralized control over all forces in all cases was paramount. Norstad's removal seemed only to cap this trend.

These feelings of frustration were heightened by the even greater deterioration of German-American relations in the spring of 1962, turning to a considerable degree on Kennedy's emerging nonproliferation policy. The lowest point perhaps was reached in the weeks just before and just after Athens, with the proximate cause being several verbatim leaks from Bonn of the most recent American negotiating packages (the purpose of the leaks presumably being to diminish the prospects of acceptance either by the Soviets or by the American people).[20] In the German view the International Berlin Access Authority and the inter-German "technical" commissions projected by the Kennedy proposal would inevitably lead to a de facto recognition of the East Germans and thus would mean the final abandonment of Bonn's long-supported demands for reunification of the German nation only on the basis of self-determination.

Further, the Adenauer government argued, Kennedy's interest in an East-West nonaggression pledge and in a universal agreement pledging the nontransference of nuclear-weapons control to additional countries would decisively weaken Western defensive strength and readiness. The first not only would produce a "false sense of security"; because of its political implications it had been consistently rejected whenever proposed by the Communists. The second would not halt the inevitable process of proliferation; it would only permit new Soviet protests against NATO arrangements and impose additional unfair restrictions on Germany's already special position with respect to nuclear weapons, without the gain of one significant counterconcession.

This was hardly a new fear or a new argument. From the beginning of Kennedy's term the German leadership had been suspicious and fearful of the new president's obvious interest in negotiations with the Soviet Union, since the negotiations purportedly were to begin "from point zero" and implied disavowal of the hard-won favorable formulation of the Herter plan of 1959.[21] New negotiations, however, did not become a serious question until the building of the Berlin Wall intensified American desires to renew communications with the Soviet Union on a European settlement.[22] The Adenauer government asserted both formally and informally its unwillingness to negotiate with the East on any basis other than the Herter plan. Yet in the face of American determination, the Federal Republic had to agree to negotiations in order to maintain any influence over either the American position or Soviet-American discussions of its future.

As the Soviet-American exploratory talks proceeded, the major targets of German criticism were several widely discussed American proposals concerning concessions with respect to nuclear weapons in Central Europe. Bonn's ambassador in Washington, Wilhelm Grewe, warned, for example, that a principal condition of Germany's entrance into NATO had been the promise of "equal treatment" in all military spheres.[23] Strauss as usual was more specific; there could be no nuclear thinning-out, disengagement, or creation of an atom-free zone within the alliance's domain.[24] It was not only that technology had rendered such concepts obsolete; NATO's political, military, and moral obligations clearly required the maintenance of a hard defensive front along the Iron Curtain, with the same commitment and armament as in all other areas.

In terms which were to become all too familiar to Washington in the coming months, the defense minister asserted that he saw no justifiable grounds for imposing further armament restrictions on Germany in hopes of appeasing supposed Soviet fears of "nuclear revanchism." The Federal Republic neither produced nor controlled atomic warheads; it no longer exercised "national military sovereignty," since all its forces were under NATO command. Any attempt to withdraw or limit further the German right to a nuclear delivery capability would in Strauss's view so impose a position of inferiority within the West that no German leader could or would accept it. Such statements brought repeated American assurances that no nuclear disengagement was being considered, but resulted reportedly in very little modification of American pressures for greater German "flexibility." [25]

What most angered Adenauer in April 1962 was the summary rebuff Kennedy had dealt the chancellor's direct entreaties on these points, thereby justifying all of der Alte's dark fears of a superpower accord that would freeze the status quo over the heads of the Germans, indeed of all the Europeans. Adenauer's ire and charges of "betrayal," however, were more than matched in Washington. The Europeanists, particularly those in the State Department, placed some hope in a conciliatory "compromise" reached with Foreign Minister Gerhard Schröder at Athens. Within days Adenauer himself publicly denounced this compromise and repudiated the actions of both Schröder and Ambassador Grewe, the chief figure in the earlier Washington negotiations. New waves of irritation and recrimination followed, only partially mitigated by subsequent bilateral discussions. [26]

Optimists in Bonn, however, still hoped that Washington soon would produce an acceptable control-sharing formula; these were primarily the group becoming known as the Atlanticists. They were led by Schröder and Ludwig Erhard and opposed through political and ideological necessity by the CDU/CSU Gaullists, with whom Strauss then was intermittently flirting. A major stimulus to their hopes was a pre-Athens meeting visit to Bonn by Under Secretary of State George Ball, who publicly and privately discussed the creation of a "sea-based NATO MRBM force under truly multilateral ownership and control." [27] At the Athens meeting itself—albeit in somewhat less enthusiastic tones—both McNamara and Rusk reaffirmed basic American support for a common force and alluded to certain staff-level "feasibility studies" then in process. The North Atlantic Council as a whole and Strauss and Schröder individually were assured that as soon as these investigations were completed, resulting information and recommendations would be shared with "interested" allies.

On June 15, 1962 Ambassador Thomas Finletter made the first official presentation regarding the MLF to a closed session of the council's permanent representatives, "for study and later discussion." The "big bulky set of detailed proposals" subsequently transmitted to the European allies presumably reflected the findings of a State Department study group that had been set down in a May memorandum to the National Security Council and of a Navy study completed in June.[28] As described by several German and American respondents, the proposals called for a fleet of missile-carrying surface vessels (rather than the submarines discussed by Ball) "truly multilateral in manning, financing, and control." The organization of this force not only would overcome many of the problems inherent in the existing multinational alliance machinery but also would be of "significant military value."

The official German response to these proposals and to the Smith-Lee MLF briefing missions to Bonn in October and December reportedly was one of "reserved enthusiasm." [29] Within the coalition leadership, the Chancellor's Office, and the Foreign Office the reaction was generally favorable—although according to interview sources in 1965–1966, there were significant shadings in the arguments advanced in private. Schröder, for example, stressed the value of such a venture for improving Atlantic relations (meaning relations with America), while those around Adenauer placed more emphasis on the securing of Germany's rightful role within the alliance and the protection against American "isolationist" or "detentist" tendencies.

Within the Defense Ministry the range of opinion was greater. Strauss—who because of his past position had been briefed extensively by MLF proponents during his June visit to Washington—was the most enthusiastic German advocate, at least in public. Throughout the months preceding his departure the minister repeatedly used a two-pronged strategy to press for an early decision of the MLF. On the one hand, he reportedly told American officials that an MLF with participation scaled to "national achievements" was the last chance to meet German strategic requirements and prevent future "destabilizing developments." On the other hand, he informed domestic audiences that whatever its final operational form only such a force would provide opportunities for the carefully "coordinated" planning and "effective" control necessary to ensure deterrence.[30]

In contrast, the attitudes of the military leadership ranged from neutral to negative. Several official position papers reportedly concluded that although the force might be of significance in tightening the irreplaceable American connection, its value as a military instrument or as a means of increasing Germany's influence over total NATO planning was "not yet clear." Surface ships were a questionable mode; mixed manning seemed an "unnatural" or "unnecessarily contrived arrangement"; the long-supported requirement for European MRBMs would still stand. In private conversations a number of prominent military men stressed the questions of cost in terms of the probable returns and the necessary cutbacks in other Bundeswehr programs—for MRBMs (air force), missile destroyers (navy), and ground-force modernization (army).

Whatever their view, there was no one in Bonn, not even Strauss, who was willing to make an immediate binding commitment to the MLF project. First, in addition to the military's objections several other major aspects were left undefined, the most notable being the precise decision-making mechanism. Second, the Kennedy administration still seemed divided regarding the most desirable American role—more precisely, the exact share in the nuclear control—to be projected for the final stages of an MLF. In August, for example, Robert Schaetzel of the State Department had stressed the necessity of "active" American participation, while in September the president's national-security assistant, McGeorge Bundy, had mentioned the possibility of "a European force, genuinely unified and multilateral, and effectively integrated with our own." [31] The Smith-Lee missions and Ball's November speech to the NATO parliamentarians meeting seemed to indicate that the Schaetzel view had prevailed, but the possibility of yet another shift could not be discounted.

Most important, the actual implementation of the proposal still was open to question. [32] The implicit American condition for further action seemed to be "wide participation"; the French and British reactions had been decidedly cool. Under these conditions would the United States still push forward? What then would be the relative advantages and disadvantages of major German participation, particularly in light of increasingly friendly Franco-German relations?

And there the matter rested, as Adenauer, under threat of forced resignation within a year, struggled to form a new government, and Strauss left the Defense Ministry under a marked shadow. The future of control sharing within the alliance was indeed still open, but in Bonn an optimistic prognosis required an act of faith.

COMMENTARY

An almost irresistible temptation to seek a single cause, a monistic explanation for these disagreements confronts the scholar. Many of the theories suggested elsewhere have focused on alleged German faults: a fundamental fear of any change, obsession with nuclear weapons, deliberate misunderstanding of the American position, or most often the dark nuclear ambitions of Strauss. Such an approach, however, obscures or ignores the basic nature of these developments and the environment in which they occurred. At issue were not one but several disagreements, the result of German but also American hopes and fears, plans and uncertainties, misunderstandings and occasional deceptions.

It is easiest to begin with the policy context, which for the German leadership and particularly for Adenauer meant the radical and dangerous revision implicit in the Kennedy approach to foreign policy. Germany's general fears of abandonment seemed substantiated by Kennedy's posture during the Berlin negotiations of 1961–1962. Erection of the wall had been shattering enough, yet the American bargaining position went further; it invalidated all the basic terms of the bargain by which Germany had joined the Atlantic alliance.[33] It challenged one by one the premises of Adenauer's foreign policy: reunification of the two Germanys obtained only through the Federal Republic's faithful membership in and receipt of the pledged support of a powerful West; an equal voice secured by treaty and achievement in all affairs affecting a future German settlement; no further concession on borders, military capabilities, or political status without at least matching gains toward eventual unity of the German people "in peace and freedom."

In retrospect this German assessment seems to have been at least broadly correct, making a substantial measure of German-American disagreement inevitable. For Kennedy the division of the German people was and for the foreseeable future would remain an accepted fact; constant repetitions of the polite words and ritualistic pledges of the past would lead only to further obscurity and delusion.[34] The concern of the West in his view must be with the present: how to ameliorate the existing situation, how to lessen the risk of war over Berlin, how to begin to establish the preconditions for a possible settlement. Germany's allegiance to the West, its understandable "state of melancholy" must be considered; but if certain "legalities" or unrealistic priorities had to be sacrificed in the interest of substance, the trade-off was just.

This basic disagreement was intensified and sometimes unnecessarily exacerbated by developments on both sides. Perhaps the most obvious cause was the simple differences in style, timing, and perspective.[35] There also were continuing problems with communication. In part this was the result of personal judgments on the highest level. Kennedy admired the chancellor, but remarked early in his term, "I sense I'm talking not only to a different generation, but to a different era, a different world." [36] The chancellor appeared to hold almost mirror-image views. Although his initial dismay at Kennedy's election abated (he found the president "engaging"), he privately questioned Kennedy's youth, his lack of experience in European affairs, his reliance on unseasoned "academic" or "prima donna" advisors.

Of far greater consequence, however, were the continuing misperceptions and misunderstandings that pervaded lower-level relations. Some of Kennedy's advisors felt that the Germans too long had exercised a veto over American policy; the United States must try to persuade, but also to lead, even if continuing pressure and a rather hard line were necessary.[37] The reaction among German advisors was similarly suspicious and dogmatic. The new faces in Washington sought only immediate decisions and concessions by Germany, new grounds for endless negotiations and detailed public statements—all impossible in terms of the dictates of diplomacy and the magnitude of Germany's problems.

Further grounds for suspicion and alienation were the short-run miscalculations by both sides. The Kennedy administration sought bilateral talks with the Soviets both as ends in themselves and as means of speeding and catalyzing agreement among the allies. The frustrations and obstructionism which the United States encountered in the latter process were not always balanced against the realistic prospects of negotiations at that point. As Theodore Sorensen reports, "Our error, J.F.K. later acknowledged, was in trying to push the Germans to accept ideas in which he could not interest Khrushchev anyway." [38] Too often the only results were increased German concern for reassurance and "influence," new fears of a Soviet-American deal at any cost, and private remonstrations along "we told you so" lines.

Also there were the many psychological and tactical errors made by the Germans, nonetheless irritating because of their origin in panic and dark forebodings. Bonn's constant complaints and requests for pledges of faith, coupled with the failure to advance positive proposals of its own, became very irritating to official Washington and especially to the president.[39]

Moreover, repeated indiscretions and inspired press disclosures hardly enhanced Germany's claims to be treated as a respected and responsible partner. In more than one American eye the Germans had proved themselves not only untrustworthy but also willing to use any method—mobilization of the president's own constituency, or even perhaps the Soviet adversary, against him—to prevent uncomfortable progress.

Internal German conflict and confusion constituted a second negative contextual factor. Some of the reasons why the Federal Republic seemed to "speak with a forked tongue" were attributable to the drastic change in Adenauer's political position after the 1961 elections.[40] Attention and support within the CDU/CSU and the nation already were shifting to the new men with new policies, to the heir presumptive, Ludwig Erhard, and to Foreign Minister Gerhard Schröder. Adenauer's frequent absences from Bonn, his recurring illnesses and lapses, his confused and often injudicious public statements (particularly during the *Spiegel* affair) only intensified and further justified this shift.

Of greater relevance for specific disagreements about strategy was the drastic diminution of Strauss's personal power and domestic prominence during 1961–1962. Without question, Strauss's violent opposition to the introduction of flexible response and to the shift in American nuclear-control policies had a substantive basis. Yet the nature and timing of his statements, the sometimes startling shifts in emphasis and intensity, are partially explicable in terms of his considerable personal and political difficulties. For Strauss even more than for Adenauer these difficulties prevented basic change or accommodation according to past patterns and intensified existing attitudes of discontent and suspicion.

Among his most salient difficulties, Strauss found himself in an increasingly isolated position within the government itself. His relations with Adenauer, cool since 1959, had reached a new low; his relations with Erhard and Schröder, his rivals for the succession, were also strained. His leadership of the CSU also was somewhat threatened within Bavaria itself; an opportunity for a test would be the provincial elections in December 1962. Moreover, interview accounts suggest that Strauss was not at the height of his powers; several illnesses as well as apparent personal difficulties and excessive drinking occasioned absences from Bonn during critical periods.[41]

The cumulative pressure of all this, plus *Der Spiegel*'s attacks, would have been difficult for any public figure to bear. In Strauss, always free-swinging in response to criticism, it seemed to occasion moments of uncontrollable rage and the loss of reasoned judgment. He also no longer held a trump card of proven usefulness: the respect and friendship of powerful figures in the United States. The position of the SPD, long vilified by Strauss for its "illusions" about military issues, was far more in tune with Kennedy's concepts and policies. Too, American demands for greater German military efforts in essence were implicit indictments of those past achievements on which Strauss had staked so much political capital. Most damaging and enraging of all were the public criticisms of Strauss himself that were being made by Kennedy and certain of his advisors.[42]

In light of these factors Strauss's more extreme statements perhaps can be viewed not only as reactions or attempts to deflect American pressure but also as actions designed to use the American connection to gain a new type of political prestige. Once again Strauss was the first to see danger, to stand up against the menacing future misunderstood by the Americans. The alliance with the United States was still vital, of course; any rejection would have denied reality, the requirements of his position, or the basic pro-American test applied to every candidate seeking German electoral success. The time had come, the defense minister intimated, for the Federal Republic to speak more frankly to its American friends and to correct them when necessary.

With respect to the specific rather than the contextual causes of policy disagreement and distrust, the shift in American nuclear strategy raised not only specific controversies but also general problems of alliance procedure. Under the conditions prevailing in 1961–1962 any such basic change, almost regardless of its particular provisions, would have engendered initial resistance on the part of all America's allies. As past experience had shown, the time lag between Washington's decisions and real understanding or acceptance by its allies was on the order of eighteen to twenty-four months. This was the period required not only to sharpen the allies' generally dim awareness of American domestic debates about strategy but also to inform, persuade, and secure acceptance by America's own officers at SHAPE and in the field. These officers then became the most direct source of education and example for the other NATO members.

In the particular case of Germany and the particular issue of flexible response the lag was certain to be at least that long. With the possible exception of a small circle around Strauss, the German military were as substantively and psychologically dependent on SHAPE as before. Independent evaluations and analyses, such as the effort leading to the air-force memorandum for January 1962, were surprising exceptions to the rule. If SACEUR, his staff, or Seventh Army contacts were hesitant about or opposed to the new approach, similar German reflections of these attitudes were hardly surprising.

A second inhibiting factor was the economic cost involved. Any basic change meant new expenditures for the European states, which were making the minimum investment necessary to "keep the Americans happy." Moreover, an increased conventional-force buildup not only would require increased government expenditures, it also would necessitate greater dislocation of the domestic economy in terms of manpower required and curtailment of allocations for the more desired dual-capable equipment. The Federal Republic, on the verge of acquiring the second largest nuclear-delivery capability in the West, clearly would be the most sensitive to any shift.

Finally, there was the somewhat intangible question of psychological commitment to past doctrine. The German army, for example, had just achieved full conversion to the 1956 phase of the strategic revolution after considerable internal opposition and debate. Even if the new strategic tenets were congenial with existing doubts, a reversal of the conversion process required not insignificant costs and effort. Moreover, for many officers a shift, in the words of one military respondent, would mean simply the replacement of one article of faith ("atomic weapons are the most effective means of defense") with another precept ("conventional weapons are the effective means below a certain level"). And there was no guarantee that still another truth would not be discovered.

As described above, statements made during the first months of the Kennedy administration did little to transform faith into reasoned commitment. There were many good and necessary reasons for the delay in detailed presentations, yet the price paid at least in terms of German attitudes was high. Any information beyond general statements by administration leaders or their representatives in Europe came from press speculations and informed rumors. Both were subject to political manipulation and were often more reflective of German fears and dire speculations than of American discussions. In a sense, German leaders (with the exception of Strauss) became so concerned with the possibility of the worst possible developments in American thinking that they either doubted or totally missed assertions of any lesser gravity or signals of reassurance.

The many initial variations in American interpretations and explanations did not ease the process. It was not a question of what Kennedy or McNamara said; it was rather what weight should be attached to this statement by a visiting White House aide as opposed to those recent statements by second-level officials at the State Department or Defense Department or by an academic of purported influence. The mixture of partial statements, generalized oversimplifications, deliberate distortions, and well-meaning declarations of inaccuracies was difficult for a domestic observer to interpret. For a European it was only confusion confounded. As one relatively well-informed CDU politician notes, "It was at least nine months before they got together on their terms and a few more months before we got a clear idea of what they had really decided."

These developments serve only as further supporting evidence for the conclusions reached by Neustadt in his Suez-Skybolt studies.[43] Each country within the alliance, but particularly the United States, assumes that its partners understand and take into consideration the basic mechanism of its own domestic political process. The occasional benefits of trial ballooning notwithstanding, an ally is expected to be aware of the techniques and modes of intragovernmental bargaining and consensus building, the difficulties and debate (often public) which precede and even follow a supposedly definite policy decision. In the 1961–1962 discussion, as in the Radford case, many American officials could not understand Germans' intense, "neurotic" reactions to insignificant or speculative remarks made for domestic consumption. Still more incomprehensible was continuance of these misinterpretations and resulting demands for reassurance even after a clear, authoritative statement on the issue by Kennedy, Rusk, or McNamara.

In the short run at least, the most frequent result was a cycle of mutual frustration. In one sense, however, all of these points beg a basic question: to what extent did German criticisms during 1961–1962 stem from deliberate misunderstandings, from a temporary disparity in strategic views, or from an inevitable and perhaps immutable difference in strategic interests? The contention here is that no one of these answers provides a sufficient explanation. Elements of each are involved and are so interrelated that only general estimates of their particular magnitude can be ventured.

Clearly, politically inspired misunderstandings and exaggerations played a major role in at least aggravating basic disagreements. In summary, the reasons for the public course chosen by Strauss (and to a lesser degree by Adenauer) were many: need for overstatement to gain support from a population tutored in dependency on America; pressures of domestic and personal problems; unwillingness to abandon or revise long-cherished programs for acquiring equipment suitable to a major power; primacy accorded the economic constraints imposed by a full-employment economy; manpower and technological interests of powerful economic communities. Of particular importance for Strauss was a factor to be treated further below: the negative implications of flexible response, with its emphasis on continuous, discriminating, centralized decision as a substitute for the long-sought "meaningful" role in control of and decision-making about nuclear weapons.

Many of these misunderstandings, however, must be interpreted as expressions of real fears about the future. The deterioration and suspicion that marked general German-American relations had loosed many of the doubts and insecurities that had always lurked just below the surface in Bonn. A supposed weakening of the American connection opened up a range of unknown and perhaps unconfrontable possibilities; it was not what the Americans currently were saying but to what this might lead. Moreover, in the political teakettle of Bonn in the early 1960s, anxieties proclaimed for political purpose quite often assumed a life of their own and were unconsciously transformed into articles of belief as well as of argument.

To a considerable degree these fears were directly related to specific German objections to flexible response. The first and apparently primary consideration focused on the doctrine's explicit assumption of possible extended conflict on, and perhaps confined to, the Federal Republic's territory. The pledge of forward defense and the guarantee against the dreaded sequence of conquest-then-liberation for all of the Federal Republic's territory were not to be redeemed even in the long run. For the military, who had long accepted implicitly the probability of some destruction, this raised questions as to whether adequate conventional forces existed, whether the plan for later phases of a war would justify or negate the sacrifices required for initial nuclear forbearance. Was not the extension and expansion of conflict inevitable? Would not initial restraint, coupled with continuing force deficiencies, mean that Germany would never benefit from the necessary later use of the superior Western strategic capability?

To the political leadership the basic idea simply was unacceptable. For what military reason had the Federal Republic joined NATO except to ensure that combat without the immediate involvement of the United States and all its forces would neither be considered possible nor ever come to pass? Given the Berlin experience, how could one expect a firm allied response to an aggression launched in pursuit of a limited gain at only German expense? Given the new strategic environment, what lasting guarantee was there of American involvement, or against America's willingness to tolerate a long European or German war if at no major costs to itself? Troops in Europe might be hostages, but they always could be withdrawn.

The necessary corollaries of these positions were the German views on the nature of deterrence and the role of tactical nuclear weapons. Since they have been described above, attention here may be directed to more speculative points. First, if conflict was seen as improbable but in any case unconfrontable, reliance on total deterrence was the only acceptable position. Bonn's insistence on the early if not immediate use of tactical nuclear weapons was motivated in large measure by beliefs in the efficacy of threats of incalculable risk or of uncontrollable escalation or in the inevitability of Western conventional-force deficiencies. But at least a semiconscious desire to take hostages against the future seems also to have existed. There must be a fixed commitment to the use of nuclear weapons, a decision about which the West and even the Germans themselves might hesitate in an actual situation of conflict.[44]

A related interpretation regarding the mounting German interest in battlefield nuclear-capable weapons may be suggested. The military's disappointment over the nondistribution of the Davy Crockett, for example, stemmed in part from judgments (fostered earlier by American army contacts) concerning the weapon's effectiveness, its ease of handling, and its marked contribution to lower-level defensive strength. Yet as interviews as late as 1968 reflected, there was also a somewhat paradoxical assessment of its value as a nuclear weapon.[45] On the one hand, it was a small weapon, capable of only limited amounts of horrifying nuclear destruction and was perhaps not an escalation trigger. On the other hand, its use would constitute a first step, would represent in essence a binding commitment to the later employment of more destructive means.

The specific limit to a German-American rapprochement on strategic issues is best left for later discussion. One result of the 1961–1962 stalemate was clear, however. Whether the result of fearful forebodings or inevitable conflict of interests, the gap in strategic conceptions only made participation in nuclear decision-making and nuclear control seem a more urgent and primary national goal. At stake was not only the broad political and military aims sought since 1958 but also the direct protection of specific defense interests now under challenge by America.

In general, German-American disagreement with respect to control-sharing was shaped by many of the same factors that bore on the dispute about strategy. Resistance to the new American emphasis on centralized control drew strength from the lessons and expectations of the past, from the fears and suspicions fostered during the necessary shakedown period of the Kennedy administration. There were similar (though not as extensive) problems in communication, often contradictory assertions of lower officials, and passionate advocacy of past positions from within the administration as well as from Americans at SHAPE. Moreover, the same psychological elements were involved: resentment and fears regarding arbitrary or imposed American actions, such as the indefinite shelving of a European MRBM or Norstad's replacement.

There were two environmental aspects, however, that took on new significance in the control-sharing context. The first was the continuing American interest in agreement with the Soviet Union, at least on a freezing of the nuclear status quo in Europe, if not on the dreaded nuclear disengagement itself. To the Germans this not only seemed to provide proof of the converging political and security interests of the superpowers, with fearful implications for the future defense and division of Europe, it also set major constraints on any participation by Germany in control-sharing and thus on any effective change in its political position within the alliance or within Europe. An agreement had not been reached, but such a pact or a similar sacrifice of German rights by America in the near future could be predicted.

Perhaps of greatest consequence in the short run was a second factor: Strauss's personal investment in and outspoken pursuit of a major nuclear role for Germany. The defense minister's campaign in December 1961 to force the issue seemed only to justify the suspicions discussed earlier—that he was willing to explore any means short of direct production that promised progress towards some form of German ''nuclear sovereignty.'' In this view, given Kennedy's nuclear-control policy, Strauss valued more highly than ever the establishment of a European MRBM force. It still might prove an acceptable first step, constitute the entrance fee, or should the force eventually break apart, even provide the hardware for an independent German effort.

Here, as before, no definite proof for or against these arguments is offered. Strauss's intensity and persistence, his dramatic declarations of deadlines, his placing of personal political capital on the line—all indicated a determination bounded at best by uncertain limits. His numerous prounouncements and proposals seemed to hint at an ultimate degree of German independence which neither the United States nor any other ally was willing to grant or perhaps even allow. Yet on more than one occasion during 1961–1962 the defense minister bowed to the dictates of political prudence and preconditions. No action could be taken until America's rethinking was completed; a minimal program might prove the best beginning; the president's right to the ultimate decision must remain inviolate; a future system could be Atlantic or Atlantic-European in nature.

The reasons for Strauss's forbearance can be found in the factors that made the control-sharing debate less acrimonious than that concerning strategy. First, continuing disagreements affecting existing force structures and tactical planning necessarily had a more urgent day-to-day priority than the related but less clearly defined interests and demands regarding future forces. The new American position on the role of tactical nuclear weapons made confirmation of German participation in this sphere a more immediate and imperative goal.

Moreover, whatever its aims, the Kennedy administration never publicly precluded either the eventual creation of an alliance nuclear force or some broadened form of participation in decision-making. The preconditions might appear unattainable—implementation of conventional goals, European definition of an acceptable control formula, extensive European financing—but the possibility was still acknowledged. Encouragement also could be gleaned both from the initial, albeit unsatisfactory, steps taken at Athens and from the personal views of prominent officials within the administration. The best German strategy, therefore, was to continue to press control-sharing demands in the present and to wait for the future.

A final point was the conviction (not limited to Strauss or to others in the German leadership) that if the alliance was to continue, American acceptance of some form of direct control-sharing was inevitable. Nuclear proliferation, at least to the major states, was a clear requirement for the future; the United States by its own logic would be forced to buy insurance against the resulting destabilizing effects. Thus once any form of significant participation was achieved, the most probable prospect—even with Kennedy's contemporary position—was the progressive expansion of competence and responsibility.

Nonetheless, during the last months before Strauss's departure from the ministry, there was limited but increasing dissent from the doctrine of inevitability. The new multilateral-force proposals (discussed further below) were interesting, but the direct benefit involved seemed unclear and perhaps even inadequate. The substantive failure of the Athens provisions led many officials to assign highest priority to participation in the tactical sphere and led some to stress the need to attain at least the same potential influence over strategic weapons.

To a small group, however, the Athens results merely reinforced the experience of discussions at SHAPE regarding possible control-sharing formulas. The United States was simply unwilling—perhaps even unable, despite their good intentions—to permit any significant participation by European allies, to allow anything more than a pro forma diminution of the American control monopoly. If it had ever existed, the Atlantic course was no longer a realistic option; a new solution on the European level must be sought.

For the most militant of this group the proof of American intransigence lay in the failure during 1961–1962 of the traditional German bargains. The Federal Republic had raised its force goals only to meet with Britain's charges of "militarism" and America's acceptance of the increase as its due, requiring no reciprocal consideration of German interests. Bonn also had increased its arms purchases and its provison of other balance-of-payments support, only to have the Americans default on previously promised armament deliveries and set new restrictions. For these militants Adenauer's strategy of gradually gaining political advantages on the basis of military achievements and economic accommodation within the alliance was simply no longer applicable.

It was a view which became increasingly attractive in future years.

EIGHT

Strategic Education & Reconciliation: 1963-1966

✠ VIEWED BROADLY, the period 1963–1966 might be called the reconciliatory phase in the development of German attitudes towards use and control of nuclear weapons. After the storms of 1961–1962, the principal goals of Erhard's Bonn were to reaffirm the American connection, to reestablish the coincidence of German and American strategic interests, to reinforce the inextricable, controlled involvement of the United States in German defense, to reconfirm American support for an appropriate German role within the alliance. Unquestionably, points of difference, both major and minor, remained. Yet most of the political leadership appeared definitely committed to muting previous disagreements and to seeking modes of compromise within new doctrines and new forms.

Perhaps the clearest example came in the discussions of nuclear control within the alliance, most particularly creation of the long-debated joint force, now called the multilateral nuclear force or MLF. Almost as soon as the first American proposal was made, the Federal Republic committed itself unequivocally to full participation. Given previous demands and calculations, a strong German interest in such a project was hardly surprising. Nonetheless, the uncertain course of discussions about the MLF, as well as the force of both external and internal opposition, increasingly made the intensity of the government's commitment the test of its faith in and willingness to give priority to the American connection.

German efforts in what has been broadly defined as the strategic sphere were similar in aim, if not in successful implementation. Bonn's fears and suspicions about the European consequences of a flexible-response doctrine remained essentially unassuaged. Its continuing disagreements with Washington were apparent, however theoretical the discussions, whether specific counterproposals or only a general call for American reaffirmation of nuclear deterrence were involved. Nevertheless, by 1966 there had been at least some narrowing of differences in every major sector—in doctrine as well as armament, in training as well as force structure. And the assured, major German role in the new alliance planning groups seemed to promise that this process would continue, if not accelerate.

Yet despite all these attempts to bridge earlier gaps, the period 1963–1966 witnessed a growing concern with the limits and costs of an Atlantic-oriented nuclear policy, with the balancing of an "American-preferred" course in nuclear affairs against other possible options. In part this awareness was the predictable product of trends discussed previously: the growing national self-consciousness born of twenty years of postwar recovery and booming economic success, and the apparent resolution of all major domestic political issues. There were also the additional years of experience in NATO, the cautious observation of the new Gaullist model in France, and not least, the protracted education of the MLF discussions themselves. More significant were the major constraints this orientation entailed, given radical changes in the European environment. Initially there was the explicit conflict of the two grand designs—that of Kennedy and that of de Gaulle—with Germany more often the prize than the balancer or mediator. Of more lasting importance was the growing atmosphere of East-West détente in Europe and, particularly, of Soviet-American global rapprochement. From Bonn's perspective this warming of the Cold War was posited not only on the present and future sacrifice of German interests but on America's unilateral revision of its alliance bargain as well. Finally, there were the harsh lessons of the MLF's denouement, the pointedly negative reaction of Britain and other allies to a proposed increase in Germany's share in nuclear decision-making.

Echoing and reinforcing these developments were the major post-Adenauer shifts within the domestic political system. The new chancellor,

Ludwig Erhard, made reconciliation with Washington a principal aim, as did the major cabinet figures Foreign Minister Gerhard Schröder and Defense Minister Kai-Uwe von Hassel. Yet the emergence of the German Gaullists as a small but increasingly vocal and effective veto group within the governing coalition marked the first major challenge to the primacy accorded to the Atlantic rather than the European orientation in security arrangements. Led by a bitter Adenauer and a recouping Strauss, the Gaullists forced continual debate and delay and, finally, played the decisive role in Erhard's fall in 1966.

Moreover, there was a growing, more reasoned resurgence of the old reunification versus nuclear-armament debate. The new formulation posed the question: What hopes could be held for Schröder's "policy of movement" toward Eastern Europe and eventual all-German union without the sacrifice of ambitions, particularly in the nuclear sphere, that best could be achieved within the Atlantic framework? The official answer, under the unofficial policy of "small steps," foresaw not sacrifice but bargaining advantage to be gained. But an ever more restive FDP, still the swing element in the government coalition, saw only illusion and continued frustration involved.

Thus the principal focus in these final analyses will be the dilemmas of a Federal Republic increasingly involved in and concerned about alliance nuclear arrangements, yet with a mounting awareness of the costs and the constraints to be accepted in hope of uncertain gains. This chapter delineates the course of the 1963–1966 debate on strategy and armament; the following two chapters treat the German aspects of the life and hard times of the much-chronicled MLF.

Perhaps the most marked characteristic of the German voice in the Atlantic alliance's debate about strategy during 1963–1966 was its tone of relative calm. It was not that major differences of opinion did not exist; in substantial measure the general disputes of 1961–1962 among the services, as well as with the United States, continued. It was rather that the dramatic public elements of confrontation were replaced by a more sober private mode of consultation. The primary emphasis was to be shifted from the full delineation of differences to the continuing search for areas of at least partial agreement and accommodation.

THE DOCTRINAL DEBATE

With respect to discussions of strategic doctrine, there were a number of in-terrelated causes for these changes.[1] Perhaps the most obvious were the cir-cumstantial factors. A considerable amount of time had passed since the promulgation of the flexible-response doctrine, time in which the Germans could overcome initial anxieties, receive American assurances, consider more extensively the specific consequences for German security. Debate also was no longer colored by the existence of a clear and present danger. Whatever the future potentialities, the defense of Berlin was not a currently pressing issue. Even from the outlook of long-resistant Bonn, the Soviet threat had begun to seem somewhat less awesome.

Moreover, the chief protagonists of 1961–1962 were no longer in of-ficial dominance. In accordance with the promise wrung from him after the *Spiegel* affair, Adenauer retired in October 1963 and was succeeded by Ludwig Erhard, the genial father of the economic miracle. Erhard's assump-tion of the chancellorship seemed to mark the official reinstatement of the Atlantic consensus after Adenauer's increasing absorption with Franco-Ger-man rapprochement. Obviously committed to a course of normalization of relations at home and abroad, the new chancellor enjoyed good relations based on mutual respect with all of the leaders of NATO countries except France, but particularly with officials in Washington. He, with his long-time ally and mentor, Foreign Minister Gerhard Schröder, favored not only greater integration of national forces within NATO but also the expansion of the European Economic Community (EEC) to include at least Britain. He also supported the launching of selective, "business-like" diplomatic probes toward all of the East's capitals except East Germany's Pankow.

Franz Josef Strauss was replaced by a man who was his antithesis in al-most every major respect. Kai-Uwe von Hassel was a reserved North Ger-man Protestant, perhaps best known as an ambitious but loyal party man within the CDU leadership.[2] His selection reflected more the govern-ment's desire to avoid the emphasis on defense so avidly sought by Strauss. Von Hassel's support and admiration of Foreign Minister Schröder's pol-icies made his appointment a clear affirmation of an Atlanticist course, of the closest possible ties with the United States.

Equally important was the change in administrative style. Like Strauss, von Hassel had done military service; as minister-president of Schleswig-Holstein he had been in contact with the problems of border defense. But he neither had nor claimed any special expertise in strategy and doctrine. Both by personal predilection and governmental decision his principal concern was to ensure full implementation and consolidation of previous plans without searching public reappraisals or great fanfare, nationally or internationally.

Within the Bundeswehr itself, on the other hand, there were several new efforts to generate and routinize expert judgment on all aspects of alliance doctrine and planning. The air force had been the first to establish a specific planning organization, with ancillary support from several small research centers. Similar (albeit still rudimentary) arrangements soon were made for the Bundeswehr as a whole, providing a somewhat more systematic input than that provided by the previous activities of the Command Staff. More important for the short run was the creation of a special political-military group, directly under the minister, having major continuing responsibilities regarding all questions about the alliance.

As discussed in earlier chapters, the principal stimulus for these activities was the growing recognition that formulation of a "German position" rather than reaction to prior SHAPE decisions was both expected and desirable.[3] Two other developments, however, provided additional incentives. The first was the program of regular Franco-German consultations begun in 1963 to foster the development of common strategic and tactical concepts.

These discussions were rooted in what Adenauer regarded as the culmination of his life's work, the Franco-German Treaty of Friendship and Cooperation, concluded with de Gaulle on January 22, 1963.[4] Military cooperation and consultation was a key element, as it had been in the treaty's political ancestor, France's Fouchet Plan for loose European union, rejected in 1962 by the four other EEC members. Owing to Bonn's continuing concern, however, the treaty explicitly urged that this cooperation be "related" to the NATO framework and mentioned not specific agreements but only "harmonization" objectives.

Although the potential scope of consultation was extremely broad (including "all important questions of foreign policy"), the mechanisms set up were rather formal and relatively rudimentary. The defense ministers were to meet quarterly; existing exchanges of military personnel and defense units were to be accelerated; joint production efforts were to be expanded. Moreover, the treaty contained no mention of cooperation in the development of nuclear weapons and was publicly interpreted as excluding it.[5]

None of these activities in themselves required more systematic German planning; most, in fact, were merely the formal continuation of limited, ad hoc arrangements begun in the late 1950s and the early 1960s. As 1963 progressed, the outlines of an emerging consensus between France and Germany on nuclear strategy and tactical doctrine were indeed clear. Such agreement of course was subordinate to their sharp, irreconcilable differences over NATO and America's role in it, however skillfully these had been blurred on the de Gaulle–Adenauer level. Nonetheless, beyond NATO itself there were no other forums in which the clear definition of German views was necessary or where these views were subject to continuing external reappraisal if not reinforcement.

The second development, institution of regular bilateral consultations with the United States, acted as a balance to the Franco-German consultations and had a more direct impact. During 1963, Washington, admittedly to offset the Franco-German arrangements, pressed a not unwilling Bonn to schedule periodic conferences between not only Defense Secretary McNamara and von Hassel but also between the chairman of the Joint Chiefs and the Inspector General of the Bundeswehr.[6] Further meetings were to be held frequently by members of their respective staffs and by other officials in areas of "common interest."

Within this new framework American pressure for the systematization of German defense planning increased. More than one consultation, according to several military respondents, consisted of detailed presentations of the background studies supporting American strategic positions and of repeated inquiries concerning similar data on the German side. Perhaps the most direct evidence of pressure was the announcement in November 1964 that (through a civilian organization) the United States would "assist the Federal Ministry of Defense in developing a greater capability in the solution of high-priority military problems through the operations research technique."[7]

Of more consequence than any of these, however, was a quite different factor, the seemingly irresolvable dilemmas of choice posed for Germany by all doctrines regarding the tactical use of nuclear weapons. The German military's basic articles of faith, discussed in chapter 6, had not changed; German officers still believed in the primacy of deterrence; the necessity of "incalculable risk" for the aggressor; the requirement of an "equal," truly dual capability of weapons down to the brigade level; the principle that an extended conventional conflict would be no less "annihilating" for the German people than a nuclear war. Yet the appreciation of the risks involved in implementing these beliefs, observed first among the army leadership in 1962, continued to grow, to suggest the need for private discussion and compromise rather than public argument and rigidity.

The most obvious dilemma has already been discussed briefly; it was the dilemma posed by Bonn's continuing (although now quieter) insistence on three related points: the doctrine of deterring by uncertain risk; the early use of nuclear weapons tactically against any Soviet conventional attack larger than a border probe, and the unavoidability of escalation. Some (but by no means all) military leaders were increasingly aware of the inherent contradictions of this position with respect to existing American reassurances regarding the eventual use of nuclear weapons. On the one hand, the position relied on what most Germans viewed as the decreasingly credible operation of American nuclear deterrence. On the other hand, it posited conditions for use of nuclear weapons which the American government clearly was unwilling to accept and which might lead to a disadvantageous restatement if not reconsideration of the basic American guarantee.

Moreover, what effect would such demands have upon a second major goal, the continued maintenance of the largest possible American military presence on German soil? When equipped with tactical nuclear weapons, six American divisions were not necessary if an immediate and escalatory response was to be automatic in all but the most limited cases. Six divisions were also many more than the number required to contain a border probe, an accident, or an autobahn confrontation.

The American commitments, nuclear and conventional, were all the more vital in view of the dilemmas involved in a third long-standing goal, effective forward defense. On September 1, 1963, after years of constant German pressure, NATO formally acknowledged the demarcation line between the two Germanys as the alliance's first line of defense under the force commitments that had been planned for through 1970. In the German view, this provided at least partial assurance that flexible response could not later be interpreted as obviously sanctioning the conduct of a "fluid defense" on the Federal Republic's territory. For purposes of nuclear deterrence if not actual defense, the allies were not committed to begin resistance at the demarcation line.

According to SHAPE planning, the minimum force necessary for such a defense was the long-discussed thirty divisions, equipped with both conventional and nuclear tactical weapons. Bonn planners again took a less sanguine view. The thirty-division figure was valid only if an immediate use of tactical nuclear weapons was planned. Any serious attempt to mount an extended conventional response to a Soviet conventional attack would require the obviously unattainable goal of thirty-five to forty divisions.

To Bonn, the prospects of implementing even an Elbe to Weser zone defense with thirty divisions seemed as negligible in the future as they were at present. Both Britain and France had vigorously and repeatedly opposed such a decision on doctrinal grounds, their final grudging approval having been gained only in the spring of 1963.[8] Neither of course was willing to provide the necessary additional forces. Britain's Conservative government had long favored a trip-wire posture, especially on economic grounds; the Labour government entering office in October, 1964, was even less willing to maintain a strong conventional capability in Germany.[9] Even payment of the recurring British demands for full troop-cost reimbursement would, in Bonn's assessment, only stabilize, not improve the level of, British Army of the Rhine deployment.

Despite repeated promises, France not only was unready to deploy its limited forces in Germany further eastward toward the border, it also had effectively announced even before its withdrawal from NATO in 1966 that no additional forces would be available for such tasks in the future because of its replacement of universal military training with a selective service system, its emphasis on "territorial defense," and above all its primary reliance on the deterring threat of massive retaliation.[10] After France's withdrawal, in almost a year of tortuous bilateral negotiations an anxious Bonn won only a French promise of "consultation" before changes were made in deployments and a French agreement to some de facto coordination with NATO planning.[11]

This left only the American and German troops as major elements in forward defense, a situation that in the German view made the immediate use of a minimum of battlefield atomic weapons against any significant conventional attack even more urgent. The Americans held another view; there must be a pause, a reliance on an effective conventional response at least until the scope of Communist intentions and commitments became known. The circle was again joined. The Germans still were very critical of American concepts and planning; yet without American involvement there could be no chance for any form of forward defense.

A final, less clearly articulated set of paradoxes centered on the inevitability of uncontrollable escalation once nuclear weapons were introduced. Throughout most of 1961–1962 the German government had emphasized this inevitability as a prime component of deterrence, a view still held by many politicians and military leaders, particularly in the air force. Others, most notably within the army leadership, had challenged this assumption on a number of grounds. Escalation might well proceed in a scalar fashion. The lower ranges might constitute a deterrent against further spiraling; the use of small nuclear weapons in this manner might in fact become necessary, given the mounting costs and political obstacles involved in a conventional-force buildup. Left unanswered, however, were numerous major questions. Might such a strategy allow for the possibility of a limited nuclear war confined to Europe or Germany? How could effective control of such escalation be maintained? Should control rest with the United States alone or be exercised in concert with others?

Much of the development of German strategic thought during 1963–1966, therefore, can be viewed as attempts to resolve or avoid these dilemmas. Without question, these efforts were limited in scope and effectiveness; they often merely offered an exchange of one set of dilemmas for another, and they continued to implicitly accord primacy to deterring by incalculable risk rather than to defense. Yet the efforts represented the first major German attempts at independent analysis and revealed more clearly than ever before the enormity of the problems at stake.

The start admittedly was rather slow-paced. Throughout 1963 the Americans' renewed calls for conventional-force strengthening prompted by their interpretation of the lessons of the Cuban missile crisis met with major opposition from the Germans on economic as well as psychological grounds.[12] Secretary McNamara's contention at the NATO meetings of December 1962, that the traditional roles of the sword and shield forces were now being reversed and that an ability to sustain conventional warfare for ninety days was necessary to cover all possible contingencies, brought forth an outpouring of a Straussian type of criticism from the German delegation. Press commentators, the most visible reflectors of official feelings, vehemently denounced McNamara's supposed belief that "horror should come in stages," that the United States would hereafter refrain from interfering in "local wars" in Europe, that the Germans would permit consignment of themselves to Fussvolk status.[13]

Statements by leading military figures continued to echo the arguments of 1961–1962, prime examples being the interviews conducted by *Die Welt* with the heads of the three services in the spring of 1963.[14] General Werner Panitzki of the air force was the most explicit, declaring in terms not far from those he had used in 1958 that the primary task of the air force was, and would always remain, the delivery of tactical nuclear weapons against the enemy's rear. A major conventional mission was impossible not only because this would be "fatal" for German security but also because Germany could not afford "the necessary number of planes, which would have to be many times the present planning goal, or the required personnel or the required number of airfields." [15]

The public declarations of the new defense minister also gave little portent of change.[16] An example was his declaration to the WEU Assembly:

The notion of graduated deterrence must not lead to a division of that deterrence into various phases nor to a distinction between conventional and nuclear systems of defense. . . . It must be impossible for the potential aggressor to calculate with any reasonable amount of reliability the proportion of risk versus the chance of success of an aggression—especially of minor aggressive action.[17]

Rumors of American troop withdrawals, sparked by the troop-transport exercise, Big Lift, also occasioned a predictable response.[18] The minister praised the technical competence involved and welcomed American reassurances of continued stationing of troops, but warned that such "strategic rotation" could never replace "forces in being" on German soil. "Only strong defensive forces in the . . . Federal Republic will force an enemy determined to wage war into such large and recognizable concentrations that the necessary conclusions—including a [later] "Big Lift"—can be drawn." [19]

The continuity in German strategic thought was most explicitly demonstrated perhaps in the presentations made to Secretary McNamara during his midsummer trip in 1963 to Germany. German officials reportedly proposed that small battlefield nuclear weapons must be used in the immediate "conventional" response against all but the most limited Soviet conventional attacks.[20] Once it was clear that the enemy planned more than a local push, "heavier" tactical nuclear weapons must be employed against his mobilization centers and his axis of march. Given the "operative" requirements of these larger weapons, the decision would have to be reached quickly—in a matter of hours. In both phases the danger of uncontrollable escalation was present, but as von Hassel himself had said, "Escalation is a possible but not . . . a necessary and automatic consequence of the limited employment of nuclear weapons. When both sides are afraid of the process of escalation into all-out war, this fear will counter the very process [as well as being] . . . an essential element of deterrence." [21]

In the midst of these developments, however, there were a few traces of changes, of a new willingness at least to discuss positions previously defined so dogmatically. In his first policy statements von Hassel stressed his intention to strengthen the Territorial Defense Force with 50,000 reservists to be enlisted by 1966—all of whom would be volunteers having previous Bundeswehr service.[22] The defense minister's move was in fact only a reactivation of the plans drawn up in 1957 and foresaw only a partial fulfillment of NATO directives regarding reserves. Yet the new priority accorded to this program, together with the emphasis on reservists rather than on new conscripts, seemed to allow at least some hope for an increase in effective strength of conventional forces.

Similar limited moves included von Hassel's support for long-discussed improvements in the Bundeswehr's effectiveness and for immediate changes to bring a 500,000-man German force up to the American standard of conventional capability.[23] Another point for "further investigation" was the divergent concepts of strategy resulting from the Germans' and Americans' differing assessments of Soviet strength. Strauss and certain of the military leadership had flatly rejected the Pentagon studies done in late 1962 that tried to disprove the "myth" of the Soviets' overwhelming nonnuclear superiority over the West.[24] These results, they argued, merely showed that the Americans or McNamara were tailoring facts to further political aims, to justify troop withdrawals and denuclearization that already had been planned. Von Hassel, however, called for a systematic review of intelligence data and announced in December 1963, with only a degree of exaggeration, that the two estimates were now "very close." [25]

Most interesting of all were the hints contained in official declarations of more differentiated views on use of nuclear weapons. Although he still stressed "incalculable risk" and "early use," von Hassel went much further than his predecessor in acknowledging at least a rudimentary concept of "phasing" or "levels." On more than one occasion the minister spelled out conditions under which "nuclear support" against a conventional attack might be necessary:

If an aggressor attacks with vastly superior forces and tries to gain as much space as possible and as quickly as possible;

When enemy reinforcements brought up to the front cannot be destroyed by any other means;

When the Western tactical nuclear potential is in danger of being lost.[26]

Bonn's stance in the NATO discussions regarding force planning for 1964–1970 was similar.[27] Albeit with reservations and after considerable American prompting, the Federal Republic agreed to draft MC 100/1, which generally provided for the imposition of a pause before a crossing of the nuclear threshold in the event of a conventional attack. Much of this assent was an obvious trade-off for the strong forward-defense provisions of the draft. The intensity of de Gaulle's opposition (forcefully expressed at the council meetings of December 1963) effectively assured Bonn of no final action by NATO. Yet interview comments suggest considerable defense-ministry sentiment in line with von Hassel's comment: "We would like to pass it, but it's not possible without our French friends. Paris unfortunately is not ready to do this." [28]

As 1964 and 1965 progressed, there was evidence of further shifts. The general cause was the continuing discussion within the ministry itself, particularly with respect to the nature of escalation.[29] This debate found its most pronounced expression in the forward-defense studies carried out by the Bundeswehr Command Staff during the spring and summer. According to an account in *Der Spiegel* that is confirmed by interview comments, von Hassel's order for the study specified (once again) that the concept to be sought must permit both the settlement of local probes by conventional forces and the defeat of attacks by superior conventional forces without large territorial loss but also without unnecessary risk of all-out nuclear war.[30]

Additional reinforcement came through the sharpened conflict within NATO concerning the common strategic concept to be adopted for the late 1960s. The principal antagonists were the United States, still stressing the need for a major conventional-force option, and France, now an explicit proponent of deterrence by massive nuclear retaliation. As developed by de Gaulle's chief of staff, General Charles Ailleret, in July, the French concept provided for immediate strategic strikes against the "roots" (Soviet cities and war potential) of any true invasion, with conventional ground forces performing only holding or mopping-up functions against the "tentacles" (invasion forces).[31] The imposition of a pause, the extensive defensive use of tactical nuclear weapons, or a substantial initial resistance at the demarcation line (or perhaps, Bonn extrapolated, even at the Rhine) were neither possible nor desirable.

In light of its political goals as much as for its strategic requirements, the Federal Republic felt its aim must be the development of a middle position.[32] Its strategy must emphasize three paramount concerns: the principle of forward defense, the restoration of the overall credibility of deterrence, and the avoidance of unnecessary destruction to German territory by design or default. And it must propound a strategy which would be implemented at an "acceptable cost," in terms of manpower and military expenditures, in terms of the "political will" of both the European allies and the United States.

The Washington visit of von Hassel and the new inspector general of the Bundeswehr, Heinz Trettner, in November 1964, saw the first detailed presentation of the German initiative. Broadly described, their proposal called for the adoption of a "ladder" or "scale" strategy. Its base was to be a series of "force intervals" determined by military requirements and political considerations rather than the rigid "firebreak" distinctions between the use of all conventional and all nuclear weapons.

More specifically, the German plan foresaw immediate conventional-force resistance at the border against any recognizable Soviet conventional attack. At an early stage limited nuclear means were to be used selectively; in von Hassel's words these should include "atomic demolition mines, nuclear air defense weapons, and, if need be, nuclear battlefield weapons." [33] These would not only help to slow and to channel the attacking forces while avoiding the unfavorable shifts in the balance of territory and forces probable in extended conventional warfare, but also would serve as "a last determined warning . . . [to] the enemy without involving escalation as a consequence." If this attempt at "secondary deterrence" and concomitant diplomatic measures failed, the West itself within days or hours was to begin nuclear escalation. Strategic exchanges would constitute the last, probably inevitable, stage.

American reactions were mixed. Among the services, the army's was the most favorable; in broad outline the German presentation paralleled recent army thinking that had been discussed both in Washington and at SHAPE. Civilian authorities at the Pentagon reportedly were at best quite skeptical. Interviews conducted at that time in Washington with participants from both the State Department and Defense Department indicated that civilians repeatedly stressed the unknown dangers of escalation resulting from the use of even the smallest weapons, the dangers of enemy preemption during the pause, and the problems involved in any Western (let alone German) decision to escalate under the hypothesized conditions.

Publicly, however, emphasis was placed on basic German-American agreement. As the final communiqué stated, "Questions relating to the manner and timing of employment of battlefield and tactical nuclear weapons received close attention. The closest agreement was reached of any recent discussions by ministers related to NATO forward defense." [34] The two governments also agreed to continue regular discussions of these questions not only on the minister–chief of staff level but also through exchanges between "coordinated" study groups focused on specific problems. Four such groups were to be established immediately, one specifically concerned with the uses and effects of battlefield weapons.

Quite unexpectedly the German proposals met with substantial domestic opposition. The cause was not the proposals in themselves, but a garbled account of their content published by Adelbert Weinstein just before a scheduled presentation of the German proposal to the North Atlantic Council meetings of December 1964.[35] Von Hassel and Trettner, he declared, wanted to establish a belt of atomic mines stretching along the zonal border, to be detonated at the first sign of enemy attack, at the probable cost of ten million German lives. Preparations had already been made for the permanent placement of the necessary munitions.

The outcry from German politicians of all parties, from newspaper commentators, and from local officials of border areas was immediate and sustained.[36] The most dramatic charge was that Bonn, after years of denouncing similar East German efforts, now was to have its own "death strip"—an assertion quickly picked up in Soviet propaganda. Government attempts at clarification proceeded slowly and with considerable effort, focusing on three main points. Such a mine belt in continual readiness had never been considered; atomic demolition means (ADMs) were to be used only in certain "noncritical" areas (to block mountain passes, to destroy bridges, or to disrupt lines of transport and communication); in peacetime the munitions always would remain under exclusive American control.[37]

As the months passed, however, public criticism—in fact all public discussion of strategic questions involving NATO—dwindled markedly. No political group, not even the Gaullist wing of the CDU/CSU, was interested in raising such sensitive and dismaying issues in a crucial election year.[38] Within NATO itself, other problems were more pressing: the fate of the MLF, de Gaulle's threat of withdrawal, the possible consequences for American deployments in Europe of America's increasing involvement in Vietnam.

Most of those interviewed in Bonn during 1965 and 1966 subscribed generally to the aims if not the specific form of the von Hassel-Trettner proposals. A somewhat sophisticated summary of the views of a surprising number of military respondents was this comment from a ranking officer:

The basic question for us is timing. We've come a long way since 1961—there's not much serious doubt that the Americans will eventually use nuclear weapons, and Mc-Namara, whatever else he's done, has increased the stockpiles. But it's a question of when—the Americans say "as late as possible"; the French say "as early as possible"; and we say "as early as necessary." The probability of escalation, of course, is the next level down, but no one can answer that with certainty.

Other, more conservative military leaders placed principal emphasis on the continuing strategic debate and the dangers that flexible response posed for German defense, given the clear impossibility of ever reaching the thirty-division goal. All but a very few older or retired officers, however, suggested that some form of agreement was still possible: "The Americans are at least becoming somewhat more realistic. They've stopped talking in terms of "pause" and "threshold" and are beginning to think in terms of what we can do with what we have."

Nonetheless, when specifically pressed, few respondents were willing to consider the German-American differences highlighted by these proposals or the disproportionate risks involved should deterrence—in this case "secondary deterrence"—fail. It was indeed possible that an aggressor would heed the warning, would halt in the face of clear evidence of Western determination to escalate further. But what was to prevent him from taking immediate advantage of his own relatively untouched tactical and strategic nuclear capabilities? What was to ensure a clear reading of the Western signal in the midst of armed conflict? Were there not other, less volatile, less destructive means to convey the same sense of determination? And would not adoption of this strategy lead to the "rigidity or response," so strongly decried during 1961–1962?

Most of the political figures, press commentators, and Foreign Office officials questioned took an optimistic view of the strategic discord. Total agreement had not been reached; neither the Americans nor the French yet understood the absolute necessity for Germany of an effective forward defense. But the remaining differences could be worked out only over time and in close and continuing consultation; the presentation of a "middle" proposal would help ease these divisions.

A few in this group went further. Debates about strategy had assumed the character of scholastic theological exercises; they were arguments, in the words of one respondent, "over the sex of angels." The continuing discussion and the exchanges of the joint study groups had led to a significant narrowing of previous differences. What was left was the "theoretically unresolvable"—questions of "Western timing, Soviet reinforcement capability, defining the firebreak, and the risks of escalation."

Even the most skeptical of the respondents, however, preferred not to examine too closely the obvious limits involved in a middle approach. The von Hassel-Trettner proposal clearly did incorporate, as Nerlich states, "elements of the American doctrine of flexibility and the French preference for early selective strikes against Soviet targets." [39] But did this combining make this proposal anything more than an uncertain melange, touching the symbols but not the essence of both positions? Was not a middle position between two such stands, based on radically different considerations, likely to prove unacceptable to the holders of both stands? And in more basic terms, even if it were not too serious an attempt, would the position be anything more than a rather inadequate political fig leaf for the balancing of the French against the Americans?

It was indeed the increasing conviction of this group that a lasting answer for Germany was not to be found in further public debate or in the promulgation of new strategic plans dependent on the agreement of "everyone else." German security goals could only be met, they argued, through assured control over the decisions that actually would be made. In Europe, such control must apply to decisions regarding the targeting and use or nonuse of tactical nuclear weapons; in the alliance as a whole, it must apply to the total scope of nuclear planning, whether with or without an MLF.

Two events in 1966 rallied more of the leadership to this position, albeit more from anxiety and frustration than because of any sudden enthusiasm. [40] The first event was de Gaulle's long-feared withdrawal of France from NATO, though it remained a member of the Atlantic alliance. For Bonn this both lessened the need for constant balancing efforts and further heightened the urgency of early use of tactical nuclear weapons to ensure forward defense. The second event was the simultaneous American offer for a de facto renewal of the alliance that would create "new opportunities" and allow broader participation in nuclear planning and control. Germany was offered a major role, first in the McNamara Committee (also called the Special Committee) and its working group on nuclear planning, and then in the permanent Nuclear Planning Group (NPG).

Official statements of support were guarded, in part because of the conspicuous failure of McNamara's earlier consultation schemes as proposed (with equal fanfare) at Athens in 1962. More immediately threatening was Washington's clear intention to substitute the consultative approach for the MLF or hardware scheme, now moribund but still an official German foreign-policy goal. Erhard, Schröder, and von Hassel carefully emphasized their view that any such planning group was a complement to rather than a substitue for an integrated force and that it should be a truly executive body without approaching the type of "global directorate" proposed by de Gaulle in 1958.[41]

Most of the German political and military leaders interviewed contemporaneously favored a wait-and-see attitude, a delay until the specific details of greater information-sharing, planning participation, and consultation were clear. Some saw the suggestions only as a tentative effort "to avoid a vacuum"; others saw them as a "rubber proposal," a tactical move primarily designed to sound out the French but from which anything could result. A few declared the suggestions to be an American end run to defuse the Soviets' constant reiteration that "the MLF gift to the revanchist Germans" was the principal obstacle to serious negotiations for a nonproliferation agreement. But almost all respondents suggested that they shared the views of one prominent SPD defense expert, who said: "It's probably worth a chance. Maybe it will be just another exercise in soul massage and numbers. And there'll probably be more talk papering over the real difference. But we'll at least be there, and that's as important as the theoretical results."

The only explicit opposition came from German Gaullists who saw the consultative-committee proposals as simply one more scheme pushed by an unreliable Washington that was unwilling to grant true partnership and was rapidly disengaging from Europe.[42] The only solution, Adenauer and especially Strauss repeatedly asserted, lay in a European defense union, with joint Franco-British control of nuclear forces and an "appropriate" role for Germany. What specific form that role would assume, however, would have to await future events, including an innovative German effort freed from American domination.

In sum, between 1963 and 1966 there was an extension of earlier strategic debates, with an even more inconclusive outcome. The mood was quieter and more reasonable; the divergent viewpoints were somewhat closer; the opportunities for developing German positions were more numerous and more demanding of analytic sophistication. But the reassurance available under a basic German-American agreement not to disagree was limited and ever vulnerable to political change.

DEBATES ABOUT ARMAMENT

German policy toward the acquisition of nuclear-capable armament during 1963–1966 on its face was merely an extension of past procurement decisions.[43] During his first trip to Washington in February 1963, von Hassel forcefully reaffirmed the American keynote set down in the earlier Strauss-Gilpatric agreements: "The Federal Republic will continue, as in the past, to make major purchases of military equipment, supplies, and services from the United States. These purchases have been largely responsible for offsetting U.S. defense expenditures in Germany."[44]

At stake was the 1961 fixing of interests mutually perceived as converging: America's interest in solving its balance-of-payments problem and Germany's concern for continued deployment of American troops in Europe and the rapid, equal armament of its forces. In 1963 Germany agreed not only to make its major arms purchases from American sources but also to contract (at relatively bargain prices) for American support and maintenance systems, provision of training sites and services, and sharing of basic research and development costs in particular areas. Within this framework Washington promised to resist financially oriented pressures for force withdrawals and to fulfill past and present promises concerning provisions of nuclear delivery vehicles for the Bundeswehr.

In the 1963 context this renewal of the pledge effectively precluded—to the relief of some officials in Washington—any significant efforts, conventional or nuclear, toward the newly proclaimed Franco-German military cooperation. As discussed above, the treaty of January 22 foresaw the expansion of joint research-and-development activities and of renewed attempts toward common production and financing. These, in the view of several respondents, were areas of special interest to France, already burdened by the heavy economic requirements of the *force de frappe* and less than pleased with its 11 percent share of Germany's foreign armament purchases during 1956–1960.[45]

As 1963 progressed, however, the underdeveloped operational state of Franco-German cooperation rendered von Hassel's Atlanticist assertion relatively meaningless. The only bilateral effort of significance was the Transall transport project begun in 1959. The program which had attracted the most attention and promised the greatest financial rewards—the development of a European battle tank—was all but officially dead. In fact, even before his visit to the United States, von Hassel had announced that he soon would recommend series production of the German prototype, the Leopard, whatever France's final decision.[46]

Indeed, one of the first new German-American projects announced in August 1963 was a joint study of follow-on tank development for the 1970s.[47] Of particular importance was to be consideration of the "newest developments" regarding firepower, maneuverability, and protection. Other agreements concerned the formulation and implementation of an integrated system of logistics, new armament purchases, and the joint development of a vertical take-off strike aircraft. Total German purchases were to reach a level of approximately $1.3 billion for 1964–1965, of which the Main Battle Tank program would account for at least $200 million.

How these funds should be divided between conventional and nuclear-capable equipment, however, was a source of continuing friction. One of the easier cases was German procurement of three long-promised guided-missile destroyers.[48] After formal WEU approval was received for German ships up to 6,000 tons, the Federal Republic let contracts for such ships in the United States, retaining the option of eventual production under license in German shipyards. According to later announcements in December 1963 and in May 1964 each ship was to require about four years for construction at a cost of around $50 million.

Two procurement requests for nuclear weapons required longer, more complicated discussion and negotiation. The first concerned Germany's considerable interest in purchasing an improved Pershing missile with a range of up to 700 miles, as well as the long-promised standard model with a 300 + mile range.[49] According to press reports and certain interview sources, officials in Washington and particularly in London consistently had opposed Germany's acquisition of additional, nonessential "strategic capability." After considerable discussion and the Germans' persistent assertion of their air-force requirements, however, an option to purchase was finally assured during the von Hassel-McNamara talks in November 1964.

A less successful campaign was directed toward purchase of the long-awaited Davy Crockett weapon. By early 1965 those interviewed in Bonn were convinced that no hope for any purchases of this type remained. Senator Goldwater's 1964 campaign proposals that the use of such small "conventional nuclear weapons" was and should be subject only to SACEUR's discretion had called forth renewed administration emphasis on the president's exclusive responsibility for control.[50] All control arrangements and deployed weapon systems were to be reexamined to assure constant, secure exercise of his rights. The obvious implication was that since the Davy Crockett was subject to permissive link control only before its issuance to the three-man operational crews, it must be considered a danger to continuous centralized control.

There were many more private indications of American intentions, the most telling being the shift in the position of American army officers on the Germans' need for this weapon. Although still Davy Crockett partisans, ranking officers in Washington and Europe had begun to accept some of the counterarguments advanced by McNamara's office. Modern conventional artillery, it was stated, would provide far more effective and accurate firepower in a greater range of situations. Accordingly, the Davy Crockett was to be progressively withdrawn from front-line deployment.[51]

Disagreement and disappointment among both the German and American military led in early 1965 to a spate of articles denouncing such action as the first step toward the tactical denuclearization first of the forward positions and then of all Europe.[52] Secretary McNamara quickly denied the existence of such plans and stated that the level of tactical nuclear-weapon stocks in Europe was now "100 percent higher" than in 1961.[53] In mid-November he was still more specific, declaring that there were now more than 5,000 warheads stored in Europe, with a 20 percent increase over the last six months alone. Announcement of these figures, however, did little to alleviate the considerable sensitivity in Bonn concerning the American denial of the Davy Crockett.

The ongoing Starfighter program evidenced similar tensions between American pressures for increased conventional strength and German interests in maintaining their nuclear-capable armament. Under the plans formulated in the late 1950s the primary function of more than half of the German F-104s was participation in NATO's nuclear-strike plan.[54] Almost as soon as the first Starfighters became operational in 1962—and increasingly throughout 1964 and 1965—Washington pressed for rapid conversion to true dual-capable status in order to increase NATO's capability for early non-nuclear interdiction missions against a Soviet conventional attack. According to several military respondents, the number of converted squadrons was to be four, all of which could be reconverted for nuclear missions.

The response was continued German opposition and criticism. Air-force officials repeatedly questioned the strategic implications involved. Their key argument ran: once such a commitment to conventional missions was made, any attrition of forces would markedly decrease Western capabilities for a swift nuclear response, should the aggressor or the West decide to escalate. In the words of one air-force respondent, "To do what McNamara wants, we need at least 6,000 tactical aircraft, not the 3,000 or so we have now. And that impossible figure might still not be enough for both missions."

Other officers interviewed stressed the many past and present difficulties involved in preparing and maintaining the Starfighters at operational readiness. Insistence now on a conventional capability would create only one more obstacle for an already beleaguered program. One civil servant interviewed in early 1966 sounded a particularly dramatic but somewhat inconsistent note: "Doesn't he [McNamara] realize they're falling out of the sky at a rate of approximately one a month and that we're lucky if more than one-third are combat ready at any one time? And now even these aren't to fulfill the mission they were designed for." [55]

These, however, were not the only German armament dilemmas in an era of dipping German growth rates. During 1963–1966 there was ever widening domestic criticism regarding the aims and implementation of armament programs. A prime example was the Starfighter criticism, focused on the extensive supplementary costs paid to the American contractor, the continuing technical difficulties, and the mounting number of unexplained crashes (twenty-six in 1965.) [56] Other major targets included failures in submarine construction and in production of armored personnel carriers.

In some respects this criticism was simply another reflection of the

Atlanticist-Gaullist split and the increasingly bitter jabs and "campaigns of embarrassment" involved. Yet there was also a new note of concern for greater rationalization and economy in armament planning. Critics of the government's efforts pointed to the enormous sums that had been wasted. Not only had the administration of particular projects been woefully deficient but also the types of purchase made seemed to have had little relation to the military role or capabilities of the Federal Republic. Some respondents spoke of the propensity to choose "the most expensive new toys," of the continuing desire of some officials within the Defense Ministry to try to enter the forbidden nuclear territory by the back door. Others criticized the ministry's tendency toward unquestioning acceptance of "whatever the Americans are trying to unload." As one ranking technician expressed it, "The Americans are playing a dangerous double game. On the one hand, they keep telling us to rationalize our planning. On the other, they offer us what is either essentially good for their balance of payments or little more than obsolescent junk.

Although similarly critical, some government supporters pressed a somewhat different argument. Armament costs were but one of the financial burdens the Federal Republic must bear in the interests of security; a population that was prosperous and thus more secure against Communist subversion was at least equally important. In a period of economic slowdown, they argued, Germany must pursue a carefully balanced financial course, postponing all but essential expenditures. The Western allies could not expect Germany to sustain, let alone increase, the level of its past burden-sharing efforts for an indefinite period.

Opinion divided as to where the necessary cuts should be made. Some circles emphasized the impossibility of pursuing so many diverse projects at once: tank development, conventional-force modernization, territorial defense, and naval construction. The few defense-policy intellectuals outside the government who were interviewed talked in terms of conventional-nuclear trade-offs. A published comment represented their feelings:

Given the actual costs [of the MLF] . . . in which the Federal Republic will have to pay the lion's share, it must be realized that sooner or later the present twelve divisions . . . will have to be reduced to ten or eight, because both—atomic and conventional armament—simply cannot be paid for.[57]

The Erhard government's response was relatively weak, emphasizing primarily that things would be different in the future.[58] As the economic situation worsened and the political splits within the cabinet widened, there was an accelerated drive toward economy, shown by these figures for Bundeswehr materiel purchases: [59]

Fiscal Year	Millions of Marks
1962	7,866
1963	9,312
1964	8,548
1965	7,294
1966	6,203
1967	7,813

Within the Defense Ministry, notice reportedly was served that any new production proposals or armament purchases would undergo the closest scrutiny and might meet with considerable delay.

A second result of the drive for economy was self-generated pressures on the government from all the political parties and the business community to reduce the level of troop-offset purchases from the United States.[60] It was not that the presence of American troops was any less essential or that Germany should not make some fair return for the costs involved. Rather, it was a growing realization, in the words of one government leader, that

every hair on every American head in Germany is not so valuable that we must pay any necessary price to keep it here. The Americans are here in our interest but also in their own interest. We have to recognize their balance-of-payments problems, but they have to think about what an economic recession means to Germany. We just can't sustain this level of military spending abroad.

Opinion within the military leadership was more restrained in public expression but equally critical in tone. Ranking officers made no attempt to conceal their displeasure over aggressive American salesmanship or, especially, over persistent Washington efforts to define independently the "primary needs" of the Bundeswehr. There was constant pressure for large new conventional-weapons purchases despite leveling off of Bundeswehr growth and still-unanswered German requests for nuclear-capable arms or joint development projects. In the view of the officers, these developments made rational spending of the $500–$600 million pledged annually for offset purchases in the United States impossible. And funds committed abroad could not be spent for more pressing Bundeswehr requirements at home.

Left virtually unconsidered in the growing Bonn acrimony were not only the past value of such arrangements but also a series of questions of greater significance for the future. Without doubt, in terms of its self-defined political and military aims the Federal Republic had a significant stake in the continuation of a dual-armament policy. Even if German leaders had unquestionably supported a major conventional capability, tactical nuclear weapons were in essence the badge of equality, the mark of a major NATO partner. Given German strategic views, they were one more indication that the necessary capability would be at hand and that national opinions concerning their use would be heard and given appropriate weight.

Nonetheless, some choices had to be made. Even the richest alliance partner had to judge the relative trade-offs between nuclear- and conventional-weapons purchases, had to deal with the problems caused by the relatively high obsolescence rate of sophisticated weapons systems. The economic resources of Germany were considerable, even with a declining growth rate. But how much longer could Bonn pursue a hit-or-miss procurement program, attempt to cover a wide arms spectrum, afford to keep buying into the next technological stage? The Erhard regime was considering an "absolute ceiling" of 20 billion DM annually for all defense costs. Under such a limitation would the creation of "credible forces" at every level be the same as the achievement of maximum effectiveness, or even of overall credibility?

But these were questions neither well articulated nor often considered in Bonn, which by then was convinced of at least some American exploitation and was visibly anxious about the failure of Erhard either to stem constant conflicts within the cabinet or to mitigate a deepening financial crisis. Unfortunately for the unhappy chancellor, these events coincided with Washington's decision that it needed increased arms sales to offset troop costs.[61] The strain of the Vietnam war on American troop deployments, especially in Europe, America's increasingly difficult balance-of-payments position, and Congress's increasing calls for a reappraisal of the American contribution to NATO led to an even stronger, more explicit bond between offset purchases and a continued American presence (of any magnitude) in Germany.[62] Meetings between German and American leaders were marked by new tensions and acrimony. The exploration of possible alternatives—joint space ventures, the earlier MRBM project, offsetting monetary arrangements, even a limited revival of the MLF—not only proved fruitless, but also further exacerbated relations by emphasizing earlier American defaults and German strategic imperatives.

In the fall of 1966 the final act was staged in Washington.[63] During his September visit to President Johnson—his third within a year—chancellor Erhard reiterated Germany's unwillingness to continue previous levels of arms purchases and proposed two alternatives: a short-term moratorium on buying and a longer-term arrangement for offsetting troop costs through monetary cooperation. Johnson was sympathetic but firm; Erhard's only achievement was a promise for extensive study with the British on future arrangements. Erhard returned home to face the long-expected gathering of his enemies, who were many. These included, to cite only the most prominent: the Gaullists; the right wing of the CDU, irritated by America's denial of the MLF and its clear preference for superpower détente in Europe through a nonproliferation treaty; those disappointed with Erhard's "political flabbiness" and failure as an "electoral engine" for his party; and members of all parties alarmed by the unchecked financial recession.[64] On October 27, 1966, the junior coalition partner, the FDP, resigned, precipitating Erhard's inevitable fall and the ushering in of the Grand Coalition and a new era in postwar German politics.

NINE

Germany
& the MLF;
the Upward Wave:
1963-1964

✠ On January 14, 1963, an "especially positive conversation" took place in Bonn between Chancellor Konrad Adenauer and Under Secretary of State and special envoy George Ball. The subject was creation of an alliance nuclear force, christened MLF and most recently put forward after the Anglo-American talks in Nassau during the preceding December. The result of the Bonn conversation was a declaration by the Germans that, as Adenauer later expressed it,

we view the Nassau agreement as a great step toward the creation of an effective NATO multilateral nuclear deterrence force. President Kennedy, through Under Secretary Ball, has informed us of his views. We have decided to cooperate in the realization of these plans.[1]

This commitment was to remain the touchstone of official German policy toward the alliance for nearly three years. As chapter 8 shows, the MLF project by no means involved the total universe of German concerns about nuclear control, especially the desires for increased participation in tactical nuclear-weapons arrangements and in NATO's military structure as a whole. But the MLF came increasingly to be the primary focus of attention, the standard against which other possibilities were to be measured, the proposal for which alternatives or supplements must be found.

As others have documented well, this development was the product as much of deliberations in Washington as in Bonn.[2] A direct but more successful descendent of the Bowie-Herter concept of December 1960, the MLF became by the autumn of 1964 the prime benchmark for all American policies toward Europe. Its proponents—skillful, commited officials, known colloquially as "the theologians" or "the cabal"—had successfully vanquished numerous national and international opponents and won the tacit approval of two presidents. The MLF's swift demise, after President Johnson's approval was explicitly withdrawn in December 1964, only pointed up the dazzling skill and speed with which its supporters had pushed this proposal to the top of Washington's hierarchy of goals.

In their missions of persuasion the traveling MLF advocates emphasized multiple and not always congruent justifications for the force: greater intergration and consultation within the Atlantic alliance, fulfillment of Norstad's MRBM requirement, a first move toward nuclear nonproliferation, revision of NATO's political structures, a future home for the British and French national nuclear forces, to list only a few. But the major selling point was always that without a tangible collective framework like the MLF, eventual development of a German national nuclear force was inevitable. No other arrangement, from shared planning to a loose union of national forces, would suffice, because, in the formulation of Robert Bowie,

the German leaders have repeatedly stated that the Federal Republic cannot indefinitely accept a second class status or discrimination. . . . Over the long pull, the 1954 WEU limitation can hardly keep Germany from demanding equal nuclear status with the United Kingdom and France. If Germany is not treated as an equal the discrimination will produce friction and discord. Aversion to a German national nuclear force would create tensions and cleavages within the alliance which the Soviets would certainly exploit. In either case the unity of the alliance would be seriously impaired.[3]

The constancy of German commitment to a project explicitly pressed as anticipating and therefore frustrating dark German desires appears at first glance somewhat paradoxical. In many respects Bonn's support for the MLF was simply the result of factors sketched in earlier chapters. With respect to the international context, the events of 1963–1966 concerning the MLF provide further proof of these seemingly endemic problems: misperception in intra-alliance communication; the Germans' hypersensitive reactions to unforeseen developments and their recurring demands for American reassurance; the implicit yet continual competition between Bonn and London for positions deemed to provide assets in Washington; Germany's relatively static cold-war conceptions of Soviet interests and intentions.

One can find similar elements of continuity in the operation of Bonn's decision-making process regarding the MLF. Once again, the broad issues of foreign policy provided the principal stuff of national politics; once again, there appeared a propensity to take option-limiting actions while decrying the limited freedom of maneuver Germany enjoyed. As before, policies tended to be personalized; the military took a somewhat diffident role in advising on "political" decisions; general public opinion, despite determined Gaullist efforts toward sound and fury, remained relatively indifferent if not untouched by the debate among the elites.

None of these points, however, touches on what has been described in all of the MLF accounts as the central question: what was the major causal factor in this confusing experience? The most widespread and contradictory assertions have focused on the MLF as a near disaster—in itself an unnecessary, inadequate, and irrelevant approach to the problem of sharing nuclear weapons within the alliance. The most prevalent interpretation is that unrelenting American pressure resulting from desires to stop nuclear proliferation kept the MLF and German interest in it afloat, and thus the seeking of antinuclear innoculation actually spread the infection. More often heard among officials then in Washington is a quite different argument: that the principal stimulus was constant German demands on the United States, outstripping even those anticipated by Professor Bowie, which, had the multilateral force been created, would have been only temporarily satisfied.

A somewhat different formulation is that the MLF discussions, more than any of the developments previously examined, had to thrust Bonn into the dilemmas of choice in nuclear affairs. First, what type of participation in arrangements for control was the most feasible or effective solution, short of the national development of nuclear weapons that was prohibited de jure and short of the independent possession of nuclear weapons that was under de facto restriction? What degree of continuing discrimination must be assumed in the face of America's currently restrictive policies in sharing weapons? Or was there no solution valid for the moment or workable in the future?

Second, what degree of balancing was required by Germany's simultaneous commitment to the three basic goals of reunification, European integration, and Atlantic security? What role would an MLF with a major German contribution to it play in fostering Atlantic solidarity? Would such participation preclude or enhance the achievement on Germany's terms of one or both of the other aims?

To lay the groundwork for consideration of these points, the often told history of the MLF is told again, but this time for the purpose of illuminating the German perspective. The analysis in this chapter and the next centers on the five stages in the German decision-making process and discusses the principal stimuli and procedural constraints, the varying attitudes and stakes of the chief actors, and German reactions to and interpretations of American, French, and British decisions. A final commentary attempts to summarize the very different "German lessons" learned from the MLF experience by the Germans on the one hand, and by American decision-makers on the other hand. Consideration of the lessons which should have been learned is left largely to chapter 11.

STAGE ONE: CAUTIOUS COMMITMENT

The conversations of January 14, 1963, of course did not mark Germany's first introduction to the MLF or Germany's first expression of interest in the creation of such a force. As was discussed in chapter 7, the German political leadership had become aware of the MLF proposal in the troubled weeks before and just after the North Atlantic Council's Athens meeting in May 1962, and on the whole had not been overwhelmingly enthusiastic. The intervening months had seen no major positive shift in German attitudes toward the force concept itself; the circumstances of the *Spiegel* affair, Strauss's departure from the Defense Ministry, and the tortuous building of Adenauer's fifth government (committed to serve no longer than one year) were sufficient to preclude extensive discussion or study. Moreover, neither the course of the December council meetings nor the somewhat contradictory reports of the Nassau discussions had evidenced any significant changes in the American MLF proposal or in responses to earlier German reservations.[4] The chancellor's unequivocal commitment was a direct response to the coincidence of four sudden developments during late December and early January.

Most foreign commentators and many of those interviewed attribute primary importance to the imminent conclusion of the treaty for Franco-German cooperation. This agreement, negotiated during the autumn, had assumed, for Adenauer at least, a far stronger anti-Atlantic or anti-American character than was originally intended. The virtual coincidence of the treaty's announcement with de Gaulle's dramatic rejection of Britain's application for EEC membership further heightened the isolationist-Europe or third-force-Europe thrust of increased Franco-German political, economic, and military cooperation. Despite continuing reservations, Adenauer purportedly intended the MLF pledge both to allay American fears of a hostile (and perhaps nuclear) enclave in Europe and to demonstrate Germany's unwillingness—whatever de Gaulle's intentions—to choose between French friendship and the American guarantee.

Clearly this coincidence of announcements was the proximate cause for the timing of the American proposal for an MLF and a point of major significance in the Bonn context. Adenauer is reliably reported to have been informed of the general thrust if not the exact content of de Gaulle's press-conference remarks about Britain and the EEC by the first days of January. The chancellor, moreover, had been made aware of America's concern about support for British entry as well as about the developing Franco-German entente that might lead to an "exclusionist Europe." [5] To both the chancellor and his advisors Ball's visit presented a dramatic opportunity for a balancing statement. There was no significant objection, after all, to the concept of an MLF; such a force promised at least a possible control-sharing formula, with possibilities for future evolution. The specific details, problems, and relation to other German concerns could be left—as in the early rearmament negotiations—to later discussions and bargaining.

Too much attention to these considerations, however, tends to obscure the importance of several other factors. Adenauer was concerned with striking a balance not only between Germany's foreign-policy goals but also between factions within his government. [6] The most clearly defined group whose objections had to be overcome were the Atlanticists, led by the heirs apparent, Ludwig Erhard and Gerhard Schröder. Waiting in the wings was a new Atlanticist, Kai-Uwe von Hassel, slated to become defense minister in mid-January. [7] In the preparations for assuming his new office, von Hassel had shown substantial interest in the MLF project. Some observers in Bonn had attributed this, rather facetiously, to his North German–maritime orientation. Other, more serious observers viewed his interest as an attempt by a politically ambitious "new boy"—about to take over a suicidal job, but perhaps only for a trial period—to espouse a project that would clearly bear his mark.

Further, the chancellor reportedly was uncertain whether he could gain substantial support even within his own party for a swift conclusion of the

Franco-German pact once de Gaulle's decisions were known. Subsequent events validated his fears. On January 18, representatives of all Bundestag parties met with Adenauer to ask him to delay his trip to Paris (the SPD's request) or to press de Gaulle to reconsider Britain's EEC application (the request of the CDU/CSU and FDP). There were also hints that if the chancellor did not do so, the Bundestag itself would take later action to prevent "misinterpretation" of the treaty's portent for Germany's Atlantic relations.[8]

Any suggestion that Adenauer believed participation in an MLF to be a major demand of any one of these parties is not valid. Most members were only dimly aware of the existence of the American proposal; even Erhard and Schröder had expressed only general support for the project. All of these discussions of balancing took place in the tense and somewhat confused post-Nassau environment.[9] The content, let alone the outcome, of the Anglo-American talks had taken the crisis-ridden fourth Adenauer government virtually by surprise, as indeed was true of most of the smaller allies. Kennedy's letter to Adenauer informing him of the offers of Polaris missiles made to Britain and France and calling his attention particularly to the provisions in the Nassau accords for multinational and/or multilateral NATO forces was essentially the first "hard information Bonn received."[10]

The initial German reaction was characteristically one of reserve, anxiety, and suspicion. To Adenauer but also to many others in the German elites, the Nassau offers bore at the very least the seeds of the NATO nuclear triumvirate proposed by de Gaulle in 1958 and still a tempting prospect for many of the French elites.[11] Under the vaguely worded communiqué, Germany and other nuclear have-nots still might participate in a multinational or multilateral force or in both. But American and British statements conveyed neither any precise impression of the proposed character of control of such forces nor any sense of commitment or agreement to the immediate implementation of either scheme. Moreover, would not a full execution of the Nassau plans formally establish two classes of alliance membership, consigning Germany to the long-feared Fussvolk status?

Indeed, by the time of Ball's visit these fears, rather than concern about French action and reaction, were paramount in Bonn. In the opposition as within the government the principal problem had become the safeguarding of German options, particularly against British efforts to preserve the revived special relationship and the continuance of its national control through creation of only a *multinational* force within NATO. An early expression of

German interest in the MLF might provide the necessary stimulus for immediate discussions regarding an integrated force, clearly preferred by the Americans, even if certain basic points remained open. Moreover, the Federal Republic thus would have guaranteed itself from the outset an equal voice in negotiations concerning the possible form or control of such forces and in any consideration of possible alternatives. "Whatever the final outcome on co-ownership (*Mitbesitz*)," one Foreign Office official declared in an interview, "we felt sure that we would gain at least one more bulwark for our demands regarding codetermination rights (*Mitspracherecht*) in alliance planning."

Less publicly visible was a third factor influencing German calculations: fears concerning the possible course of Soviet-American relations after the Cuban missile crisis. There were some immediate grounds for concern, namely, Kennedy's remarks in November 1962 to Adenauer concerning his hopes for "new momentum" in arms control negotiations and Secretary Rusk's general observations to the December North Atlantic Council meeting about "capitalizing on the lessons of Cuba." For an already suspicious chancellor, these comments were sufficient to revive the anxieties of 1961 and 1962 about wide-reaching settlements in Europe that might be negotiated without prior consultation and might sacrifice vital German interests. Interview accounts also suggest that although all previous difficulties had been smoothed over publicly, the chancellor was now convinced that Kennedy would never listen seriously to any expression of German interest or anxiety.

From several perspectives German involvement in an MLF seemed to promise a hedge against such developments. If nothing else, such a structure would force more regular consultation by America with its partners. Continuous German participation in planning for the MLF and "related forces" would also militate against any sudden American force withdrawals or thinouts. Finally, full membership in a common nuclear force would not only provide a new bargaining lever for reunification negotiations, it would also make a denuclearization of Germany without its consent virtually impossible.

STAGE TWO: THE WARMING TREND

During the weeks that followed January 14 the MLF remained the subject of continuing, often confused and confusing discussions in Bonn. The terms of public debate were relatively unspecific, the primary focus being only the broad significance of German participation. Responses by the government in these debates were phrased as usual in general, reassuring terms. Adenauer declared that German participation involved no question of choice politically or militarily, that it was based only on desires "to share full responsibility" and "to make . . . war . . . impossible." [12] Only Defense Minister von Hassel mentioned military requirements, declaring that the force would represent a "considerable reinforcement of the atomic defense power of NATO in Europe." [13]

In private, nonetheless, intragovernmental debate on the many "technical" problems involved in the MLF proposal ebbed and flowed. In a letter to Kennedy and in his conversations with Ball, Adenauer had made clear that full German satisfaction would depend on the successful resolution of a number of objections. Ball reportedly reassured him on three counts: the MLF was not designed to facilitate an eventual denuclearization of Europe; it would assure an "equal" German role, perhaps as a member of a five-nation "executive control committee"; it eventually would be placed under SACEUR's rather than SACLANT's command. [14] Still unresolved, however, were a number of major points: the questionable choice of surface vessels over submarines, the unnecessary complexity of the mixed-manning formula, the future status of the American veto, and the plans to go beyond the MLF's 200 missiles to provide deterrence against Russia's 700–800 MRBMs.

As spring neared, the course of both private and public debate was significantly affected by what the Adenauer government perceived as hardening of American policy on the MLF. Perhaps the first sign taken seriously was the creation in late January of a special MLF task force, headed by special Ambassador Livingston Merchant, to assist NATO Ambassador Thomas Finletter in the presentation and negotiation of American proposals. [15] Bonn's embassy in Washington also reported that President Kennedy purportedly had ordered a speedup in MLF planning as a matter of the "highest priority."

Considerable evidence suggested that a concerted push to launch the MLF was in the offing. For several months, most officials in Washington reportedly had viewed the alliances's primary problem as the need to give new public stimulus to Kennedy's Grand Design, to create a new symbol of the NATO unity so brutally rejected by de Gaulle. Clearly, most MLF proponents argued, the force as proposed would be militarily superfluous. [16] Yet creation of such a force would provide a dramatic riposte to those Gaullist arguments that seemed to justify national nuclear development for all. It would demonstrate to all the allies, but particularly to Germany, that an effective solution to the problems of common control could be found, that a start could be made toward eventual European-American partnership.

In this general environment, a number of accounts indicate, the influence of the MLF's ardent State Department supporters increased.[17] Now possessing a bureaucratic foothold and limited presidential approval to brandish before their Pentagon critics, they vigorously sought to build support both at home and abroad, using a variety of complex, often contradictory arguments. Still central, however, was their commitment to Atlantic partnership and their perception of eventual difficulties with Germany if this was not soon achieved. Their arguments emphasized that under existing conditions within the alliance Bonn's moderate leadership would find itself under increasingly irresistible pressure to seek, first, the unattainable national control of nuclear weapons, and then full nuclear production—alone or under the Franco-German treaty. Immediate all-out support for the MLF therefore was needed to capitalize on the German interest in this force, on Bonn's willingness at the time to accept binding "integrative safeguards" against diversion of weapons or independent actions.

From a safe postdictive perspective, however, it seems clear that a skilled neutral observer of Washington infighting might have spotted major areas of softness if not opposition. The president himself, at his press conferences in February and March, took great pains to express the "tentative" and "exploratory" nature of the American proposal. There were many difficult problems which would have to be resolved;[18] the Europeans might well decide that some other arrangement was less costly yet equally beneficial;[19] the MLF was a good proposal but not "essential to the security of the United States."[20] Although relatively silent during this period, presidential national-security advisor McGeorge Bundy and Secretary of Defense McNamara reportedly held similar views. And the predictable sources of congressional opposition to any nuclear-sharing proposal, the JCAE and liberal members of the Senate, apparently had not been consulted.

The official German perspective encompassed none of these doubts; the American position was interpreted as being quite fixed. Beyond discussions ongoing within NATO, strong evidence seemingly was gathered from the constant round of German-American visits touching upon MLF problems that went on throughout the February–June period. A rough tally culled from press and interview sources suggests that at least nine high-ranking American officials—almost all supporters of the MLF—came to Bonn, while at least five Germans—the most prominent being Defense Minister von Hassel—visited Washington. American acitivity included both the numerous conversations of individual high-status emissaries and the extensive efforts of two "technical briefing" groups—the Merchant mission in March and that led by Admiral Claude Ricketts in April.[21] Further technical information was provided through a Washington conference of German and American naval experts.

Within this framework a shift in the official German position was highly predictable; by early May almost all official reservations to the MFL proposals apparently had been withdrawn. Adenauer, it was reliably reported, had given "full approval" to all aspects, including a secret formula for control and staffing.[22] Von Hassel's statements during the military-budget debate in the Bundestag and later to the WEU Assembly were more revealing.[23] The minister in particular recalled the history of Norstad's land-based MRBM requirement and reaffirmed continuing German support for this demand. But, he declared, "at present, it is rather pointless to argue about the matter since there are as yet no [such] MRBMs . . . and if there were . . . there would be an immediate political strife with the communities near which the . . . missiles would be emplaced." [24]

Although von Hassel reiterated his stand on an eventual change in voting procedures, the tone and structure of his arguments seemed to indicate yet another shift. Clearly, the United States could not at present give up its insistence on unanimous agreement. What must be sought was rather "some [other] kind of construction" for the future. This would not only "maintain the effectiveness of deterrence," but also provide an incentive for French reconsideration "once a certain point in development was reached."

All these public endorsements tended to obscure the continuing skepticism if not direct opposition within the government leadership. Schröder, von Hassel, and to a lesser extent Erhard were the only constant supporters of the MLF in the cabinet, and although they would almost certainly lead the new government, they did not yet enjoy decisive influence. Most of the other members supported the basic concept of a new physical bond with the United States, the need for a balancing of French and American ties, and the opportunity for a major German role. But at best they expressed only a tolerant acceptance of the specific characteristics of the MLF itself, of the arguments why such a costly effort should be mounted.

There are a number of indications that Adenauer himself held a similar view. Interviews, as well as contemporary press accounts, emphasized his continuing doubts. The chancellor not only declared that the MLF did not represent a "final stage" in Atlantic development but also reportedly questioned "whether the United States had purposely made the MLF difficult to accept." [25] As one official then in the Chancellor's office observed,

Adenauer never really seemed to understand what the MLF was all about. He heard all the arguments, raised the same objections over and over again, and then gave his consent. Unlike von Hassel, he never went into "fire and flames" over the thing, and right up to the end he remained suspicious about American willingness to make any significant concessions.

The skepticism of the military leadership was at least equally intense. Despite the numerous American briefings, few officers had changed their earlier convictions that such a force was neither technically feasible nor of any significant military value. In contrast to some of their American opposite numbers, German naval officers remained almost unanimously unenthusiastic. Several days after the Merchant briefing in March, the Navy inspector declared that the briefing had demonstrated "what an unbelievable number of problems were posed by such a project." [26] Characteristically, however, the military either made no attempt to express their views publicly or limited themselves to minor criticisms of the government's position.

Within the Bundestag the general trend of opinion was vaguely pro-MLF because of the American bond involved.[27] Few Bundestag members, however, were aware of the specific details of the MLF proposal or of the continuing negotiations, and those who were informed were at best unenthusiastic supporters. Their reported views were perhaps best summarized by Fritz Erler of the SPD shortly after a spring visit to the United States that included extensive briefings on the MLF:

It is right that the Federal Republic participate in [these] discussions . . . for two reasons: first, to show that the Federal Republic is not seeking national development—perhaps with France, as the press has claimed; second, to show that . . . the highest value is placed on the closest possible integration of the American potential. . . . But what is involved is perhaps only a politically unavoidable detour so that, finally, a serious start will be made toward European participation in the planning and preparations for emergency decisions with respect to the total alliance potential.[28]

A quite different view of the MLF's "political necessity" was propounded by certain younger SPD figures—most notably Helmut Schmidt—as well as by many liberal press commentators.[29] They repeatedly challenged von Hassel's continuing assertions that "the planning doors will not be opened without financial participation" [30] and the MLF was a "good and clear-cut instrument" to counteract both American isolationist tendencies and European pressures for American withdrawal.[31] Participation in the MLF, wrote Theo Sommer in *Die Zeit,* had become a kind of "loyalty demonstration" or even "support for an illusion." [32] Since the force would add little to the total Western strategic capability and the United States would never agree to majority control, the Europeans would indeed be paying more but not deciding more. A far more essential goal for Germany was an assured, decisive influence over total planning for the alliance, to be achieved through an extension of the "Athens approach."

More conservative press opinion reflected similar objections.[33] The MLF was a "farce" or a contrived "technical nightmare"; it was a device primarily designed to alleviate American balance-of-payments problems or to mask the gradual withdrawal of American weapons from the Continent. Surface ships or perhaps even Polaris submarines could not and should not be accepted in lieu of European-controlled, land-based MRBMs. Most important, the willingness to pay "a lion's share" of the costs (perhaps as much as 40 percent) meant that other Bundeswehr programs—particularly force and equipment modernization—must be cut back. Whether participation in an MLF was "fashion" or "necessity," there must be no threat to a stable domestic economy.

The only direct opposition to German participation in the MLF, however, came primarily from two other sources. The most active of these was the small group of German Gaullists, drawn almost exclusively from the CSU. The keynote for their campaign was set by the remarks in January of Deputy Karl Theodor Freiherr von und zu Guttenberg (a CDU/CSU foreign-policy expert by then often speaking for the Gaullists) to the effect that the Nassau agreement had been only "an attempt to maintain the American nuclear monopoly" at the cost of European security.[34] At stake was the basic goal of Atlantic partnership between two equal, atomically armed participants. France's *force de frappe* could provide the nucleus of a European force, a basis for a two-key Atlantic system. Germany's contribution to the costs of an MLF might better be put toward furthering a truly European solution.

Franz Josef Strauss, in his newly assumed Gaullist garb, put forward a somewhat different proposal. In a speech in June the former minister declared,

We Europeans should not place blind confidence in the reliability and trustworthiness of the Americans, who do not wish without more ado to let themselves be drawn into an atomic war. . . . So long as Europe has no nuclear weapons, Europe has no sovereignty. The only solution is to pool the British and French weapons—which should be fully supported by the full transfer of American know-how. Thus in the long run a European atomic force would come into existence under the precondition, of course, of political union.[35]

In the midst of this debate the official commitment to participation stood firm. But by the time of Kennedy's visit to Europe in June it was apparent that Bonn was the only European government that had reached such a decision. The president and the chancellor discussed the proposal at some length and agreed to make every effort to further this "vital project." By common consent and with apparently no great regret, however, no definite action was to be taken until a "broader base" could be established.[36] And with the Profumo scandal in Britain, no government in Italy, and major skepticism among the Scandinavians, such an achievement did not seem imminent. The MLF, in the public view at least, seemed on the way to limbo.

STATE THREE: TOTAL CONVERSION

Twelve months later, a new chancellor, Ludwig Erhard, and a new president, Lyndon Johnson, in a joint communiqué agreed that

the proposed multilateral force would make a significant addition to this [Atlantic] military and political strength and that efforts should be continued to ready an agreement for signature by the end of the year.[37]

Officially, the only shift in the intervening period had been a German retreat on the long-disputed question of MLF voting procedures. Beginning in the fall of 1963, Defense Minister von Hassel carefully emphasized that although a change in the unanimity principle was vital, such a change was to be considered "once the MLF has come into being." [38] In private talks with American officials, Germans stressed, rather disingenuously, that the issue was not the eventual lifting of the American veto. It was rather the Federal Republic's concern for the veto power of other, small contributors, who might be less willing to risk defending German interests.

Over the twelve-month period, however, the number of committed MLF supporters in both capitals had increased measurably. It was believed that Johnson himself had given full approval to the project in April, authorizing intensive discussion and persuasion abroad but not at home.[39] Reportedly he had two motives: continuation of Kennedy's basic foreign-policy program until after election in his own right, and basic sympathy for a meeting of German desires.

The shift in Bonn's position had been far more intense, moving, in the words of Alastair Buchan, "from one of intelligent interest to something more closely resembling a demand." [40] One reason for this shift was education, the result of the extensive "information and persuasion" effort launched by the United States with full German approval in the summer of 1963. Formulated after the somewhat disappointing results of the earlier Merchant and Ricketts briefing missions, the program's goal was to use every available channel and means to present the rationale of the MLF. Repeated and often summary presentations of American findings alone would not ensure favorable attitudes. The bases for these conclusions must be demonstrated and, if necessary, recalculated to the satisfaction of the skeptical.

Those Germans most affected by these efforts were the military, particularly the officers involved in the continuing Washington discussions.[41] In interview after interview, respondents referred to "conversions" to a position of tolerant acceptance (by the army's leadership, reportedly) if not to one of full conviction (the navy's position, reportedly). As one of the participants remarked, "For me, I think the turning point was the working through of the Washington feasibility study—in contrast to the April briefings on survivability and mixed manning, which had seemed just so much talk and American sideshow. . . ."

Discussing the experimental mixed-manned voyage aboard the U.S.S. *Ricketts,* an observer (outside the government and less than enthusiastic about the MLF) advanced a somewhat different view. The American educational program, he remarked, had really a two-fold strategy: "The Americans not only told them what they should know, but also got them . . . to 'role play.' How could they help but become convinced?"

A second, more significant factor bearing upon German attitudes about the MLF was the renewed crisis in German-American relations. The initial focus of mounting German concern was the American effort, in the post-Cuban missile crisis environment, to reopen the arms control dialogue with the Soviet Union.[42] As Kennedy formulated it, the immediate goals were to avoid the political dilemmas which had plagued the 1962 Berlin talks, to seek instead limited agreements in areas of "common interest." The principal American target was adoption of a ban on testing of nuclear weapons, long and fruitlessly discussed since 1956.

As before, the position of the federal government was one of reluctant support for the American initiative. Adenauer privately warned the Americans of the dangers inherent in any negotiation with the Soviets. There was widespread concern about the bilateral (later trilateral) basis of the talks and repeated requests to the United States for full and frequent consultation. Even Schröder, the architect of Germany's tentative policy of movement towards the East, spoke of the need to gain "something in return."

On the whole, however, the Federal Republic raised few specific objections to the ban itself. As one respondent expressed the judgment of a number of respondents.

They really didn't pay too much attention to what was going on. First of all, nobody thought anything would come of it. Then too, it didn't really seem "relevant." Some Foreign Office brain has set down the rule: global disarmament measures are good; those limited to Europe are bad because they fix the status quo. And they followed that tactic, never looking back, almost down to the end of the negotiations.[43]

The final form of the test-ban agreement concluded in Moscow in late July provoked expressions of anxiety and sustained criticism from all segments of the German leadership.[44] On the very day of signature the federal government announced that it had not yet decided whether it would accede to the treaty or not. Many, both within and outside the coalition, attacked the treaty as a "Soviet trick" to gain de facto recognition of East Germany as one of the signatories exercising "national sovereignty." A small number of CDU/CSU spokesmen—chiefly Gaullists led by former foreign minister von Brentano—went further. There was no reason for Bonn to sign, they said, since it had renounced ABC weapons production in 1954, a voluntary restriction pledged to its allies and as yet unmatched by any other state.

Within the government the principal focus was the frightening lack of consultation among the allies during the crucial Moscow negotiations. Weeks after both President Kennedy and Secretary Rusk officially had stated that accession involved no legal recognition—then or in the future—of any other signatory, two criticisms still were being raised. First, the United States had kept its allies almost totally uninformed about the course of negotiations and even had not shown Bonn the final draft until after American, British, and Soviet agreement had already been reached. Second, without any prior consultation the United States implicitly had agreed to the exploration of several arms control measures bearing directly on Germany's political and military position. As Chancellor Adenauer told Secretary McNamara at the height of the debate, the Federal Republic would not discuss or accept any agreement that involved further discrimination against Bonn, that offered no immediate direct concessions on reunification, or that was negotiated without prior consultation.[45]

Slowly the crisis ebbed away; the Federal Republic on August 18 announced its intention to sign the test-ban treaty. The next few months, however, saw continuing crises over such "appropriate consultation" procedures as troop withdrawals and the Big Lift exercise.[46] The net effect of these upsets was to increase the determination of most German leaders to use every possible means to fix the American connection even more inexorably and to ensure major, continuing German influence over Washington decision-making. The ultimate aim must be the long-discussed reform of the alliance's political and military arrangements. For the moment, the most promising if not the only available solution lay in the swift implementation of the MLF proposal. Despite its many problems, the MLF would permit at least immediate de facto modification of the existing system.

This view, however, was not shared by the total leadership; therein lies a third major factor affecting German attitudes toward the MLF. With the election of Ludwig Erhard to the chancellorship, the long-simmering disputes within the CDU/CSU became increasingly intense and visible publicly. As discussed previously, the split had little to do with nuclear-weapons control, but was rather a debate between the ins and the outs.[47] The principal Gaullist challenge concerned the government's failure to grant primacy to Franco-German cooperation. Schröder, rather than the supposedly popular, vote-getting Erhard, was the chief public target; increasingly there were strident cries for the replacement of this "unrepresentative" foreign minister, and every available medium was used to mount scathing criticisms or sibylline warnings.

One of the major arguments in the Gaullist campaign was the need for far-reaching Franco-German military cooperation, particularly in the nuclear area. The basic arguments remained those cited above. The *force de frappe* must be recognized and fostered as the nucleus for a European force, the only real basis for forcing the United States to grant true partnership. France seemed interested in immediately making a start toward a real sharing of control, in contrast to the "sham" or "makeshift" solution of an MLF.[48] The Franco-German treaty had established a legal basis; all that was needed to initiate serious discussion was a clear expression of German interest.

Throughout 1963 and early 1964, several statements by French officials and in the French press lent some credence to this argument. In earlier years, the question of the *force's* impact upon Germany had been raised only by de Gaulle's domestic critics, particularly those often characterized as Little Europeans. Over the long run, they had argued, a French national effort must necessarily stimulate latent German aspirations.[49] The public response of the de Gaulle government was one of cool denial; France's present concern must be with achievement of its own goals; Germany's position in nuclear matters had been set in 1954 and would not be significantly affected by French developments. Perhaps the clearest statement came at the joint press conference following formal signature of the Franco-German treaty. As the official *Bulletin* reported,

In the military provisions, it is not explicitly noted that cooperation in this area will not extend to atomic armament. Such a restriction, [French] Secretary Lebel said, was not necessary in the text itself because the [German] federal government had pledged itself in 1955 [sic] not to undertake atomic armament. . . . The French government had full confidence in the federal government and had, therefore, waived inclusion of such a proviso.[50]

Beginning in March, 1963, a number of scattered statements signaled a clear shift in emphasis.[51] The French effort, it was argued, was but a first step. Once Europe had "strengthened its political structures," the *force* would be the "keystone" in the effort to secure a common and autonomous defense policy. Direct questioning about possible timing and the extent of a German role elicited only general, vague answers, however. French Foreign Minister Maurice Couve de Murville, like many other leaders, stressed that there was still a "long way yet to go" toward creation of the requisite "European political authority."[52]

In the judgment of certain German Gaullists, the private views of French officials were quite different. As one respondent close to the French described the situation,

Of course there were only hints, never a firm offer. That wasn't possible in terms of the French or the German political scene at the time. But Strauss and Guttenberg were always told, "Your ideas aren't those of your government, and therefore we can't take your interest seriously." The clear implication was that if official policy had been different, something could have been arranged.

All of these developments met with little interest from the Erhard-Schröder-von Hassel faction. That group's line of argument emphasized that although there was no "basic contradiction" involved in seeking cooperation with both France and the United States, Germany's security requirements could be met only "within the Atlantic framework." [53] On several occasions, Erhard and von Hassel were more explicit. France had never suggested German participation in the *force de frappe,* and in von Hassel's words, "if we are asked, we will of course say no." [54]

Such reports quieted but did not halt Gaullist charges and challenges. As the months passed, Chancellor Erhard was forced to reply to renewed attacks upon Schröder and increasingly upon himself. The MLF was indeed the "touchstone," the sticking point for the political future of the Atlanticists. If, as Erhard reportedly told Johnson in June 1964, an MLF agreement was not signed by December 1964 and submitted to the Bundestag before the federal elections in September 1965, there could be no assurance of German agreement or even of an Atlanticist Germany.

In summary, by June 1964 there had been a significant qualitative change in German attitudes toward the MLF. For the Erhard government the creation of this force as soon as possible had become the only available means to meet both its national and international political requirements. Almost all of the necessary preparations had been completed; all that was needed was a final push to galvanize the somewhat diffident allies, particularly the British. It was hoped in both Washington and Bonn that the pledge of June 1964, which underscored the determination to proceed with the MLF despite the remaining objections, would provide the necessary spark.

Germany
& the MLF;
the Downslope:
1964-1966

✠ ALMOST IMMEDIATELY after the pledge of June 1964, the MLF proposal began to die a slow death in Germany as well as in the United States. By December 1964 the Erhard and Johnson governments still were officially viewing the project as a vital "instrument of unity" and as an "effective military force." [1] But statements by them were couched in terms of obtaining allies' agreement "soon," of maximizing participation, of giving the force a "more viable character." [2] The swift-paced chronological development and the broad interrelated causes of Washington's shifts have been well and frequently discussed. The effort here, as in the previous chapter, is to explain, in case-study format, the particular constellation of factors affecting Germany's decision-making about the MLF.

In most essential respects the interaction pattern remained the same as in the earlier phases. The multisided character of the debate with other countries emerged more clearly, as in later 1964 and 1965 when de Gaulle, British Prime Minister Harold Wilson, and the Soviets increased their anti-MLF activities. Despite some role reversals, however, the principal decision centers remained Bonn and Washington, each viewed as being at one and the same time the moving sine qua non of a successful control policy and the primary threat to any successful arrangement. Finally, the interpenetration of the domestic debates and the debates within the alliance continued to be just as thoroughgoing and seemingly as little amenable to division or resolution as before. Positions on the MLF still served as testing points for political and official futures, however remote these considerations may have seemed from the perspective of a rational actor.

The few new elements were those often noted during any crisis in bilateral relations or even in the more general class of phenomena somewhat mistakenly labelled as bureaucratic politics. As an atmosphere of crisis deepened—with the missed cues, the overworked communication channels, the invocation of "safe" standard operating procedures, the almost automatic attachment to positions previously questioned—all the elements of crisis decision-making were present. Perhaps the most significant development on the German side was also predictable: the ever firmer, more exclusive identification of personality and political stakes with a policy position. For the weaker partner in the debate within the alliance, for the status quo forces in the domestic arena, this inevitably involved increasing cost. And as Chancellor Erhard painfully discovered, at stake was a game not only of win or lose but also of no withdrawal.

Underlying this growing sense of frustration and irresolution was the dilemma that is emphasized in the concluding commentary to this chapter as throughout the entire study. So long as the Federal Republic remained even only formally committed to the scope and ordering of the three Adenauerian foreign-policy goals, the hope of gaining either decisive success or freedom from external pressure (i.e., blackmail) was illusory. For the unanswerable questions turned less on the need constantly to decide within situations defined by others than on Bonn's decided ability to perpetuate choice without choosing.

STAGE FOUR: COLLAPSE BEFORE CHOICE

It is clear from the public record alone that for Bonn the principal new factor was sudden, massive French opposition to German participation in the MLF. As discussed above, the previous French position had been one of official tolerance, coupled with vague hints about a European alternative. The period from July through December of 1964, however, saw a revised French strategy, one designed to force a choice between immediate German involvement in the MLF and Bonn's hopes for its other foreign-policy goals, namely, eventual reunification and progress toward European integration.

The opening phases of the French campaign were essentially a tandem effort by de Gaulle and the German Gaullists. The French president came to Bonn in early July, obviously determined, according to one commentary, "to jolt the Erhard-Schröder . . . assumption of Atlantic priority." [3] The president placed special emphasis on the many failures in military cooperation under the Franco-German treaty. He not only referred to these generally, but also was more specific about the many reasons why the MLF was not appropriate for Germany. According to a number of respondents, some of whom were quite close to these conversations, Erhard then raised the question of eventual joint control over the use if not the development of French nuclear weapons. [4] General de Gaulle reportedly stressed the "essential French nature" of the *force de frappe,* but reiterated his pledge of "immediate protection" for Germany and left open the question of common planning.

Within hours of de Gaulle's departure, the German Gaullists, led by Adenauer, Strauss, Krone, and the CDU party manager, began to take up the cry. There must be an immediate move toward political union with France to bring an end to Foreign Minister Schröder's "do-nothing" European policy and to Soviet-American efforts to play "great-power politics" over Europe's head. [5] Erhard's response was swift and drastic. He had full confidence in and responsibility for Schröder's policies, he said; the only way to change this course was for the Bundestag to compel the chancellor's resignation. The attack continued, but in a far more muted tone. [6]

A statement by Erhard himself on a possible "bilateral" MLF was the proximate trigger for the second phase of the Gaullist campaign. Questioned at a Berlin press conference about rumors that if necessary Washington and Bonn might be the sole participants in the initial stages of the MLF, the chancellor replied, "I cannot give you a flat 'yes' but I cannot deny it." [7] It was clear, he added, that "a beginning has to be made," although "we hope that the doors will stay wide open for other European countries to join."

Despite subsequent disclaimers and modifications issued by the Federal press office and the chancellor himself, the debate on the budget a week later saw the Gaullists make their first major challenge to foreign policy within the Bundestag itself. Strauss and Guttenberg passionately argued that until there was a united European voice, NATO remained "a guarantee system of the strong for the weak . . . not an alliance." [8] There were repeated rumors that Erhard was losing support, that his rigidity in foreign policy coupled with recent CDU losses in state elections would cause his removal after the national elections in September 1965.

Far more effective, however, was the pressure applied publicly and privately by the French government that in essence posed threats to the Federal Republic's most basic advances in postwar foreign policy. During the last weeks of October this pressure took the form of a series of measures—long-considered but now announced with great fanfare—demonstrating the costs involved in noncooperation with France. On October 21, de Gaulle announced that he not only would prevent further progress in the Kennedy Round of negotiations to reduce barriers to international trade, but would boycott the Common Market itself unless the Federal Republic gave up its long-debated resistance to common grain prices.[9] On October 26, France announced the conclusion of a five-year trade pact with the Soviet Union, signaling the renewal of "traditional ties." On October 31, highly reliable sources reported that France also was seriously considering withdrawal from NATO.[10]

In early November, participation in the MLF clearly was made the central test of German intentions. In a speech to the French Assembly on November 3, Foreign Minister Couve de Murville declared that it was necessary to know "whether this force, far from strengthening the alliance, will not introduce . . . a germ of division for which . . . France is not responsible . . . whether there will still then be some possibility for progress towards a European political union." [11]

In a speech in Strasbourg on November 22, de Gaulle himself struck the most dramatic public blow. His eloquent warnings on the risks inherent in renouncing the goal of a "European Europe" in all areas but particularly in the defense sphere were perhaps best summarized in a concluding statement. How could a European people, he asked,

take the role of an auxiliary and rely decisively for its very existence on a power assuredly friendly but situated in a different world? . . . In a time of atomic threats and escalation, there is no other way to assure eventually the initial safeguarding of the old continent, and consequently to justify the Atlantic Alliance, than to organize a Europe which will be self-sufficient, especially for its defense.[12]

Private Franco-German conversations throughout this period revealed still another threat. Politely phrased, the French argument ran: If the Federal Republic continues its single-minded pursuit of a nuclear role, it will effectively preclude any prospects for eventual reunification. Blunter terms were used on at least one occasion, as recounted by a respondent: "I was told that unless we gave up the MLF, France would make common cause with those Eastern European states that feared a nuclear Germany in any form." [13]

Bonn's response to what was seen as an ultimatum was marked by consternation and conflict. Numerous private discussions were held with French and American officials; Gaullist attacks mounted; Adenauer journeyed to Paris as a self-appointed "envoy of amity"; articles challenging the premises of the MLF began to reappear in the liberal press. On November 11, the decisive step was taken. Under Adenauer's leadership and despite Erhard's objections, the CDU Fraktion, encompassing both cabinet and Bundestag members, voted for an undetermined "delay" before any German participation in an MLF.

In the following days Erhard and Schröder repeatedly declared that the delay was only temporary, that the Federal Republic was still firmly committed to the principle of the multilateral force. Both agreed with Ball and then with Rusk that a delay until early 1965 was in fact advisable to permit sufficient consideration of some recent British initiatives. Moreover, recent French developments were understandable but not decisive. In Schröder's words, "The Federal Government is not thinking of loosening its ties with the United States in the coming MLF negotiations as a counterbalance for France's backing down on the grain-price issue." [14]

But from all accounts the die was cast, at least for the foreseeable future. Whatever his hopes for change, Erhard simply did not have enough votes under existing circumstances to secure passage of an MLF treaty. Quite apart from the Gaullists, support was lagging among certain members of his own party and, as the subsequent SPD conference in Karlsruhe showed, among some segments of the loyal opposition. [15] More important, to many within the government the MLF was not worth an unwanted and impossible choice among Germany's Atlantic and European goals. There could be no decision until this threat of final choice was lifted or at least until the first election of the Erhard government, in September 1965, had been completed successfully.

But even for those few German enthusiasts willing to push forward with the MLF despite French recalcitrance, two other developments indicated that the game might not be worth the candle. The first was the shift in British policy signaled by the close Labour Party victory in mid-October; the second was the uncertain drift of American policy regarding immediate creation of the MLF.

In Bonn's view, British policy towards the MLF had always seemed ambivalent, if not overtly hostile. The Conservative government had continually played a waiting game, reluctantly agreeing to enter into preliminary negotiations, refusing to undertake any definite commitment on participation until all of the preparations were completed. It also had repeatedly attempted what could only be considered diversionary tactics. The first had been pressure for the multinational force approved at the Ottawa meetings of the North Atlantic Council; the latest was the plan of June 1964 for the mixed manning, joint financing, and common control of the strike aircraft and missiles deployed in Europe.[16]

From the beginning, the Federal Republic had considered British participation in the MLF to be essential and not only because such participation was a sine qua non for the United States. A Britain outside the force, with its independence in nuclear affairs unimpaired, would mean no real leveling of the special relationship, no real change in Germany's political status within the alliance, no inducement (however minimal) for eventual French coordination if not participation.

Nonetheless, there were three essential areas where basic British policy decisively undercut German goals. First, Britain was unwillingly (and, because of its Polaris purchases under the Nassau agreement, unable) to pay more than 10 percent of the cost of the new force; any further contribution would be made up of existing or projected nuclear forces that would remain under national control. Yet the British were equally unwilling to accept any control formula that provided for representation proportionate to financial contribution—in short, the formula that assured Germany a greater role. Second, London was opposed to any control provision, for the present or the future, that provided for dilution of the unanimity principle or at least diminution of the British and American vetoes. Third, England opposed the assignment of any force (whatever its form) to SACEUR, who was "but one" of the NATO commanders.

To some officials in Washington and a few in Bonn, Labour's victory presaged a fundamental shift in British policy concerning the MLF. Prime Minister Wilson had campaigned on the pledge to divest Britain of its "pseudo-independent" nuclear force, especially through a renegotiation of the "ill-fated" Nassau agreement. Participation in the MLF or some variant seemingly would offer a convenient substitute or receptacle for existing equipment. Labour, to be sure, had opposed the force, but Wilson himself had said he would reluctantly support it if it were "the only way" to wider nuclear consultation within NATO.[17]

Most members of the German government were less optimistic, however. Even if Labour would or could honor its pledge to "divest," there were few grounds for hoping that it would revise its stand on the MLF or retreat from the previous Conservative stand on control arrangements. Labour's left wing had been the most committed anti-German group in British politics; it had consistently opposed anything that suggested a German finger on the trigger and had supported plans for a nuclear disengagement in Central Europe. Wilson himself had been widely reported as preferring a "real sharing in decision-making" and as viewing the MLF as a whet to German nuclear aspirations. "If you have a boy and wish to sublimate his sex appetite, it is unwise to take him to a strip-tease show," he was quoted as having said.[18]

Confirmation of these estimates was not long in coming. Wilson's first week in office gave rise to three highly reliable rumors.[19] The prime minister opposed the MLF in its proposed form; he favored discussion of a modification that would include Britain's nationally controlled and manned Polaris system; he had assigned first priority to new arms control negotiations with the Soviet Union, particularly with regard to nonproliferation of nuclear weapons. By late November the rumors were substantiated in the form of Britain's proposal for a broader-based ANF (Atlantic, then Allied Nuclear Force) and Wilson's declaration in the House of Commons:

We believe that a mixed-manned surface fleet adds nothing to Western strength . . . is likely to cause a dissipation of effort in the alliance . . . and adds to the difficulties of agreement with the East. . . . There is the question whether the fleet involves a German finger on the trigger.[20]

For the Bonn Atlanticists the only hope of overcoming British objections lay in a firm stand by Washington. During a hectic round of diplomatic talks in October and November, statements by leading American officials—particularly Rusk, Ball, and McNamara—seemed to meet this requirement fully.[21] All of the Americans noted the necessity of granting full consideration to the British proposals, but reaffirmed the centrality of genuine pooling of men, money, and control. The MLF theologians reportedly promised a new push for MLF once the travails of the presidential election were over. Nothing, it was felt, could be firmer than Ball's statement on November 15: "The United States stands ready now to join with other members of the alliance, nuclear and non-nuclear alike, in a combined effort to create and manage a multilateral nuclear force." [22]

There were indications of growing opposition in Washington, however. According to official German reports, the principal obstacle was Congress, which, although it had not yet been formally consulted, was less than committed to the MLF's creation. A few senators publicly had expressed support for some form of MLF,[23] but others, particularly some who had written to President Johnson on this matter in September, were in favor of a "thoroughgoing congressional review" of the assumptions and characteristics of the force. A second major center of opposition was the Joint Committee on Atomic Energy, whose members had long expressed doubts about the force and about any German participation, as well as opposition to any change in the McMahon Act.[24]

The decisive factor, however, clearly was the position of the just-elected president. In the past, Johnson's commitment to the MLF had seemed unequivocal. In light of this, many members of the Erhard faction reportedly found Johnson's postelection statements confusing. On November 28 the president reaffirmed American interest in the sharing of responsibility for nuclear deterrence through the currently proposed "multilateral forces," but suggested that his administration would not be "adamant in our attitudes." [25] On December 3, however, the president seemed to take a firmer and more welcome stand. Emphasizing the need to treat Germany "as an honorable partner of the West," he told a Georgetown University audience: "Those of us who are ready to proceed in common ventures must decide to go forward together—always with due deliberation, with due respect for the interests of others, and with an open door for those who may join later." [26]

Bonn thought the crucial test to be the Johnson-Wilson discussions on December 8. According to interview sources, German diplomatic communications and private hopes regarding the outcome were somewhat ambivalent. A firm American stand along the lines of the Georgetown speech would hopefully put an end to any British attempts at diversion or "death by discussion." Yet too definite a demand for immediate action on any specific proposal might force the choices many officials in Bonn wished so desperately to avoid for the moment.[27]

In certain respects the president's approach to Wilson met these paradoxical requirements. The United States undertook no binding commitment to any specific formula. The British proposals were interesting, but Bonn's legitimate, reasonable demands for effective sharing had to be thoroughly discussed with other potential partners, principally Germany. A definite decision could then be made, hopefully within the near future.

Johnson's basic point, however, was quite different, as the subsequent National Security Council memorandum deliberately leaked by him to the *New York Times* demonstrated.[28] For the present and the future, American policy on nuclear sharing was to be determined in light of four basic principles. No plan would be approved which (1) was not acceptable to both Britain and Germany and not previously discussed with France, (2) would be interpreted as an attempt to oppose European economic or political integration, (3) would include the use of "pressure tactics," the establishment of "special arrangements" with any single ally, or the imposition of "deadlines" for the acceptance of American proposals, (4) would not leave the door open for accession at any time by any ally, particularly France. This declaration clearly was directed as much toward the competing factions within the administration as toward the NATO allies. There was no reason to conclude, the MLF supporters in the State Department immediately argued, that the multilateral concept itself had been wholly abandoned. Yet to some in Bonn (though not all), Johnson's point was clear. The MLF proposal as the central focus of American nuclear policy for NATO was moribund. It was now just one possible proposal to be discussed, debated, and compared, without haste or pressure. A German commitment was interesting, welcome, and worthy of consideration, but it was a necessary rather than a sufficient condition.

STAGE FIVE: THE DENOUEMENT

In the nine months that followed Johnson's decision in December 1964, the initials MLF all but vanished from the vocabulary of Bonn's political discussions. There were still scattered official references and more frequent mention in continuing Gaullist oratory. But as one respondent remarked, in comparison to the public and private deliberations during the fall of 1964, "the silence was deafening."

The principal reason was to be found in Erhard's directives to his CDU partisans and in his informal communications to members of the alliance, particularly the United States. The MLF was to remain on ice until after the September parliamentary elections. The broad issue of nuclear control-sharing could be discussed in terms of Germany's desire for an appropriate and effective role. There must be no new opportunity, however, for public confrontation with de Gaulle and thus for a further dramatic split within the barely united CDU/CSU electoral coalition. Moreover, under existing conditions Bonn could do little else but wait. Within the ministries themselves, MLF was still discussed, but in what were reported to be markedly subdued tones. The events of December had been a shock to most; time was needed to reappraise earlier arguments and to gain insight into the "fresh thinking" Rusk had emphasized in his presentation to the December meetings of the North Atlantic Council. Some of those who had been merely tolerant of the MLF had already begun the slow process of disassociation. Among those most committed, a number had adopted an air of cautious reserve. As one high-ranking military man close to von Hassel said in a 1965 interview,

The United States and Germany climbed up the mountain and then they—we—climbed back down again. In terms of time, money, personnel, and prestige, neither of us can afford that again.

What extended consideration did occur within the bureaucracy was in response to external developments. The primary stimulus was the somewhat desultory British campaign to sell an ANF. Basically, the ANF package was what Wilson had discussed earlier: a mixed force composed of some existing national elements (the British Polaris submarines, the American Polaris submarines currently assigned to SACLANT, some of Britain's V-bomber force) and a new, "integrated" force of ten MLF-type vessels. Although vaguely defined, the proposed control system provided for an intermeshing of an American and a collective European veto, the latter to be based on a formula positing Anglo-German equality. There was also some suggestion of what one Foreign Office official called "an open-ended grab bag" for the future, namely, the possibility of eventually incorporating other elements, such as a portion of SACEUR's land-based dual-capable forces.

The German response was one of interest but not enthusiasm. In accordance with a Foreign Office proposal worked out in January, Bonn reportedly was willing to accept a mixed force in which the multilateral component would be between twelve and eighteen rather than twenty-five ships.[29]

Its basic objections, however, remained as before. The Federal Republic was not willing to accept the creation of a special force that would lead to a de facto denuclearization of SACEUR; it favored the extension of the mixed-manning principle to "as many units as possible"; it would oppose the inclusion of major tactical weapons systems in any such force. Most important, it would insist on an equitable sharing of burdens and responsibilities with respect to all units of the force.

Although the Paris Working Group on MLF resumed sessions in May, discussions, in the view of most German observers, clearly were proceeding "in a downhill direction." Moreover, at the May meeting of the alliance members' defense ministers, Secretary McNamara formally resurrected another discussion topic, the establishment of the Special Committee on nuclear planning.[30] The Erhard government promptly recorded its initial approval, but carefully emphasized the view that this group was a complement to rather than a substitute for an integrated force.

It was in relation to the Geneva negotiations for a nuclear nonproliferation treaty that MLF received the greatest public attention in Germany. The Germans' requirement for such a force was publicly and purposefully restated in a special anti-NPT interview granted by Foreign Minister Schröder in early July.[31] Although the Federal Republic had decided not to seek national nuclear weapons through any guise, Schröder asserted, it would accede to this treaty only upon the fulfillment of two conditions. First, German security against the uncountered Soviet MRBM threat must be assured through creation of an MLF or some similar integrated force; second, German acceptance of these new restrictions must be matched by some new concessions from the East regarding reunification.

Schröder's declaration was in itself nothing new. Almost from the first discussions in 1963, the Soviet Union had branded the MLF as a device to give the Federal Republic nuclear weapons of its own and had threatened that creation of an MLF would vitiate any progress toward German reunification or toward the long-proposed nondissemination agreement.[32] At least as early as December 1963 Schröder had told the allies, in a clear reference to the test-ban experience, that Bonn would accept no further restrictions on nuclear matters without prior consultation and clear guarantee of its demands regarding the sharing of responsibility in nuclear matters and the shaping of Germany's political future.[33] In subsequent communications with the Soviet Union, the allies had duly reaffirmed Germany's sovereign right to participate in a multilateral force, while emphasizing their strong interest in non-proliferation measures.

The timing and the warning implicit in Schröder's assertion were significant. The declaration came less than a month before the resumption of the Geneva disarmament talks where nonproliferation was certain to be the principal topic of discussion, given the trend of British and Soviet policy. More disturbing to Bonn was the seeming ascendancy of the arms controllers in the Johnson administration. The most disturbing evidence was an article in *Foreign Affairs* by William C. Foster, chief American negotiator at Geneva and less than an MLF proponent.[34] Although his argument was phrased in somewhat ambivalent terms, Foster seemed to suggest that the United States was willing to accept some "erosion of alliances" in the interest of the primary goal of halting further spread of nuclear weapons. The anxiety level displayed in all of the interviews conducted during this period was further heightened, first, by a speech in the Senate by Robert Kennedy that stressed the necessary priority of a nonproliferation agreement over any specific form of nuclear sharing within NATO,[35] and second, by the leak to the *New York Times* of similar recommendations made in the secret report of the Gilpatric Committee.[36]

Despite a renewed Soviet propaganda effort and the Western press's speculations about Germany's "real nuclear aspirations" that followed,[37] Schröder's tactic was relatively successful from the Atlanticist viewpoint. There were new statements of reassurance from both Washington and London and new attempts to encourage a "fruitful" exchange of views both within NATO and on a bilateral basis. On August 17, it was the American rather than the British delegation which submitted a draft nonproliferation treaty, with the "qualified support" of the other Western members and the unofficial support of the nonparticipating Federal Republic.

The carefully phrased provisions of the American plan allowed for the possibility of both an MLF and an eventual European force. First, there was to be no transfer of nuclear weapons "into the *national* control of any non-nuclear State, either directly or indirectly through a military alliance." And second, there would be a promise by all signatories "not to take any other action which would cause an increase in the *total* number of States and other organizations having independent power to use nuclear weapons." [38]

Nonetheless, the range of opinion in Bonn was negative if not anxious about the Geneva proceedings.[39] The American proposal did not contain two provisions for which Germany had long fought: a nonrecognition clause regarding signatory procedures and a token linkage to progress in the German question. British support for the compatibility of the MLF with any agreement on nonproliferation seemed less than firm. This was even more alarming when viewed in relation to Britain's unilateral decision, announced in late August, to replace its obsolescent nuclear-capable Corporal missiles deployed in Germany with conventional artillery. Most worrisome was a speech given in closed session on August 24 by the chief Canadian negotiator at Geneva. He called essentially for due consideration of "legitimate" Soviet security interests with respect to NATO's nuclear arrangements and suggested the convening of East-West talks on European security.

The total impact of these developments set off new waves of anxiety and debate in Germany's already tense preelection atmosphere. As before, the bitterest reaction came from the German Gaullists, especially Adenauer. At rally after rally, the former chancellor denounced the Western role in the nonproliferation discussions. Representative comments were these:

> The American plans are so horrible that in the long run Europe will be delivered over to the Russians. . . .
>
> There are good Americans and then there are others. Among the good was John Foster Dulles; among the others, Mr. Morgenthau, who in 1945 wanted to turn Germany into a pasture land. . . .
>
> If this treaty comes into being, NATO is finished. England is then in the atomic club for good, despite its many debts, which will be paid for with our money.[40]

Franz Josef Strauss advanced a somewhat different formulation. Striking a note common to less partisan critiques, the former defense minister protested vigorously against attempts, both Communist and Western, "to discriminate against Germany" and "to force it to accept a fait accompli with no return." His most dramatic warning stated that if Germany were made to undergo a "military Versailles, one could calculate from historical experience alone when a new Führer-type would promise and probably also require nuclear weapons or worse, for a Germany treated in this way." [41]

The response of the Atlanticist leadership to these and the many more reasoned criticisms of the Geneva developments was a twofold defensive campaign. On the one hand, the leaders attempted to gloss over these arguments by reiterating—without specific mention of the MLF—the demands they had presented to the Western allies. On the other hand, they attempted to defuse the issue by emphasizing their expectation that Washington would safeguard vital German interests. In Schröder's words,

We are no protectorate . . . but rather the reliable friend of our friends. Without the United States, there would be no security for Germany and Europe, there would be no reunification, and there would also be no German right to codetermination (*Mitsprache*) in the area of nuclear responsibility.[42]

The election of September 19 brought this phase of public discussion to a close. To the surprise of some observers, the CDU/CSU garnered 47.6 percent of the votes and 245 seats in the Bundestag. This was 4 seats too few to avoid another coalition with the shrinking FDP (9.5 percent of the votes compared with 12.8 percent in 1961), but was more than enough to constitute a personal electoral victory for Erhard, thereby assuring his undisputed reelection by the Bundestag as chancellor.

The MLF and the whole nuclear-sharing complex was one of the principal self-defined issues confronting the chancellor in the first weeks of his new term. There could be no further delay; the external environment was hardly more receptive than that in the fall of 1964; Erhard was to visit Washington in December.[43] Of principal concern were the changes which had occurred in French and American positions. In the months past, de Gaulle's opposition to German participation in any integrated nuclear force had become even more explicit and intractable.[44] The impact of his opposition was heightened not only by France's assiduous courting of the Communist states but also by two related tactics. The first was de Gaulle's candid remarks in February about the prospects and conditions for German reunification. Partition was a source of continuing unrest, concern, and suffering, but

what must be done will not be done, one day, except by the understanding and combined action . . . [of] the European peoples. . . . Certainly, the success of such a vast and difficult undertaking implies many conditions. . . . First of all, Germany must recognize that any settlement of its frontiers and its armament will be in agreement with all its neighbors, those on the East and those on the West.[45]

The second tactic was de Gaulle's formal declaration that at least by 1969 France would call for a "revision" of the North Atlantic Treaty organization along "long-proposed" lines.[46] More specific indications of intention followed: first, French opposition to the construction of a new integrated military headquarters for NATO near Paris and, second, the publication of a proposal for reform of NATO in *Politique Etrangère*, a magazine long considered an official sounding board.[47] Broadly sketched, the plan provided for creation of two alliances: a traditional, loosely coordinated Atlantic pact and an integrated European system centered in and limited to German territory, within which the only nuclear elements, the *force de frappe,* would remain under exclusive French control.

Far less clear and therefore more disturbing was the American position on nuclear sharing. Officially, there seemed no fixed administration line but rather an unresolved collection of conflicting views, concepts, and schools of thought on how to proceed. To many officials in Bonn, the MLF complex now seemed the focus of debate between two major groups: those who gave priority to détente with the Soviet Union versus those (particularly in the State Department) who placed primary value on recementing the Atlantic alliance. To others, and particularly to the chancellor's advance men sent to the United States, there seemed at least three sets of related trade-offs at issue, trade-offs between nonproliferation progress and new alliance measures; between an immediate and a delayed confrontation with de Gaulle; and between a hardware and a political solution for sharing nuclear decision-making. The lines cut across all departments; the probable outcome, except for the certainty that the old MLF formula would not be revived, was still uncertain.

Any decision clearly was to be the president's, and characteristically, Johnson had forcefully expressed his intention to keep his hand free. The emphasis was on waiting, on the careful, unhurried exploration and comparison of various possible partial answers. Moreover, the White House seemed to view the December meeting as an occasion for a German initiative. Erhard's tentative indications that he would present no new proposals brought a prompt reminder that the president was most interested in hearing specific German views.[48]

Domestic prospects for formulating and gaining approval for such proposals, however, were anything but encouraging. Despite his personal electoral victory, Erhard had faced momentous problems even in constituting a government made up of the warring CDU, CSU, and FDP.[49] An Atlantic arrangement for nuclear sharing was clearly one of the issues on which the equilibrium was most fragile. The battle over the relevant portion of the inaugural Government Declaration consumed many days and was fought both in secret discussions and in the press. The basic lineup reportedly arrayed Schröder and von Hassel against most of the other political leaders in insisting on a specific declaration in support of—at the very least—a "common integrated weapons system."[50]

Erhard's speech in the Bundestag on November 10 reflected his almost unqualified success. Declaring that sharing must be in proportion to the dangers and burden borne, the chancellor said:

We are thinking in terms of a joint nuclear organization, and we are participating in relevent deliberations with the allied powers. We have repeatedly made known that we do not desire national control of nuclear weapons.

We should, however, not be kept out of any nuclear participation simply because we are a divided country. The partition of Germany is an injustice. It must not be augmented by another injustice, by making it more difficult for us—who are rendering substantial contributions to the Western alliance—to defend ourselves against the open threat from the East. Such views weaken the alliance and simultaneously encourage the Soviets to insist on the partition of our continent.[51]

But these words indicated only a direction, not a proposal, and could only gloss over, not reconcile, four broadly defined divergent points of view which interview after interview of German respondents revealed. The first was held by a small group of "MLF purists," located primarily within the Defense Ministry. Following what many conceived to be von Hassel's lead, the purists considered the MLF plans already hammered out to be the best solution to the nuclear-control issue, if not the only one possible. A second group, with significant support among members of the Foreign Office, the Defense Ministry, the SPD, and the Erhard wing of the CDU, were the "convinced multilateralists." [52] The MLF, in this view, was clearly moribund, but it must be kept alive long enough to allow discussions on a more acceptable solution based on the principles of "common property, common financing, common control, and common manning." The reason for this position, as one prominent CDU business leader explained in an interview, was simply that

improved information and consultation practices as in the McNamara Committee are fine and necessary but just not enough. Under the best possible arrangements, there's no guarantee that a German voice—a nuclear outsider—will carry enough weight. It's just like in business . . . even if a stockholder holds only five percent, I must listen to him.

Characteristically, however, there was little agreement within this group as to what precise form such a force should take.

The hallmark of the third group—in essence the forerunner of the coming Grand Coalition—was definite opposition to any revival, even in modified form, of the MLF proposal.[53] Although such a force might once have been considered tolerable, they argued, events especially since October 1964 had dramatically disproved every agrument advanced for its usefulness. Furthermore, the intensity of Germany's interest in MLF participation had severely hampered the implementation of the policy of movement towards Eastern Europe, of incipient Ostpolitik. Schröder's tentative efforts to establish economic ties and to create diplomatic flexibility with Eastern Europe would hardly be successful if the Soviet Union could use the specter of a nuclear Germany "to frighten its satellites back into line." France, moreover, had been quick to follow the Soviet example and had gained its "Eastern successes" essentially at Germany's expense.

Most important of all, whatever naive overestimation had initially existed, the continuing discussions had clearly shown that "copossession" (*Miteigentum*) in MLF entailed no necessary involvement in total planning for the alliance. It was this involvement that was crucial to Germany's long-run political and military interests; in the words of one officer close to the SPD,

It's like having a choice between owning three guns in a battery or sitting in the central control station. Both would be best, but that's not possible. If you buy the guns, you get to say what's to be done with them, but nothing about the rest—the other weapons with related targets, the overall battle plan of which you're just a tiny and perhaps expendable unit.

Few of those interviewed were able to describe precisely the necessary or desirable limits of a German share in nuclear control within the alliance beyond the rather vague and often interchangeably used terms *Mitsprache, Mitbestimmung,* and "crisis management." Most talked only in terms of the need for influence, perhaps through a McNamara Committee, on the targeting of all nuclear weapons, the predetermined battle rules, the specific operation of the American guarantee, and the steps to be taken in a crisis before military action was begun. A few proponents, however, stressed the need for a veto (in German given the paradoxical name of "negative veto") over the firing of any nuclear warhead—from American or German launcher—that was stockpiled on German soil.[54]

The views of the fourth group, the Gaullists, remained essentially those described above.[55] The shifts in the French position produced few public changes; the *Politique Etrangère* article, for example, was said merely to prove that it had been German unwillingness to cooperate that had forced France into its two-alliance position. A somewhat different view was expressed by one Gaullist figure close to Strauss: "I know that today France isn't willing, that there isn't a chance. But if we stop trying, if we accept the MLF force or the restrictions sponsored by the Geneva nuclear club, then for once and for all, Europe is finished."

Extensive consultations on the "Washington package" were held in mid-November and again after the Bundestag debate in early December. The final decision was that Erhard again should present a strong case for the hardware approach as well as endorse the cooperation in planning begun with the McNamara Committee. Interviews with Foreign Office and Chancellor's Office figures, as well as press sources, suggest that Erhard's principal proposal provided for the combination of American and British Polaris submarines into an integrated ten-ship fleet, to be owned, controlled, financed, and manned—after American legislative approval—in common.[56]

Johnson's response is perhaps best revealed by the wording of the final communiqué:

The President and the Chancellor gave close attention to the nuclear problems confronting the alliance. They agreed that the Federal Republic of Germany and other interested partners in the alliance should have an appropriate role in nuclear defense. . . . [They] noted with satisfaction that the defense ministers of a number of NATO countries have started discussions on the possibility of improving present nuclear arrangements. . . .[They] agreed that discussion of such arrangements be continued between the two countries and with other interested allies.[57]

Nine months later, the fall of the Erhard government and the advent of the Grand Coalition marked the end of official German endorsement of the MLF concept. The MLF proposal—in both its German and American phases, in both its original and altered forms—finally was dead.

COMMENTARY

Without question, the arguments raised in the beginning of the previous chapter about the causes and contradictions of the MLF proposal are too starkly formulated and hardly susceptible to conclusive verification even through the mills of history. All that will be attempted here is to draw together certain tentative conclusions about the interplay of German and American policies regarding the MLF.

With respect to the argument about unrelenting American pressure, there is little doubt that from 1963 to 1964, the MLF at least seemed to be the ultimate goal of American policy regarding nuclear sharing within the alliance. Clearly, not every American official held this view; neither Kennedy nor Johnson believed himself to be committed to any specific formula. But those whose stake was greatest—the MLF theologians—used every resource at their command to demonstrate and propound the necessity and the sufficiency of this solution. Visiting missions, repeated briefings, elaborate study groups, trials at sea—all were employed to affix not only the American seal of approval but also the mark of "what the United States wants."

Certainly the German leadership—both those favorably and those unfavorably disposed to the MLF proposal—believed that the MLF represented an important American goal. Although interviewed in the somewhat ex post facto environment of 1965–1966, all respondents spontaneously mentioned this belief. All but a very few respondents cited American desires as the primary reason for initial and continuing German support of the MLF.[58]

At that point these interviewed German leaders also expressed either surprise or disdain at the multiplicity of arguments—not all mutually compatible—that were used to cajole, to demonstrate, to persuade. This may have resulted in part from the natural tailoring of briefings to the specific groups involved or from the varying points of view held by American MLF supporters. But clearly there was a tendency to gloss over difficulties, to slide over possible present and future contradictions, to meet objections and queries with a practiced grace. To cite only one example, a respondent reported, "Every time they sent someone over, we asked them about the congressional prospects, particularly about the McMahon Act restrictions. The standard answer was either 'Don't worry; we'll take care of that when the time comes' or 'That's already been settled.' "

To a significant degree these selling efforts were quite successful at the time. The structural as well as the political difficulties plaguing intra-Bonn communication tended to dampen down the contradictions. Many of the American advocates, particularly those from the State Department, were not only respected officials but men intimately involved in relations with Germany throughout the entire postwar period. Telling phrases in official statements, points of emphasis in presentations to the Bundestag, extended comments in private interviews—all tended to reflect the direction if not the very structure of American arguments.

After an initial period of iciness, American influence seemed even more pronounced in the military sphere. This study's general findings, as well as those echoing other, earlier interview studies, were an almost point-for-point reproduction of American arguments regarding the MLF's military usefulness, particularly its value as a "secure second-strike force." Perhaps the only original German argument put forward concerned the MLF's role as a "European theater force," which might—with American approval—be used independently of other strategic forces. But this suggestion, too, seemed to be a garbled version of Norstad's MRBM force or of some American arguments about the MLF's future uses.

Of far greater importance than the specific arguments advanced was the tremendous widening of interest in and attention to NATO nuclear arrangements that the American campaign produced. The campaign was clearly not the only cause, nor did it significantly alter the saliency, of the nuclear-sharing problem for the top German leadership. There is little question, however, that for many Germans, particularly in the middle ranges of government and in the general attentive public, the push for an MLF forced the first semiserious consideration of technical problems and of Germany's proper role under various formulas.

As one respected Bonn generalist expressed the point,

You Americans were really quite clever. When you argued that unless the sharing question was solved the Federal Republic might eventually follow the French example, most said, "Who, us?" You probably moved the discussion up a few years, but it clearly would have come anyway and under conditions considerably less favorable to American interests.

The truth of these statements, however, does not permit the conclusion that American pressure was the sole or even the sufficient condition for sustained German interest in the MLF. Although perhaps reaching new levels of intensity, the role of the American salesman after all was a role that conformed to German expectations and experience. As leader of the alliance, the United States was the initiator of proposals, the driving force for implementation, even the purveyor of arguments. More important, as the investigation above shows, specific German interests that made Bonn both susceptible and amenable to American proposals were involved at every stage of the MLF campaign.

Some observers contend that this latter condition did not necessarily affect German policy during the initial discussions in 1963.[59] According to this view, the major advocate of participation in an integrated strategic force, Franz Josef Strauss, was no longer in power and few other figures in

Bonn were so enchanted with the prospect of such participation. If Washington had presented another proposal—an earlier-day McNamara Committee or even greater influence over planning and use of tactical nuclear weapons—Bonn would have been at least as interested and committed to that American proposal. In fact, given the strategic disagreements of 1961–1962, such a proposal might have aroused even greater interest and commitment from Bonn.

In many respects this view is an attractive hypothesis, but one that is hard to prove. First, that the MLF concept had already attracted a small, diversified, but committed group of supporters must not be forgotten. Some Germans wanted to buy into the strategic game merely because it was there; others (apparently a well-camouflaged few) hoped that as MLF evolved or declined, it might lead to "acceptable" or "legitimized" national acquisition of a nuclear capability. Still others were attracted by the possibilities of the Europeanization of Europe's defense, of political trading with the Soviet Union, of obtaining at least some revision in the alliance's structure, frozen since 1952. A number of Germans thought only in terms of "this until something better comes along." The MLF in Germany as in the United States seemed to hold out the promise of all things to all men.

Whatever these individual hopes and calculations, a physical multilateral solution also had a broad appeal to Bonn as the means that would best fulfill general operational goals pursued at least since the late 1950s. The MLF was both a *new* and an *integrated* force, long considered the best means to fix the American commitment to the defense of Western Europe and simultaneously gain recognition of Germany's contribution to the alliance. The MLF promised access within a definite framework to at least some aspects of nuclear planning, a factor to be highly prized in view of the failure of the type of consultation proposed at Athens. Finally, involvement in the strategic sphere not only signified Germany's right to total participation in the alliance, but also constituted an essential defense against the discrimination that would be caused by the political use of the *force de frappe* within Europe and the British national forces within the alliance.

As discussions continued, as external opposition to a major German role increased, Bonn's commitment to the MLF as the only available means to the above-stated goals increasingly hardened. By 1965, the force, its specific characteristics, or even the option for a new multilateral effort were more than ever of secondary importance. The crux was, rather, "full valuation" of the "New Germany," respect for the rightful demands of a faithful ally, recognition of the ally's unwillingness to accept further restrictions or closure of any of its options without consent and compensation.

In all phases, in 1965 as in 1963, the German leadership was totally aware that American approval and support were primary requirements. The MLF in the broadest sense represented one instance of pro-American choice. There were many others: the Bundestag's preamble to the Franco-German treaty, the final grudging accession to the test-ban treaty, the position regarding European preparations for the Kennedy Round, the refusal to consider extensive Franco-German cooperation in areas of current or potential conflict between Paris and Washington. Even as the MLF faltered, as doubts about the strength of the American connection versus America's interest in détente grew, the primary consideration was still to find some arrangement, on an alliance or bilateral basis, to secure that connection, to guarantee German influence over American decisions.

Yet this awareness alone was sufficient neither to reduce the foreign-policy dilemmas the MLF posed for Germany nor to force an ultimate choice in favor of the United States. Perhaps the clearest proof was Bonn's reaction to de Gaulle's policy. The Erhard government totally opposed French efforts to make progress on European integration and reunification of the two Germanys dependent on either the acceptance of French terms for future military cooperation or the rejection by Germany of the MLF. The government privately denounced France's flirtation with the East and its avowed intention to disrupt if not dismantle the carefully constructed alliance structure, the sine qua non for German security.

But in the final analysis Bonn would not take any action which effectively precluded future if not present cooperation with France in any sphere. In 1964, de Gaulle's opposition and its German echo forced a delay. In 1965, the Erhard government clearly was more willing to discount French objections, but still it attempted to take certain limited insurance measures as well as offer concessions in European matters. There were continued efforts to emphasize the preservation of, rather than the demand for, the multilateral option, to suggest German willingness to forgo "certain weapons" and perhaps participation in the MLF as well, in return for real progress toward reunification.

The determination not to choose between America and France was far more pronounced outside the Erhard group. Quite apart from the Gaullists, few of those interviewed—whether from the ministries, the Bundestag, or the political parties—were ready to support measures that seemed to renounce even for the short run the striving for European or French support for reunification. Such action would entail not only risk of electoral suicide but also contradiction of the hallowed bases of postwar foreign policy.

Moreover, there was an increasing number of officials in Bonn who wished even more than is usual with competent policy makers to give no hostages to an uncertain future. The prospects for an effective Atlantic arrangement seemed dim; any solidifying of the American interest in détente probably would involve the sacrifice or at least the disregard of German interests. Reunification might eventually prove to be an impossibility; the coin for which the reunification prospects of 1954 had been tendered—support of the Atlantic allies against the Soviet Union—would be valueless. While not taking any action which challenged or weakened the American connection, this group argued, the Federal Republic must seek to maximize its freedom of choice, to keep all options—Atlantic, European, and perhaps national— open for the future.

But the word option, whether used by the government or by its critics, keynotes the harshest dilemma revealed by the MLF experience. As generally used in German as in English, the word implies a clear perception of what is necessary as well as desirable, of what is probable as well as possible. It further suggests an awareness of the relative trade-offs involved in various arrangements and the willingness to make a choice, if not at present, at least at some future point.

Throughout the MLF discussions but particularly during 1965, the position of the Erhard government did not reflect fulfillment of any one of these conditions. Within the framework of a specific American proposal German leaders had indeed raised certain objections, had sought certain revisions and assurances. When the MLF project began to founder, however, they were faced with the seemingly insoluble task of defining minimum German requirements, of suggesting desirable alternatives regarding nuclear sharing. Albeit prepared in haste, their final decision in 1965 was merely a warmed-over version of the original project, buttressed by familiar arguments and designed to resolve few if any of the previous objections or outstanding dilemmas at home or abroad. They had, in essence, no fallback position except to await new American initiatives.

The position of their critics was hardly more considered. Increased consultation on planning and use of nuclear weapons and the assurance of veto rights unquestionably were desirable. But how would these rather general concepts be put into operation? What would be the limits and the political costs and risks involved? In the long run, what other measures or actions would be necessary, desirable, or possible?

To sum up, in death as in part of its life, the MLF proposal confronted the Federal Republic with a pair of dilemmas. Some initiative clearly was required, for to do nothing was to run the risk of further discrimination or sacrifice of German interests. Yet taking any action required choices regarding the three German goals of security, equality, and reunification, choices that the Federal Republic was still unwilling if not unable to make.

ELEVEN

Commentary: 1954-1966

✠ To DRAW TOGETHER what has been a long and occasionally discontinuous examination of a decade of German deliberations about the use and control of nuclear weapons, it seems appropriate to go beyond a simple summation of points already made.[1] Accordingly, this concluding commentary deals only in its first part with the overarching theme of this study: the significance of nuclear-policy decisions both as a primary issue area and a telling indicator of the modes of Adenauerian foreign policy. Attention then is given to a theme developed only at points in the text itself: the degree to which German nuclear policy during the Adenauer era is indicative of the policy choices and decision-making modes of a broader group of states, namely, the middle powers and what here have been called second-tier states, those middle powers of continuing significance for all interactions in the international system as a whole and among the major powers (or central system) in particular. The commentary does not explicitly deal with the Neustadt hypotheses about alliance relationships, leaving the testing and the extension of his findings described in chapters 2 and 6 to stand as basic statements.

NUCLEAR POLICY AS A TESTING POINT
OF ADENAUERIAN FOREIGN POLICY

Broadly defined, the basic argument of this study has turned on two major points. First and most simply, for Adenauerian Germany (just as for France and Britain during the same period) policies toward the use of and access to nuclear weapons were determined in light of the perceived requirements of broad foreign-policy goals and were almost never purely a function of analysis of prevailing strategy and doctrine. With increasing prosperity, returning national awareness, and a lessening of a direct Soviet threat, Germany pursued nuclear policies designed primarily to attain greater influence with and political security through its principal ally, the United States. Not surprisingly, these policies were framed almost exclusively in terms of supporting or expanding NATO's framework and of improving Germany's status within the alliance. The strategic terms and emphasis often so prominent in German pronouncements or positions in the debate within the alliance merely were acceptable vehicles (and sometimes the only vehicles) for the expression and protection of basic German interests.

The second and more significant point is that the complex nature of Adenauerian foreign policy made the German search for an appropriate and acceptable stance on nuclear issues a process fraught with continuing and occasionally irresolvable problems of political choice. Without question, the range of feasible and credible options available to the Federal Republic was and would continue to be more limited than that available to France or Britain or any other major industrialized state except perhaps Japan. This was true not only because of the constraints imposed by the nuclear nonproduction pledge of 1954 but also because of the determined continuing opposition, from ally and opponent alike, to any direct or independent access by the Federal Republic to nuclear weapons. But more basic restrictions were imposed by the conflicting requirements of the goals Adenauer had set as the primary touchstones of German foreign policy, his declaratory commitment to the necessary interrelationship between efforts to eventually attain reunification of the German nation, European integration, and Atlantic partnership. Or in the shorthand, somewhat different formulation used in this study, the stated simultaneous, equal, and inseparable goals of unity, equality, and security were to be sought in Germany's relations with the East, with its Western European peers, and with its American guarantor.

This study has concluded that any German discussions of policies concerning use or control of nuclear weapons during this first decade after rearmament involved more than the reexamination of the operational priorities that of necessity had to be assigned the three goals. Choices must be made which explicitly or by implication would lead to postponements, sacrifices, or irreversible foreclosings of at least two of the three goals. In part Germany's experience reflected the nature and dominant assumptions of the international, and especially the Western, system that the Federal Republic was gradually reentering. Questions about nuclear weapons were significant questions, status questions. In the short run, national positions could be used as levers or lures to decisively influence the behavior of others, particularly allies. Bonn's interest lay in avoiding any policy that would reduce this flexibility or maneuverability without simultaneously allowing major progress toward broad foreign-policy goals. Similarly, it was in the interest of Bonn's opponents and some if not all of its allies to reinforce the constraints on an increasingly powerful and rehabilitated Germany, to reduce uncertainty about future German behavior by emphasizing the hard consequences of any flexibility in treatment of the Federal Republic for eventual attainment of German goals.

Largely, however, these policy dilemmas were the product of the basic Adenauerian foreign-policy strategy, perhaps best described as one of almost all balls in the air at all times. Adenauer's personal and political preferences were clear. He was a Westerner, a Christian European who feared the potential follies of his countrymen nearly as much as the expansionist tendencies of the atheistic Communists to the east. In nuclear matters as in general foreign policy, he and his successor left no question about their estimates of the improbability (and for Adenauer perhaps the undesirability) of a return to the boundaries of the Germany of 1937. And progressively the prospects for a united Western Europe, the Europe of Jean Monnet if not of Charlemagne, appeared equally dim.

Yet in Adenauerian terms as perhaps in reality, the simultaneous-triad approach was probably the best possible as well as the only allowable choice for the Federal Republic in the immediate postwar decades. It involved a formal commitment to seek at least future gains in the national and European spheres. In every specific instance that required the explicit balancing of conflicting goal requirements regarding future unity, equality, and security, however, it permitted a decision—a particular pragmatic variant of choosing without choice—that acknowledged security's present priority and, most often, American preferences. The virtue of necessity notwithstanding, this strategy offered the greatest opportunity for full political rehabilitation and increased freedom of maneuver without serious risk to the substantial gains in domestic prosperity and political stability already won or to the total exclusion of future choice or change. Put most simply, into the early 1960s Germany's American connection was based on congruent national nightmares as well as converging national interests. It brought the greatest possible political and military support for all German goals at the least present costs, with the fewest liabilities for or restrictions on the future direction of German foreign policy.

In the final analysis, the costs of choosing without choice were high, of course, even if calculated only in terms of the tension and confusion that Adenauer and Erhard had to endure in maintaining such a stance. Decisions had to be presented publicly as noncumulative or as not affecting the basic definition of the other two goals, just as the three goals themselves were continually described not only as inherently and eventually noncontradictory ends but also as necessary, interactive, mutually required conditions in some ultimate *logique d'etat*. Even if the task was only one of maintaining surface or formal rationality, as Adenauer was so often accused of saying, such a task required a major expenditure of effort internally and externally: review and infinite refinement of myriad political formulas, engagement in what one critic of Bonn privately called "legalistic doublethink." Quite apart from the inherent perceptual confusion among an officialdom doing what it said it was not doing, the task represented an enormous drain on Bonn's time, creativity, and political resources at home and abroad. The more logically exclusive a decision seemed objectively, the more emphatic had to be the insistence that there had been no irrevocable choice or change in either the public or elite consensus concerning foreign-policy goals or priorities.

To be sure, once the initial rearmament bargain had been struck, few Germans, even in the political elite, devoted serious (let alone equal) attention to all three of the goals or to the minimum present requirements for their future realization. The usual style of Bonn vacillated between the most legalistic frameworks and the most pragmatically operational perspectives. Rhetoric was cheap and most plentiful around election time, if only because a focus on foreign-policy choices, some analysts have added, helped to obscure basic disagreements within the CDU/CSU on domestic goals and structures or to reduce the programatic advantage of the SPD.

Yet even the commitment to reunification—objectively the most theoretical and least security-related of the three goals—placed definite limits on German decision-making. It was hardly a positive guide to policy, as the absence of any major continuing consideration of the necessary concomitants of future unity for nuclear decision-making indicates. But as Bonn's eventual decisions in 1955, 1958, and 1962 document, clear constraints were recognized. There could be no German action which decisively weakened NATO's support of Bonn's reunification stance (whatever its particular content), since under the policy of strength this support was deemed the primary means toward unity. Moreover, the Western wartime partners, and most particularly Britain and France, explicitly had linked their acceptance of a semi-independent German political position to the continuation of general military dependency and control and specifically to a nonnuclear status.

As the decade passed, and especially after the grey finality of the Berlin Wall, future unity of the German nation clearly was an ever less salient or definable goal. Schröder and Erhard began the first cautious Ostpolitik, well behind increasing public expressions of unconcern for the fate of "the brothers and sisters in the East." But until the end of the Erhard era, formal commitment to unity "as soon as possible" remained a goal which the official leadership believed it could neither abandon nor allow the Western allies to abandon as a consequence of its security requirements or policies.

Another constraint was not so clear: the degree to which Bonn must take into account Eastern policies and threats regarding the unity-security nexus. There were the Soviet assertions in 1966 as in 1954 that direct German association with nuclear weapons would vitiate any hope of future reunification. More invidious was the continuing utility in the 1960s of purported "German nuclear revanchism" for recementing not only Eastern solidarity but also East German claims as the sole regulator of all of the Federal Republic's relations with Eastern Europe. For Adenauer himself there seemingly was never any question; under the assumptions of the policy of strength, any action which increased the Federal Republic's value as an equal Western partner only further ensured a decisive role in future East-West negotiations. Yet ever more members of the ruling coalition saw this adherence as eventually precluding any direct bargaining by Bonn in the East or the West, as obviating any hope of interim normalization or marginal gain in economic or political matters.

Adenauerian logic indeed suggested that regardless of the form or timetable envisioned, any concept of future unity provided a number of incentives for at least formally holding open a national option. If reunification would come only through negotiations, Germany must neither take nor allow any action that would further formalize partition (as imposed Rapacki-like nuclear-free zones seemed likely to do in the 1950s) or that would sacrifice any bargaining counter of possible future value (as any share, no matter how limited, in an Atlantic or European force of the 1960s undoubtedly would have done) without adequate present compensation or promise of future changes.

Moreover, the Federal Republic had a formal obligation, as the self-proclaimed legitimate spokesman for the whole German nation, to hold open as much as possible of the future. Bonn had to be able with credibility to offer to trade further restrictions for specific new concessions, to threaten effective balancing measures should anything happen in East Germany, or eventually to assert the right to negotiate on an independent basis. And as was implied more and more often even among Adenauerians during 1965–1966, should some acceptable form of Germanic reassociation finally prove not feasible, on what grounds should Bonn be further bound or considered less trustworthy in nuclear affairs than, say, Paris?

It was of little wonder that by the mid-1960s and the end of the MLF, most of the German populace simply had tired of the game. For the elite, however, this public balancing act among conflicting requirements faded in significance before the problems endemic to maneuvers directed at holding open future options that were given only broad definition. How, for example, was Bonn to prevent its allies from bargaining its bargain away? If the ultimate value of all German security efforts was dependent on the role Bonn was assigned under NATO doctrine or on the degree of its access to or control of Washington's nuclear decision-making procedures, then Bonn's bargaining power on reunification or even on a future united Europe was always subject to Washington's prior definitions. When the Kennedy administration began its search for "rationality" in Soviet-American relations and its program to limit purported German veto rights held over from the Dulles era, Bonn's potential bargaining counters, as well as its immediate freedom of maneuver, shrank measurably.

All of the allies were better able than Bonn to negotiate the conditions and limits of German partnership, as de Gaulle, Wilson, and eventually Johnson amply demonstrated in 1964–1966 with respect to the MLF. Moreover, they were rather willing to do so, particularly because of British and French interests in retaining against German challenge the Western status hierarchy frozen at the time of the alliance's founding. Denuclearization of Germany, for example, was a cheap and attractive bargain for London and Paris in light not only of Eastern interest in détente and accommodation but also of the fears and prejudices of their own domestic audiences.

A more telling difficulty was that in the international system of the 1950s and 1960s Bonn's three foreign-policy goals hardly were susceptible to static definition nor dependent to any significant degree on Germany's action alone. This was commonplace wisdom in Bonn, yet Adenauer seemed at times to underestimate the limits of possible systemic change or to overestimate the defenses Bonn could mount against any threatening shift in policy. Flexibility of definition and focus, perhaps the characteristic most antithetical to the later Adenauer vision, constituted the key.

To touch on only one instance, a nuclear flirtation with France in the name of a European-security or equality option as in 1957–1958 was simply no longer credible, let alone broadly acceptable, once de Gaulle raised his banner of national autonomy. Indeed, as Bonn's experience from 1964 to 1966 painfully demonstrated, any attempted German effort at a Paris-Washington version of Schaukelpolitik would be possible only so long as neither partner demanded exclusively or threatened an immediate direct balancing of costs and benefits to the alliance. In a situation of forced choice, even though the operational priority of the American connection was clear, Bonn could only lose.

Fundamentally, the basic definition of Germany's options—in nuclear matters as in general foreign policy—was imbedded in a gradually changing context: broadly speaking, the cold-war confrontation of East and West in Europe. All Adenauerian calculations posited, first, the continued, irresolvable conflict of Soviet and American interests over the future shape of the German nation as well as over a general European settlement; and second, the congruence of American and European interests in an allied—perhaps integrated, but clearly controlled—Western Europe within which the Federal Republic was inextricably bound. By at least 1962 this context had changed decisively under the cumulative impact of perceived strategic parity between the superpowers, the rebirth of European nationalism made possible by de Gaulle, and in a very real sense the first peaceful settlement of the German question in more than a century through the rearmed, controlled partition of the German nation. The Federal Republic then found itself forced increasingly not only to redefine the meaning and cost of its foreign-policy options but also to bear alone the heavy costs both of current errors of calculation and of unlimited mortgages on the future.

There were numerous specific reasons, of course, for the rigidity in late Adenauer-Erhard foreign policy: the crisis of succession, the obfuscations of tendencies toward legalism, the unnecessary problems caused by Kennedy's commitment to reality above the process of bilateral communication, the simple inertia of past conceptions and policies, to name only a few. Yet the basic issues were policy dilemmas that although now increasingly visible and costly had been foreseeable from the Federal Republic's inception. First, what was the proper stance for a Bonn that was committed to a particular future revision in the international or specifically European system, but that viewed all possible current changes in that system as inimical to attainment of its future vision? Second, what strategy was open to a Bonn that was committed to achieving the status of *primus unter secundes* in the West, but was rehabilitating itself at a time when the status of all second-tier states was being more clearly, permanently, and restrictively defined, at least in the military-strategic sector?

Stated simply, Adenauer's postwar bargain had accomplished its purposes but lost its meaning. Germans came to question the profit in suffering restrictions and liability to manipulation for the sake of formally preserving options that no longer really existed or of maintaining bargains on which others had seriously defaulted. Regardless of achievement or performance as a true ally, every European state by 1966 had more options, more room for diplomatic maneuver and negotiation across previously closed lines. Any significant German action would have to be set within the framework of Soviet-American détente, on which Bonn could expect to have only limited indirect influence. What specifically German bargain must or could now be sought?

Given all of this, it is hardly surprising that the Washington or RAND type of projections of inevitable proliferation of nuclear weapons in the early 1960s were hardly relevant for understanding German nuclear policy-making from 1954 to 1966. At no point in the multitudinous deliberations of this decade was there any official or discoverable unofficial effort toward acquiring a national production capability or a capacity for hair-trigger development, nor was there any serious expectation in Bonn of attempting such in at least the foreseeable future. Indeed, the Federal Republic's policy toward use and control of nuclear weapons did not solely or primarily turn on the desires of this second-tier state for what has been traditionally defined as enhanced international status or for national autonomy or for national security. It is hard to imagine a more dramatic counterexample, a national case in which the real and perceived international structural constraints on national acquisition were not more salient.

Moreover, the evidence seems sufficiently clear to overcome distortions resulting from the idiosyncrasy of a case study of Germany or from the developmental lag to be expected in the case of any defeated great power that is only slowly regaining legitimacy within the international hierarchy. The evidence strongly suggests that these Washington projections of rational behavior fail to allow for differences in states' perspectives and motivations toward nuclear-weapons acquisition, differences that necessarily pertain in an international environment characterized by: a limited, determinedly exclusive nuclear club that has been in existence for some years; the gradual dissolution, under conditions of purported strategic parity, of tight bipolar alliances; and widespread dispersion of the requisite nuclear technology and delivery capability.

To touch on only the most salient point from a structural perspective, Bonn's experience at no time approximated that projected for an $N + 1$ country, stimulated if not forced to emulate the example of the last entrant into the nuclear club. Without question, Adenauer's Bonn did view the nuclear status of Germany's allied and competitive peers, Britain and France, as disadvantageous to its search for political rehabilitation and as sources of discrimination both in European and transatlantic relations, both in present negotiations and future prospects. When opportunities arose, neither British nor French decision-makers gave their opposite numbers in Bonn much reason to think otherwise.

But British and French nuclear status was not a constant concern of Bonn nor always of first-order priority; and it never constituted an undeniable goad towards national development in order to gain similar advantages or to offset imposed discrimination. This was true if only because in the second decade of nuclear weaponry any $N + 1$ contender risked costly, determined opposition from the previous successful entrants into the nuclear club; opposition to a suspect, only gradually rehabilitated former enemy under a very special form of direct military control was certain to be intense. And by 1966 some officials in Bonn could see that status in the European political hierarchy of the 1970s, measured in terms of respect commanded, freedom of diplomatic maneuver, and available national-power resources, would be inversely related to the magnitude of national efforts toward nuclear self-sufficiency in the 1950s and 1960s.

In no small part such constraints resulted from the deliberate Soviet and American attempts to change the probabilities involved in what might be called the earlier "European nuclear domino theory." Most decisive perhaps was the Soviet-American campaign of the 1960s to retard if not restrict future nuclear proliferation and the joint commitment by 1966 to a détente based on a freezing of the status quo, at least in Europe. There also were several unilateral measures; perhaps the most successful was Kennedy's effort to counteract the nuclear lessons taught the allies in the 1950s while simultaneously offering the prospect of an Atlantic control system that would allow for sharing, if not for backdoor acquisition. And there was the impact of the stability created by growing East-West strategic symmetry. Superpower and middle power alike saw the continuance of this stability and therefore of the prevailing distribution of influence and the division of the German nation as both their greatest defense and their greatest opportunity.

But acknowledging these explicit external limits on future possibilities for Germany should not obscure the continuing impact of the conclusions that the Federal Republic and indeed other second-tier states reached on issues involving possession of nuclear weapons. For Erhard as for Adenauer and all actors on the Bonn stage, opportunities for gaining physical control could not be separated from or allowed to supersede German stakes in Washington decision-making. This was true for all aspects of the German question, for the role that the West (i.e., Washington) assigned to nuclear weapons in deterrence or defense against threats to German territory. As has been discussed above, the primary reason for this tying together of these issues in second-tier states was not to be found in an elaborate, commonly espoused, political-military rationale or in a studied comparison of objective capabilities and strategic requirements. Rather the reason was that the geographic and the political realities of what Willy Brandt later called Germany's era of "political dwarfdom" allowed little room for any other definition.

Indeed, Bonn's principal opportunity came to lie in exploiting these very assumptions about inevitable proliferation, in finding ever new ways to trade upon the commitment not to develop nuclear weapons now or in the future. Bonn had to convince its Western partners of (and thereby demonstrate to its Eastern opponents) its legitimate need for compensation in the form not just of strategic doctrines congruent with German security interests but also (1) of a potential veto over all steps towards German unity and therefore all negotiations with the East about the course (or end) of the Cold War, and (2) of a German right to full Atlantic equality of status and eventually to leadership of the Western second tier. And as this study documents, all of this was to be in exchange for nonexercise of an option which—international constraints to one side—was from 1954 to 1966 neither an immediate certainty in technical terms nor irresistibly appealing to any large number within the Federal Republic's attentive public or political elite.

On balance the Adenauer-Erhard governments were remarkably successful in maintaining the credibility of the bargain. Considerable diplomatic skill was involved, although as American nonproliferation policies tightened in the 1960s, stridency and frequency became perhaps more marked hallmarks of German demands. To a degree, however, little action or conscious conspiracy was required of Germany. The key elements of the inevitability model had indeed been designed to account for the German case or indeed for the action of any major industrialized state. Further aids to credibility were the Germans' very real fears about eventual American unreliability (if not abandonment), the elite's conviction that no technology could be penned up or kept nationalized forever, the widespread fixation on deterrence rather than defense, and perhaps most basically, the Adenauerian bargaining tradition set by the 1950–1954 trade-offs of rearmament promises for specific and immediate political gains.

In the international system of the late 1950s and the 1960s, however, bargaining on the basis of nonpursuit of any option to go nuclear was an attractive device for any middle power.[2] Status within the Atlantic alliance undoubtedly constituted a major intervening variable; success also would seem to have been contingent upon the definition of specific, limited, or defensive goals tied to a specific regional or alliance hierarchy. But the costs involved would be attractively moderate at least in the short run, particularly when measured against the dilemmas and risks Britain (and later France) faced in running ever faster to keep in the same nuclear place.

There were nonetheless major costs in maintaining a credible option for development, costs which increased rather than decreased with time and imputed proximity to the level of a nuclear threshold state. In asserting its option—as in all of Adenauer's strategies for at least the declaratory maintenance of his three general foreign-policy goals—the Federal Republic faced an increasing number of complex and eventually irresolvable contradictions. Those actions which contributed most to credibility—the trumpeting and intrigues of Strauss, the constant exploration of alternative arrangements within the letter of the 1954 nonproduction pledge, the constant demands for equality, Adenauer's late-in-the-day stress on *rebus sic stantibus*—were in the end those which often prevented compromise and concession. In both friend and opponent alike they called forth determined resistance based perhaps on objective fears but also clearly on the resulting possibilities for political manipulation and blackmail at Germany's expense.

What this study has found more significant in the short run was that these actions tended to undermine or hamper Bonn's objectives in those nuclear areas on which its current security turned more directly. When coupled, as in the 1960s, with dramatic attacks upon the flexible-response doctrine, such demands raised Washington's doubts about the seriousness of Bonn's own commitment to its self-defined security needs. On the one hand, the Federal Republic demanded the maximum number of American troops; yet on the other hand, it denied the conventional mission for which they were designed and desired by Washington. Objectively Bonn stood not only to lose the American guarantee but also to put into question the value of its efforts to build a conventional force. If this achievement was not of significance in strategic terms, on what basis did Bonn press its extensive claims to American protection, to equality and sharing within the alliance?

If the German nuclear bargain still was proclaimed as potentially revocable, critics could also question the benefit of current concessions to German demands for a significant voice in Washington or for new alliance-wide consultative or control-sharing arrangements. Did not Bonn's repetitive emphasis on the equality theme contain echoes of earlier German insistence on a leading international role—the "rightful place" searches of the Wilhelmian as well as the Nazi era, with their tragic denouements? Logically this implied claims for ultimate nuclear development, even if the relevant measuring stick was the British or French example and not that of the United States. If the interest of Bonn in nuclear affairs was so all-consuming, how long could it or would it be satisfied with less holistic guarantees? And in the interim the West would have to consider well why or how to trust the Germans in broader-gauged security deliberations, why or how to allow them a share in decisions and tactics in pursuit of East-West détente (let alone a commanding voice in or control over the use of nuclear weapons during a war).

GERMAN NUCLEAR POLICY AND DECISION-MAKING
IN SECOND-TIER STATES

With respect to the specific modes of German policy-making on nuclear issues, it might well be argued that timing alone produced most of Bonn's difficulties with questions concerning use and control of nuclear weapons. In broad terms, Bonn had the misfortune of entering the Western alliance and the postwar revolution in strategic warfare during a period of rapid flux in American strategic development. It began its rearmament at the height of the age of nuclear euphoria, when Washington's assumptions about the inestimable advantages of nuclear weapons (particularly tactical nuclear weapons) for deterrence and personnel replacement and about the inevitability of their eventual development by all major military powers were dominant. Whatever Bonn's doubts or specific military interests, it had to adopt the prevailing American concepts in order to attain its principal aim: political capital in Washington and thus within the alliance. When the Kennedy administration's push for flexible response and centralized nuclear control came, the Federal Republic stood to lose much of the psychic, material, and domestic political investments it had already made. But given the Adenauerian interpretation of Germany's goals, it had no choice but to shift its views and bear the costs, however grudgingly or painfully.

Even such a summary underemphasizes the almost totally reactive and goal-instrumental tendencies that characterized all German national-security deliberations of the period. In what was by 1966 Europe's largest conventional military power, there was almost no evidence of serious independent concern with what Washington or RAND or American civilian strategists would and did posit as the central issues and choices of German national-security policy. There was little country-wide consideration of the specific requirements of a forward-defense strategy or of the repeatedly promised protection of civilians, of the implications of a rapidly changing strategic nuclear environment for force size and structure, or of the constraints on nuclear targeting and deployment implicit in Bonn's claim to represent both parts of the German nation. Statements about defense that reached the public—whether at home or within the alliance framework, whether in the form of announcements or inspired leaks—hardly touched on such questions even in the broadest terms. For most of the first decade after rearmament, there was little organizational capacity in the Defense Ministry, Foreign Office, or Chancellor's Office with which to sustain the dialogue about strategy with Washington, let alone to attempt independent strategic analysis of the RAND type.

What perhaps is more surprising is the evidence presented in this study that indicates that the private German deliberations were only slightly more focused, informed, or concerned with specific strategic choices or trade-offs. The German opposite numbers for any transatlantic dialogue were always far fewer than Washington or RAND ever expected; they mostly were limited to the professional military and individual politicians or elite analysts with previous American education in strategy and doctrine. The domestic political context always was one of official and elite apathy, if not active lack of interest, even at points of great crisis like the Radford, Berlin, or MLF crises. And for all of Washington's carrot-and-stick efforts to induce greater rationality and conformity with the decision-making model preferred by Americans, the decade saw little change.

A central conclusion of this study is that such American norms and expectations provided not only an inaccurate but also a largely irrelevant guide to the substance and the process of German defense policy-making. Partly responsible were what Adenauerian Bonn knew to be the more basic political requirements of its national security. For far longer than most other Europeans the Germans perceived themselves as exposed to direct, unswerving Soviet threats in their role as the West's front line against the overwhelming conventional superiority of the Warsaw Pact countries, against blackmail by Soviet MRBMs, and against Eastern "salami tactics." But they also saw the primary if not the only hope for security in the inextricable commitment of the United States to the integrity of German territory, a commitment backed up by American strategic and increasingly tactical nuclear weapons, by American European-based forces hostage to the basic deterrence guarantee. For all but a handful of the postwar leadership, the question to be asked first was "what must be done?" or "what is the minimum needed?" to secure this tie. Only thereafter (if at all) did the continuing contradictions between NATO doctrine, force, structure, or equipment and German territorial requirements assume relevance; only then did information about new technologies or possible shifts in American positions have any meaning or salience. And no matter how necessary to meet limited military goals, there must be no German military effort sufficient to justify the long-threatened American withdrawal from Europe or even a significant reduction in troop presence.

Underlying but also undermining application of this principle was the second basic element in Bonn's consensus on defense matters: belief in the necessary Armageddon quality of any future European war, however improbable such a war might be. The idea of conventional armed conflict in the sense of a repetition of the horrors of World War II was simply un-confrontable. All but a few in the German leadership believed and in a sense hoped that any military engagement would inevitably mean immediate involvement of the superpowers, immediate exchange of nuclear shots, and immediate overturning of all planned limits on weapons, targets, geographic bounds, or timing of escalation. Security therefore lay in making certain such conflicts never occurred, in Western maintenance of "holeless" deterrence, and in the nonrecognition in declaratory policy of any limitations, spatial or temporal, on use of nuclear weapons or on the targets of retaliation. And if war nevertheless occurred, popular and even elite wisdom added, all simply would be lost.

Whenever these two principles conflicted, the Adenauerian strategy prescribed resolution along instrumental lines. Policies were to be recast in lines with American preferences and couched at least superficially in American-defined terms. In the dispute regarding flexible-response doctrine of the 1960s, for example, Bonn did increase its conventional-force strength and did begin conversion of its almost exclusively nuclear-focused air force to conventional missions, however slowly. But this strife, as with other kinds, dramatically reemphasized Germany's primary stakes in the bolstering of the American deterrent as a hedge against the future. And this in turn intensified Bonn's search for some form of acceptable, continuous, equal access to American decision-making and control of nuclear weapons. The technical details and particular scope, in the final analysis, were of secondary importance.

This reactive tendency was exacerbated by the nature of the domestic political interplay on defense questions. Manifestly, the political rules of Adenauer's Kanzlerdemokratie and of German business's economic miracle discouraged the taking of national initiatives in strategic matters. What was to be gained by the preparation of independent national position papers or even by the establishment of a large, conspicuously independent and efficient defense ministry? In the West even more than in the East there indeed was much to lose in terms of military protection, national image, and opportunities for rapid political rehabilitation, facts which an ambitious Strauss, for all his constant probing and concern for increased Hausmacht (personal internal bureaucratic power) and international bombast, obviously recognized. Quite apart from Germany's objective dependence on others for its security, a policy of almost total reliance on prior alliance (i.e., American) directives and proposals in the making of military policy provided more than guidelines for review (or even for later dispute) in areas of little expertise and provided more than protection against the many domestic and international critics fearful of Germany's military past as well as its present efforts. Such a policy also constituted a political cover that both met minimum demands of the other allies and permitted concentration of national energies in a more politically and electorally productive sector, domestic economic growth. And money always helped to allay further fears and meet further burden-sharing requirements.

Even when the alliance's dictates were unmistakable, Bonn of course did not fulfill all of the requirements set, did not hesitate to delay or dispute or even plead necessary noncompliance in the face of adverse domestic political consequences. To mention only a few nuclear-related examples, the stretchout in 1956 of the timetable for the force buildup, the choice in 1958 of the Starfighter as Germany's primary nuclear-capable aircraft, and the early push for participation in the MLF were greatly influenced by the following: the ability of the business community and the CSU to veto courses of action; particular interservice rivalries and enshrined military traditions of superiority; and the political style of a particular personality, a von Hassel rather than a Strauss. But much more often than not—for agreements as well as disagreements, for nuclear as well as nonnuclear issues—the basic outlines were set by decisions of the United States that already had been hammered out in Washington and were being transmitted via the alliance. And the argument was most often not about the detailed *what* to be accepted but about the limits and timing of that acceptance.

However, a more fundamental argument here is that for the Bonn of 1954–1966, defense-policy deliberations indeed were something other than simply a watered-down, less competent, more dependent, and thus clearly constrained version of the Washington process. It is not at all clear from the available evidence, for example, that German positions on use of nuclear weapons or on force structure would have been markedly more rational in the idealized sense advocated by Washington or RAND, or would have been subject to broader, more democratic pressures, had Bonn been given more specific information or instruction in American strategic rationale or even a more attentive American audience. Such would probably not have been true even if Bonn had been given a key to the alliance's tactical nuclear weapons, assumptions of the late 1950s and early 1960s about the educational and constraining effects of physical nuclear control notwithstanding. At most, there would have been only side benefits: improvements in the style and tone of the Bonn-Washington or Bonn-Paris dialogue, lowered levels of anxiety about change, and a somewhat less isolated role for the German military in domestic and international deliberations.

For example, all of the cost factors that Washington continually expected would impel rational choice among carefully considered alternatives—the large scope of the rebuilding forces, the considerable magnitude of defense expenditures, the probable military consequences of investing heavily in almost exclusively nuclear-capable equipment for the Bundeswehr—faded in significance before the broadly held view that defense questions concerned only the downpayment required *by others* for an untroubled future. These cost factors were to be calculated in terms of the minimum acceptable levels and with due regard to prior domestic economic constraints. In terms of future options and present cost-effectiveness the strategy had to be essentially one close to the traditional paying of tribute, of being America's most loyal ally and nothing more.

Or perhaps the only real alternative was to do something very different, something that from a traditional or narrowly rational national-security perspective would appear to be next to nothing at all. Unquestionably Bonn's available freedom of maneuver was considerably more restricted than that of other middle powers or second-tier states; German neutrality or withdrawal from the Atlantic alliance probably would have been as subject to direct international sanctions as would have been the raising of a million-man force or the decision to pursue national nuclear development. But as the SPD and some military men tried intermittently and often confusedly to argue, once the option of functioning as even a quasi-independent national military actor in a bipolar nuclear age was closed or forsworn, were not the logical alternatives effectively limited to making a downpayment to the Alliance or to raising limited forces organized in a very different way and sufficient only to ensure internal order and perhaps balance the East Germans? And as fear of Soviet attack diminished to the vanishing point, as by 1966 strategic duopoly increased within an atmosphere of broad diplomatic détente and multipolar economic competition, was not even the time for sizable, persuasive downpayments at an end?

These were choices most officials in Washington from 1954 to 1966 and beyond alternately rejected or misperceived. To be sure, there were

points of understanding—at various times in the late 1950s and in the denouement of the MLF—and splendid rhetoric relating to partnership and education, most pointed perhaps in the Kennedy-McNamara era. But in confirmation of the Neustadt hypotheses discussed throughout this study, few
American officials did more than project onto German decision-making their
own version of the Washington game or, still worse, their version of an
idealized policy-making model for success for which Bonn needed only more
education. Most Washington officials never saw that, however equivalent
their titles or functions, all but a handful of the central actors in German national security matters simply marched to a very different drummer—
whether they were government leaders, members of parliamentary commit-
tees, the press, the bureaucracy, economic pressure groups, the attentive
public, or members of the most visibly concerned (even when sometimes in-
coherent) SPD opposition and the reconstructed military establishment.

Any attempt to generalize from the German case must be a cautious
one. Many of the data needed to draw reliable comparative conclusions are
simply unavailable; indeed, a good portion of the supporting German evidence falls outside the scope of this particular study and has not been treated
fully elsewhere. Yet these findings of reactive, "irrational" policy-making
under conditions of high risk and significant cost nevertheless seem applicable to a broader class of states, the middle powers and what here have been
defined as second-tier states. Such phenomena are not unknown; salient and
measurable parallels in certain nineteenth-century phenomena within the European alliance system can be found. Yet if only similar present behavior by
actual or potential second-tier states—a group in 1974 including at least
Japan, India, Brazil, Italy, Sweden, South Africa, and Australia,[3] as well as
Britain, France, and Germany—is considered, the significance for international and regional balances is enormous.

Unquestionably, close alliances with a superpower heightens the tendency to and the value of reactive decision-making. Just as in prenuclear alliances between somewhat unequal powers, realistic national-security assessments have to begin with the leader's position and the willingness of the
lesser powers to sacrifice. For example, NATO's Annual Review, which
sets force levels and requirements, always in the last analysis turns on
American expectations about acceptable contributions and prescriptions
about the needed operational doctrine. There may be opposition, shortfalls
and even operational defections, but only within limits deemed tolerable.

And the impact implicit in the role of holder of both the principal nuclear umbrella and the control-sharing keys needs no further comment.

Also, such close alliance exacerbates the structurally related problem of strategic lag. Even Britain and France, committed to a degree of national military autonomy, have at times been unable to follow the leader in matters of current doctrine or strategic shifts, let alone proceed on their own. The specific causes have included: restricted or outdated information, particularly on things nuclear; the inevitable discontinuities in consultation or in the Europeans' monitoring of brewing American developments; or simply the gaps in expertise when considering complex issues such as possible common control procedures. But the more general cause is that even doctrinal innovation—often a serious and compensating activity for lesser powers in the past—is now directly correlated with a state's ability to force technological development and therefore to make continuous qualitative improvements (in Samuel Huntington's sense) in its military posture.[4]

In the short run, however, a reactive posture becomes almost a closed-loop phenomenon—surprise, anxiety, and crisis becoming recurring characteristics of the national-security policy-making process. If the terms of the bargain are to be set elsewhere, there is always the threat of external, unilateral change, of a sudden imposed renegotiation of installment payments, and specific guarantees. Support for the status quo is clearly the usual response among second-tier states, even in a strategic shift like the one in 1961–1962, which offered opportunities for what objectively might be seen as reduced human and material costs, should war occur. Such savings hardly outweighed the problems involved in recalculating the psychic and political investments already made in the existing military posture, in security reaffirmation of the central security guarantees thus seemingly put into question, or in renegotiating external status hierarchies and perhaps the domestic national-security consensus as well. There was, in short, a basic, time-consuming if not ultimately disruptive asymmetry within the alliance, an asymmetry which might eventually be papered over but which neither concerned nor was resolvable through explanations of the latest strategic rationale.

Indeed, the German case from 1954 to 1966 suggests that America's demands for verbal as well as material compliance from its partners whenever its strategic rationale shifted added a number of unnecessary hindrances to an already difficult process. The demands made the inevitable initial confusion even more pointed and intractable, allowing ample time for the casting of the most pessimistic projections (relatively automatic in the German context of the 1950s and early 1960s) and for the mounting of opposition, often involving deliberate misunderstanding. These sentiments then had to be overcome, but even the new rationale was open to real or manipulative confusion or misinterpretation. Perhaps most critical for security policies regarding use of nuclear weapons were the constraints these asymmetric compliance-seeking and reactive tendencies placed on the unlearning of past doctrinal lessons, often the stuff of basic political debate among near-equals.

Yet there is a more basic question, namely, the degree to which this is symptomatic not just of the policy process but of broad policy trends in all advanced, industrialized, democratic states.[5] The German case is perhaps the most dramatic, given the acceleration inherent in the cycle of defeat and separation followed so quickly by rearmament and political rehabilitation. For all these states, however, there have been the mounting pressures for change perceived in the nuclear revolution (crudely analyzed, perhaps) and in new unrestricted popular demands for increasing amounts of butter whatever the number of guns, in growing unwillingness among the young and some of the old to equate nationality or patriotism with the right and the obligation to military service, in a lack of interest in if not rejection of the concept of national identity itself. Together these have forced fundamental changes in definitions of national security, in definitions of the means deemed appropriate to obtain it or even of the amounts available to democratic central governments for these purposes for any extended period of time.

There still are military establishments, military plans and priorities, military applications of the newest in technology, all analogous to those in the prenuclear, economically leaner, less democratized eras. But in those states broadly classified as democratic—by now, in all perhaps but the United States—these military phenomena only mask the fundamental relegation of the war-fighting or conflict-deterring business to a second-order goal, no longer to be a parameter value for all national efforts and most especially for the domestic economy. At this time, it is indeed difficult to construct a believable scenario—even one including a high-probability threat of direct invasion—under which a decisive (however temporary) reversal of this trend in advanced industrialized states could be predicted.

Clearly, however, such speculation goes far beyond the evidence presented here. The conclusions of this study can function at best as indicators of the more general effects of international structure in a nuclear era on alliance behavior and national security policy-making. They provide at least a starting point for much-needed further investigation on a broad-gauged comparative basis. In the last analysis, only some of the German dilemmas of 1954–1966 that arose over use and control of nuclear weapons were indeed specific to country and time. Now, as then, the end of these dilemmas for the Federal Republic, as presumably for other second-tier states, is by no means certain.

TWELVE

A Look Forward

✠ To INVOKE IN THE SAME BREATH Germans and nuclear weapons seems in the mid-1970s an outdated if not totally irrelevant exercise. The almost-decade since the MLF's demise has witnessed unparalleled transformations in the nature and direction of interaction between nations. The Cold War has been finally and ceremoniously buried; the era of détente, negotiation, and nuclear peace seems now in full flower. The threat to international stability predicted by the earlier prophets of proliferation—an irreversible series of new nuclear powers by 1980—has failed to occur; despite the Indian developments, such a series appears ever less probable under the freezing impact of the NPT and the first round of the Strategic Arms Limitation Talks (SALT I). The principal impetus for change in both East-West and intra-West relations comes rather from "low politics," through factors only indirectly related to military power as classically defined or to present or potential nuclear status.[1] In the short run at least, the principal readjustments in the international hierarchy are a function of monetary and fiscal capacities, relative trade position, physical and technological resources, and even comparative social cohesiveness.

More often than not, the Federal Republic has been a principal actor, indeed at the cutting edge of these developments. Its elevation from political dwarfdom in some measure has been the result of the coincidental weakness or inattention of others, notably of Germany's principal allies, France and the United States. However, the transformation has also reflected the redirection of national attention and consciousness under Willy Brandt's SPD, as junior and then senior partner in three successive governments. Brandt's commitment to the normalization of Germany's international status and to active rapprochement with the East has garnered a Nobel peace prize and overwhelming electoral ratification. And however stormy the domestic debate may have been, however uncertain (or unknown) the long-term outcome may appear, the treaties with Moscow, Warsaw, and East Berlin must rank among the most significant accords negotiated since 1945.

To suggest now that all of this has been done despite (or even because of) dark urges for direct control of nuclear weapons, or that in the near future all of this may be traded for a national nuclear trigger, would hardly follow from the conclusions of this study. Yet to suggest that everything has now definitely changed (presumably for the better, in terms of nonproliferation criteria at least) would seem equally foolhardy. Indeed, viewed from a somewhat longer-term perspective, many of these changes raise issues regarding the future nuclear status of Germany that are different in detail but not in kind from those of the past.

To touch on only three: What recompense or new protection must or can be afforded Bonn to offset the forced denuclearization apparently inherent in any wide-ranging East-West agreement on mutual balanced force reductions (MBFR) or a successor concept? What role would be both possible (nonthreatening to the Soviet Union) and acceptable (equal or predominant) for the Germans in any European defense arrangement that might follow eventual American withdrawal or strategic decoupling from Western Europe? And however mechanistic, what are the prospects regarding Germany's objective nuclear-development capacity, for the physical option increasing as a function of prosperity, time, and technological application?

One chapter, however forward looking, cannot deal seriously with all of these questions. The aim therefore will be to deal briefly and generally with only two areas: the principal factors that have led to a new definition of German options, summarized by the catchwords NPT, NPG, and Ostpolitik, and the broad parameters for future German policies set by these and other foreseeable developments, internal and external.

DEVELOPMENTS SINCE 1966: REAPPRAISAL OF NUCLEAR POLICIES

THE IMPACT OF OSTPOLITIK

The most radical shift in the post-1966 universe of German foreign policy has been of domestic origin, the active pursuit of Ostpolitik, an attempt to realistically adapt the Adenauerian triad of foreign-policy goals to the requirements of European détente. The driving force clearly has been the SPD, with its first postwar governing responsibilities, eager to fulfill past

promises and to win new rewards. Success has been mixed; at times movement for movement's sake has seemed to be the principal goal and short-
term result. Yet it has been this framework which has marked if not allowed
the emergence of the Federal Republic as an independent, assertive, diplomatically skilled leader in both the Western European and all-European
spheres—and all in less than a decade.

Only a few points about Ostpolitik need restatement in this context.[2]
First, it is too easy to overestimate the newness and radical character of
Ostpolitik's aims. Whatever the secret hopes of the most devoted supporters
and even of the critics, neither rhetoric nor behavior has suggested more
than a (perhaps only interim) reordering of German foreign-policy attention.
Second, Ostpolitik from 1966 to the present indeed has been a generic policy category subsuming a wide range of acts, current and potential, associated with the unfreezing of Germany's relations with the East. This flexibility in intention and expectation has been alternately a source of strength
and weakness—in the context particularly of continuing Atlantic indeter-
minism and European stalemate or confusion.

Perhaps within the Grand Coalition before the invasion of Czechoslovakia, the attraction of Ostpolitik indeed was its revitalization of old (but
called new) options. The new leadership faced a paucity of opportunities to
make its mark in NATO's post-MLF phase and in a European sphere still
dominated by an obdurate de Gaulle. Of particular interest to CDU supporters in business and industry were the potential new applications in the
East for Germany's formidable economic and technological strength—never
in doubt, but now a major tradeable asset in the traditional Eastern markets.
For the SPD, Ostpolitik provided a new framework for discussing if not
solving the German question. The final outcome could not be anticipated,
but any change would constitute both progress in human terms and a much-
needed revision of such Adenauerian incrustations as the Hallstein doctrine.

Domestically, however, the limits of change were set by the limited
basis of coalition agreement. With Brandt in command (if not always in control) of the Foreign Office, the SPD was able to push exploration of a wide
range of opportunities, to begin talks at multiple points, to probe and promise.[3] But as the question of a German signature on the nonproliferation
treaty forcefully demonstrated, in the final analysis fulfillment was dependent on CDU/CSU acquiescence. To the despair of supporters (and sometimes opponents as well), the party rarely reached a decision without in-

tended-for-the-electorate theatrics or marked intraparty dissensions. The weak stewardship of Chancellor Kurt Georg Kiesinger and the studied irresponsibility of a returned Finance Minister Strauss hardly helped. The result was a withering of the early diplomatic and trade successes under what was in effect a double veto system—by the SPD, with its commitment to "can-opener" policies of wide-ranging normalization, and by the CDU, with its determination to divide the Eastern countries and isolate East Germany at almost any cost.

This approach shifted dramatically in the post-Czechoslovakian invasion period and after the 1969 elections. Despite a non-majority coalition with the FDP (shaky indeed in the Ostpolitik area), the SPD explicitly promoted a changed perception within the Federal Republic of the international environment and of Bonn's legitimate, crucial role.[4] Not only had overarching Soviet-American nuclear hegemony stabilized Europe's political-military division, it had vitiated all policy which did not explicitly accept the status quo and proceed on that basis. In all areas but that of basic security, Bonn must normalize, to the minimum level of relations with the West, all of its relations with the East—even with that other state within the German nation. The aim must be to maximize Germany's current national freedom of maneuver, while eventually undermining the status quo through its acceptance.

Exports of capital and technology to the East therefore would provide necessary but not sufficient conditions for changed relations. The costs of political normalization, judged in terms of past practice, would be high, whether the quid was recognition of the Oder-Neisse line, an implicit denunciation of the Munich Pact of 1938 with all of the legal implications of such a denunciation, or comembership with East Germany in the United Nations. But these costs could and should be structured to gain the greatest diplomatic independence possible, with effects in all of the three Adenauerian-defined spheres.

In both phases of Ostpolitik, however, Bonn's posture on nuclear-control questions was perceived as a point of inescapable cost. The Soviet anti-German thrust within the NPT debate is explored below; logically derivable were similar Eastern European fears which the Soviet Union had long mobilized to justify tighter Soviet control. As Georgi Arbatov heavy-handedly warned a German representative at a conference in 1970 that occurred more than six months after Bonn's signature of the NPT:

I hope Mr. Jelinek understands what the results would be if the East European countries learn that you have in West Germany one or two nuclear bombs. It would really change the whole situation in Europe.[5]

More concretely, by 1969 Moscow had expressed its willingness to measurably improve normalization prospects for the Federal Republic vis-à-vis all Eastern European states once every aspect of direct access to nuclear weapons was abjured. Bonn of course would have to meet the NPT conditions: no extra-territorial production, no importation, no direct uncontrolled sharing in the production systems of others. It would also have to exhibit self-regulation in all areas of contact with nuclear materials—the most acceptable form being a multilateral approach in all civil research and development endeavors that could have even remote potential for national military use.

Bonn's behavior seems to have conformed to these conditions, although the specific motives at work cannot be conclusively isolated. In this, as indeed in all aspects of Ostpolitik, it is hard to define authoritatively the prime factors for the degree of change or even the degree of success independently attained. The timing from 1966 to 1969 was propitious for German initiatives, given the character of the general East-West context. The United States was committed to bridge-building and to pursuing a holding policy in NATO while mired deep in the Vietnam quicksand The Soviet Union was primarily interested in attaining superpower parity, but was caught in the competing strictures of domestic modernization and exclusive supply of capital and technology to an economically restive Eastern Europe.

As mentioned before, Western Europe was similarly constrained. By 1966 the French were unable to sustain either de Gaulle's push in Eastern European relations or his chosen role as détente maker. Much to de Gaulle's and then Pompidou's chagrin, the French found that they had merely legitimated subsequent German efforts. A concerted Western European campaign, even one arrayed around Bonn's thrusts, simply was impossible, given the state of disorder within the European community. And Britain's final entry into the EEC only worsened the prospects for foreign-policy coordination, let alone joint nuclear cooperation, in the near future.

The impact of the new direction and style of leadership provided by the SPD and the Brandt group, however, was unmistakable. In nuclear-policy questions, as in many areas, they provided the stimulus for reevaluation and for directed change at precisely those points where the Adenauer-Erhard foreign-policy consensus had become too rigid or had broken down completely. The result was a far more open and in a sense positive approach to the external world, one that stressed Germany's actions as well as its options, its responsibilities as well as its legal rights.

Change, of course, was the order of the day, the means through which the rewards, defined internally and externally, were to be garnered. The floundering CDU/CSU, essentially leaderless and too often hysterically irresponsible, and the minute, schizophrenic FDP were from 1966 to 1974 hardly in competitive or even comparable positions. The SPD was a party relatively disciplined and refreshed after four decades' rest from office and after ten years of relative consensus regarding foreign-policy goals. Moreover, the number of critical areas not touched by the sweep of the new broom, even since 1969 when the SPD assumed the commanding coalition role, far surpasses those which have been affected.

On balance, Brandt's creative continuity with past party positions and statements of priorities was impressive. To take only the areas most important for this analysis, the considered relation of Ostpolitik moves to current policies—on nuclear sharing, on tactical doctrine, on civil nuclear development—has been striking; and the degree of explicit popular toleration if not support for these positions has been surprising. In the face of continuing American carping, European suspicion, continuing bureaucratic sabotage, and debilitating party defections, the stance has been firm and skilled. And in contrast to Adenauer's no-experiments approach, evolution and policy change were even at times desired and innovative, not reactive, and determinedly continuous.

EXTERNAL INFLUENCES AND CONSTRAINTS: THE NPT AND THE NPG

As during 1954–1966, the principal factors inducing change in German nuclear affairs have been direct functions of external developments, especially in American policy.[6] For some officials in Bonn, Adenauer's long-avoided nightmare—superpower hegemony on the basis of the division and control of the German people—has been fulfilled. In SALT as in the NPT, on Vietnam as on Czechoslovakia, in formal agreements or through informed signaling, the superpowers have agreed to be more than just increasingly cooperative adversaries committed to constrain mutual damage capabilities. They have moved directly to limit, through attenuation or isolation, the risks to stability posed by restive allies, to defuse to whatever degree possible the chances of uncontrolled, undesired escalation, and to freeze both the present international hierarchy and the boundaries of existing spheres of influence.

For Germany as for all the middle powers, the result has been the deliberate constraining of all present and future policy choices. Quite surprising, therefore, has been the publicly flexible, adaptive German response.[7] There are still obvious anxieties; Chancellor Kiesinger's charge in 1967 of Soviet-American "nuclear complicity" was an obvious low point. But if pressed not too hard, almost every German politician of the major parties would swiftly admit basic dependence on Washington for present security and the irreplaceability of the American nuclear umbrella, whatever its credibility. Distressed calls from Bonn for reassurance or public condemnation of inadequate American consultation have not only become more private matters, by all indications the number of them has declined.

More striking has been the increasing German tendency to treat, at least explicitly, each new proposal for Soviet-American agreement or for a new negotiating forum as a framework for the active advancement of German interests. Involvement at various steps in the long-feared trend toward hegemonic détente has allowed, for example, the lightening of Bonn's "militaristic" reputation in Eastern Europe (through the "imposition" of the NPT), the enhancement of German leadership within the NATO Eurogroup (for example, in preparations for MBFR discussions), and the easement, especially with domestic critics, of the building of new German bridges to the East (for example, the coupling of the Berlin agreements with acceptance of the Moscow and Warsaw treaties, and the less successful devaluation of the Berlin clause in the Czechoslovakian accords).

THE NPT: COSTS AND BENEFITS

In large measure it was the painful lessons of 1955–1966 and especially of the MLF period that has finally brought about adaptation in German policies. Beginning with the Grand Coalition and continuing through the SPD-FDP governments, German leaders apparently have updated the basic Adenauerian principle: extract maximum political virtue from externally imposed necessity. Given the patent futility of the MLF experience, of the increasingly rigid American priorities on the European force balance and on control of nuclear proliferation, there was no rational goal-seeking purpose in maintaining and stressing nuclear options that were neither real nor realizable. By at least the mid-1960s all payoffs for Germany were within the widening of détente, not outside of it.

To be sure, such conclusions now suffer the risks of postdiction and the glaze of historical inevitability. Contrary evidence to this perhaps overly rational interpretation can be found in the bitter and protracted German debate, internal and external, over the aims and conditions of the nuclear nonproliferation treaty.[8] The stream of criticisms and denunciations of this "Soviet-American effort" heard before Erhard's fall quickly became a roaring tumult, with perhaps the greatest disturbances coming first in the late 1966–early 1967 period and then again in 1969. Judged both quantitatively and qualitatively, the debate was a composite of all the discussions and anxieties of the late 1950s and early 1960s, with perhaps the only major differences being the length devoted to one topic (intermittently for more than three years) and the greater extragovernmental scope of the debate.

As in the past, internal political calculations caused a substantial part of the debate and much of its acrimony. Viewed narrowly, the debate on the NPT was only a proximate legitimate framework within which to do battle for the Adenauerian legacy. The Center parties were most obviously concerned, with Schröder and the former Atlanticists basically but grudgingly for signature and Strauss and the CSU against it. The fundamental issue, however, was control of the party leadership, with both groups powerful enough to veto any decision but neither sufficiently strong to force acquiescence or to recement the loose coalition of groups, regions, and notables that Adenauer had constructed so skillfully. The SPD's partisan involvement was of a very different character: the testing of its leadership qualifications and skill on a set of issues associated in the mind of both the electorate and the party's membership with past emotional and "neutralist" party positions. Although always committed to early signature, Brandt and his colleagues felt constrained to demonstrate their defense of German national interests and of the national groups most concerned, especially the business community so long identified with the CDU.

This domestic context lends greater meaning to the specific objections to the treaty that Bonn repeatedly raised during the negotiation phase and to the nineteen specific interpretations Brandt issued at the time of signature. Certain issues were points of Grand Coalition friction hidden in legalistic definition, like the issue of the discriminatory "double jeopardy" for the European states subject to inspection by both Euratom and the International

Atomic Energy Agency (IAEA) or the safeguarding of the opportunity for a
"European option." Other issues touched upon the specific concerns of the
business and scientific communities, both eager to preserve German
strengths in research and export. Their concerns included assured access to
nuclear-fuel supplies for both domestic and export purposes, avoidance of
industrial espionage by potential IAEA multinational inspection teams
through a mechanical follow-the-flow system, and freedom to continue research (in breeder reactors, for example) unhampered by stringent definitions of what constitutes a nuclear weapon. The differential timing of such
constituency demands, together with such political exigencies as test state
elections, only made a complex process more difficult. For external observers at least, it was ever more suffused with an aura of grandstanding and
stage managing.

The central common concerns of the coalition, however, were patently
three: untouched continuance of the American nuclear guarantee; unhampered German participation in all nuclear arrangements (as in NATO's Nuclear Planning Group [NPG] or the physical deployment of nuclear weapons
or joint civil nuclear projects) on an equal, assured-access basis; and full
recognition of Germany's status as a major power, albeit currently and
for the foreseeable future a nonnuclear power. These were issues in what
for Germany was the central negotiating arena: the bilateral talks with the
United States. The end result was judged differently by the participants;
Washington eventually agreed to issue its six-point statement of "interpretation" in response to pressures from Germany and other allies; the CDU still
hedged its bets on full acceptance of the conditions until well after the end
of the Grand Coalition; and the SPD consciously made signature one of its
first official acts after the 1969 elections.

On a somewhat different level there were marked departures from the
past in both the style and process of the external negotiations. Largely owing
to the stance of the SPD, there was never any official bluff about not signing. Reportedly on threat of withdrawal from the coalition, the SPD argued
from the first days that to threaten even temporarily not to sign was to ignore
the realities of the American connection and especially the obvious dominance of arms controllers in Washington, to allow continued Soviet definition and manipulation of the "German menace," and to restrict the Federal
Republic to only negative impact on the treaty's specifications. During the
first months of the coalition (late 1966 through the spring of 1967), this

position came under continuing public attack, as shock waves of anger at the first, virtually unanticipated Soviet-American draft radiated through Germany.[9] But by the fall of 1967 the signature question for all but the CSU had become when rather than whether.

German movement on a number of fronts showed skillful, relatively smooth, unrelenting pressure applied with considerable skill, albeit with a considerable difference. Bonn was for the first time explicitly bargaining with both superpowers. With Moscow, the official tone was cool, constant rejection of an anti-German NPT, with more heated responses reserved for such obvious tactics as Moscow's reassertion of its rights of intervention in former "enemy states" and its intrigues during the sagging of détente that followed the Soviet invasion of Czechoslovakia. Vis-à-vis Washington, the approach was cool but insistent, with far fewer German demands focused solely on the respective rights and obligations of an ally and far more concern for the coordination of admittedly divergent interests. Throughout both sets of relations the Kiesinger-Brandt government skillfully orchestrated a variety of approaches: official presentations and informal visits, bilateral bargaining and multilateral caucusing, the soothing of domestic unrest and the citing abroad of the resulting difficult pressures, the requirements of future political uncertainty, and the dictates of present technical developments.

Indeed, whatever the degree of actual German interest involved, official criticisms of successive drafts of the treaty were far more sophisticated statements than ever before.[10] Detailed questions of both a political and technical nature were raised (e.g., the famous seventy-six questions of 1967); more often than before, the government drew on domestic resources for supporting research and evaluation (e.g., the black-box inspection system to foreclose espionage that eventually was developed at Karlsruhe); possible alternatives or acceptable forms of reassurance were articulated with some degree of originality (e.g., the proposed nuclear-blackmail clause). Information and tactical points, in this era of new diplomatic flexibility, were shared and discussed with other nuclear-threshold states, with Japan, India, and Italy in particular. Bonn and Brandt by 1968 had indeed emerged as leaders of the ill-starred Non-Nuclear Conference.

It is hard to assess the specific impact of this markedly different German approach either on the final form of the NPT or on the growing tolerance for ratification among domestic elites and masses. In the latter case, probably the more significant variables were simply the passage of time and the intrusion of more central or dramatic issues of domestic economy or Ostpolitik. Even partial fulfillment of the educational or issue-clarification goals which the SPD so consciously sought in the debate would be hard to demonstrate, except by omission. CSU calculations about public sensitivities (if not hysteria) to the contrary, the reaction of elite opinion as well as the more predictable public opinion to direct questions dealing with nuclear issues today reportedly approaches that of boredom or dismissed irrelevance.

Perhaps a better indicator of success is the continuing adoption of this basic negotiating position, nationally and internationally. Soviet-American negotiations in SALT I were met with little publicly observable criticism and suspicion. True, once European topics were excluded, there was the familiar phenomenon of European lack of interest except on such fanciful thoughts as a possible European antiballistic-missile (ABM) system. Nevertheless, Bonn's desires for prior briefings and ongoing consultation were from all reports relatively well satisfied within both the bilateral and alliance frameworks.

The truer test, of course, will come with the successful handling of the problems inherent in the necessarily more complicated and threatening follow-on rounds of East-West talks.[11] At Russian insistence SALT II was to have dealt with the postponed topic of Western forward-based weapons systems (FBS)—largely the Pershing missiles and quick-reaction nuclear-capable strike aircraft (QRAs) stationed on German soil and in part owned by Bonn. There is also the all-too-familiar issue of the 800 plus MRBMs (fixed and mobile) in western Russia, admittedly largely targeted on the Federal Republic's territory. At Vladivostock, these demands were withdrawn. At this junction it is far from clear whether the FBS will be handled in MBFR or in a related bilateral form, or what, if any, additional negotiating capital German participation in the MBFR talks (discussed further below) will yield.

Yet there are a number of indications that at least an SPD-led Bonn will continue to prefer an approach to negotiation with Washington that is lower in key, more mixed in form, more technically based, and more free-wheeling than before. Legalisms still abound; considerations of option maintenance, however expensive or inoperative in the short term, still occasionally rise to the surface. However, it can be repeated that by almost any measure the Federal Republic under Schmidt is a far more confident, innovative, diplomatically independent actor than 1963 or 1966 or perhaps 1968 would have suggested.

THE NPG: FORUM AND SAFETY VALVE

Not to be overlooked in this respect is the general devaluation that nuclear issues have undergone in NATO itself. This is hardly surprising in the case of the military organization of an alliance that has been committed for the past decade to the "active pursuit of détente," that has been implicitly convinced, despite the Czechoslovakian invasion, of the waning of a purely military threat from the East, and that has been "enthusiastically" engaged (whatever the level of allies' doubts) in negotiating with its erstwhile opponent about balanced (if not necessarily symmetrical) reductions in military capability. Perhaps the more direct causation, however, has been the lack of American leadership against which to flail or react. The MLF has spawned no hardware successors (and perhaps never will); the Johnson and Nixon administrations have been only too happy to bury flexible response.

For the Federal Republic a further dampening factor has been the operational achievements of NATO's Nuclear Planning Group and the substantial German role therein.[12] Taken as a whole, the group perhaps has enjoyed mixed success in view of the expectations of 1966—far more than the simple burial of the MLF foreseen by the group's critics, yet far less than the ultimate triumph of the education-consultation-conversion approach endorsed by its supporters. The direct output has been a series of papers or perhaps role-playing exercises produced primarily by those participating allies—England, Turkey, Germany—who have expressed most discontent with the official flexible-response doctrine formally if belatedly adopted in 1967. Several of these papers, however, particularly the Anglo-German efforts on tactical nuclear guidelines, have been adopted officially as alliance policy and operationally as the best possible interim solutions to old, perhaps irresolvable transatlantic or national differences.[13]

For Bonn, the NPG has served primarily to broaden Germany's diplomatic maneuverability and domestic flexibility. If nothing else, it has served to withdraw issues concerning use of nuclear weapons from the domestic arena and to spur the development of greater domestic expertise, confidence, and planning capability. There has been more (although reportedly still not enough) transmission of information about weapons and about American intentions. National perspectives also have been introduced, at far less cost and even with the hope of some mobilizable support, in this multilateral forum, thus easing or overcoming earlier bilateral strains and misconceptions. And establishment of the group assured another form of continuing American presence, however great the pull, first, of Vietnam and, second, of Senator Mansfield.[14]

More important in the long run, its role in the NPG was a major stimulus to Bonn's recent fundamental reexamination of doctrine.[15] It was not that the carrying through of NPG assignments to develop, for example, guidelines for use of tactical nuclear weapons or to study projected use of ADMs on German soil was a sufficient condition for change. Rather these tasks converged with those imposed by the budget strictures set forth after 1967 in the Middle-Term Financial Plan, which decisively limited the growth of the defense budget, and by the long-held convictions about strategy and the innovating style of Germany's second postwar professional defense minister, Helmut Schmidt. The publicly observable results were a series of three Defense White Papers, remarkable for Germany (or indeed for any second-tier state) in scope and detail and in the maturity of the analysis.[16]

This new German self-confidence and sense of broad support within the NPG has changed the methods for dealing with German-American doctrinal differences. Indeed, it is not without parallel that Bonn has been the chief voice raised against the de facto abandonment of flexible response, against the seeming willingness of the Nixon administration and to some extent the Johnson administration to gradually replace manpower with technology, especially tactical nuclear weapons. Some degree of the strategic lag, of lessons too well learned, that was observed in the 1954–1966 period may indeed still be at work. But the principal reason for its opposition seems to be Bonn's continuing paramount concern: the maintenance of graduated, credible deterrence coupled firmly to American military force. The Soviet Union is still the primary threat to be constrained, with the possibility of political pressure and nuclear blackmail all too conceivable even if direct invasion is not.

The doctrinal reexamination begun by Schmidt has led, however, to a number of significant shifts regarding use of tactical nuclear weapons. By 1970 the Federal Republic had at least publicly abandoned its earlier call for rights of veto over all weapons on its soil; further, it had decisively rejected widespread use of or the prepositioning of ADMs on its territory. While nuclear-capable equipment still is sought on the basis of needed military "equality," equipment purchases are to be fewer, because of budget stretch-outs, and are to meet more exacting specifications (e.g., the "cleaner" Lance missile is to be procured for the 1970s).

German doctrinal preferences were formulated best perhaps in Schmidt's first white paper, released in 1970. Nuclear weapons in Europe "must not be used except as a last resort and even then only with restraint and on a selective basis." [17] Under graduated deterrence, lower-level nuclear responses must be designed primarily to impose political restraints on the enemy, whether in "direct defense" (a NATO-defined response in kind) or in deliberate excalatory moves ("demonstration use"), whatever the specific area, intensity, or timing involved. Official Bonn is well aware that this limited, selective use "as early as necessary" again runs counter to the American preference to delay as long as possible and then to begin "decisive" use. But in contrast to the past, these differences appear less critical during a period of détente and less reconcilable in a period of divergent national perspectives. German political and military leaders (and not only they) see no realistic alternatives to an early, clearly restricted crossing of the nuclear threshold in view of the combination of the necessarily inviolable commitment to the earliest possible forward defense of the Federal Republic's territory at the lowest collateral cost with the increasingly irremediable gap in Western conventional strength, most pronounced in the areas of tank forces and tactical air capabilities.

This aura of cautious conservatism reflects in part German uncertainties about possible and perhaps even desirable outcomes for MBFR. For the longer term, German governments can be expected to seek, for budgetary reasons alone, to make major cuts in the twelve thinly spread German divisions, to reduce new armament expenditure, to reduce the army's dependence on inadequate, politically troublesome conscription, if costs will permit, and to depart from basic planning dependence on the all-service "American expeditionary force" model. [18] As is discussed below, there also are a few groups interested in returning to an all-conventional/limited forces strategy, structured (as in the original von Bonin proposals in 1955) on not matching Eastern force directly, tank for tank or plane for plane, but on antitank, antiaircraft defensive principles.

The calculus of the 1954–1966 period indeed still dominates. Unilateral action will adversely affect German stakes in the bargaining over a continued American presence in Europe and undoubtedly will set off another round of force "restructurings" on the central front. For all the reasons developed earlier, it is still preferable, whatever the cost, to retain a sizable multinational layer-cake defense on German soil with a firm attachment to American strategic forces. Smaller German forces might indeed prove lesser burdens both at home and in Eastern Europe, but there is still the problem of maintaining trading cards for future exchange.

For the last half-decade, therefore, Bonn has been willing to use almost every means to hold the relative East-West balance of forces steady until the bargaining could at least begin. To cite only the strategies most frequently used against Washington primarily, but also against London and Paris, the Germans have used suasion, example (development of the Lance missile, multirole combat aircraft [MRCA], and even in a somewhat different way the Main Battle Tank), direct grants (purchase of securities, expenditure of $200 million for improvements in foreign-troop barracks), leadership in pledges to increase shares of the alliance burden (Eurogroup in general and the European Defense Improvement Program [EDIP] in particular), and discreet political blackmail (over French deployments and potential tactical nuclear forces on German soil). The rate of short-term success, particularly when the Federal Republic has been willing to bear substantial proportions of the costs involved (averaging perhaps 40 percent), has been considerable.

But once even a first-stage Soviet-American bargain is achieved with respect to MBFR, Bonn is more than certain that there will be another round of lessons on use of nuclear weapons to be learned. Even in the post-Vietnam cautionary approach to alliance commitments, the end of conscription in the United States already means less American manpower available for European defense; the political benefits to be gained in Congress as in the electorate from a considerable reduction in European-deployed troops are purportedly substantial. Quite apart from the chain reaction of restructurings that would occur, the best available result probably would be a turn back toward a tripwire or firebreak strategy. Other outcomes considered probable and arranged in order of anxiety engendered in Bonn include: withdrawal from German soil of large numbers or classes of tactical nuclear weapons; institution of weapon-deployment zones (as in the Rapacki plans) that would effectively denuclearize German territory, German forces, and their American counterparts; the drawing down of American forces below even the often discussed two-division level; and an explicit Soviet-American agreement on a no-first-use doctrine in Europe or on coordinated strategic decoupling from destabilizing European crises and battles, conventional or nuclear. Whatever the actual probabilities, each one of these events would require a radical recasting of NATO and German thinking about defense requirements, if not about continued deterrence itself.

THE FUTURE AND ITS OPTIONS

The ramifications of such events for future German policies concerning nuclear control clearly would be enormous. Viewed from perhaps the most dire perspective, these events taken in series constitute an updated, intensified version of the inevitability scenario much favored in the early 1960s. In the face of (1) a continuing political if not direct military threat from the Soviets, and (2) attenuation of the credibility of America's nuclear guarantees of presence, plus perhaps (3) a marked destabilizing increase in Soviet strategic capabilities vis-à-vis American capabilities, or (4) the nonavailability of acceptable alternative security systems (e.g., European or Franco-German), Germany will be pushed to use its long-available material and technical potential to develop national nuclear forces, and most probably will do it clandestinely and in the shortest possible time.

The argument here has been that in a post-NPT world, as before, acquisition in this fashion of a national nuclear capability would be counterproductive for all German foreign-policy goals. Moreover, it is far from clear that the bargaining potential involved in even the discussion of such a dramatic scenario by German leaders (or perhaps their adversaries) can ever again attain a high positive value.[19] Let the focus therefore shift to those future options that are most discussed and are most plausible as implementers of presently defined German foreign-policy goals.

NUCLEAR ABSTINENCE *IN EXTREMIS*

One option of course would be to confront squarely some of the hard questions about the inherent relationships between nuclear weapons and the physical security of a middle power, questions that have been swept aside since the early 1960s. Over the past few years, for example, the FDP has fitfully asked itself and its coalition partner: What are the requirements of deterrence which can and must be met by the Federal Republic?[20] In an age of strategic parity and superpower hegemony, what is the value of a German arsenal of nuclear-capable weaponry? Short of diversion or seizure, its use depends entirely on the wishes of the American president, wishes almost totally independent of German choices. As Defense Ministry officials have been emphasizing, forward defense must begin at the very outset of any war; over one-half of the Federal Republic's industrial work force is employed within a region that can be covered by tanks in less than eight hours after their crossing of the demarcation line. Consequently would not a strong, imaginative conventional antitank defense—as critics suggested as early as the 1950s—be a better guarantor of forwardness and ultimate German survival than even the cleanest battlefield nuclear weapons or ADMs? Moreover, does not the Federal Republic in the 1970s have all the requisite leverage and equality in American or NATO decision-making that is due its economic position alone? Its role in the NPG, for example, is hardly the mere result of its possession of the second largest but essentially empty nuclear delivery capability in the West.

More broadly, what evidence does the last twenty-five years present for the necessity for presence or contiguity or border deployment of nuclear weapons or for masses of foreign troops to ensure the functioning of deterrence? In the 1970s, how many buckets of blood should constitute a sufficient guarantee of external involvement? As has been suggested only partly in jest, will not the annual net American investment of capital funds in Europe amounting to billions of dollars stand as an adequate surrogate for troops, or could not trust be placed in a series of interlocking agreements—present and future—which would be self-enforcing because of mutual expectations and reciprocal guarantees? A list might include related proportionate pledges between the United States and the Soviet Union on the one hand, and on the other hand, between France, England, the two Germanys and at least one other Eastern European state (Poland or a rehabilitated Czechoslovakia, for example).

All present indicators suggest that abstinence options such as these have not been considered very seriously, despite the flood of such basic reappraisals. At most, the options are seen as possible negotiated outcomes of MBFR discussions or SALT II, with appropriate compensation for sacrifice of Germany's interests. For most officials in Bonn, it is not yet time to voluntarily cast aside long-held bargaining cards.

THE EUROPEAN OPTION, STRATEGIC AND TACTICAL

A somewhat more probable and pragmatic option would seem to be the long-discussed Europeanization of nuclear defense, subsuming or at least drawing together existing British and French forces.[21] As discussed in detail earlier, the form most often proposed in the 1960s was the coordination or combination of these two increasingly complementary capabilities into a Eu- ropean deterrent that would be relatively independent of American forces and subject to a united European command, actual or surrogate. More recent Anglo-American discussions have placed greater stress on transatlantic coor- dination—in targeting, regularized modernization of equipment, and even direct control itself. Another more current proposal foresees British and French tactical nuclear weapons (under joint "trusteeship") as supplement- ing and eventually replacing existing American-controlled systems, includ- ing custodial arrangements with the Germans.

Whatever the form, the hindrances to and the doubts about such ar- rangements are legion, just as they were before. To start with the most obvi- ous problem, little—and all of it negative—has been heard from the French. Almost all of the recent discussion has originated in Britain, now presum- ably interested in the maximum exploitation and sharing of the burden of its Polaris submarines and aged V-bomber force. Even with a minimal degree of interaction, some common ground for ongoing discussion and negotiation would have to be found.

All-too-familiar questions remain about a European force's efficiency and effectiveness when taken in isolation. Despite the implicit boost of the limitation on ABMs negotiated under SALT I, neither the British nor the French force can reach even the 5 percent level on the maximum-assured- destruction scale. There is no evidence to support (and much to belie) the "whole is greater than the parts" argument; "tearing off an arm," crude calculation suggests, simply will not be even minimally effective more than 50 percent of the time.[22]

Without doubt, one can almost endlessly conjure up problems inherent in the creation and operation of a European force. What about existing American restrictions on sharing of technical information and on custodial control? The problems of a European NPG? A strict interpretation of the NPT's clause concerning the creation of joint forces only after a new politi- cal entity has been established?

One of the central questions, however, remains the role of the Ger- mans—a role that will prove both appropriate and acceptable. Theoretical proposals have suggested that the Federal Republic would be the major fi- nancial supporter of a European force but one bound by every possible prohibition, legal and self-imposed, against direct access to weapons or significant commingling of men and material. The extent to which the force would be committed to the forward defense of all of the Federal Republic's territory is less clear, since French proposals in particular have been characterized by references to their own borders or perhaps the Rhine line at best.

For Bonn in the 1970s and the 1980s the most probable response would seem to be "Why bother?" Almost any American arrangement would seem preferable in terms of effectiveness alone. A role in a NATO nuclear planning group in which the Americans still participated clearly would yield greater influence. The telling arguments from the past seem irrelevant. A Germany which is the acknowledged economic and perhaps diplomatic leader of Europe hardly need fear either French efforts to overvalue an increasingly cut-down *force de frappe* or a discriminatory Anglo-French pact aimed specifically (once again) at constraint and control of the Germans.

On the verbal level at least, there is still considerable support for Europeanization in Bonn among the CDU and especially the CSU. The fundamental argument is familiar: to build a Europe, one must make a start and take risks. Willingness to sacrifice now, especially on the part of the Germans, will not only advance the process, it will lead ultimately to a lifting of restrictions and to future benefits. There are indications, however, that this approach is partially an artifact of party inertia (or nostalgia). Strauss, long and most vocal advocate, has had little to say recently; indeed, so has most of the internally divided CDU leadership.[23]

Even if one posits the nearly worst possible case—total withdrawal of American forces but not American deterrent guarantees—Bonn in the near future seemingly would garner as many advantages within an all-European security arrangement as within one confined to Western Europe.[24] Much, understandably, would depend on the mode and bargaining regarding America's departure. Yet there still would be relief from the arranging of an acceptable unified command (or set of structures) or internation coordination deemed so essential in the West. Given its position and potential, the Federal Republic still would be one of the major actors within (and influencing) the framework agreed upon by the superpowers.

There might also be considerably less direct economic burden; increased political influence and interaction on relatively nondiscriminatory terms in East and West would be assured.

Unquestionably, the probability of such an arrangement occurring is ex-

tremely low; but given both the changes in underlying conditions necessary
to bring it about and the general guidelines set out in the domestic struggle
over Ostpolitik, there would seem at least an even chance of a positive German response.

As before, the primary variable would be the direction of American
policy, as reflected in NATO guarantees and doctrines. Viewed from one
perspective, Brandt's Westpolitik (and that of Schmidt and his presumptive
successors in all parties) was a commitment to constancy within change.[25]
Its minimal operational definition is an indefinite American veto over all
German security arrangements (however loosely defined) so long as the
American commitment remains firm.[26] Recent press reports suggest that
Washington is distrustful of if not unprepared for any sweeping change in
the status quo. This is true whether the discussion focuses on eventual European outcomes—which are seen as involving all the risks of the political *im-
mobilisme* of the 1930s—or on various Western European schemes, the latter having been questioned publicly by Washington in terms of unity and
efficiency with with overtones reminiscent of earlier cold-war prohibitions
against second-tier collusion or risk taking.

ACQUISITION BY DISPENSATION

Perhaps the only serious option left to consider is one often discussed in
the 1970s with respect to Japan: the development of a national nuclear capability through the cooperation or at least the active tolerance of the United
States.[27] The most favored scenario in the Japanese case foresees an arrangement technically like the Anglo-American conventions but allowing (if
not encouraging) assumption of independent responsibility in the East Asian
military/foreign-policy balance. Warheads and delivery systems might be directly provided or produced under license sponsorship, thus exploiting recent research developments yet fulfilling both the NPT requirement and the
intricacies of the more stringent nonproliferation pact that America implicitly has concluded with the Soviet Union.

Clearly the fit of this scenario with what this analysis has considered
the primary elements in the existing European security system is far from
perfect. The demonstrated *idée fixe* of the Soviets about Germany's access
to nuclear weapons alone seems sufficient hindrance now and in the future.
A second Rapallo on Soviet terms would seem the only possible gating factor. The probability of that occurring between a state now formally accorded

worldwide parity with the United States and a state that still views its American connection as the major element in its security would seem to approach zero.

It is almost as hard to conceive of the changes in American policy concerning access to nuclear weapons that would make such sharing appear both necessary and desirable. American policies concerning nuclear-weapons access have often been ambiguous but never openhanded or free from hegemonic control, even in the British case. Even if wide-ranging superpower agreement is posited, what manipulable controls outside of double keys and physical custody would Washington find acceptable? And while in a five-pole world a case might be made for Japan, any such intrusive development in Central Europe could only be destabilizing in terms of several balances, regional and global.

But it is hardest to imagine any but the most extreme or unknowing German leadership in the future accepting such an arrangement for Germany alone—perhaps the most revealing measure of changes since 1966. Such an arrangement would put into question all the normalization moves towards the East, raise again the easily exploited specter of an expansionist, revanchist Germany. Patently it would restore a degree of dependency on the United States that might fatally constrict Germany's new freedom of diplomatic maneuver. Most important of all, logic would suggest good grounds for Bonn's suspicions of any Soviet-American agreement that would allow this arrangement to occur. If indeed it was not based on superpower coordination, then such a program either would entail maximum risk for minimal gain or would be totally irrelevant.

PRODUCTION POTENTIAL

The scope of speculation has now moved full circle, returning to the point where this analysis started, namely, the inescapable fact of the possession by Germany of a significant potential for nuclear-weapons production. To cite only a recent rough yet dramatic estimate, by 1980 or sooner, the Federal Republic will produce annually an estimated 1,000–4,000 kilograms of plutonium (exploitable for one hundred to two hundred nuclear weapons annually) through nuclear power-generation programs alone.[28] A critical further note is that during the past six or seven years Bonn's civil nuclear program has become, in the words of one estimate, "second to none outside the nuclear weapon powers." [29] It now has all of the research skills and technical facilities—enrichment and reprocessing facilities being the most recently acquired—necessary for an autonomous production takeoff. The only element lacking is a domestic source of uranium, a handicap which India at least found negligible.

Challenge to this type of argument about a de facto just-under-the-threshold option is relatively easy. Most simply, the argument ignores (or cannot contemplate) the easier roads to national nuclear capability: seizure of the inactive (controlled by permissive action links), thinly guarded American stocks of warheads on German soil, careful diversion of the nuclear fuel now in use and provided from external sources, or exploitation of the large civil nuclear-fuel stockpile wrung from Washington during the NPT debate as a hedge against an uncertain future. Each of these routes, of course, involves risks of detection and indeed of program failure. Yet all, and especially the second and third, would seem far more effective short-run solutions, if only in end-running the buildup of hostile external coalitions.

To touch briefly on only one other aspect, all the new ventures of the NPT and post-NPT periods explicitly have been designed by Bonn with reassurance and control in view. Development of gas ultracentrifuge technology for uranium enrichment is proceeding jointly with Britain and the Netherlands—with no facilities on German soil—under an agreement carefully cleared with the United States and concluded after Germany's signature of the NPT.[30] The fuel reprocessing plant is small and is deliberately tied to France and others under a series of interlocking agreements. All of this development of course is also embedded in the most extensive and sophisticated external control system now in operation, with on-site follow-the-fuel and record checks of facilities by the multiple external sources involved, who reportedly make an average of five visits a year.[31]

The list of problems, as the NPT debate proved, is endless. There are problems of unnoticed enrichment that achieves the level of weapon-grade material, of the vociferous scientific community still firmly committed to the noninvolvement pledge of 1957, of credible rhetoric without an adequate testing program, of secrecy in what one official interviewed described as the ultimate transparent society.

Still open, however, are the questions that plagued nonproliferation advocates long before the NPT. To what extent must potential for production be considered to be at least the first step toward acquisition of capability?[32] To what extent in the 1970s will not potential, in and of itself, signify an op-

tion politically created and held in reserve? And even if not totally inten-
tional, will not potential constitute a resource of "last resort?"

As this study has indicated, these are essentially unanswerable questions, since the impact of political will is not subject to reliable prediction
even through the most advanced methods of measurement. Viewed only
from the technical perspective, the rapid development and competitive com-
mercial (cum status) diffusion of nuclear technology have made impossible
any definitive categorization of a particular investment or even a series (e.g.,
dependence on fast breeder reactors or natural uranium reactors), as it would
tend to seem tantamount to a decision to develop a national nuclear weapons
program. The NPT notwithstanding, the possibilities for unauthorized diversion, secret development, or even wholesale importation, once the political
decision has been made, are incalculable. In the 1970s even a moderately industrialized state willing to spend throughout a decade $100–500 million in
start-up costs can acquire a small nuclear capability with indeed decreasing
technical difficulty. For the Federal Republic these technical and cost calculations would be largely academic questions.

As argued throughout this study, the more difficult relationship to spec-
ify is the influence of external and internal expectations on this interaction of
capability with intention. One clear ground for caution is the fact that a significant portion of the world's elites (including some in Germany) believe
proliferation is indeed an inevitable process that currently is under only temporary constraint. Given the penalties that military development most probably would call forth, a significant divertable civil program is the precedent
and indeed the most probable first step. There may be some sweeping
changes in the international system of the 1970s; the general consensus now
is that the number of serious near-nuclear or contender states is considerably
fewer than those endless series portrayed in the early 1960s, only partially
for effect. Yet it would seem a safe bet that by the 1980s a nuclear-threshold
option within the NPT framework might prove to have a political weight
somewhat comparable to an obsolescent or totally dependent nuclear force.

Within this context, the Federal Republic will in all probability face a
set of all-too-familiar dilemmas and paradoxes that will be different in intensity but not in kind from those of the past. Germany by the early 1970s had
indeed ceded its position as the leading nuclear contender (given its level of
technological skill) first to India and then to Israel and Japan, and its position as potentially the greatest disrupter of the present world order among

the nuclear candidates to perhaps Israel. Yet expectations based on past behavior, the fact of objective technological capability, and the objective and
perceived inconsistency in the Federal Republic's international status will
keep the question of German access to nuclear weapons one of continuing if
no longer predominant concern.

To sum up, this continuance of concern will prevail despite the perception and the acknowledgement in Bonn that should the Federal Republic
choose even a multilateral framework for direct access, it will face higher
risks and more direct costs, both specific and general, than almost any other
contender state. A German government, *rebus sic stantibus,* would win few
points at home and assuredly none abroad. Rational calculus—never a primary guide for policy—suggests that acquisition of a nuclear-weapons capability would add nothing to Germany's present military security and a questionable (or perhaps marginal) amount to its international political assets.
Even if status alone is the criterion, the Federal Republic will be hard put to
justify a mere repetition of the Indian or the expectable Japanese or Israeli
breach of the NPT proscriptions. Justification seemingly would require an
even more improbable stimulus—a nuclear-armed Italy or Poland or indeed
East Germany.

Yet one does not have to believe in the conspiracy theory of world politics to foresee that some few Germans may sincerely argue that an option of
direct access to nuclear weapons must be kept alive. Short of fundamental
new arms control agreements, the continued restraint and constraint of Germany regarding nuclear issues will prove increasingly less possible and less
acceptable, whether viewed in national or in more systemic terms. There is
the still unresolved question of the appropriate definition of German national
identity in a world of nation states, of the necessary workability of the self-
imposed limits on Germany's extra-European role, recent flirtations with
China notwithstanding. And there are the basic unresolved questions of the
effective leverage open to a second-tier state (second-tierness itself convey-
ing an uncertain status) in an international system in which the use of force
had been a seriously constrained and for major states a markedly less
frequent, less legitimate instrument of policy, but in which no replacement
for military potential as a prime component and indicator of national power
has yet emerged.[33]

To predict German policy beyond the end of the 1970s would seem a
foolish task; in an era characterized by both negotiation and serendipity,

forecasting for half a decade is at best a chancy exercise. But if the present firm commitment to policies of cautious nuclear strategy and of total abstinence from direct access to nuclear weapons has only reduced past nuclear dilemmas, there seems little reason to expect their total elimination by 1980. Choices will still be hard and in need of constant recalculation. And although greatly lessened, the underlying German predilection to give no major hostages to an uncertain future will—and perhaps should—die hard.

APPENDIX: SOURCES

✠ Interview Data, Press Accounts, Official German Publications, and Strauss Collection

All material, written or spoken, obtained by the author in the German or French language was translated into English by her.

INTERVIEW DATA

THE SAMPLE

Three considerations guided the drawing of the sample of respondents to be interviewed for this study. The first and more usual consideration was reaching the German actors who had played a central role in, or who were knowledgeable about, one or more phases of Adenauerian nuclear policy-making from 1954 to 1966. The second was the need to secure reliable reports from a number of respondents (the minimum level being set at four) on what previous analyses suggested were critical points in these deliberations. And the third was the desire to compare Germans' interpretations of events with those of closely involved actors in the United States and in other European states in the Atlantic alliance.

As with most elite interviewing done for interpretive purposes, the first problem was to define the population. The compiling of a brief historical survey and some preliminary interviewing done in Washington and Cambridge, Massachusetts, in early 1964 yielded a list of some 50 possible names. About 20 more were added on the basis of available information about the panel of German elite members used by Daniel Lerner [1] and the elite sample drawn for the Yale Arms Control and Disarmament Agency project, then in the preliminary stages.[2] By the end of 1964, after the first round of full-scale interviews of Americans, the list of possible interviews had grown to almost 100. Preliminary requests for interviews were addressed to some 25 Germans, with hope of interviewing perhaps only some 40 in all.

Three months of research and interviewing in Germany, conducted at the invitation of the Deutsche Gesellschaft für Auswärtige Politik from the base of its Forschungsinstitut in Bonn, led to a radical revision of both the list and the interview plans.[3] A considerably larger number of both German

TABLE 7
Interviews with German Respondents by Category and Frequency

Category	1965–1966		1968
	Number	Multiple interviews	Reinterviews
Elite Interviews			
Politicians			
Total	**15**	**6**	**7**
by function:			
Legislators	10	4	5
Party officials	5	2	2
by party:			
CDU/CSU	8	3	2
SPD	6	2	4
Other	1	1	1
Military officers			
Total	**26**	**11**	**6**
Serving officers	19	9	5
Retired officers	7	2	1
Public officials			
Total	**27**	**9**	**8**
by type of appointment			
Civil servants	18	7	6
Appointees	9	2	2
by ministry			
Foreign Office	11	4	3
Defense Ministry	9	3	3
Other	7	2	2
Interest-group leaders			
Total	**11**	**2**	**1**
Business	7	1	1
Trade union	2	1	0
Other	2	0	0
Reference interviews			
Journalists			
Total	**17**	**7**	**5**
Daily press	8	3	2
Other	9	4	3
Intellectuals, independent analysts	**19**	**4**	**4**
Grand Total	**115**	**39**	**31**

TABLE 8
Location of Interviews or Reinterviews
with German Respondents

	1965–1966	1968
Bonn	59	20
Elsewhere in the Federal Republic	29	0
Paris	11	0
Washington	14	7
London	2	2
Brussels	0	2
Total	115	31

and non-German respondents seemed to be needed in order to overcome the problems of widespread lapses in memory and the not surprising caution and reticence being encountered. Moreover, there was by then a snowballing of names, based on interview references, elite referrals, and increasing personal contacts, largely through the Gesellschaft and its distinguished study group on international security and arms control. By mid-1965 the list of possible respondents, divided now into elite participants and knowledgeable intellectuals and journalists, numbered some 200 Germans and 100 non-Germans.

As tables 7 and 9 show, approximately two-thirds of that number (115 Germans, 70 non-Germans) eventually were interviewed over the two-year period. The author's 23-month stay in Bonn and Paris under a Ford Foundation grant made reinterviews both possible and extremely useful. A number of respondents, particularly in Bonn, even volunteered a second conversation. This often resulted from their checking of their files or came in the wake of a significant happening, say, in the denouement of MLF or the creation of the McNamara Committee.

A second round of interviews (31 Germans; 10 others) was conducted in 1968 under a grant from the Institute of War and Peace Studies, then concerned with the broad problem of European security.[4] Most were reinterviews, since the aim was both to probe recollections of the 1965–1966 period and to gain insight into the impacts of the NPT discussions and Ostpolitik developments. Again, those reinterviewed were selected primarily in terms of probable knowledge and accessibility. As shown in table 8, proportionally more of these interviews were conducted in Washington.

TABLE 9
Interviews with Non-German Respondents
by Category, 1964–1966

	Americans	British	French
A. *Elite interviews*			
Politicians	3	2	4
Military	11	2	5
Public officials	9	3	10
B. *Reference interviews*			
Journalists	7	3	5
Intellectuals	5	7	4
Total	35	17	28

INTERVIEW TECHNIQUE

Appointments for interviews were made either through a written request or increasingly by 1966 through personal referral or contact. In each case a special effort was made to fully identify the author, the nature of the projects, and the proposed focus of the interview. Few requests—approximately fifteen, eight with Americans—were denied outright.[5]

Preparation for interviews with elite respondents focused on their known or suspected role in a particular policy-making phase. A considerable effort was made to check career details and reported relationships with other key actors. Talks with knowledgeable scholars and journalists were less structured and functioned more as reference interviews.

The interviews with Europeans proved surprising in a number of respects. Most exceeded the suggested time limit, with the average interview of Germans lasting more than an hour. One interview indeed involved intermittent questioning throughout an eight-hour visit. Almost all interviews were conducted in the respondent's native language or in a mixed format; all quotations from these interviews incorporated into the text are translations by the author. Although most interviews were confined to the office of the respondent or the author, more than a dozen interviews in Germany took place in more informal settings.[6]

A variety of interviewing approaches were used. Only the first and last questions were common to every interview and comparable to those used by the Lerner or Yale group. From the first question, depending on the respondent, the interview might follow a stylized recounting of a historical event or a general discussion of the technical requirements of nuclear sharing. The general tactic was to learn as much as possible about the respondent's personal perspective. Accordingly, very few topics were common components of more than twenty interviews.[7]

In general, the interviews flowed well, with only six ending abruptly or with obvious irritation on the part of the respondent. The greatest initial problems lay in offsetting disdain for "yet another questionnaire." In Europe, the promise of nonattribution and the taking of only minimal notes were clearly crucial elements.

Each interview therefore had to be written up as soon after the event as possible. As those who have done it know, one can gain the ability to conduct an interview for an hour and immediately thereafter write down the respondent's remarks almost verbatim. Opportunities for additional interviews and for reinterviews also proved helpful.

Possible respondent error or bias, however, remained a continuing concern. To meet the requirements of both validity and reliability, efforts were made to cross check the accounts of at least four major participants in each key phase, to compare interview accounts with contemporaneous press accounts (see below), and to compare these accounts with those given to other investigators at an earlier or even later point.

PRESS ACCOUNTS

The following newspapers were examined by the author for the periods listed. The indicated abbreviations are those used in the footnotes to this study.
Bayern Kurier, 1958–1968
Christ und Welt, Stuttgart, 1962–1966
Christian Science Monitor, 1963–1965
Die Welt, 1956–1966
Die Zeit, 1954–1962, 1965–1966
Die Zeit (NA): *Die Zeit,* North American edition, 1963–1964, 1967–1969
FAZ: Frankfurther Allgemeine Zeitung, 1954–1968
France Observateur, 1956–1960
General Anzeiger (Bonn), 1965–1967
Le Monde, 1954–1966
New York Herald Tribune, 1956–1960

NYT: New York Times, 1954–1973
NYT (E): *New York Times,* European edition, 1964–1966
NZZ: Neue Zürcher Zeitung, 1954–1966
Rheinische Merkur, 1960–1966
SDZ: Suddeutsche Zeitung, 1954–1966
Times (London), 1954–1966 *passim*.

OFFICIAL GERMAN PUBLICATIONS

Verhandlungen: Stenographische Berichte is the official record of proceedings in the Bundestag and is published by the Bundestag; it is cited in the footnotes to this study as *Verhandlungen.* (*Verhandlungen: Anlagen zu den Stenographische Berichte* is a compilation of supplementary documents and reports and, although consulted by the author, has not been cited in this study.) *Bulletin* is published daily (in German) by the Presse- und Informationsamt, the press and information office of the federal government. *The Bulletin* is an English-language weekly publication of the BPIA; it is cited in this study as *Bulletin* (Eng.). All of these periodicals are published in Bonn.

STRAUSS COLLECTION

The author extensively examined a private collection formerly in Bonn that includes all of Franz Josef Strauss's known writings and speeches from 1956 to 1962. For the analysis in chapter 3 and subsequent chapters, persons who had worked on major or controversial speeches by Strauss were interviewed, so far as was possible, and their impressions of the content or intent of his remarks checked against the written record. Most of Strauss's output eventually was published in some form; citations in the footnotes are to the private collection only for speeches or writings that were never published.

NOTES

INTRODUCTION

1. This study is a substantially revised and expanded version of the author's doctoral dissertation, "German Nuclear Dilemmas: 1954–1966," submitted to the Political Science Department of the Massachusetts Institute of Technology in September 1967. Further references to this earlier work are cited as Kelleher, MIT.

2. See the appendix for further information on how these individuals were identified and a sample chosen for focused-interviewing purposes.

3. This study was explicitly designed to be only broadly comparable to two extensive, authoritative data sets on German elite attitudes: that imaginatively gathered by Daniel Lerner from 1954 to 1966 and presented by him and Morton Gorden in *Euratlantica* (Cambridge: MIT Press, 1969); and that collected by Karl W. Deutsch, Lewis J. Edinger, Roy C. Macridis, and Richard L. Merritt under a grant from the Arms Control and Disarmament Agency (ACDA) during 1964–65 and presented in *France, Germany, and the Western Alliance* (New York: Scribner, 1967). Although exact figures are not available, there is presumably considerable overlap in respondents between these two sets and that used in this study in all but the military sector, obviously more heavily exploited here.

4. The standard citation to any invocation of the rational-actor model must be to Graham T. Allison's Model I as discussed in his *Essence of Decision* (Boston: Little, Brown, 1971).

5. An early analysis of these assumptions and the relations they bore to postwar German reality is Hans Speier's classic *German Rearmament and Atomic War* (Evanston: Row, Peterson, 1957).

6. See, for example, the kinds of technical emphasis evident in an otherwise commendable first "objective" effort, Leonard Beaton and John Maddox, *The Spread of Nuclear Weapons* (New York: Praeger, 1962). Throughout the text of the present study, such political and technological determinism regarding nuclear proliferation is referred to as the inevitable proliferation model. The first thoroughgoing critique of this model was William S. Bader, *The United States and the Spread of Nuclear Weapons* (New York: Pegasus, 1968). But the tradition still persists, as shown in George F. Quester, "Some Conceptual Problems on Nuclear Proliferation," *American Political Science Review*, June, 1972, 490–97.

7. Richard E. Neustadt, *Alliance Politics* (New York: Columbia University Press, 1970).

8. Even those authors purportedly engaged in such a review find themselves mired down by this earlier focus on historical repetition and technological requirements. See, for example, the slippage between the promises of such a review and the actual achievement mustered throughout most of Johan J. Holst (ed.), *Security, Order and the Bomb* (Oslo: Universetetsforlagt, 1972).

CHAPTER I. PROLOGUE: 1945–1954

1. Protocol III, on the Control of Armaments, Annex I (incorporating the provisions of Annex II, paragraph 103), reprinted together with the other protocols modifying the Brussels and North Atlantic treaties in Senate Committee on Foreign Relations, *Protocol on the Termi-*

nation of the Occupation Regime in the Federal Republic of Germany and Protocol to the North Atlantic Treaty on the Accession of the Federal Republic of Germany, Executives L and M, 83rd Cong., 2nd sess. (1954) (hereafter referred to as Senate, *Protocols*).

2. Cf. the Soviet "legal" arguments analyzed by Zbigniew Brzezinski in his "Moscow and the MLF: Hostility and Ambivalence," *Foreign Affairs,* October, 1964, 126–34, with the standard Western interpretation presented by Mason Willrich in "West Germany's Pledge on Nuclear Weapons," *Virginia Journal of International Law,* December, 1966, 91–100.

3. The high-probability sites have at various times been reported to include Spain, then-French-controlled Sahara, South Africa, and Argentina.

4. "The Objectives of Germany," in *A World of Nuclear Powers?,* ed. Alastair Buchan (Englewood Cliffs: Prentice-Hall, 1966), 41.

5. For Adenauer's 1965 impressions of this encounter, see his interview with Thomas J. Hamilton, *New York Times,* European edition [*NYT* (E)], October 14, 1965. A somewhat fuller account is in his *Erinnerungen, 1953–1955* (Stuttgart: Deutsche, 1966), 346–47.

6. This section is particularly indebted to the work of two German scholars who were resident fellows of the Forschungsinstitut of the Deutsche Gesellschaft fur Auswärtige Politik in Bonn during the author's 1965–66 tenure there. They are Dr. Gerhard Wettig, author of *Entmilitarisierung und Wiederbewaffnung in Deutschland 1943–1955* (Munich: Oldenbourg, 1967); and Dr. Arnulf Baring, author of *Aussenpolitik in Adenauers Kanzlerdemokratie* (Munich: Oldenbourg, 1969).

7. Control Council for Germany, *Official Gazette* (Berlin: Allied Secretariat for Germany), Law 25.

8. For a more detailed description of the German atomic energy program and the allies' fears, see Samuel A. Goudsmit, *Alsos* (New York: Henry Schuman, 1947); David Irving, *The German Atomic Bomb* (New York: Simon & Schuster, 1968); and Robert Jungk, *Brighter Than a Thousand Suns* (New York: Grove Press, 1958), especially 48–105, 214–20.

9. Goudsmit, *Alsos,* especially 176–86.

10. Quoted in Jungk, *Thousand Suns,* 219.

11. Jungk describes and supports this argument, in explicit opposition to Goudsmit's thesis; *ibid.,* 92–104.

12. Quoted in Robert Batchelder, *The Irreversible Decision, 1939–1950* (New York: Macmillan, 1961), 32.

13. The definitive discussion of American plans and expectations in this period, as throughout the initial stages of the Eisenhower New Look, is contained in the essays which comprise Warner R. Schilling, Paul Y. Hammond, and Glenn H. Snyder, *Strategy, Politics, and Defense Budgets* (New York: Columbia University Press, 1962).

14. See U.S. Department of State, *Germany, 1947–1949: The Story in Documents* (1950).

15. See "Agreement on Prohibited and Limited Industries" in *ibid.,* 64. The severity of these prohibitions can best be measured by noting that uranium's critical mass is approximately 22 pounds and that of plutonium, approximately 2.5 pounds.

16. Leo Brandt, *Staat und friedliche Atomforschung* (Cologne: Westdeutscher, 1956), 17.

17. See the interesting summary of the opposition's position in Hans Speier, *German Rearmament and Atomic War* (Evanston: Row, Peterson, 1957), chapter 8.

18. For a more detailed treatment of the structural and operational difficulties faced by Amt Blank, see Baring, *Aussenpolitik,* part 1, especially 21–30; and Wettig, *Entmilitarisierung,* chapters 3 and 4, *passim.*

19. The basic source on the EDC period, albeit with an almost exclusively French orientation, remains Daniel Lerner and Raymond Aron, *France Defeats EDC* (New York: Praeger, 1957). Wettig's chapter 4, "Das Scheitern der EVG und der Beitritt der Bundesrepublik zum Atlantikpakt," sections 1 and 2, in *Entmilitarisierung,* 523–89, adds considerable new material from the German perspective.

20. Konrad Adenauer, *Erinnerungen, 1945–1953* (Stuttgart, Deutsche, 1965), 395. See also Baring's incisive treatment, *Aussenpolitik,* 48–62 *passim.*

21. Wettig, *Entmilitarisierung,* 244–45. Known as both a military scholar and a diplomat, Speidel had been Rommel's chief of staff in France and an associate of the unsuccessful 20th-of-July plot to assassinate Hitler. His influence during the entire rearmament process was substantial; in 1957 he became the first German commander to hold a major NATO post, that of Commander, Allied Ground Forces, Central Europe.

22. James P. Warburg, *Germany, Key to Peace* (Cambridge: Harvard University Press, 1953), 184, quoted in Wolfram F. Hanrieder, *West German Foreign Policy, 1949–1963* (Stanford: Stanford University Press, 1967), 47. For further discussions of early rearmament considerations, see Laurence W. Martin, "The American Decision to Rearm Germany," in *American Civil-Military Decisions,* ed. Harold Stein (Birmingham: University of Alabama Press, 1963), 646–49; Jules Moch, *Histoire du réarmement allemand depuis 1950* (Paris: Laffont, 1965), 15–42; and Wettig, *Entmilitarisierung,* 234–51, 265–81.

23. Perhaps the best-known and most dramatic evidence of Adenauer's basic mistrust of his fellow Germans, this pessimistic prediction about the return of German militarism and nationalism was stated at an informal gathering during the London conference after the EDC's fall; it was overheard by journalist Lothar Ruehl and reported in *Der Spiegel,* October 6, 1954, 5–7. See Baring's analysis of this mistrust in terms of Adenauer's perspective as a Rhinelander, a Francophile, and a "compleat civilian" in *Aussenpolitik,* 54–60.

24. Charles de Gaulle, *Memoirs of Hope,* trans. Terence Kilmartin (London: Weidenfeld & Nicolson, 1971), 177. Given de Gaulle's sense of his historical place, it is interesting that he mentions at this point his statement to Adenauer of the four preconditions of French support of German policy: Bonn's acceptance of its existing frontiers, an attitude of good will in its relations with the East, complete unilateral renunciation of atomic weapons, and unremitting patience concerning reunification. Despite some rhetorical ambiguity and a few incidents of Franco-German nuclear dalliance that are reported on in chapter 5, these preconditions remained the basic cornerstones of de Gaulle's and his successors' German policy.

25. See Great Britain, Foreign Office, *The European Defense Community Treaty,* Cmd. 9127 (London: 1954), especially articles 87, 89, 101–11, 114, 115, 120, and the provisions on the strategically exposed areas in article 107 and its annex II.

26. Wettig, *Entmilitarisierung,* 472–73. At London in 1950, reliable sources have suggested, there was further discussion of an earlier proposal to designate all areas east of the Rhine as strategically exposed. Parts of Holland and Belgium reportedly were later included within this category.

27. See Wilhelm Cornides and Hermann Volle, "Die Einbeziehung der Bundesrepublik in die Europäische Verteidigungsgemeinschaft," *Europa Archiv,* 13–14/1952, 5020–40.

28. Johann Graf Kielmansegg, "Der Vertrag über die Gründung der Europäischen Verteidigungsgemeinschaft," *Europa Archiv,* 13–14/1952, 5016. Colonel von Kielmansegg, later general and commander of all NATO land forces in the Central Region, was at that time an important member of the nascent Defense Ministry, called Amt Blank, although it still officially was the "Office for Questions relating to the Increase of Allied Troops." See further discussion below, chapter 2.

29. Basic sources on this rather frantic period include Konrad Adenauer, *Erinnerungen, 1953–1955,* 315–80; and Anthony Eden, *Full Circle* (Boston: Houghton Mifflin, 1960), book 1, chapter 7. For a more detailed description, see Hermann Volle, "Die Agonie der Europäischen Verteidigungsgemeinschaft," *Europa Archiv,* 23/1954, 7115–26. For further details concerning national positions and the course of negotiations before the London conference, see Roscoe Drummond and Gaston Coblentz, *Duel at the Brink* (Garden City: Doubleday, 1960), 102–8; Hermann Volle, "Die britische Europapolitik nach dem Scheitern der EVG," *Europa Archiv,* 2/1955, 7231–42; Wettig, *Entmilitarisierung,* 590–606; and F. Roy Willis, *France, Germany, and the New Europe, 1945–1967,* rev. ed. (New York: Oxford University Press, 1968), 185–201.

30. Wettig, *Entmilitarisierung,* 602–4, discusses this proposal in detail.

31. *Erinnerungen, 1953–1955,* 347.

32. Quoted in Sommer, "Objectives of Germany," 41, and confirmed by interview comments in 1966.

33. Only a handful of those interviewed in 1965–66, however, admitted that they took these French ambitions even semiseriously. All were from the "French" wing of the CDU; several had been in the Foreign Office. But as Lawrence Scheinman well documents in his *Atomic Energy Policy in France under the Fourth Republic* (Princeton: Princeton University Press, 1965), even French politicians were not then so convinced of an atomic future. See his chapter 4 and Konrad Huber, "Die friedliche Verwendung der Atomenergie in Frankreich und die französiche Stellungnahme zur Europäischen Atomgemeinschaft," *Europa Archiv,* 23–24/1957, 10340–42; and Jean Planchais, "La France et les armes atomiques," *Le Monde,* April 14, 1954.

34. These, of course, were only a small fraction of the more than sixty points made at the Brussels meetings. See Wettig, *Entmilitarisierung,* 574; *Le Monde,* August 24, 1954; and Scheinman, *Atomic Energy Policy,* 103–11.

35. Eden, *Full Circle,* 169. Several former officials who were present commented in 1965 that Luxembourg made a similar declaration. None of these offers was made public or was annexed to the final treaty.

36. Adenauer, *Erinnerungen, 1953–1955,* 347. See also his general discussion of all the negotiations, *ibid.,* 313–80, generally confirmed by American and German sources interviewed in 1965–66.

37. Cf. Adenauer's own account, *ibid.,* 347–48, with the research of Wettig, *Entmilitarisierung,* 604ff., and Scheinman, *Atomic Energy Policy,* 103–11.

38. Cf. Protocol III on the Control of Armaments and Protocol IV on the Agency of Western European Union for the Control of Armaments, in Senate, *Protocols.*

39. Willrich suggests in his analysis that the possibility of revision of prohibitions of ABC weapons by unanimous vote of the WEU Council was implied in the treaty negotiations and accepted by the United States; see "Germany's Pledge," 97.

40. See Konrad Huber, "L'utilisation pacifique de l'énergie atomique en Allemagne," *Politique Etrangère,* 6/1956, 678, and the rather bitter comments about the shortness of the period by M. Alfred Coste-Floret in National Assembly, *Journal Officiel,* December 22, 1954, 6771. Few of those then in the Chancellor's Office or Foreign Office revealed in later interviews any knowledge of the letter—some indication of its minimal value at least to the German side.

41. For a full discussion of the ratification debates in both France and Germany, see Willis, *France, Germany,* 188–197. For a discussion of the motives underlying French Assembly positions, see Nathan Leites and Christian de la Malène, *Paris from EDC to WEU,* RM-1668-RC (Santa Monica: RAND, 1956).

42. Leites and de la Malène, *Paris from EDC,* 97–98. See especially the debates in the National Assembly on December 22, 27, 1954, and the discussions in the Council of the Republic on March 24, 26, 1955.

43. It is worth noting that under both the EDC formula and the WEU treaty all Continental states agreed to controls over production on their soil only. Given contemporary concerns, any broader formulation would have been at best irrelevant.

44. There unquestionably was some partisan twisting of memory once Adenauer (assisted by Franz Josef Strauss) began to publicize his version during the 1965 federal election campaign, which is discussed below and in chapters 9 and 10. But interview respondents in 1964 in Washington and in early 1965 in Bonn also confirmed at least the general outline of Dulles's remarks —often with a shaking of the head.

45. Coral Bell, *Negotiation from Strength* (London: Chatto & Windus, 1962), 87, quoting John Foster Dulles, *War, Peace, and Change* (London: Macmillan, 1939), 47, and "Security in the Pacific," *Foreign Affairs,* January, 1952, 183.

46. See chapter 5 *passim.*

47. For Adenauer's 1965 impressions of this encounter, see his interview with Thomas J. Hamilton, *NYT (E),* October 14, 1965. The first public reference to this political strategy, significantly, was in Franz Josef Strauss, "An Alliance of Continents," *International Affairs* (London), April 1965, 200.

48. Without question, this was the most straightforward (or cynical) comment on this issue recorded in any of the 1965–66 interviews, whether with Germans or Americans. By 1968—presumably after the battles and benefits associated with NPT and a clear shift in American nonproliferation policy—such a detached view of the potential for manipulation was heard more frequently. But in 1965–66 the issues at stake were NATO, MLF, the American guarantee, and even the French *foederator*—all too serious for any Foreign Office or Defense Ministry official, or even many left-wing politicians, to take lightly.

CHAPTER II. THE TRANSITION: 1955—1956

1. For a more detailed discussion of this maneuver and its political consequences, see Hans Speier, *German Rearmament and Atomic War* (Evanston: Row, Peterson, 1957), chapter 10.

2. See *Süddeutsche Zeitung* [SDZ], June 29, July 12, 1955.

3. Federal Republic of Germany, Bundestag, *Verhandlungen: Stenographische Berichte,* February 25, 1955, 3736 [hereafter cited as *Verhandlungen*].

4. Cf. his *Keiner kann den Krieg gewinnen* (Bonn: Schimmelbusch, 1955); his Carte Blanche columns, *Frankfurter Allgemeine Zeitung* [*FAZ*], June 22, 24, 28, 1955; and his later commentaries, *FAZ*, July 7, 12, 1955.

5. See, for example, the speeches by Ollenhauer, Erler, and Blachstein in *Verhandlungen*, July 16, 1955, 5598ff. For a more detailed discussion of the debates on the Volunteers Bill, see Gerhard Loewenberg, *Parliament in the German Political System* (Ithaca: Cornell University Press, 1966), chapter 6, *passim;* and Speier, *German Rearmament*, chapter 10.

6. For the speeches of Blank, Strauss, Kliesing, and others, see *Verhandlungen*, July 16, 1955, 5589ff.

7. *Ibid.*, July 16, 1955, 5603–10, especially 5605.

8. See Speier, *German Rearmament*, part 1. For a further discussion of the activities and organization of Amt Blank see Gordon Craig, "NATO and the New German Army," in *Military Policy and National Security*, ed. William W. Kaufmann (Princeton: Princeton University Press, 1956), 1956), 201–18; Speier, *German Rearmament*, *30*–41; Gerhard Wettig, *Entmilitarisierung und Wiederbewaffnung in Deutschland 1943–1955* (Munich: Oldenbourg, 1967), 400–409, 438–43; and Arnulf Baring, *Aussenpolitik in Adenauers Kanzlerdemokratie* (Munich: Oldenbourg, 1969), chapter 1.

9. *Bulletin,* (official publication of the Press and Information Office of the Federal Government, July 2, 1955. For a more detailed account of the evolution of Heusinger's position, see Catherine M. Kelleher, "German Nuclear Dilemmas: 1954–66," (Ph.D. diss., Massachusetts Institute of Technology, 1967), chapter 2 [hereafter cited as Kelleher, MIT].

10. For a brief but confirmatory discussion, see Speier, *German Rearmament*, 146.

11. A more detailed description of these difficulties can be found in Kelleher, MIT, chapters 1 and 2.

12. It was significant, as Speier points out, that both reports came from American news agencies (UPI and AP); Speier, *German Rearmament*, 192–93. Given the framework of German military discussions, however, it was equally significant that there was no official denial and that both stories and follow-ups were reported in the cautious *FAZ*, December 29, 31, 1955.

13. *FAZ*, December 15, 1955.

14. For press reports on the Radford proposal and the resulting controversy, see *New York Times* [*NYT*], July 13–15, 17, 19, 1956; and *Washington Post*, July 17–19, 1956. A more extensive but partisan treatment of the background is contained in Maxwell D. Taylor, *The Uncertain Trumpet* (New York: Harper, 1960), 39–43. It is widely believed in Germany and the United States that circles close to Taylor were responsible for this preemptive leak.

15. Taylor, *Uncertain Trumpet*, 40.

16. For Adenauer's own pungent account of this crisis and its political implication, see his *Erinnerungen, 1955–1959* (Stuttgart: Deutsch, 1967), 197–214; 222–25. Contemporary press reports can be found in *FAZ, SDZ, Neue Zürcher Zeitung* [*NZZ*] and *NYT* for July 15–30, 1956. In his memoirs, *Ein unordentliches Leben* (Dusseldorf: Econ, 1967), 451–460, Felix von Eckardt, one of the chancellor's then closest aides and one of those sent on an unofficial reporting mission to the United States during the crisis, gives a somewhat different perspective. His mission was primarily concerned with securing for Adenauer the pledge of leading Democrats not to support this "conversion" or continue it if Stevenson was elected in November.

17. For a more detailed discussion of these debates, see Speier, *German Rearmament*, chapter 11.

18. This was a dramatic reversal in position, since the SPD—like all established socialist parties—had traditionally opposed the creation of a professional military class. For a commentary on the party's decision, see *Economist*, April 7, 1956.

19. *Verhandlungen*, July 6, 1956, 8777–78. Interview comments from 1965, as well as the author's earlier conversations with Erler, suggest that he was particularly close to American sources at this period, having contacts with Democrats and academic strategists. His own expertise was well respected on both sides of the Atlantic.

20. See, for example, Strauss's article, "Fur eine Qualitatsarmee," *Die Zeit*, May 10, 1956. For the statements by Blank, see *Verhandlungen*, May 4, 1956, 7480–84; and for those by Berendsen, Adenauer, and Kiesinger, *Verhandlungen*, July 6/7, 1956, 8766–72, 8782–84, 8810–15. As Richardson notes, it is significant that the first-string military experts of the CSU, Strauss and Jaeger, did not speak on these issues in the Bundestag; James L. Richardson, *Germany and the Atlantic Alliance* (Cambridge: Harvard University Press, 1966), 45. No speaker, either for the government or for the opposition, referred to a possible German acquisition of tactical delivery systems.

21. *Verhandlungen*, July 6/7, 1956, 8783.

22. *NYT*, July 19, 1956. See Richardson's brief but enlightening discussion of this point, *Germany and Atlantic Alliance*, 46.

23. See Eden's description of these debates and the simultaneous private discussions of long-range planning; Anthony Eden, *Full Circle* (Boston: Houghton Mifflin, 1960), 414–25.

24. The article was first published in the *Westdeutsche Rundschau* and in *Der Tag* (Berlin) on July 27, 1956. It was reprinted under a new title in the official *Bulletin*, August 21, 1956. It is of interest that in *Der Tag*, there was an additional sentence after "all energy should be used to make a nuclear war impossible." It read, "It would be unrealistic to always assume the largest possible war." Several ranking civil servants interviewed in 1965 placed particular emphasis on the chancellor's uncharacteristic reliance on the press in this instance.

25. Quoted with some smugness in Franz Josef Strauss, *The Grand Design* (New York: Praeger, 1966), 95. Confirmation was obtained in 1965–1966 interviews with Strauss partisans and critics alike.

26. *Bulletin*, September 27, 1956; italics added.

27. For the government's statistics, see Press and Information Office of the Federal Government, *Warum brauchen wir die Wehrpflicht?* (Bonn, 1956). These revisions, in essence, forced acceptance of a Bundeswehr of only 350,000 men.

28. *FAZ*, October 18, 1956; *Times* (London), October 18, 1956.

29. Speier, *German Rearmament*, 211–23; Gerald Freund, *Germany Between Two Worlds* (New York: Harcourt Brace, 1961), 144–51. Interviews in 1964–65 with involved Americans and especially Pentagon officials found considerable congruence between their views and the Freund-Speier interpretation.

30. Neustadt's thesis is developed in fullest detail in chapters 4 and 6 of his *Alliance Politics* (New York: Columbia University Press, 1970).

31. *Ibid.*, 118. It might be well to recapitulate here Neustadt's brief explanations for this paradoxical self-containment: "game" positions are defined domestically; men necessarily

grow up "at home," and their incentives to "other" learning are weak; careers are made or broken, at least manifestly, at home, whatever the effects of external happenings.

32. For a more extended discussion on this point, see chapter 9 of this study. The terminology is Warner Schilling's formulation.

33. Further details on this point and others not fully developed in this chapter may be found in chapter 2 of Kelleher, MIT.

34. A partial list of these forums would include meetings at SHAPE, a meeting of the NATO Standing Group, with the French representative presenting the German case, and a special WEU Council meeting called in September at Adenauer's enraged insistence.

35. This argument is made in explicit contrast to the thesis advanced by Richardson: that German reaction primarily represented a plea for an alliance strategy not unlike that eventually presented by the Kennedy administration as "flexible response"; Germany and Atlantic Alliance, 42–48. Neither direct examination of some of the supporting documentation prepared in the Chancellor's Office in 1956 nor twelve extended interviews with knowledgeable civil servants or military men involved in the 1956 discussions supported the Richardson interpretation.

36. See below, chapters 3 and 5 passim.

37. The standard sources of course are Baring, Aussenpolitik; and the earlier, well-documented analysis offered by Karl W. Deutsch and Lewis J. Edinger, Germany Rejoins the Powers (Stanford: Stanford University Press, 1959), especially part 1.

38. The longer-range findings of Daniel Lerner and Morton Gorden in Euratlantica (Cambridge: MIT Press, 1969), and those of Deutsch and Edinger, Germany Rejoins the Powers, especially chapter 12, provide additional confirmation on this point.

39. Interview comments were the only sources of detailed information about the nature and frequency of these trips. What can be established is that there were a number of sponsors for these trips—the State Department, the broad occupation-based exchange-of-persons program, the "consultants program" of the American military services, and the Pentagon itself. For all, the aims seem to have been the same: education by example, friendship through exposure, and support through direct American recognition. The establishment and education of a "defense constituency" in Germany was, in the words of one long-time State Department official, one of the "special, high-priority targets" of this broad effort during the Eisenhower-Dulles period. It had been of continuing interest, however, since the first days of the Cold War.

40. For Adenauer, as for most of the CDU leadership and all of the Foreign Office-Defense Ministry officialdom, members of the general press were only one step above those who engaged in assassination for a living or who dealt in irresponsible rumormongering. See on this point the comments throughout Adenauer's Erinnerungen as well as the analysis by Baring, Aussenpolitik, and Deutsch and Edinger, Germany Rejoins the Powers, chapter 8.

41. See on this point Speier's comment in his German Rearmament, chapters 2 and 3.

42. It is a mark of the changed status of the German military that in the more than twenty-five interviews done with ranking military men, no one failed to mention these limits in the first five minutes of the interview or to reassert them at least once during subsequent comments. This was true whether the respondent was a leading "rehabilitated" commander, a colonel returned in 1955 from Siberia, an SPD adherent, or an avowed nationalist who looked forward to reunion with Austria within the next century.

43. See Baring's commentary on the structures and techniques which made this possible, Aussenpolitik, part 1.

CHAPTER III. GERMANY GOES NUCLEAR: 1957–1960

1. Strauss is the subject of an ever increasing body of political literature. Among the most important efforts, perhaps, are two pro-Strauss volumes, Lutz Hermann, *Die Trommel im Ohr* (Bonn: Berto, 1962); Karl F. Grau (ed.), *Appropos Strauss* (Stuttgart: Seewald, 1965); and four highly critical works, Hans Frederik, *Franz Josef Strauss: Das Lebensbild eines Politikers* (Munich-Inning: Humboldt, n.d.); Erich Kuby, *Im Fibag-Wahn* (Reinbek bei Hamburg: Rowohlt, 1962), Erich Kuby (ed.), *Franz Josef Strauss: Ein Typus unserer Zeit* (Munich: Desch, 1963); Samuel Wahrhaftig, *Franz Josef Strauss* (Munich: Scherz, 1965). Two other and more scholarly studies are David Schoenbaum's analysis of Strauss's behavior in the *Spiegel* crisis of 1962 in his *The Spiegel Affair* (New York: Doubleday, 1968); and Gebhard Schweigler's perceptive "The Grand Designs of Franz Josef Strauss: A Political Biography," mimeographed (Cambridge: Harvard University, May, 1969).

For the most recent examples of Strauss's efforts at self-interpretation, see his *The Grand Design* (New York: Praeger, 1966), especially 89–105; and *Challenge and Response* (London: Weidenfeld & Nicolson, 1969), especially chapter 10.

2. Klaus Epstein, "The Adenauer Era," in *A New Europe*, ed. Stephen R. Graubard (Boston: Beacon, 1967), 132.

3. Richard Crossman, "A Talk with Franz Josef Strauss," *New Statesman*, April 12, 1958, 460. Crossman's phrasing was: "He had the good fortune to be too young to have a Nazi past. An SA Obersturmfuhrer Strauss, a prisoner of war in Siberia perhaps until 1950—what would have become of him?"

4. See the comments in Strauss, *Grand Design*, 94–96.

5. For a somewhat different view, see Raymond Albright, "The Defense Ministry of the Federal Republic of Germany" (Ph.D. diss., Harvard University, 1960).

6. Strauss's critics delight in listing his numerous failures in choosing personnel. See, for example, the list in Frederik, *Strauss*, 110–32, and Kuby's speculations throughout *Fibag-Wahn*.

7. Every military officer interviewed, whether active or retired, a Strauss supporter or critic, mentioned Strauss's outstanding academic record, particularly his accomplishments at the prestigious Maximillian Gymnasium in Munich. In contrast, few political figures or Foreign Office officials volunteered this information.

8. The text of the memorandum was reprinted in the official *Bulletin* (published by the Press and Information Office of the Federal Government), August 20, 1960. A comprehensive analysis is contained in Albright, "Defense Ministry," 291–94. A less familiar case was Strauss's interest in "voluntary" military participation in his ill-fated "psychological defense" campaign, Rettet die Freiheit. Although the campaign's express purpose was to increase popular appreciation of defense problems, the principal thrust of its many publications and "documentations" seemed to be condemnation of "atheistic Communism" and repudiation of the antinuclear campaign launched by the SPD. See Frederik, *Strauss*, 165–70. Even by 1965–1966 comments made by interviewed military officers about this campaign can best described as intense.

9. See Gerald Freund, *Germany Between Two Worlds* (New York: Harcourt Brace, 1961), 63. Arnulf Baring's forthcoming analysis of the von Brentano papers will shed further light on this complex triangle.

10. The most striking examples were with respect to national armament production, and his original plans for the Territoriale Verteidigung (home defense) buildup, both discussed in

chapter 4. Rettet die Freiheit encountered similar difficulties, according to some Foreign Office and Defense Ministry officials interviewed in 1965.

11. Flora Lewis, "Franz Josef, German Question Mark," *New York Times Magazine,* May 1, 1960, 19ff.

12. The analysis in this and subsequent chapters is the result of extensive examination of a private collection that includes all of Strauss's known writings and speeches from 1956 to 1962, crosschecked against data from interviews with persons who worked on his speeches; see appendix.

13. Quoted in Albright, "Defense Ministry," 305. This purportedly was said to von Brentano.

14. "Einheit und Freiheit," *Politisch-Soziale Korrespondenz,* February 15, 1957.

15. Wahrhaftig, *Strauss,* 11.

16. For further discussion on this point, see chapter 5 *passim.*

17. Perhaps the most detailed description of the debate within NATO can be found in Robert E. Osgood, *NATO: The Entangling Alliance* (Chicago: University of Chicago Press, 1962), 102–211 *passim.* Valuable sources for the critical American discussions include Samuel P. Huntington, *The Common Defense* (New York: Columbia University Press, 1961), 88–112; Maxwell D. Taylor, *The Uncertain Trumpet* (New York: Harper, 1960).

18. Franz Josef Strauss, interview in *Der Spiegel,* January 2, 1957, 21.

19. *Ibid.* One measure of that political will was suggested in a later analysis by Strauss of the 1956 situation: "There was no differentiation between local action, limited war, or general war. If there was an attack on the NATO area—regardless of where—if the invasion forces had not drawn back to their standing point by sunrise the next day, there was to be retaliation with strategic weapons." Franz Josef Strauss, "Verteidigungskonzeption in atomaren Zeitalter," *Deutsche Korrespondenz,* February, 1960.

20. *Bulletin,* January 8, 1957. See also *Frankfurter Allgemeine Zeitung [FAZ],* February 12, 1957.

21. *Times* (London), October 11, 1957. See also *FAZ,* March 20, 1957, for a brief discussion of the views of Army Inspector Hans Röttiger on nuclear-weapons use and the problems of escalation.

22. The plan not only received wide coverage in the international press but also became a major element in Strauss's speeches after 1958. See *New York Times [NYT],* October 10, 1957, January 5, April 17, 1958.

23. For the full text of Norstad's statement and a thorough analysis of its content, see Malcolm Hoag, "The Place of Limited War in NATO Strategy," in *NATO and American Security,* ed. Klaus Knorr (Princeton: Princeton University Press, 1959), 98–126.

24. See, for example, the interviews quoted in *NYT,* October 12, 1957; and in *Bulletin,* October 17, 1957. Interview comments from 1966 attest to this combining of the new with the old as being a conscious strategy of Strauss.

25. *Bulletin.*

26. *Ibid.*

27. *FAZ,* June 9, 1958. Panitzki, a known airpower advocate who had been the acting airforce inspector during 1955 and early 1956, spoke at a conference on European security prob-

lems sponsored by the Europa Union. There is some 1965–66 interview evidence to suggest that Panitzki was a reliable public spokesman for those air-force leaders, including General Josef Kammhuber, who identified themselves both as supporters of Strauss and as the most "modern" of the Bundeswehr's leadership.

28. Strauss's initial comments were contained in a speech announcing revisions in Bundeswehr planning, *Neue Zürcher Zeitung [NZZ]*, June 21, 1958. A more explicit discussion is to be found in his "Der Preis des Friedens," *Wehrtechnische Monatshefte*, September, 1958, 393–95, especially 395; and his "Sinn und Aufgabe der Wehrpolitik," *Bulletin*, November 14, 1958. For a more detailed analysis, see Catherine M. Kelleher, "German Nuclear Dilemmas: 1954–1966," Ph.D. diss., Massachusetts Institute of Technology, 1967), chapter 3 [hereafter cited as Kelleher, MIT].

29. Strauss, "Preis des Friedens," 394.

30. *Ibid.*, 395.

31. See, for example, Adelbert Weinstein's critique in *FAZ*, July 16, 1959.

32. For further details, particularly with respect to the impact on equipment and training, see the brief treatment in chapter 4 and the more extended treatment in Kelleher, MIT, chapter 4.

33. Kammhuber was a Bavarian and a close associate of Strauss. Long a convinced airpower advocate, under Blank he had submitted a long memorandum specifying the requirements of a "modern" air force. Interview respondents critical of Strauss often identified Kammhuber as one of the principal military figures in the anti-Blank *fronde* of 1956.

34. See Strauss's comments on the army's position made in an interview conducted by Weinstein, *FAZ*, October 19, 1960. In contrast to the other services, the army did not simply adapt NATO tactical manuals, but produced its own *Truppenführung*. See, for example, General Heusinger's speech to the Bundeswehr command in 1959, "Die Aufgabe des Soldaten," in Adolf Heusinger, *Reden, 1956–1961* (Boppard am Rhein: Boldt, 1961), 16–17. Like the American army, the German army showed continuing interest in the development of battlefield nuclear weapons, particularly small launchers for battle units and atomic demolition means (ADMs). See *Süddeutsche Zeitung [SDZ]*, April 20, 1957; Heusinger's 1958 speech, "Militarische Fragen der Verteidigung," in his *Reden*, 18–34; and the discussion of ADMs in *Der Spiegel*, January 6, 1965, 16–25.

35. Cf. Osgood, *NATO*, 389, n. 72. British commanders, on the other hand, reportedly could not conceive of a war in Europe without the use of nuclear weapons. Some indication of what the German military have considered "sufficient" was recounted in several interviews with military officers and confirmed in a fragmentary report in *FAZ*, November 2, 1960. A Defense Ministry study done in 1958 supposedly concluded that even with nuclear disarmament the West still would be able to counter Soviet conventional superiority below a 3:1 ratio in numbers and firepower. One of the principal reasons advanced, it was reported, was the German experience on the eastern front during World War II.

36. One striking example of German intensity on this point was a controversy which erupted in May 1959. An American commander, General Clyde Eddelman, told a Bonn meeting that a troop withdrawal to the Rhine under a "disengagement" would mean "no essential change" in the present strategic concept. There was an immediate and sharp German protest, one remembered by several Defense Ministry respondents as late as 1966. Strauss declared that he had received a personal assurance that the general had been discussing a "purely military" hypothesis. *NZZ*, May 10, 1959.

37. See, for example, Norstad's comments in *NYT,* April 6, 1959; and his speeches to the NATO parliamentarians' meeting and the WEU Assembly, *NYT,* November 22, December 1, 1960.

38. Secondary accounts confirming in broad outline the limited comments garnered by the author from interviews of both French and German respondents are John Newhouse, *De Gaulle and the Anglo-Saxons* (New York: Viking, 1970), and Jack M. Schick, *The Berlin Crisis, 1958–1962* (Philadelphia: University of Pennsylvania Press, 1971). It is unquestionably symptomatic of the state of German defense policy-making at this point that a determined search uncovered only a handful of 1958–1960 German press accounts that even mentioned a *German* view on the military implications of the Berlin crisis. Almost every other account began by attributing the responsibility to the three Western powers and then never mentioned the matter again.

39. Reprinted as ''Abgestufte Abschreckungsstrategie'' in *Kriegsgeneration in unserer Zeit* (Bonn: Defense Ministry, 1960).

40. See, for example, the problems discussed by General Heusinger in his speech at the NATO Defense College on October 5, 1960, ''Bundesrepublik—Brennpunkt der NATO-Verteidigung,'' in his *Reden,* 55–56.

CHAPTER IV. ADAPTATION AND CONTROVERSY: 1956–1960

1. Perhaps the most extensive recent expositions of these theories of economic causation, real and purported, are Steven Rosen (ed.), *Testing the Theory of the Military-Industrial Complex* (Lexington, Mass.: Lexington Books, 1973), especially the essays by James Kurth and by Arnold Kanter and Stuart Thorson; and Sam C. Sarkesian (ed.), *The Military-Industrial Complex: a Reassessment* (Beverly Hills: Sage, 1972), especially the contributions by Charles Moskos, Charles Wolf, and Stanley Lieberson. The work of the Frankfurt group under Dieter Senghass represents perhaps the most extended German effort in this direction; see, for example, Dieter Senghass, *Rüstung and Militarismus* (Frankfurt/Main: Suhrkamp, 1972).

2. For details of the general NATO pattern, consult Robert E. Osgood, *NATO: The Entangling Alliance* (Chicago: University of Chicago Press, 1962), chapter 5.

3. *New York Times* [*NYT*], April 6, 1957. Cf. Adenauer's own account in his *Erinnerungen, 1955–1959* (Stuttgart: Deutsche, 1967), 296ff.

4. Bad Boll speech, paraphrased in *Frankfurter Allgemeine Zeitung* [*FAZ*], February 13, 1957.

5. *FAZ,* April 3, 1957.

6. *Bulletin* (official publication of the Press and Information Office of the Federal Government), April 6, 1957. See similar remarks by the CSU's Richard Jaeger, *FAZ,* March 3, 1958, and by Strauss in the Bundestag in Federal Republic of Germany, Bundestag, *Verhandlungen: Stenographische Berichte,* March 25, 1958, 1107–15 [hereafter cited as *Verhandlungen*].

7. *Verhandlungen,* March 20, 1958, 843.

8. *NATO Letter,* December, 1956, 37.

9. *NYT,* May 2, 1957.

10. *Ibid.,* February 26, 1958. The full text was reprinted in *Bulletin,* March 4, 1958.

11. See Jack Raymond in *NYT,* February 1, 1957.

12. *Times* (London), December 14, 1956; *Le Monde,* December 15, 1956. The latter report noted that Strauss had asserted that these weapons should be held at the divisional rather than the Army-group level. German forces were to serve in "integrated" Army groups.

13. See chapter 5.

14. *Bulletin,* November 10, 1956.

15. *FAZ,* November 6, 1956.

16. *Ibid.,* December 21, 1956.

17. For further discussion, see pp. 128–31.

18. *FAZ,* November 15, 1957.

19. Two particularly valuable and data-rich sources for the evaluation of the German equipment program are Gerhard Brandt's specific analysis, *Rüstung und Wirtshaft in der Bundesrepublik,* vol. 3, *Studien zur politischen und gesellschaftlichen Situation der Bundeswehr,* ed. Georg Picht (Witten/Berlin: Eckart, 1966), especially 203–339; and the broader series of studies done under the aegis of the Institute for Strategic Studies, *Defence, Technology and the Western Alliance* (6 vols.; London, 1967), especially vol. 2, C. J. E. Harlow, *The European Armaments Base: a Survey,* 2 parts.

20. *NYT,* October 26, 1957.

21. Quoted in Ernest Leiser, "Germany's Would-Be Strong Man," *New York Times Magazine,* June 1, 1958, 10ff. Similar remarks were made by both British and French respondents in 1965–1966.

22. See *NYT,* April 12, 1959. Interview comments by American civil servants as late as 1964–1966 suggested that Strauss's semiannual visits were always marked by high dudgeon, hectic scheduling, and hard bargaining.

23. Cf. Brandt, *Rüstung und Wirtshaft,* 164–77; *NYT,* August 19, 1957; and Strauss's description of the contract system in "Zu Problem der Wehrwirtschaft," *Bulletin,* October 21, 1957.

24. Perhaps the most extensive treatment of the continuing problem of offset arrangements is in Horst Mendershausen, *Troop Stationing in Germany: Value and Cost,* RM-5881-PR (Santa Monica: RAND, 1968), especially chapters 4–6. The Brandt and Harlow studies cited in n. 19 also include discussions and data on this problem.

25. For fairly detailed but frankly biased accounts of the Starfighter decision, see "Starfighter: Ein Gewisses Flattern," *Der Spiegel,* January 24, 1966, 21–36; and Kurt Johannson, "Starfighter und Mirage," *Der Monat,* April, 1966, 26–41. Interview accounts of this process almost without exception were influenced by the subsequent poor performance of the F-104.

26. Perhaps the first mention was in a dpa (German wire service) interview in London; see *FAZ,* October 18, 1956. Cf. also Bulletin, January 10, 1958; and the more detailed analysis presented in Catherine M. Kelleher, "German Nuclear Dilemmas: 1954–1966," (Ph.D. diss., Massachusetts Institute of Technology, 1967), chapter 4, [nereafter cited as Kelleher, MIT].

27. As is discussed in greater detail in chapter 5, common nuclear-weapons production was at least contemplated under F 1 G.

28. In addition to the sources cited in chapter 5, there is the account, which includes the quoted phrases given in John Newhouse, *De Gaulle and the Anglo-Saxons* (New York: Viking, 1970), 16.

29. See, for example, articles throughout 1959 by Arthur Olsen, the Bonn correspondent of the *New York Times*, in which this interpretation appeared almost weekly.

30. See *FAZ*, November 25, 1959; *NYT*, November 26, 1959; and Strauss's "Wirtschaft und Rüstung," *Bulletin*, December 3, 1959.

31. More detailed chronological accounts of these developments and their relation to shifting Washington coalitions within the American government is given in Newhouse, chapter 4; and in chapter 4 of Kelleher, MIT. See also chapter 5 of this study.

32. *Die Welt*, June 24, 1959.

33. *NYT*, April 14, 22, 1960. A few scattered comments in 1965–1966 from past and present Foreign Office officials suggested, however, that cabinet support for the Gates' proposal was less than unanimous.

34. *NYT*, June 8, 1960; *Die Welt*, June 23, 1960.

35. *NYT*, July 5, 1960.

36. See articles throughout 1959 by Arthur Olsen in *NYT;* and chapter 5.

37. *FAZ*, November 25, 1959; *NYT*, November 26, 1959; and Strauss's "Wirtschaft und Rüstung."

38. *Die Welt*, June 24, 1959, confirms the broad outlines of the evidence gathered in Bonn interviews in 1965–1966.

39. This was the so-called "Herter concept" of a joint nuclear force within NATO, the legendary ancestor of the still-more-legendary MLF. See chapters 5 and 9.

40. An analysis of the precise implications of adoption of nuclear weapons for the organization, training, and political position of each of the three services and the territorial-defense force can be found in chapter 4 of Kelleher, MIT.

41. After a slowdown for purposes of "extensive review" (and, one suspects, achieving a decisive victory in the September, 1957 federal elections), reorganization plans for the new Bundeswehr were announced in late 1957. For the air force's announcement, see *FAZ*, February 8, 1958.

42. See, for example, the analyses in *NYT*, March 22, 1957, and June 20, 1958.

43. *Bulletin*, October 14, 1953; *NYT*, September 28, 1958. See Strauss's critique, *FAZ*, October 11, 1953; Adelbert Weinstein's critique, *FAZ*, September 23, 1959; and Hanson Baldwin's critique, *NYT*, February 11, 1960. It was a rating which would continue—to the embarassment and chagrin of the military leadership—into the mid-1960s.

44. The argument here will touch on the more detailed hypotheses developed in the standard works on these developments. For the domestic opposition, this would include Douglas A. Chalmers, *The Social Democratic Party of Germany* (New Haven: Yale University Press, 1964), especially 59–72; and Wolfram F. Hanrieder, *West German Foreign Policy, 1949–1963* (Stanford:Stanford University Press, 1967) 207–12. For the development of the disengagement concept, see Charles R. Planck's two works, *Sicherheit in Europa* (Munich: Oldenbourg, 1968) and *The Changing Status of German Reunification in Western Diplomacy: 1955–1966* (Baltimore: Johns Hopkins Press, 1967); and Eugene Hinterhoff, *Disengagement* (London: Stevens, 1959).

45. For concurrent views, see Osgood, *NATO*, chapter 10; Planck, *Changing Status;* and James L. Richardson, *Germany and the Atlantic Alliance* (Cambridge: Harvard University Press, 1966), part 5.

46. Signers of the Göttingen Appeal included Max Born, Walther Gerlach, Otto Hahn, Werner Heisenberg, Fritz Strassmann, and Karl Friedrich von Weizsäcker. Excerpts of all documents relating to the scientists' effort can be found in *Die Politische Meinung*, May, 1957, 55–60.

47. *Ibid.*, 56. Italics added.

48. See, for example, the estimates of congruence between SPD elite opinion and mass public opinion given by Karl W. Deutsch and Lewis J. Edinger in their seminal work, *Germany Rejoins the Powers* (Stanford: Stanford University Press, 1959), as summarized in table 16.1, 206–7.

49. See Chalmers, *Social Democratic Party*, especially 59–72; and Deutsch and Edinger, *Germany Rejoins the Powers*, 70–74.

50. Cf. Uwe Kitzinger's definitive account of the 1957 election, *German Electoral Politics* (Oxford: Clarendon Press, 1960), especially 87–90 and 94–95.

51. Cf. *Verhandlungen*, May 10, 1957, 12052–74; Gerald Freund, *Germany Between Two Worlds* (New York: Harcourt Brace, 1961), 70ff; and Gerhard Loewenberg, *Parliament in the German Political System* (Ithaca: Cornell University Press, 1966), 397–98.

52. Document 72 in Karl Bauer's excellent document collection, *Deutsche Verteidigungspolitik: 1945–1963* (Boppard am Rhein: Boldt, 1964), 154. (Italics added.)

53. See, for example, *Blaubuch: Dokumentation über den Widerstand gegen die atomare Aufrüstung der Bundesrepublik* (Dusseldorf: Friedenskommittee der Bundesrepublik, 1958).

54. *Bulletin*, July 3, 1958. For a report of earlier discussions, see *Neue Zürcher Zeitung* [*NZZ*], March 7, 1958.

55. Strauss had drawn this distinction before; see, for example, *Die Zeit*, April 13, 1957. But he had not often done so, and he was virtually the only government spokesman who did it. Cf. a later discussion on this point, *FAZ*, March 17, 18, 1961. SPD leaders for obvious tactical reasons were ambivalent about developing this distinction.

56. See, for example, two statements by Erler, a Saar Radio interview of July 22, 1960, and "Sicherheitspolitik," *Vorwarts*, July 27, 1960, both excerpted in *Keesings Archiv der Gegenwart 1960* (Bonn: Siegler, 1961), 8534, 8547.

57. The basic sources for the period are touched on in n. 44. To these might be added the invaluable documentation of Hermann Volle and Claus-Jürgen Duisberg, *Probleme der internationalen Abrüstung* (2 vols., Frankfurt/Main: Metzner, 1964), the stimulating analysis of Karl Kaiser, *German Foreign Policy in Transition* (New York: Oxford University Press, 1968), and Thomas Wolfe's comprehensive *Soviet Power and Europe: 1945–1970* (Baltimore: Johns Hopkins Press, 1969).

58. See the discussion in chapter 5, of the opposing views developed in the post-Sputnik era by Kurt Georg Kiesinger and Eugene Gerstenmaier. Gerald Freund, *Germany Between Two Worlds*, 203–9, recounts one conciliatory gesture by Adenauer in December 1957 that quickly drew severe criticism from both Dulles and the American press.

59. Here is Wolfram F. Hanrieder's formulation of essentially the same point: "Following West Germany's accession to NATO, the Soviet Union persistently tried to further solidify the *political* line of division in Central Europe . . . and to blur, at the same time, the East-West military boundary running through Germany. . . ." See his *The Stable Crisis* (New York: Harper Row, 1970), 96, as well as Adam B. Ulam, *Expansion and Coexistence* (New York: Praeger, 1968).

60. Volle and Duisberg, *Probleme,* vol. 2, 649–50. Hanrieder views it as significant for Adenauer that the first Rapacki plan was presented to the United Nations the day after the first Sputnik was launched. See his *Foreign Policy,* 174–75.

61. Cf. Osgood, *NATO,* 247–52.

62. See Planck, *Changing Status,* 8–23.

63. See, for example, Franz Josef Strauss, "Entspannung und Wiedervereinigung," *Politisch-Soziale Korrespondenz,* March 1, 1958.

64. Cf. statements by Foreign Minister von Brentano, Strauss, and Kurt Georg Kiesinger in *Verhandlungen,* January 23, 1958, 302–3, 381–83; March 20, 1953, 870–71, 912–13.

65. Cf. Planck, *Changing Status,* 25–29.

CHAPTER V. THE SEARCH FOR CONTROL-SHARING: 1957–1960

1. Four basic sources for the debate among the allies about control of nuclear weapons during this period are Robert E. Osgood, *NATO: The Entangling Alliance* (Chicago: University of Chicago Press, 1962); Harold L. Nieburg, *Nuclear Secrecy and Foreign Policy* (Washington: Public Affairs Press, 1964); John Steinbruner, "The Mind and the Milieu of Policy-Makers: A Case Study of the MLF" (Ph.D. diss., Massachusetts Institute of Technology, 1968; to be published by Princeton University Press), and Thomas C. Wiegele, "The Origins of the MLF Concept," *Orbis,* Summer, 1968, 465–89.

2. *Frankfurter Allgemeine Zeitung [FAZ],* December 21, 1956; *Neue Zürcher Zeitung [NZZ],* December 22, 1956.

3. For a more extensive discussion of French worries and demands in 1956, see Lawrence Scheinman, *Atomic Energy Policy in France under the Fourth Republic* (Princeton: Princeton University Press, 1965), especially chapters 4 and 5; and Wilfrid L. Kohl, *French Nuclear Diplomacy* (Princeton: Princeton University Press, 1971), chapter 1.

4. See, for example, Spaak's speech in Paris in June, 1956, quoted in Scheinman, *Atomic Energy Policy,* 142, and the account in John Newhouse, *De Gaulle and the Anglo-Saxons* (New York: Viking, 1969), 21ff., 60ff.

5. Cf. his interview in *Der Spiegel,* January 2, 1957, 21–25.

6. As Adenauer told French Foreign Minister Michel Debré in 1960, "I've won three elections with it anyway"; Konrad Adenauer, *Erinnerungen, 1959–1963* (Stuttgart: Deutsche, 1968), 75.

7. Cf. Adenauer's own account of his related comments with those made in Washington by Foreign Minister von Brentano, *Erinnerungen, 1955–1959* (Stuttgart: Deutsche, 1967), 260–65; 274–75.

8. See Adenauer's continuing comments throughout his *Erinnerungen, 1955–1959,* and especially those on the occasion of Dulles's death, 471–78.

9. Paraphrased from *ibid.,* 426. A comment made to de Gaulle in 1962 is in some respects even more startling; as Adenauer retold it, "For a non-American, a non-Frenchman, and a non-Briton, it's a feeling that only two powers in the world make the decisions about these things [nuclear weapons]. When one knows how problematical the party system, the democracy, the executive bureaucracy, the lawmaking process, particularly in social areas, still are, then one has to be worried. Therefore, I was very glad that de Gaulle had very calmly continued development on his atomic weapons." *Erinnerungen, 1959–1963,* 205.

10. Cf., for example, his comments found in *Erinnerungen, 1955–1959*, 292–96, 323–32, 334–39, and 424–36, and in the fragmentary *Erinnerungen, 1959–1963*, 14–21, 54–67, 70–88, 101–2, 138–40, 205–7.

11. *New York Times* [*NYT*], March 25, 1957. According to Nieburg, *Nuclear Secrecy,* 174, the British implied that if American assistance was not forthcoming, they might be "forced" to join a "military" European nuclear-energy consortium, like the then-forming Euratom. Under the accords London received direct dual-key control; the Royal Air Force was to have an equal share in control over both the Thor launchers and their warheads. For one relatively accurate view of how this arrangement contrasted with that offered the Continental states, see Irving Heymont, "The NATO Nuclear Bilateral Forces," *Orbis,* Winter, 1966, 1025–41.

12. *NYT,* July 17, 1957.

13. For Gruenther's remarks, see *NYT,* August 26, 1957. Part of the Gaither Committee report was subsequently made public; it was vague on the issue of sharing.

14. For a more detailed account of the generation of Norstad's proposed force, see Steinbruner, "MLF," 61–83. Both Steinbruner and the author were told by several close associates of Norstad that the distinction between his MRBM force and the IRBMs suggested by Washington was deliberately designed to attract political support as a "new" and "European" concept.

15. *NYT,* October 26, 27, 1957. The source of this report was Agence France Presse, and it was the subject of formal discussion within the North Atlantic Council; *ibid.,* November 21, 22, 1957. Drew Middleton commented on a similar proposal somewhat earlier; *ibid.,* November 5, 1957.

16. See paraphrases in *FAZ,* November 6, 11, 1957, and reports in *NYT,* December 10, 11, 1957. Speaking at the heated NATO parliamentarians conference, Spaak made perhaps the most forthright statement of European demands: "It is not indispensable, for the prestige of the European countries, to reinvent what the United States has already discovered. . . . The security of the United States will not be imperiled if it makes known to its friends what its enemies already know." *NATO Letter,* November 1957, quoted in Nieburg, *Nuclear Secrecy,* 176.

17. Cf. Wiegele, "MLF Concept," 468–71.

18. Dulles's "Report to the Nation," *NYT,* December 24, 1957.

19. See, for example, remarks by Foreign Minister von Brentano, *NYT,* November 5, 1957, and by Strauss, *FAZ,* November 17, 1957, and *NYT,* December 8, 1957.

20. Reports from Defense Ministry and Foreign Office sources interviewed in 1965 suggest that Alain Clement's article in *Le Monde,* December 11, 1957, contains a good summary of the study's general conclusions.

21. The text of the letter was reprinted in *Europa Archiv,* 1/58, 10440–44. Cf. comments by James L. Richardson in his *Germany and the Atlantic Alliance* (Cambridge: Harvard University Press, 1966) and by Charles R. Planck in his *The Changing Status of German Reunification in Western Diplomacy, 1955–1966* (Baltimore: Johns Hopkins Press, 1967). In his *Lebenserinnerungen eines Botschafters* (Cologne: Kiepenhauer & Witsch, 1967), 383ff., Hans Kroll, Bonn's ambassador to the Soviet Union from 1957 to 1962, writes that later in 1958 Moscow was indeed prepared to make such a trade for a permanent renunciation of ABC weapons by the Federal Republic and that only the intervention of Washington prevented the start of exploratory discussions. Adenauer in his *Erinnerungen, 1955–1959* (337–92 *passim*) describes a far more limited "realistic" assessment by Bonn of Soviet intentions, an assessment formed primarily

for purposes of bargaining with the alliance. Foreign Office sources interviewed in 1965 confirmed this and alluded to the cool reception given a visit by Mikoyan.

22. Cf. his personal working paper for the 1957 meetings, reprinted in *Erinnerungen, 1955–1959,* 334–37.

23. Adenauer at least suggests in his memoirs that he believed a transfer of nuclear weapons to SACEUR's control was within the McMahon Act restrictions; *ibid.,* 336. Officials then in the Chancellor's Office suggested in 1965–1966 interviews that Adenauer pressed this point repeatedly with Dulles and others.

24. This theme was clearly reflected in a speech by Adenauer in Amsterdam in late November; *NYT,* November 24, 1957. For Strauss's contemporary argumentation, see chapter 4.

25. See Adenauer's account of his private conversation with Italian Defense Minister Paolo Taviani on this point and his report of von Brentano's strong representations on the need for a "British loophole"; *Erinnerungen, 1955–1959,* 260–61, 264–65.

26. On Strauss's conversations and the details of a specific French proposal, see *Le Monde,* November 22, December 14, 1957, as well as material below in this chapter. Adenauer's account of his remarkably open discussions with Faure is in *Erinnerungen, 1955–1959,* 323–331. Cf. also *Times* (London), November 21, 22, 1957; Edgar S. Furniss, *France: Troubled Ally* (New York: Praeger, 1960), 248–49; and Kohl, *French Nuclear Diplomacy,* chapter 2.

27. Comments in interviews with both civil servants and journalists indicated that the substance of these considerations was reported in a number of "inspired" articles, stressing German hesitation about a tempting prospect. See particularly those in *FAZ,* November 25, 27, 1957, and in *NZZ,* November 28, 1957.

28. Cf. Strauss's careful phrasing, reported in *NYT,* November 15, 1957.

29. For further evidence, see Robert Osgood, *NATO,* 222ff.

30. Cf. Nieburg, *Nuclear Secrecy,* 177–84; Wiegele, "MLF Concept", 471–73; and William B. Bader's authoritative account in his *The United States and the Spread of Nuclear Weapons* (New York: Pegasus, 1968), chapter 1.

31. Testimony before the Joint Committee on Atomic Energy (JCAE) on April 17, 1958, reprinted in *Department of State Bulletin,* May 5, 1958, 741.

32. *Ibid.* See also the telling excerpts from Dulles's testimony and his secret briefing of the American mission chiefs in Europe cited in Bader, *Spread of Nuclear Weapons,* 26–27, 30–32.

33. *Erinnerungen, 1955–1959,* 332. See also C. L. Sulzberger's discussion of de Gaulle's veto of a "secret" Franco-German agreement, *NYT,* November 18, 1964; and discussion below in this chapter.

34. See, for example, reports in *NYT,* November 15, 1958, January 2, 1959, November 18, 1959.

35. See Secretary of Defense Neil McElroy's comments. *NYT,* November 14, 15, 1959.

36. For a detailed examination of the chronology of the Berlin crisis and of Western discussions, see Richardson, *Germany and Atlantic Alliance,* chapters 12, 13, and 16; John Mander, *Berlin: Hostage for the West* (Harmondsworth: Penguin, 1962); and Jean Edward Smith, *The Defense of Berlin* (Baltimore: Johns Hopkins Press, 1963).

37. See, for example, Strauss's harsh debunking of the spirit of Camp David in "Die Verantwortung nimmt uns keiner ab," *Bulletin* (official publication of the Press and Information Office of the Federal Government), January 5, 1960, and in "1960—Ein Jahr der Bewährung," *Wehrtechnische Monatshefte*, January, 1960, 1–2. According to interview accounts gathered in 1965–1966, Adenauer's reaction ranged from one of despair to burning rage. Quite apart from his political difficulties at home, he felt betrayed by the Americans at a crucial point in Germany's development and attributed much of this to the failure of Dulles's successors. See *Erinnerungen, 1955–1959*, 471–82; *Erinnerungen, 1959–1963*, 48–51.

38. Cf. *Erinnerungen, 1959–1963*, 71–72, 119, and especially 182.

39. An interesting but limited treatment of Norstad's central role in this period can be found in Steinbruner, "MLF," chapter 1, section 3; and in the highly sympathetic articles of Charles Murphy in *Fortune*, especially "NATO at a Nuclear Crossroads," December, 1962, 84–87ff.

40. *NATO Letter*, January, 1960, 10.

41. This section draws heavily on Steinbruner's original analysis in "MLF," 61–83. Wiegele, "MLF Concept," 479–84, presents a somewhat different view, which was not confirmed in either the primary or secondary materials uncovered by this study.

42. There reportedly was great interest on the part of the Defense Ministry in this suggestion.

43. See Murphy, "NATO at Crossroads," 222, for a description of sharing formulas considered at SHAPE, which of course set the parameters for discussions within the German government.

44. See also Steinbruner, "MLF," 72–76.

45. As Norstad later expressed it, a NATO system might not "influence the desire of some nations [i.e., France] to pursue their own quest for an atomic weapons capability," but it "might very well remove a good part of the motivation ot the others [i.e., Germany] to do so." Quoted in Osgood, *NATO*, 229.

46. For more details on the decision to remain silent, see Catherine M. Kelleher, "German Nuclear Dilemmas: 1954–1966" (Ph.D. diss., Massachusetts Institute of Technology, 1967), chapter 5 [hereinafter cited as Kelleher, MIT].

47. Two examples were his *Wehrtechnische Monatshefte*, January, 1960, 2; and his "Verteidigungskonzeption in atomaren Zeitalter," *Deutsche Korrespondenz*, February, 1960.

48. *NZZ*, October 31, 1959.

49. *Die Welt*, August 6, 1959, quoted in Erich Kuby (ed.), *Franz Josef Strauss: Ein Typus unserer Zeit* (Munich: Desch, 1963), 27.

50. *NATO Letter*, January, 1960, 10.

51. *NYT*, February 4, 1960. Cf. Osgood's discussion, *NATO*, 231–32.

52. See Steinbruner's authoritative account in his "MLF"; Bowie's own later remarks, cited in Wiegele, "MLF Concept," 484–85; and later press reports in *NYT*, October 30, November 17, 24, 1965. Steinbruner suggests that Gerard Smith, then head of the State Department's Policy Planning Staff, commissioned the study to be done by Bowie because of his increasing unease about uncontrolled German access to tactical nuclear weapons—actual and as proposed by Norstad; "MLF," 72–76. Interview accounts from some American officials in 1964 confirmed Steinbruner's assertion.

53. Wiegele, "MLF Concept," 478.

54. See Steinbruner, "MLF," 71. It was apparently this arrangement—presumably under SACEUR's direct control—which Barry Goldwater during the 1964 election campaign proposed as a model for future NATO arrangements. See his interview with *Der Spiegel* reprinted in *NYT*, July 9, 1964. Disclosures in 1965 that such practices were still common (albeit apparently with permissive action links installed) caused substantial uproar and embarrassment in both Washington and Bonn. See chapter 7.

55. See chapter 4.

56. This WEU speech was printed as "Abgestufte Abschreckungsstrategie" in *Kriegsgeneration in unserer Zeit* (Bonn: Defense Ministry, 1960). There were, of course, numerous inspired articles—by Adelbert Weinstein and others, especially after France's first atomic explosion—stressing the need for change in the direction of greater Atlantic or European rather than national responsibility. One in *FAZ*, February 6, 1960, declared that it was "unthinkable that one of the NATO states in Central Europe could use atomic weapons on its own and without decision with the other allies"—a decidedly anti-French statement.

57. *Erinnerungen, 1959–1963*, 54–67. See also Albert-Paul Lentin in *France Observateur*, October 13, 1960; editorial in *NZZ*, November 27, 1960.

58. One account suggests that Adenauer instructed Herbert Blankenhorn, ambassador to Paris, to keep him constantly informed of any developments and in August sent the State Secretary in the Foreign Ministry, Hilger von Scherpenberg, to confirm his own impressions with French Foreign Minister Maurice Couve de Murville. See Dieter M. Mahncke, "Nuclear Participation: The Federal Republic of Germany and Nuclear Weapons, 1954–1966" (Ph.D. diss., Johns Hopkins University, 1968), 88–89. A revision of this work was published as *Nukleare Mitwirkung* (Munich: Oldenbourg, 1971).

59. Cf. Adenauer's account in Erinnerungen, 1959–1963, 71–72, with C. L. Sulzberger's report in *NYT*, November 23, 1960.

60. *Erinnerungen, 1959–1963*, 70–76.

61. *FAZ*, October 19, 1960. A second interesting comment was Strauss's response to a charge made by the SPD that the atomic armament of the Bundeswehr constituted a de facto increase in the number of nuclear nations. The defense minister declared that the Federal Republic had always supported the American view on nonproliferation and added: "An atomic proprietor can only be one who produces atomic warheads for himself or receives atomic warheads from producing states in such a fashion that he himself has full control over them. That is not the situation here." "Die klare Konzeption," *Politisch-Soziale Korrespondenz*, October 15, 1960.

62. Characteristically, Adenauer waited almost until the American election had been decided. See his speech to the German-British Press Institute, *NZZ*, November 2, 1960; his speech to the Foreign Press Association, Bonn, *NZZ*, November 11, 1960; his speech to CDU leaders, *Bulletin*, November 18, 1960. See also a commentary in *Le Monde*, November 20/21, 1960, and in *NZZ*, November 27, 1960, and a speech by Ambassador Herbert Blankenhorn to the Diplomatic Press Association in Paris, Le Monde, November 30, 1960.

63. Interview probes in 1965–66 failed to produce any further information about preferences among formulas at that point. See a report in *FAZ*, December 19, 1960, and Strauss's hints in his recommendations for the December meeting in *NYT*, December 2, 1960, for the only public references.

64. This last provision was Norstad's condition for supporting the Herter concept, according to one American military source.

65. *FAZ*, December 19, 21, 1960. The German proposal was supported by Canada and Greece, but at least one press report (*FAZ*, December 29, 1960) suggested that the other allies were uncomfortable about, if not opposed to, any transfer of control from the American president to the council and/or SACEUR.

66. Reprinted in *Department of State Bulletin*, January 9, 1961, 40.

67. For one British view on the nature of this relationship, see Donald C. Watt, *Britain Looks to Germany: British Opinion and Policy Towards Germany since 1945* (London: Wolff, 1965).

68. Horst Mendershausen's account of this protracted argument in his *Troop Stationing in Germany: Value and Cost* RM-5881-PR (Santa Monica: RAND, 1968), especially section 4, is the most comprehensive to date.

69. *Erinnerungen, 1955–1959*, 256.

70. See Adenauer's pungent remarks on this in *ibid.*, 294–302, especially his remarks to French Premier Guy Mollett in February, 1957, on British attempts to finance their nuclear force by leaving the heavy burdens to others, with the consequence that "England is then the only nuclear power in Europe and thereby the strongest political power (*Potenz*)"; *ibid.*, 274.

71. A public reflection of the anti-German sentiments reported in the later Bonn interviews of 1965–66 is represented in articles appearing in the (London) *Times* throughout late October and November 1960 that stressed the problems which control-sharing would pose in terms of effective military use of weapons and of a future disarmament agreement. Cf. also *NZZ*, November 27, 1960.

72. For the Euratom case, see the discussions in Bertrand Goldschmidt, *L'aventure atomique: ses aspects politiques et techniques* (Paris: Fayard, 1962), 128–35 and Nieburg, *Nuclear Secrecy*, 169–74. The British initiative to replace F-I-G cooperation with "less divisive" WEU cooperation was reported in *NYT*, April 15, 1958.

73. See, for example, his remarks in *Erinnerungen, 1955–1959*, chapter 14.

74. *Ibid.*, 294–95; *NZZ*, May 26, 1957.

75. See the figures for British purchases in table 5, chapter 4.

76. *Erinnerungen, 1955–1959*, 263.

77. This account is drawn from scattered interview materials as well as the sources cited in n. 72 and in Wilhelm Cornides (ed.), *Die Internationale Politik, 1956/1957* (Munich: Oldenbourg, 1961), 280, 363–65; Jacques Vernant, "Die Kernwaffen und die Europäische Union," *Europa Archiv*, 12/1962, 411–16; F. Roy Willis, *France, Germany, and the New Europe, 1945–1963* (Stanford: Stanford University Press, 1965), 250–51.

78. For a more detailed, chronological examination of these and later Franco-German conversations, see chapter 5 of Kelleher, MIT, especially 308–12; 319–20; 327–38. Interview accounts have been checked against and confirmed by the evidence cited in Kohl, *French Nuclear Diplomacy*.

79. Strauss of course was on an official visit and brought with him General Adolf Heusinger, then Inspector General of the Bundeswehr, and a very prestigious delegation. Although

these accords were signed only by the defense ministers, Strauss later asserted that he had obtained Adenauer's specific approval and presumed that Premier Mollet also had been consulted. Heusinger also formally advised the other NATO states. Cited in Edmund Taylor, "The Powerhouse of German Defense," *Reporter,* April 18, 1957, 25–27.

80. Questioned by an American journalist in March, Strauss said that reports of European atomic production were "premature," but that such a project was not "excluded" from the Franco-German program. He then discussed his own views on the control problem: "I don't believe that any one European nation should be authorized to produce atomic weapons and neither should they be in the sole possession of any one nation." *Ibid.* Strauss later declared that he had been misquoted by Taylor in this and other respects.

81. *NYT,* May 25, 1957.

82. *Erinnerungen, 1955–1959,* 323–32. Adenauer also mentions (p. 332) a confidential French General staff memorandum by General Lavaux expressing support for such cooperation.

83. *Ibid.,* 339. Dulles reportedly also suggested direct cooperation with those states which "have already had experience." This seems quite consistent with his views on nuclear-weapons sharing (chapter 1).

84. "Plain Talk by France on the United States and World Problems," *U.S. News and World Report,* January 3, 1958, 60–63.

85. Strauss made these statements in response to questioning by the SPD in the Bundestag on January 23, 1958; see Federal Republic of Germany, Bundestag, *Verhandlungen: Stenographische Berichte,* 384.

86. *FAZ,* February 8, 1958. See also *NYT,* February 28, 1958.

87. Interview in *Daily Mirror,* April 2, 1958, quoted in Hans Frederik, *Franz Josef Strauss: Das Lebensbild eines Politikers* (Munich-Inning: Humboldt, n.d.), 190. Richard H. S. Crossman omitted this section of the interview in his subsequent and longer "A Talk with Franz Josef Strauss," *New Statesman,* April 12, 1958, 460–62, out of "courtesy," given Strauss's denials. Gerald Freund, however, asserts that Strauss told him approximately the same thing at approximately the same time; see his *Germany Between Two Worlds* (New York: Harcourt Brace, 1961), 154–55.

88. Strauss himself discussed this on his return; see *FAZ,* March 19, 1958. See also his later discussion in an interview in *Die Zeit,* April 8, 1966, where he suggested that the common interests had been focused primarily on the development of small reactors and on nuclear ship propulsion.

89. In light of subsequent events, it is interesting to note a press commentary in *France Observateur* on December 4, 1958. Commenting on the general French attitude of "unconditional support" for Adenauer, the unknown author speculated that one reason was "the desire of French diplomacy to strengthen the chancellor against the machinations of his defense minister. . . . He appears to the French delegation to be an extremely dangerous man, ultranationalistic, today anti-Soviet to the extreme, but who one day could take a swing around to conclude an agreement with Moscow behind France's back."

90. Cf. Adenauer's account of each in *Erinnerungen, 1955–1959,* 424–36; *Erinnerungen 1959–1963,* 15–21, 42–48, 59–67, 80–88, 101–11, 119–33, 136–50, 158–74, 177–84, 198–210, 221–30. Significantly, these accounts form the bulk of this last, incomplete document.

CHAPTER VI. DISCORD OVER STRATEGY: 1961-1962

1. For this and subsequent discussions of developments in American strategic thinking the author is particularly indebted to William W. Kaufmann's account in his *The McNamara Strategy* (New York: Harper & Row, 1964). Considerable material concerning the American political background has been drawn from Arthur M. Schlesinger, Jr., *A Thousand Days* (Boston: Houghton Mifflin, 1966), especially chapters 16, 17.

2. Originally published in the *Washington Star,* the report appeared in the *New York Times* [*NYT*] on February 28 and March 1, 1961.

3. The immediate focus was the defense-appropriations budget for fiscal 1962; see Federal Republic of Germany, Bundestag, *Verhandlungen: Stenographische Berichte,* March 15, 1961 [hereafter cited as *Verhandlungen*]. Cf. the often biting critiques of perceived American policy in the official *Bulletin* (published by the Press and Information Office of the Federal Government) of this period, especially the March 3, 1961, issue.

4. See Strauss's statements in *Verhandlungen,* 8628.

5. *Ibid.,* 8633.

6. *Ibid.*

7. See on this point Wilhelm Cornides, "Die Überprüfung der Amerikanischen Strategie und die Reformen McNamaras," in *Die Internationale Politik, 1961,* ed. Wilhelm Cornides and Dietrich Mende (Munich: Oldenbourg, 1964), 48.

8. For a discussion of Norstad's formulation of this argument, see Charles Murphy, "The Education of a Defense Secretary," *Fortune,* May, 1962, 273-74.

9. *NYT,* April 11, 1961.

10. Cf. Adenauer's own account of this first meeting in his *Erinnerungen, 1959-1963* (Stuttgart: Deutsche, 1968), 91-99. See also *NYT,* April 16, 18, 1961.

11. For Norstad's remarks, see *NYT,* April 18, 1961. For some of Strauss's comments, see his interview with Adelbert Weinstein in *Frankfurter Allgemeine Zeitung* [*FAZ*], May 13, 1961; and his speech to the Bund der Deutschen Industrie, "Nato und unsere Sicherheit," *FAZ,* June 13, 1961.

12. See also *FAZ,* April 27, 1961; *Bulletin,* May 3, 1961.

13. See, for example, *Neue Zürcher Zeitung* [*NZZ*], June 28, 1961.

14. This was merely one more example of Strauss's leaking of details of the top-secret MC-70 plan, a tendency which more than once prompted complaints and criticism from NATO officials. See David Schoenbaum, *The Spiegel Affair* (New York: Doubleday, 1968), chapter 3.

15. Speech to the conference of German-Belgian parliamentarians at Köln-Wahn airport, November 11, 1960, private collection (see appendix). See his earlier remarks to the Bundestag on March 25, 1958, *Verhandlungen,* 874-75.

16. For further details on all of these discussions, see Sorensen, *Kennedy,* 657; and Schlesinger, *Thousand Days,* 381.

17. Excerpted in Sorensen, *Kennedy,* 188-98.

18. *Ibid.,* 193.

19. *McNamara Strategy,* 67.

20. See, for example, *NYT*, July 15, 23, 28, August 1, 1961; *NZZ*, August 1, 1961; *FAZ*, August 3, 5, 1961.

21. "Glaubhafte Sicherheit durch Abschreckung."

22. The remarks in *Der Spiegel*, October 10, 1962, 44, confirm the broader interview data.

23. See Kaufmann, McNamara Strategy, 73ff.

24. Although John Steinbruner, "The Mind and Milieu of Policy-Makers: a Case Study of the MLF" (Ph.D. diss., Massachusetts Institute of Technology, 1968; to be published by Princeton University Press), is now the definitive source on these discussions (see his chapter 1, section 5, in particular), three of the many earlier discussions on this point are Alastair Buchan, *The Multilateral Force: a Historical Perspective*, Adelphi Paper, no. 13 (London: Institute for Strategic Studies, 1964), 4–6; Wilhelm Cornides "Überprüfung," 94–100; Schlesinger, *Thousand Days*, 850–56.

25. See Kaufmann, *McNamara Strategy*, 11; Charles Murphy, "NATO at a Nuclear Crossroads," *Fortune*, December, 1962, 220.

26. For a detailed description of the German buildup, see FAZ, September 29, 1961; *NYT*, October 25, 29, 1961; and Wallace C. Magathan, "West German Defense Policy," *Orbis*, Summer, 1964.

27. *FAZ*, September 29, 1961.

28. See *Der Spiegel*, October 10, 1962, 46; and Schoenbaum, *Spiegel Affair*, 52–55. It was this memorandum that was to be the indirect cause of the *Spiegel* affair in October (discussed below in this chapter). Schmückle's article, entitled "Eine Betrachtung über das Kriegsbild in Europa: Die Wandlung der Apokalypse," appeared in the prominent Stuttgart weekly *Christ und Welt* on March 4, 1963.

29. See, for example, Speidel's interview with Weinstein, *FAZ*, December 30, 1961; and Heusinger's interviews with Weinstein, *FAZ*, December 16, 1961, March 27, 1962.

30. One article explicitly establishing the connection was Gerhard Elser, "United States Army, 1961," *Wehrkunde*, April, 1962, 178–85.

31. Wolf Graf von Baudissin, "Das Kriegsbild," *Wehrwissenschaftliche Rundschau*, July, 1962, 373.

32. Uwe Nerlich, "The Nuclear Dilemmas of the Federal Republic of Germany," 10–11 (unpublished revision of an article prepared earlier for the Stanford Research Institute and published in German under the same title in *Europa Archiv*, 17/1965, 637–52).

33. The most detailed but certainly partisan accounts were two articles in *Der Spiegel*, June 13, 1962, 16–19, and October 10, 1962, 32–53.

34. *NYT*, March 1, 1962. For the tone of Washington's assessments, see *Time*, March 9, 1962, 27–28; Joseph Kraft, *The Grand Design* (New York: Harper, 1962), 54. For German reactions, see *Verhandlungen*, April 6, 1962, which prints the military-budget debate that provided the framework for the SPD's attack.

35. McNamara's subsequent speech at Ann Arbor is generally accepted as being an unclassified version of his remarks at Athens. See Kaufmann, *McNamara Strategy*, 114.

36. *Ibid.*, 119–20.

37. "Athens, a New Start," Defense Ministry press release, May 7, 1962. Another of Strauss's reported formulations perhaps is closer to the classic American model of the 1950s:

"An atomic bomb is worth as much as a brigade and costs much less." Quoted in *Der Spiegel,* October 10, 1962, 50.

38. *NYT,* April 14, 1962. See also the discussions in James L. Richardson, *Germany and the Atlantic Alliance* (Cambridge: Harvard University Press, 1966), 63–65; Henry A. Kissinger, *The Troubled Partnership* (New York: McGraw-Hill, 1966), 70. See *NYT,* May 8, 10, 13, 15, 19, 1962; *NZZ,* May 10, 1962; Gordon Craig, *From Bismarck to Adenauer* (New York: Harper & Row, 1965), 106; Sorensen, *Kennedy,* 629–30.

39. Cf. C. L. Sulzberger, *NYT,* July 30, 1962; Murphy, "NATO at Crossroads," 86. Theo Sommer, discussing the general nature of the alliance dialogue after the announcement of Norstad's recall, suggests that two items of particular European concern were projected removal of Thors and Jupiters and American thinking about withholding at least the Davy Crockett warheads from the European allies' forces; *Die Zeit,* North American edition (NA), August 10, 1962.

40. Maxwell D. Taylor, *The Uncertain Trumpet* (New York: Harper, 1960), 145.

41. *NZZ,* August 1, 4, 1962; *Bulletin,* August 10, 1962; Murphy, "NATO at Crossroads," 219. Interviews in 1964 with Washington participants indicated that the Germans repeatedly were told that Lemnitzer was being "kicked upstairs" because of his "failure to advise" at the time of the Bay of Pigs fiasco. Those few German respondents who admitted the existence of such messages uniformly suggested that Kennedy had advanced a good excuse to mask his antipathy to the pro-European Norstad.

42. *Bulletin,* July 25, 1962; Speech to International Students' Conference at Bonn University, July 28, 1962, private collection (see appendix); *Bulletin,* August 4, 5, 1962; *FAZ,* August 9, 1962; *Hamburger Abendblatt,* August 11, 1962; *Münchener Merkur,* August 11/12, 1962; *Welt am Sonntag,* August 14, 1962.

43. Two rather different approaches to the affair are presented by Schoenbaum, *Spiegel Affair,* and the comparatively less detailed Ronald F. Bunn, *German Politics and the Spiegel Affair* (Baton Rouge: Louisiana State University Press, 1968).

44. Cf. chapters 2 and 3.

45. Officially known as the Bundesnachrichtendienst, the Gehlen Organization was responsible to the Chancellor's Office. Its founder and head, General Reinhard Gehlen, was head of the "Eastern" *Abwehr* during 1941–1945 and established a postwar intelligence system—even before the founding of the Federal Republic—with substantial American assistance. The American connection is popularly believed to have been one of its continuing sources of strength; interview data, although limited, would seem to contradict this. See Marion Grafin Donhoff, "Gehlens Geheimdienst," *Die Zeit* (NA) August 2, 1963.

CHAPTER VII. THE DEBATE ABOUT CONTROL-SHARING: 1961–1962

1. Quoted in William W. Kaufmann, *The McNamara Strategy* (New York: Harper & Row, 1964), 106–7. Steinbrunner suggests that the multilateral-force offer was included much to the chagrin of nonproliferation advocates within the administration and was largely the effort of one man, Henry Owen, later to be known as one of the fathers of the MLF. See John Steinbruner, "The Mind and Milieu of Policy-makers: a Case Study of the MLF" (Ph.D. diss., Massachusetts Institute of Technology, 1968; to be published by Princeton University Press).

2. Perhaps the two most authoritative accounts of this debate are Steinbruner, "MLF," and John Newhouse, *De Gaulle and the Anglo-Saxons* (New York: Viking, 1970), chapters 3–4.

3. Quoted in Steinbruner, "MLF," 384.

4. *Ibid.*, 385.

5. See chapter 6 for a discussion of the other related presentations at Athens.

6. Interview with Adelbert Weinstein, *Frankfurter Allgemeine Zeitung* [*FAZ*], May 8, 1962.

7. Quoted in Steinbruner, "MLF," 396.

8. See Newhouse's account on this point in *De Gaulle,* chapter 6.

9. See chapter 5.

10. See *New York Times* [*NYT*], April 16, 18, 1961; and Konrad Adenauer, *Erinnerungen, 1959–1963* (Stuttgart: Deutsche, 1968), 91–99.

11. *NYT,* November 17, 1961.

12. *Regierungserklärung,* November 29, 1961, translation in *NYT,* November 30, 1961. This statement, according to one report, was a major point in the bargaining to form the coalition; *NYT,* November 5, 1961.

13. See Strauss's comments in *Neue Zürcher Zeitung* [*NZZ*], December 4, 1961; interviews with Weinstein, *FAZ,* December 5, 14, 1961; *NYT,* December 13, 1961. See also on this point the Erler-Strauss exchange in a later Bundestag debate in Federal Republic of Germany, Bundestag, *Verhandlungen: Stenographische Berichte,* April 6, 1962, 920, 939 [hereafter cited as *Verhandlungen*]; and the general statements in Charles Murphy, "NATO at a Nuclear Crossroads," *Fortune,* December, 1962, 220.

14. Frank Nash Memorial Lecture, "National Sovereignty and the Alliance: the European States in NATO," delivered at Georgetown University on November 27, 1961, printed in the official *Bulletin* (published by the Press and Information Office of the Federal Government), December 1, 1961. For a discussion of the circumstances of the speech, see Wilhelm Cornides, "Der Grand Design der Atlantischen Partnerschaft," in *Die Internationale Politik, 1961,* ed. Wilhelm Cornides and Dietrich Mende (Munich: Oldenbourg, 1964), 95–98. For Strauss's personal assessment, see his remarks in *The Grand Design* (New York: Praeger, 1966), 103. His other principal speech during this visit was an address to radio and television executives in New York on November 29, 1961.

15. Strauss declared that for "many European states" this would be "an easier path" than that to a United Europe.

16. His text was reproduced almost verbatim in an article by Weinstein in *FAZ,* December 16, 1961. See also in *FAZ* other articles by Weinstein on December 14, 16, 1961, and an interview with Strauss on December 21, 1961.

17. In the interview in *FAZ,* December 21, 1961, Strauss alluded to "two proposals"; in an article in *NYT* on December 13, 1961, he was quoted as having four or five possible solutions to present.

18. *Verhandlungen,* April 9, 1962, 939–42. See also his "Frieden für Europa," *Bulletin,* April 7, 1962; and reports of his comments to Bundeswehr commanders at Mainz, *Die Welt,* March 30, 1962; *NYT,* March 31, 1962; and *NZZ,* April 11, 1962.

19. *FAZ,* May 7, 10, 1962; *NZZ,* May 11, 1962.

20. See *NYT,* April 14, 1962; and the discussion in Henry A. Kissinger, *The Troubled Partnership* (New York: McGraw-Hill, 1966), 70.

21. See chapter 5.

22. Cf. Wilhelm Cornides, "Grand Design," 76.

23. Wolfgang Wagner, "Das Geteilte Deutschland," in *Die Internationale Politik, 1961,* ed. Wilhelm Cornides and Dietrich Mende (Munich: Oldenbourg, 1964), 176.

24. *FAZ,* September 29, 1961; *NZZ,* October 8, 1961.

25. In his authoritative monograph to which this discussion is indebted Charles R. Planck notes that after the first round of Western discussions the United States clearly excluded any zonal disarmament proposal from the American-Soviet exploratory talks. See *The Changing Status of German Reunification in Western Diplomacy* (Baltimore: Johns Hopkins Press, 1967), 41–48. See also *NYT,* October 25, 1961.

26. See *NYT,* May 8, 10, 13, 15, 19, 1962.

27. Speech to the Deutsche Gesellschaft für Auswärtige Politik, Bonn, April 2, 1962, printed in *Department of State Bulletin,* April 23, 1962, 666–73.

28. Theo Sommer, *Die Zeit,* North American Edition, (NA), November 8, 1963.

29. See *NZZ,* March 17, 1963.

30. See, for example, reports in *Bonner Rundschau,* June 27, 1962; *Bulletin,* August 5, 14, 1962; *FAZ,* August 9, 1962; *Münchener Merkur,* August 11/12, 1962; *NYT,* October 17, 1962.

31. Several interview sources reported that Bundy's speech in Copenhagen, from which the quotation is taken, was generally regarded by most circles in Bonn as an authoritative but not necessarily believable summary of Kennedy's thinking.

32. Alastair Buchan makes the contradictory statement that Rusk presented to the North Atlantic Council a plan for a force to be composed of Polaris submarines and a new medium-range mobile land-based missile known as "Missile X," which had been under reluctant development by the Pentagon since 1961. See his *The Multilateral Force: a Historical Perspective,* Adelphi Papers, no. 13 (London: Institute for Strategic Studies, 1964), 7.

33. Whatever the validity of this German view, it seems relevant here to recall Sorensen's statement: "The truth is that Kennedy himself did not look upon either the Alliance or Atlantic harmony as an end in itself. He cared about the concrete problems which the Alliance faced . . . but he tended to look upon the rest of the Alliance in somewhat the same light as he looked upon Congress—as a necessary but not always welcome partner, whose cooperation he could not always obtain, whose opinions he could not always accept, and with whom an uneasy relationship seemed inevitable." Theodore Sorensen, *Kennedy* (New York: Bantam, 1966), 633–34.

34. See on this point Kennedy's revealing discussions with President Kekonnen of Finland in the fall of 1961, as quoted in Arthur M. Schlesinger, Jr., *A Thousand Days* (Boston: Houghton Mifflin, 1966), 379–80, 398–99.

35. Cf. here the interpretations offered by Fritz R. Allemann in "Arger mit den Verbundeten," *Der Monat,* June 1962, 22–28; James L. Richardson, *Germany and the Atlantic Alliance* (Cambridge: Harvard University Press, 1966), 63–67; Kissinger, *Troubled Partnership,* 68.

36. Sorensen, *Kennedy,* 630; Arthur Schlesinger, *Thousand Days,* 403–4. Adenauer's own account is a masterly reflection of the differing perspectives of the two men and the dif-

ficulties involved in harmonizing even their respective time frameworks. For example, Kennedy repeatedly poses questions about the present and the future in highly pragmatic terms; Adenauer replies in terms of answers he has previously given to John Foster Dulles or in terms of tactics proven successful in the past. Cf. *Erinnerungen, 1959–1963,* 91ff. Adenauer was also extremely piqued that Willy Brandt, mayor of Berlin but also the SPD's candidate for chancellor in the elections of September, 1961, paid an official visit to the White House before he did. See *NZZ,* February 16, 17, 1961; Wagner, "Geteilte Deutschland," 130–31.

37. See, for example, Sorensen, *Kennedy,* 672; Schlesinger, *Thousand Days,* 399; Steinbruner, "MLF," chapter 1, sections 5 and 6.

38. Sorensen, *Kennedy,* 673.

39. See, for example, Kennedy's "suspicious wife" simile regarding German behavior, as cited in Schlesinger, *Thousand Days,* 403.

40. See Wagner, "Geteilte Deutschland," 169–171; Richard Hiscocks, *Germany Revived* (London: Victor Gollancz, 1966), 207–8; Terrence Prittie's reports in *New Republic,* July 22, October 27, 1962.

41. A number of those interviewed—political figures, journalists, and military men—discussed particular incidents in which they were personally involved and concluded that Strauss seemed to be "a different man."

42. Several Defense Ministry respondents alleged that at least one member of Strauss's staff made sure that the minister was fully aware of all criticism raised directly or in major American press commentaries. Although such behavior seems to smack of the conspiracy theory of history, it is not precluded by the atmosphere in the ministry, especially during 1962.

43. Richard E. Neustadt, *Alliance Politics* (New York, Columbia University Press, 1970). See the discussion of Neustadt's propositions in chapter 2.

44. The weak response of Bonn and its allies to the erection of the Berlin Wall would seem to constitute a prime example. For an even more "psychological" interpretation, which draws a relationship between reliance on battlefield weapons and the experience of the Eastern Front, see Conrad Ahlers, "Fallex und Baudissin," in *Zwanzig Jahre Danach,* ed. Helmut Hammerschmidt (Munich: Desch, 1965), 297–300.

45. These sentiments were strongest among middle-level army officers and were not without parallels in the attitudes of American army officers interviewed at about the same time (albeit for another project) in both Washington and field situations.

CHAPTER VIII. STRATEGIC EDUCATION AND RECONCILIATION: 1963–1966

1. The subsequent analysis owes a particular debt to Uwe Nerlich, "The Nuclear Dilemmas of the Federal Republic of Germany" (manuscript, 1966, of which an earlier version was published under the same title in *Europa Archiv,* 17/1965, 637–52). A good introduction to the subject is provided by Wallace C. Magathan, "West German Defense Policy," *Orbis,* Summer, 1964, 301–15; an interesting Eastern view is Julian Lider, *West Germany in NATO* (Warsaw: Zachodnia Agencja Prasowa, 1965), 170–202; a partisan but thoughtful German critique is Dieter Göbel, *Ist Westdeutschland zu verteidigen?* (Dusseldorf: Econ, 1966).

2. Cf. "Porträt des Monats: Kai-Uwe von Hassel," *Wehrkunde,* February, 1963, 109.

3. See Ulrich de Mazière, "Die national Verteidigungsverantwortung," *Wehrwissenschaftliche Rundschau,* March, 1964, 129–40.

4. The full text is to be found in the official *Bulletin* (published by the Press and Information Office of the Federal Government), January 24, 1963, and the preamble adopted by the Bundestag in *Bulletin*, May 17, 1963. See also Adenauer's notes on the genesis of the treaty in his *Erinnerungen, 1959–1963* (Stuttgart: Deutsche, 1968), chapter 14, and the account of F. Roy Willis in his *France, Germany and the New Europe: 1945–1967*, rev. ed. (New York: Oxford University Press, 1968), chapter 10.

5. Cf. Wilfrid L. Kohl, *French Nuclear Diplomacy* (Princeton: Princeton University Press, 1971), chapter 7.

6. *Die Welt*, August 8, 1963; *Neue Zürcher Zeitung* [*NZZ*], December 6, 1963; *Bulletin*, May 19, 1964.

7. *New York Times* [*NYT*], November 15, 1964.

8. *Ibid.*, March 19, May 15, 1963. Deputy George Kliesing (CDU) suggested in the Bundestag debate of April 15, 1964, that one implicit condition of formal recognition had been the growth of the Bundeswehr to the 400,000-man level; Federal Republic of Germany, Bundestag, *Verhandlungen: Stenographische Berichte*, 5797 [hereafter cited as *Verhandlungen*].

9. Cf. Alastair Buchan and Philip Windsor, *Arms and Stability in Europe* (New York: Praeger, 1963), 83–86; "The British Army in Germany," *Times* (London), October 17, 1963; and the statements by Labour Defense Minister Dennis Healey, cited in *NYT*, March 4, June 1, 1965.

10. See *NYT*, July 9, 29, November 4, 1964; the National Assembly speech by Defense Minister Pierre Messmer on December 1, 1964, in the *French Affairs* series, no. 171, and the National Assembly speech by Premier Georges Pompidou on December 2, 1964, in the *Speeches* series, no. 169, both published in New York by Ambassade de France, Service de Presse et d'Information.

11. The highlights of these and later Franco-German exchanges are reprinted in Karl Bauer's useful documentary collection, *Deutsche Verteidigungspolitik: 1946–1967* (Boppard am Rhein: Boldt, 1968), 269–84; 292–93; 318–23.

12. Cf. *NZZ*, December 17, 1962; *Die Welt*, January 18, 1963.

13. Cf. *NZZ*, December 18, 22, 1962; *Le Monde*, December 29, 1964. A similar speech by Paul H. Nitze on March 2, 1963, produced a similar reaction; see *NZZ*, March 4, 1963. Everyone seemed to have forgotten that Strauss himself had once spoken of such a "reversal"; see above, 79.

14. *Die Welt*, January 18, March 19, April 9, 1963.

15. *Ibid.*, January 18, 1963.

16. Cf. *Die Welt*, February 6, 17, 21, March 1, 1963; *Verhandlungen*, May 9, 1963, 3569–70.

17. Defense Ministry Press release, June 6, 1963.

18. For a more detailed discussion of the Big Lift crisis, see below, 243.

19. *NZZ*, October 30, 1963.

20. One version of this proposal was that subject by Lothal Ruehl in *Die Welt*, October 30, 1963. A somewhat different account was contained in "Atomare Kleinkamptruppen," *Wehrkunde*, October, 1963, 561.

21. Speech to the WEU Assembly, Defense Ministry press release, June 6, 1963.

22. Cf. two articles by Heinz Schneider: "Neue Wege in der Landesverteidigung der Bundesrepublik," *Wehrwissenschaftliche Rundschau*, November, 1963, 638–43, and "Aufgaben und Wesen der 'Territorial Reserve,' " *Bulletin*, February 21, 1964. See also chapter 3, 84.

23. Cf. von Hassel's Bundestag remarks, *Verhandlungen*, May 9, 1963, 3568.

24. For more details, see excerpts from and comments on a speech by Paul H. Nitze on March 2, 1963, in William W. Kaufmann, *The McNamara Strategy* (New York: Harper & Row, 1964), 1932; and Secretary McNamara's speech to the Economic Club of New York, *NYT*, November 19, 1963.

25. *NYT*, December 5, 1963. Comments by several respondents indicated that although there were continuing differences regarding estimates of the rate and scope of Soviet postattack mobilization, the two ministers were agreed on the level of forces to be stationed in central Europe.

26. Speech to the WEU Assembly, Defense Ministry press release, June 6, 1963.

27. See on this point, *Die Welt*, December 14, 18, 19, 1963; Gerhard Baumann, "Wehrdoktrin in Widerstreit," *Wehrwissenschaftliche Rundschau*, March, 1964, 160–76. The principal negotiations took place during General Heusinger's service as chairman of the NATO Military Committee.

28. *Die Welt*, December 14, 1963.

29. For one officer's dissent from von Hassel's position on escalation, see Oberst Hellmuth Roth, "Zum Problem der Eskalation," *Wehrwissenschaftliche Rundschau*, October, 1963, 554–65.

30. *Der Spiegel*, January 6, 1965, 16.

31. "Flexible Response: A French View," *Revue de défense nationale*, August-September, 1964, reprinted in *Survival*, November–December, 1964, 258–65. See also *NYT*, July 29, 1964.

32. Nerlich, "Nuclear Dilemmas," 11; Kai-Uwe von Hassel, "Organizing Western Defense," *Foreign Affairs*, January, 1965, 210–11.

33. Von Hassel, "Organizing Western Defense," 211; *Der Spiegel*, January 6, 1965, 16–25.

34. *NYT*, November 15, 1964. See also von Hassel's comment in his "Organizing Western Defense," 211.

35. *Frankfurter Allgemeine Zeitung [FAZ]*, December 16, 1964. See also *NYT*, December 17, 19, 23, 1964. Just as in the *Spiegel* affair, an official investigation was launched to determine whether Weinstein's disclosures had been treasonable; *NYT*, January 20, 24, 1965.

36. See *Der Spiegel*, January 6, 1965, 19.

37. A report by Drew Middleton alleged that the prime target areas were the Fulda gap and the Bohemian forest region not far from Munich; *NYT*, January 30, 1965.

38. For further discussion of this and following points, see chapter 8, 254–59. A familiar point regarding the German Gaullists warrants repeating here. Their support for General de Gaulle's policies in essence was a matter of domestic political infighting and of selective perception. They were, for example, in favor of a European nuclear option and a weakening of discriminatory Atlantic bonds, but were totally opposed to any bridge-building to Eastern Europe or to the "atheistic" Soviet Union.

39. Nerlich, "Nuclear Dilemmas," 11.

40. Cf. the discussion here with William T. R. Fox and Annette B. Fox, *NATO and the Range of American Choice* (New York: Columbia University Press, 1967), chapter 6; Walter Schultz, "Die Politik de Gaulles und die erzwungene Neuordnung der NATO," *Europa Archiv*, May 10, 1966, 31–24; and the special issue "NATO 1966," *Politische Studien*, September–October, 1966.

41. Cf. von Hassel's view in March in *Christian Science Monitor*, March 8, 1966, Erhard's view in June in *NYT*, June 5, 1965, and Schröder's view in his July interview with *Dusseldorfer Nachrichten*, reprinted in *Europa Archiv*, 15/1965, D 384ff.

42. See below, 262–63.

43. The basic sources in English for this subject are C. J. E. Harlow, *The European Armaments Base: A Survey*, vol. 2, Institute for Strategic Studies; *Defense, Technology, and the Western Alliance* (6 vols., London, 1967), especially part 2, "National Procurement Policies," 39–50; and Horst Mendershausen, *Troop Stationing in Germany: Value and Cost*, RM-5881-PR (Santa Monica: RAND, 1963) chapters 4 and 5. See also chapter 4 of this study.

44. The *Bulletin* (official English-language publication of the Bundes Presse- und Informationsamt), March 5, 1963. A similar assurance had been given in February to visiting Deputy Secretary of Defense Roswell Gilpatric; *Die Welt*, February 15, 1963. See also Mendershausen's discussion in his *Troop Stationing*, 74–76.

45. Cf. *Der Spiegel*, January 24, 1963, 20–22; *NYT*, February 11, 1963; *Die Welt*, February 16, 1963; Jean Planchais's article in *Le Monde*, August 17, 1963, translated as "France and Germany: Military Collaboration" in *Survival*, November–December, 1963, 249–50.

46. For a detailed description of the Leopard, see *Wehrkunde*, August, 1963, 448–50.

47. Defense Ministry press release, August 3, 1963; *Economist*, August 10, 1963.

48. For a more detailed description of this program and the entire naval modernization effort, see *Die Welt*, August 8, 1963; *NZZ*, December 6, 1963; Fritz E. Giese, "Braucht die Bundesmarine Grössere Schiffe?" *Wehr und Wirtschaft*, December, 1963, 499–500; *FAZ*, January 20, 1964; *NYT*, May 12, November 15, 1964; *Der Spiegel*, July 8, 1964, 26–34.

49. *NYT*, November 22, 1964.

50. Perhaps Senator Goldwater's most publicized statements were those made to a *Spiegel* interviewer, reprinted in *NYT*, July 9, 1964. See also the comments of a Republican Party study commission, *NYT*, August 6, 1964; President Johnson's remarks in his Labor Day address, *NYT*, September 8, 1964; and a review by Jack Raymond, *NYT*, September 23, 1964.

51. *NYT*, November 8, 1964.

52. Cf. the review in *Die Welt*, May 25, 1965.

53. *NYT*, May 26, November 28, 1965.

54. See chapter 4, 108–9.

55. A somewhat different calculation was advanced by SPD Deputy Helmut Schmidt in the Bundestag debate about the Starfighter on March 24, 1966. He argued that less than 20 percent of the 800 Starfighters eventually purchased (100 more than originally planned) were combat ready; *Verhandlungen*, 1548.

56. Cf. *ibid.*, May 9, 1963, especially 3571–72, March 24, 1966, 1510–1603. For a more detailed discussion, see *Der Spiegel*, January 24, 1966, 21–36; and Kurt Johannson, "Starfighter und Mirage," *Der Monat*, April, 1966, 26–41.

57. *Wehr und Wirtschaft,* 6/1964, 256, quoted in Gerhard Brandt, *Rüstung und Wirtschaft in der Bundesrepublik,* vol. 3, *Studien zur politischen und gesellschaftlichen Situation der Bundeswehr,* ed. Georg Picht (3 vols., Witten/Berlin: Eckart, 1966), 260. See Brandt's further discussion of Germany's "second armament phase," *ibid.,* 259–272. Although somewhat slighted in this discussion, British demands were equally involved.

58. See, for example, von Hassel's comments before the Bundestag on June 1, 1966; *Verhandlungen,* 2609ff.

59. Cf. table 1, chapter 4, 98.

60. Cf. *NYT,* November 24, 1965. Cf. the different conclusions but similar data in Wolfram F. Hanrieder, *The Stable Crisis* (New York: Harper & Row, 1970), 21–28; Mendershausen, *Troop Stationing,* chapter 4 *passim,* and Harlow, "National Procurement Policies," 39–40.

61. Harlow, "National Procurement Policies," suggests that in 1965 Washington decided to double the value of its arms exports and began a form of bargaining with Germany "hardly distinguishable from blackmail." His remarks are echoed in a volume of the same series, John Calmann, *European Co-operation in Defence Technology: the Political Aspect,* vol. 1, Institute for Strategic Studies, *Defence, Technology, and the Western Alliance* (6 vols., London, 1967), 12–13; and in Theo Sommer, "Bonn Changes Course," *Foreign Affairs,* April, 1967, 477–91. Sommer suggested that Secretary McNamara "appears to many as a tireless arms merchant with shockingly high-pressure sales techniques"; *ibid.,* 483.

62. Cf. report of an exchange on May 13, 1966, between von Hassel and McNamara in *NYT,* June 9, 1966.

63. Compare reports in *NYT,* September 28–30, 1966.

64. See Erhard's report to the Bundestag and the subsequent pointed debate; *Verhandlungen,* October 5, 1966, 2941ff.

CHAPTER IX. GERMANY AND THE MLF; THE UPWARD WAVE: 1963–1964

1. Federal Republic of Germany, Bundestag, *Verhandlungen: Stenographische Berichte,* February 6, 1963, 2576 [hereafter cited as *Verhandlungen*]. It is a matter of historical fascination to most MLF analysts that the Adenauer-Ball conversation took place on the same day as General de Gaulle's famous press conference rejecting Britain's bid to enter the Common Market and as Kennedy's first formal endorsement of the MLF project in his State of the Union address.

2. By 1975 the literature dealing with the history and lessons of the MLF has become voluminous, with no end in sight. Three accounts of particular value for this analysis were Alastair Buchan, *The Multilateral Force: a Historical Perspective,* Adelphi Papers, no. 13 (London: Institute for Strategic Studies, 1964); Wilfrid L. Kohl, "The United States Proposal for a Multilateral Force" (M.A. essay, European Institute, Columbia University, 1964); Theo Sommer's four articles in *Die Zeit:* "Raketenflotte: Hell, Yes," North American edition (NA), November 8, 1963; "Eine Perle in der Atlantischen Auster," (NA), November 15, 1963; "Was Erhard erwartet," November 19, 1965; "Das nukleare Dilemma," November 26, 1965.

Perhaps the most definitive treatments thus far of the involved and somewhat incredible American discussions are John Steinbruner, "The Mind and the Milieu of Policy-Makers: Case Study of the MLF" (Ph.D. diss., Massachusetts Institute of Technology, 1968, to be published by Princeton University Press); and the authoritative "MLF—or, How He Does It," chapter 7 of Philip Geyelin, *Lyndon B. Johnson and the World* (New York: Praeger, 1966).

3. Quoted in Steinbruner, "MLF," 384.

4. Cf. Buchan's contradictory statement, *Multilateral Force,* 7.

5. Cf. *Neue Zürcher Zeitung [NZZ]*, January 30, 1963; and Adenauer's remarks during the second and third Bundestag reading of the Franco-German treaty in *Verhandlungen,* May 16, 1963, 3753.

6. For a descriptive examination of the interplay of these factions even before 1963, see F. Roy Willis, *France, Germany, and the New Europe: 1945–1967,* rev. ed. (New York: Oxford University Press, 1968), chapter 11. See also Waldemar Besson, *Die Aussenpolitik der Bundesrepublik* (Munich: Piper, 1970) and to a lesser degree, Fred Luchsinger, *Bericht über Bonn, 1955–1965* (Zurich: Fretz & Wasmuth, 1966); and Karl Kaiser and Roger Morgan (eds.), *Britain and West Germany* (London: Oxford University Press [for the Royal Institute of International Affairs], 1971).

7. On this point, see Rolf Zundel, "Das Strauss Erbe aus Kiel," *Die Zeit,* December 28, 1962.

8. Cf. Robert Strobel, "Der Pariser Vertrag," *Die Zeit,* February 1, 1963.

9. *Verhandlungen,* February 6, 1963, 2574–83, especially 2576–77.

10. See *Le Monde,* December 25, 1962. The frightening prospect of yet another exclusive Anglo-American bargain, however, had clearly worried many in Bonn. One indication was the very stiff tone taken by the German representatives at the December sessions of the North Atlantic Council; another was an article in the official *Bulletin* (published by the Press and Information Office of the Federal Government) of December 19 (the second day of the Nassau meetings) reiterating the "no German footsoldiers for American atomic knights" position of the previous summer.

11. Cf. *Die Welt,* January 4, 1963. Unfortunately, Adenauer's only account of this period concerns his meeting with de Gaulle in Paris later in January. In that meeting the principal accents clearly are placed on the unreliability of American foreign policy and perfidy of Macmillan in concluding yet another special arrangement just as Britain supposedly wanted to enter Europe. See Konrad Adenauer, *Erinnerungen, 1959–1963* (Stuttgart: Deutsche, 1968), 198–210; NZZ, January 6, 1963; *Die Zeit,* North American edition (NA) January 11, 1963.

12. *Verhandlungen,* February 6, 1963, 2577.

13. "Atlantische Partnerschaft," *Politisch-soziale Korrespondenz,* March 13, 1963, reprinted in *Bulletin,* March 14, 1963.

14. Cf. *Die Zeit* (NA), January 11, 25, 1963.

15. *New York Times [NYT]*, January 24, 1963. The two men responsible for the original MLF briefings, Gerard C. Smith of the State Department's Policy Planning Staff and Admiral John M. Lee, were appointed to the Merchant mission.

16. Steinbruner, "MFL," 114 reports that Pentagon studies done before the Athens meetings in 1962 indicated that an MLF-like force would yield only a very small percent increase in damage-limiting effectiveness.

17. Cf. Arthur M. Schlesinger, Jr.'s critical "first-hand" account in his *A Thousand Days* (Boston: Houghton Mifflin, 1966), 871–73, with Steinbruner's analysis in his "MLF," chapter 1, section 8.

18. *NYT,* February 15, 1963.

19. *NYT,* March 7, 1963.

20. *NYT,* March 22, 1963.

21. *Die Welt,* April 17, 1963; *NZZ,* May 8, 1963.

22. *NYT,* May 5, 1963; *NZZ,* May 8, 1963. The author could find no other public evidence on this point.

23. For Bundestag statements, see *Verhandlungen,* May 9, 1963, 3574–76; for speech to the WEU Assembly, see Defense Ministry press release, June 6, 1963. See also related statements in an interview with Adelbert Weinstein in *Frankfurter Allgemeine Zeitung [FAZ],* May 25, 1963.

24. *Verhandlungen,* May 9, 1963, 3574.

25. See, for example, reports in *Die Welt,* March 9, 1963; *Die Zeit* (NA), March 22, 1963; *NYT,* April 11, 1963.

26. Interview with Vice Admiral K. A. Zenker, *Die Welt,* March 19, 1963.

27. This attitude was very much in line with the preamble which the Bundestag, not entirely against the government's wishes, had affixed to the Franco-German treaty during ratification. The preamble contained the phrases, "the preservation and consolidation of the unity of the free nations, and in particular of a close partnership between Europe and the United States" and "collective defense within the framework of the North Atlantic Alliance and the integration of the armed forces of the States bound together in that Alliance." The treaty was ratified on May 16, 1962, with only four negative votes and four abstentions. An English translation of the preamble was reprinted in *The Bulletin* (official English-language publication of the Press and Information Office of the Federal Government), May 21, 1963 [hereafter cited as *Bulletin* (Eng.)]. Numerous sources indicate that the American embassy in Bonn exerted great pressure for the inclusion of such a statement. See, for example, the account of George M. Tabler in his *John F. Kennedy and the Uniting of Europe* (Bruges: College of Europe, 1969), 119–20, 122–23.

28. *Verhandlungen,* May 9, 1963, 3564.

29. Schmidt's views were particularly interesting at that point not only because of his role as the SPD's defense expert second only to Erler but also because of his authorship of perhaps the first attempt at modern political-military analysis in German, *Verteidigung oder Vergeltung,* published in English as *Defense or Retaliation* (New York: Praeger, 1962). His views, however, were not markedly different from the arguments raised in his two-part article, "Die unvermeidbare neue Strategie," *Die Zeit,* August 17, 24, 1962.

30. *Verhandlungen,* May 9, 1963, 3573.

31. Speech to WEU Assembly, Defense Ministry press release, June 6, 1963.

32. Articles in *Die Zeit* (NA), February 15, March 3, 22, 1963. Similar points were made by Kurt Becker in *Die Welt,* March 3, May 10, 24, 1963.

33. For a good review of the conservative press, see *Le Monde,* March 8, 1963; *NYT,* April 11, 1963; *NZZ,* May 8, 1963. Cf. also Marian Grafin Donhoff's analysis in *Die Zeit* (NA), April 12, 1963.

34. *Die Welt,* January 22, 1963.

35. *Ibid.,* June 10, 1963. This was Strauss's first public statement on security questions since his forced departure from the Defense Ministry and the government. See also *Die Welt,* May 1, 1963.

36. Cf. Steinbruner, "MLF," chapter 1, sections 8 and 9. Steinbruner reports that although Kennedy adopted a laissez-faire attitude toward the debate on the MLF and other force proposals, he could never quite believe that once the Germans understood the immutability of the American veto for the foreseeable future, they would be willing to assume such a large financial share for so little incremental sharing of control. Kennedy was not forced to make a final decision about an MLF or any other sharing formula, but he seemed to expect the survival of such a veto until creation of a single voice in Europe—presumably a president of the United States of Europe.

37. English text in *Bulletin* (Eng.), June 16, 1964.

38. Interview in *Christ und Welt,* October 23, 1963.

39. Cf. Geyelin, *Lyndon Johnson,* 160.

40. *Multilateral Force,* 9.

41. They were not the only "target audience," of course; others included legislators, party officials, business leaders, communicators, and interested intellectuals. One striking case of conversion was that of Theo Sommer, who in November, 1963, presented a long detailed defense of the MLF as a valuable and significant "clamp for the Alliance." See his *Die Zeit* articles cited in n. 2.

42. Cf. Theodore Sorensen's discussion in his *Kennedy* (New York: Bantam, 1966), 818–26.

43. See the related points raised by Fritz Erler during the second reading of the test-ban treaty in *Verhandlungen,* January 22, 1963, 4934, and in his introduction to David Mark's enlightening *Die Einstellung der Kernwaffenversuche* (Frankfurt/Main: Metzner, 1965).

44. See *Economist,* August 10, 24, 1963; *Die Zeit* (NA), August 16, 23, 1963.

45. *Die Zeit* (NA), August 16, 1963; *Die Welt,* August 19, 1963. Cf. *NYT,* October 1, 1963; and remarks by CDU Deputy Johan Gradl during the final reading of the treaty in *Verhandlungen,* June 5, 1964, 6264.

46. By what seems to have been a coincidence, Washington almost simultaneously announced the withdrawal of 40,000 troops, mobilized during the Berlin emergency in 1961, and the start of Big Lift, an exercise demonstrating the rapid air transport of a division from the United States to Europe. Big Lift was not the first such exercise. Its predecessor, Operation Long Thrust, carried out in January, 1962, had occasioned similar fears and criticisms; *FAZ,* January 16, 1962. Cf. "Big Lift," *Wehrkunde,* October, 1963, 619–20; *Die Welt,* October 22, 28, 1963; *NZZ,* October 27, 1963; *Economist,* October 26, November 19, 1963; above, 212, 243.

47. Above, 204–6.

48. Cf. the statement by Richard Jaeger, CSU deputy and chairman of the Bundestag Defense Committee, cited in NZZ, November 29, 1963.

49. See, for example, Pierre Uri's argument in *Le Monde,* February 26, 1963.

50. *Bulletin,* January 24, 1963. Lebel was the chief press secretary of the French Foreign Office. See also a related statement by Maurice Couve de Murville to the National Assembly on January 24, in the *Speeches* series, no. 186 (New York: Ambassade de France, Service de Presse et d'Information, 1963) [hereafter cited as *Speeches*].

51. Some of the more publicized signals included a statement by Minister of Information Alan Peyrefitte, *NYT,* March 20, 1963; an article by Defense Minister Pierre Messmer, "Notre

Politique Militaire,'' in *Revue de défense nationale,* May, 1963, translated in the *French Affairs* series, no. 155 (New York: Ambassade de France, Service de Presse et d'Information, 1963), especially p. 12; speech of Michel Habib-Deloncle, Secretary of State for Foreign Affairs, to the European Consultative Assembly, *Speeches,* no. 194, 1963, especially p. 4); the remarks of General Gallois to the *Wehrkunde* conference in Munich, cited in *Le Monde,* December 3, 1963. For a detailed discussion of all Franco-German nuclear-control probes during this period, see Wilfrid L. Kohl, *French Nuclear Diplomacy* (Princeton: Princeton University Press, 1971), chapter 7; and John Newhouse, *De Gaulle and the Anglo-Saxons* (New York: Viking, 1970).

52. Cited in *Die Welt,* July 24, 1963.

53. See, in particular, Erhard's Bundestag speech on January 9, 1963, *Verhandlungen,* 4842–46.

54. *Die Welt,* March 8, July 10, 1963; *NZZ,* July 11, 1963. Cf. *FAZ,* February 1, 1964; and Erhard's interview with the Bonn *General Anzeiger,* quoted in the *World Journal Tribune,* March 7, 1967, and in *NZZ,* March 8, 1967.

CHAPTER X. GERMANY AND THE MLF; THE DOWNSLOPE: 1964–1966

1. See, for example, the McNamara-von Hassel communiqué, *New York Times* [*NYT*], November 15, 1964; and the Rusk-Schröder communiqué, *NYT,* November 27, 1964.

2. Rusk-Schröder communiqué, *NYT,* November 27, 1964.

3. *Economist,* July 11, 1964. See also F. Roy Willis, *France, Germany and the New Europe* (Stanford: Stanford University Press, 1965), 318–20; *Le Monde,* July 7, 1964; *NYT,* July 10, 1967. See also Waldemar Besson, *Die Aussenpolitik der Bundesrepublik* (Munich: Piper, 1970).

4. Somewhat contradictory contemporary press reports regarding this conversation were given in *Economist,* August 1, 1964, and *NYT,* August 31, 1964. Interviews gathered for this study are on the whole congruent with the findings reported in Wilfred L. Kohl, *French Nuclear Diplomacy* (Princeton: Princeton University Press, 1971), chapter 7.

5. *NYT,* July 9, 10, 1964; *Economist,* July 18, 1964.

6. See *Economist,* August 8, September 26, 1964.

7. *NYT,* October 7, 1964. A number of respondents alleged that Erhard's statement was the result of a slip, that he misunderstood a Foreign Office memorandum regarding an unofficial stance to be taken vis-à-vis the reluctant allies. A few suggested that this indeed had been the meaning of the pledges cited in n. 1.

8. Guttenberg's remarks are in Federal Republic of Germany, Bundestag, *Verhandlungen: Stenographische Berichte,* 6892–93 [hereafter cited as *Verhandlungen*]; Strauss's in *Verhandlungen,* 6828–30. For other related comments, see Erler's statement on the same day, *Verhandlungen,* 6901; the analysis of *Economist,* October 17, 1964; and Franz Josef Strauss, ''An Alliance of Continents,'' *International Affairs* (London), April, 1965, 191–203.

9. For further details on this and subsequent developments in October and November, 1964, see *L'Année Politique 1964* (Paris: Presse Universitaires de France, 1965), 293–99, 300–11.

10. *Ibid.,* 301.

11. *Ibid.,* 302.

12. *Ibid.*, 311.

13. Couve de Murville reportedly pursued a similar line of argument at the North Atlantic Council meeting in December. Interview reports indicate that the German Gaullists were easy targets for such an approach, because of their militant anti-Communist stance.

14. Response during Bundestag question hour, quoted in *NYT*, November 13, 1964.

15. For account of the SPD convention and the abortive attempt to get acceptance of a party declaration supporting the MLF, see *NYT*, November 23, 1964.

16. The British proposal had been the subject of special talks in London. See Alastair Buchan, *The Multilateral Force: A Historical Perspective*, Adelphi Papers, no. 13 (London: Institute for Strategic Studies, 1964), 10–11.

17. *NYT*, March 4, 1964.

18. In C. L. Sulzberger's column, *NYT*, March 4, 1964.

19. Cf. *NYT*, October 19, 24, 27, 1964.

20. Speech of November 23, 1964, quoted in *New York Herald-Tribune*, November 29, 1964.

21. See, for example, Rusk's speech upon the return of the *Ricketts* (*NYT*, October 21, 1964), the McNamara-von Hassel communiqué (*NYT*, November 15, 1964); and two statements by Ball (NYT, November 16, 17, 1964).

22. *NYT*, November 16, 1964.

23. Cf. statements by senators Fulbright and Javits, *NYT*, November 20, 1964.

24. Cf. statement by Chairman Chet Holifield, *NYT*, December 1, 1964.

25. *NYT*, November 29, 1964.

26. *NYT*, December 4, 1964.

27. For other evidence, see Philip Geyelin, *Lyndon B. Johnson and the World* (New York: Praeger, 1966), 171–72.

28. *NYT*, December 21, 1964; Geyelin, *Johnson and World*, 171–72.

29. Interview probing with both Foreign Office and Defense Ministry officials at that time elicited no basic justification for the Germans' particular numbers other than the obvious fact that they were fewer than twenty-five.

30. *NYT*, June 1, 1965. See also chapter 7. Cf. Erhard's reported comments during his June visit to Washington, *NYT*, June 5, 1965.

31. Interview in *Dusseldorfer Nachrichten* on July 3, 1965, excerpted in *Europa Archiv*, 15/1965, D. 384ff, and discussed in *NYT*, July 4, 13, 1965.

32. See, for example, *NYT*, July 2, October 23, 1964.

33. *Neue Zürcher Zeitung* [NZZ], December 18, 1963; *Die Welt*, December 19, 1963. According to *Frankfurter Allgemeine Zeitung* [FAZ], January 3, 1964, Schröder and Erhard had discussed this position with Johnson during their December visit to the United States.

34. "New Direction in Arms Control and Disarmament," *Foreign Affairs*, July, 1965, 587–601.

35. *NYT*, June 24, 1965.

36. *NYT*, July 1, 1965.

37. *Sunday Times* (London), for example, reported that Germany wished to buy nuclear weapons; quoted in *Die Welt,* July 13, 1965.

38. Quoted in *NYT,* August 18, 1965. Italics added.

39. Reports regarding Germany's growing uneasiness and displeasure (*Die Welt,* August 19, 23, 25, 30, 1965; *FAZ,* August 11, 19, 1965) only faintly reflected the sentiments expressed in contemporaneous interviews.

40. *Die Welt,* August 20, 1965; *Der Spiegel,* September 1, 1965, 19, 21. It was in this connection that Adenauer himself first publicly mentioned the conditional or *rebus sic stantibus* clause to the 1954 renunciation of nuclear weapons; see chapter 1.

41. *Rheinischer Merkur,* August 26, 1965; see also *Die Welt,* August 23, 1965. Strauss's explicit reference to another Hitler ignored one of the taboos of political discourse in the Federal Republic.

42. *Die Welt,* August 30, 1965.

43. Contemporaneous interview comments indicated that Erhard felt that to assure maximum attention a German initiative had to be launched before the next round of Soviet-American nonproliferation negotiations. A further consideration was that the initiative must occur before the McNamara Committee became an "entrenched solution" or a de facto settlement.

44. See, for example, C. L. Sulzberger in *NYT,* October 29, 1965; *NYT,* November 17, 1965; *Christian Science Monitor,* November 24, 1965. French officials reportedly no longer merely castigated Germans for their "non-European" outlook or alluded vaguely to the eventual creation of a "European" force. In numerous private conversations with Western as well as Eastern visitors, they purportedly accused the Germans of seeking access to nuclear weapons in order to force reunification and the return of the territories east of the Oder-Neisse line. This, a number of respondents were forcefully told, France (together with the Soviet Union and the Eastern European states) would never allow.

45. Press conference of President de Gaulle on February 4, 1965, in the *Speeches* series, no. 216 (New York: Ambassade de France, Service de Presse et d'Information, 1965). The General was perhaps more direct when during Gromyko's visit to Paris in the spring of 1965 he stressed the mutual interest of France and Russia, as nuclear "continental" powers, in a non-nuclear Germany, echoing the earlier remarks to Adenauer reported in chapter 5.

46. Press conference of September 9, 1965, quoted in *NYT,* September 10, 1965.

47. *Politique Etrangère,* 3/1965, translated as "Must We Reform NATO?" in *Survival,* January, 1966, 2–8, and discussed in *NYT,* October 17, 1965.

48. Cf. *Der Spiegel,* November 10, 1965, 28; Geyelin, *Johnson,* 174–80.

49. Cf. *Die Zeit,* October 15, 1965; *Die Welt,* October 27, 1965.

50. According to one knowledgeable respondent, the opposition came from a mixed group: President Heinrich Lübke, incoming Interior Minister Paul Lucke, and chancellor advisor Ludwig Westrick, as well as Strauss and Heinrich Krone. All were hardly Schröder partisians.

51. The *Bulletin* (official English-language publication of the Press and Information Office of the Federal Government), November 16, 1965.

52. Cf. the views advanced by the SPD's Fritz Erler and, in part, by Foreign Minister Schröder in the Bundestag debate of late 1965 in *FAZ,* November 30, December 1, 1965.

53. Representative variations on this third theme include Theo Sommer, "Das nukleare Dilemma," *Die Zeit,* November 26, 1965; Uwe Nerlich, "The Nuclear Dilemmas of the Federal Republic of Germany (manuscript, 1966), especially 12–31; and Helmut Schmidt's remarks in the Bundestag debate of late 1965, *FAZ,* December 1, 1965.

54. Schmidt advanced this argument before the Bundestag (*FAZ,* December 1, 1965) and received somewhat surprising support from Franz Josef Strauss, who declared the guarantee of a "negative veto" to be Germany's most pressing goal in the Atlantic sphere (*ibid.*). Cf. Uwe Nerlich's critical appraisal of this concept in his "Nuclear Dilemmas," 13. Most of the German elites interviewed, however, believed such an arrangement to be impractical if not impossible. As one knowledgeable military commentator remarked sarcastically during a contemporaneous interview: "They're essentially asking for the right to preemptive surrender. If that's what they really want, why not do what's been discussed in England—make the American battalions the first target?"

55. For further information, see Strauss's statement in the Bundestag (*FAZ,* December 1, 1965); and his *The Grand Design* (New York: Praeger, 1966), especially chapters 3 and 4.

56. Cf. *Der Spiegel,* December 15, 1965, 33; *NYT,* December 31, 1965.

57. Text quoted in *NYT,* December 22, 1965.

58. For a report of similar findings during the summer and fall of 1964, see Lewis J. Edinger, "Patterns of German Elite Opinion," in Karl W. Deutsch, Lewis J. Edinger, Roy C. Macridis, and Richard L. Merritt, *France, Germany and the Western Alliance* (New York: Scribner, 1967), especially 142–153; and Daniel Lerner and Morton Gorden, *Euratlantica* (Cambridge: MIT Press, 1969). Alastair Buchan mentions a related personal observation in his *Multilateral Force,* 9.

59. This is Alastair Buchan's argument in his "Nassau Reconsidered," *New Republic,* March 2, 1963, 23.

CHAPTER XI. COMMENTARY: 1954–1966

1. This chapter owes much of its logic and clarity to the probing questions and suggestions of William T. R. Fox and Warner R. Schilling.

2. Although explicitly outside the scope of this study, this device almost surely will be of more limited utility in the 1970s given: deliberate changes in superpower policy, such as controlled Japanese development under the often discussed pentagonal concept; a critical and increasingly problematical bunching of just-under-the-threshold states; the improbable but still possible evolution of new regional arrangements like a joint European force, which still would have to devise a legitimate role for Germany.

3. A related but somewhat different classification can be found in two recent works: Marshall Singer, *Weak States in a World of Powers* (New York: Free Press, 1972); and Steven L. Spiegel, *Dominance and Diversity: The International Hierarchy* (Boston: Little, Brown, 1972). A somewhat longer list might be drawn by relaxing the criteria of a major member of an alliance (bearing more than a 25 percent share of burden after subtraction of the superpower's share) or a major regional power (possessing more than 30 percent of the total available military capability). It would then include some or all of the following: Argentina, Mexico, Belgium, Netherlands, Spain, and Israel. A second major constraint is specification of a semiautonomous national-security decision-making process; otherwise, Czechoslovakia, East Germany, and Poland might be included.

4. For a somewhat more extended discussion on this, see Samuel P. Huntington, "Arms Races: Prerequisites and Results," in *Public Policy,* ed. Carl J. Friedrich and Seymour Harris (Cambridge: Harvard University Press, 1958), 41–68. For interesting recent efforts to assess the increasing British and French shortfalls and abortive attempts at technological one-upmanship, see Spiegel, *Dominance and Diversity,* 61–70; Wilfrid L. Kohl, *French Nuclear Diplomacy* (Princeton: Princeton University Press, 1971); and Andrew Pierre, *Nuclear Politics* (New York: Oxford University Press, 1972).

5. This would certainly follow from the much-cited analytic framework suggested by James H. Rosenau in his "Pre-theories and Theories of Foreign Policy," in *Approaches to Comparative and International Politics,* ed. R. Barry Farrell (Evanston: Northwestern University Press, 1966), 27–92.

CHAPTER XII. A LOOK FORWARD

1. For two converging statements on this phenomenon, see Edward L. Morse, "Crisis Diplomacy, Interdependence, and the Politics of International Economic Relations," in *Theory and Policy in International Relations,* ed. Raymond Tanter and Richard H. Ullman (Princeton: Princeton University Press, 1972), 123–50; and Alastair Buchan, "The End of Bipolarity," in *The Super-Powers and the Context,* part 1, *East Asia and the World System,* Adelphi Papers, no. 91 (London: International Institute for Strategic Studies, 1972), 21–30.

2. See Catherine M. Kelleher and Donald J. Puchala, "Germany, European Security, and Arms Control," in *European Security and the Atlantic System,* ed. William T. R. Fox and Warner R. Schilling (New York: Columbia University Press, 1973), 157–96. Other perspectives are ably presented in Laurence L. Whetten's encyclopedic *Germany's Ostpolitik* (New York: Oxford University Press, 1971), and Roger Morgan's broad-ranging "West-East Relations in Europe: Political Perspectives," *International Affairs* (London), April, 1973, 177–89.

3. Brandt had to overcome sabotage-by-leak almost continually from 1966 to 1974. Internal memos on negotiation positions, preparatory draft treaties, even telephone-call transcripts with the East have unerringly found their way into the conservative Springer press (*Die Welt* especially) or into the regional newspapers that are under CSU protection. The short-run effect always has been a flurry of cries of betrayal, followed by bureaucratic investigation, followed by no punitive action. In hindsight, such leaks may have enhanced the long-run effectiveness of Brandt's approach by both drawing opponents' fire early and demonstrating the government's determination to proceed whatever the criticism.

4. This nonmajority coalition led of course to the CDU's nearly successful attempt to force a no-confidence vote against Brandt in April 1972. Two CDU abstentions—one the focus of the so-called Steiner scandal of 1973—led to defeat of the motion and ultimately to the elections held in the autumn of 1972. Although the primary electoral issues turned on the state of the domestic economy, Brandt's victory was widely interpreted as a mandate for Ostpolitik.

5. Quoted in Mason Willrich (ed.), *Civil Nuclear Power and International Security* (New York: Praeger, 1971), 85.

6. For a further exposition of the author's views on the post-Cold War transformations in superpower relations, see Warner R. Schilling, William T. R. Fox, Catherine M. Kelleher, and Donald J. Puchala, *American Arms and a Changing Europe* (New York: Columbia University Press, 1973), especially chapters 1 and 3.

7. Philip Windsor arrived at similar conclusions in his *Germany and the Management of Detente* (London: Chatto & Windus [for the Institute for Strategic Studies], 1971).

8. Although several manuscripts are in progress, there is as yet no significant work describing the full course of the German debate or analyzing the NPT's importance in the redefinition of postwar foreign policy by any of the middle powers. A good overview of the treaty's development and impact on a number of near-nuclear states is contained in chapters 9 and 10 of the Stockholm International Peace Research Institute's *World Armaments and Disarmament: SIPRI Yearbook* (New York: Humanities Press, 1972) [hereafter cited as *SIPRI Yearbook*]. The details of the German case are at least introduced in Horst Menderhausen, "Will West Germany Go Nuclear?" *Orbis,* Summer, 1972, which is largely derived from the author's earlier analysis. Significant documents from the debate are contained in the official *Treaty on the Non-Proliferation of Nuclear Weapons: German Attitude and Contribution* (Bonn: Press and Information Office of the Federal Government, 1969). A clear statement of the CSU critique can be derived from Marcel Hepp, *Der Atomsperrvertrag: Die Supermächte verteilen die Welt* (Stuttgart: Seewald, 1968).

9. Interviews conducted in Germany in 1968 identified December, 1966, through March, 1967, as the time of maximum outrage and semisincere anger within official circles. Several respondents argued that articles and statements made during this time—as for example Wilhelm Grewe's outspoken "Über den Einfluss der Kernwaffen auf die Politik," *Europa Archiv,* February 10, 1967 should therefore be interpreted only as "heated reactions of the moment."

10. This evaluation was offered spontaneously by both German and American officials interviewed in Washington, Bonn, and Brussels in 1968. Those Americans associated with arms control efforts tended to regard this development with some suspicion and disfavor. On the other hand, military men and some State Department officials tended to view this as a welcome sign of long-delayed maturity.

11. See on this point two articles in *Foreign Affairs,* April, 1972: Herbert Scoville, "Beyond SALT One," and Walter F. Hahn, "Nuclear Balance in Europe." Some of the most informative writing on MBFR has been done by Christoph Bertram in his *Mutual Force Reductions in Europe: the Political Aspect,* Adelphi Papers, no. 84 (London: International Institute for Strategic Studies, 1972), and in his "The Politics of MBFR," *The World Today,* January, 1973, 1–7; and by John N. Yochelson in his "MBFR: The Search for an American Approach," *Orbis,* Spring 1973, and his "MBFR: West European and American Perspectives, mimeographed, Cambridge, Mass., 1974.

12. Two valuable sources on the NPG are Harry George Harris's dissertation (based in part on his own official role), "The Special Committee of NATO Defense Ministers: A Study of Political Consultation in the Atlantic Alliance," (Ph.D. diss., Harvard University, January, 1970); and Thomas C. Wiegele's more general "Nuclear Consultation Processes in NATO," *Orbis,* Summer, 1972.

13. See, for example, Harris's discussion of the ADM report of 1966–1967 in "Special Committee," 208–12; and of the joint British-German tactical-guidelines and threshold-specification study of May–November, 1969 in *ibid.,* 243–56.

14. Although clearly subject to private disclaimer or later revision, the official German position is that contained in the Defense White Papaer of 1970 (English ed. [Bonn: Defense Ministry, 1970], 41), namely, that Bonn has "fully adequate means of representing German interests in consultation on the possible release of nuclear weapons."

15. For an assessment of the crucial role of Schmidt and the SPD in this process, see Helmut Schmidt, *The Balance of Power* (London: Weidenfelt & Nicolson, 1970); and the background information collected in Udo F. Lowke, *Für den Fall, dass: Die Haltung der SPD zur Wehrfrage, 1945–1955* (Hannover: Verlag für Literatur und Zeitgeschehen, 1969).

16. The first (1969) was prepared under Schröder's tenure in the Defense Ministry; the next two were prepared at Schmidt's order by the newly created Plannungstab first chaired by Theo Sommer and later by Hans Georg Wieck.

17. 1970 Defense White Paper, English edition, 42.

18. The 1972–73 report of the Defense Force Structure Committee, however, clearly suggests that this will not be possible. See *The Force Structure in the Federal Republic of Germany: Analysis and Options,* English ed. (Bonn: Defense Ministry, 1973), especially 106–27; or the excellent summary of the paper published in *Survival,* January–February, 1973, 35–38.

19. Cf., however, the similar conclusion reached in *SIPRI Yearbook,* and by Mendershausen, "Germany Go Nuclear?" with the more pessimistic view based on technological grounds alone offered semiseriously in Walter B. Wentz, *Nuclear Proliferation* (Washington: Public Affairs Press, 1968), 28–30.

20. Similar questions were posed in 1967–1969 by the now dormant National Democratic Party (NDP), which on far more nationalistic grounds advocated Bundeswehr rejection of all American influences and control. Virtually the only treatment of this is Rudolph H. Brandt, *Die Militärpolitik der NPD* (Stuttgart: Seewald, 1969). Nuclear abstinence has from time to time also attracted support from within the CDU; see, for example, von Wrangel's statement in Olaf von Wrangel and Dieter Schwarzkopf (eds.), *Chancen für Deutschland* (Hamburg: Hoffman un Kampfe, 1965), 101–5.

21. The literature on Europeanization has reached a substantial if not always serious level. Perhaps the best is still Ian Smart, *Future Conditional: The Prospect for Anglo–French Nuclear Cooperation,* Adelphi Papers, no. 78 (London: International Institute for Strategic Studies, 1971). See more recently Bernard Burrows and Christopher Irwin, *The Security of Western Europe* (London: Charles Knight, 1972); *Towards Nuclear Entente* (London: Conservative Political Centre, 1970); Andrew Pierre, "Nuclear Diplomacy: Britain, France, and America," *Foreign Affairs,* January, 1971; and the special issue of *The Round Table* on this subject in April, 1972, 139–98.

22. The reader is invited to try the calculations for himself on the basis of the technical data available in the latest edition of the International Institute of Strategic Studies, *The Military Balance,* and of the calculation methods so clearly presented in Lynn E. Davis and Warner R. Schilling, "All You Ever Wanted to Know about MIRV and ICBM Calculations but Were Not Cleared to Ask," *Journal of Conflict Resolution,* June 1973. For comparison, the reader might check his figures against the pre-SALT calculations of Geoffry Kemp and Ian Smart in their "SALT and European Nuclear Forces" in *SALT: Implications for Arms Control in the 1970's,* ed. William R. Kintner and Robert L. Pfaltzgraff (Pittsburgh: University of Pittsburgh Press, 1973), 199–235.

23. Strauss's best exposition of his "nuclear triangle" scheme was contained in his *The Grand Design* (New York: Praeger, 1966); his later *Challenge and Response* (New York: Atheneum, 1970) contains little new. Far more representative of current CDU centrist thinking is Walter Leisler Kiep's low-key treatment in *Good-bye Amerika—was dann?* (Stuttgart: Seewald, 1972), 164–70, which declares a continued American guarantee to be a sine qua non for German security.

24. See, for example, Gerda Zellentin's argument in her *Europa 1985* (Bonn: Europa Union, 1972).

25. See Brandt's own statement on this in his article "Germany's 'Westpolitik,' "

Foreign Affairs, April, 1972, and Helmut Schmidt's related piece, "Germany in the Era of Negotiations," *Foreign Affairs,* October, 1970.

26. See, for example, the broad overview prepared for a specific target audience in R[obert] Ball, "Rethinking the Defense of Europe," *Fortune,* February, 1973, 60ff.

27. Perhaps the best brief view of the various Japanese scenarios is Wayne Wilcox's insightful "Japanese and Indian National Security Strategies in the Asia of the 1970's: The Prospect for Nuclear Proliferation," in *The Regional Powers,* part 2, *East Asia and the World System,* Adelphi Papers, no. 92 (London: International Institute of Strategic Studies, 1972). A somewhat fanciful application to the German case, foreseeing possible French and/or Soviet donations as well, can be found in Mendershausen, "Germany Go Nuclear?" 429–32.

28. See the comparative statistics given for the other near-nuclear states in *SIPRI Yearbook,* 296–97 as well as the somewhat earlier estimates contained in the expert report of the Secretary-General of the United Nations, *Effects of the Possible Use of Nuclear Weapons and the Security and Economic Implications for States of the Acquisition and Further Development of These Weapons* (New York: United Nations, 1968).

29. *SIPRI Yearbook,* 338.

30. See, for example, the statements by Dr. Peter Jelinek, a member of the responsible advisory board, on the timing of the British-Dutch-German joint gas centrifuge development project in Willrich, *Civil Nuclear Power,* 33, 39.

31. See a report in the *Süddeutsche Zeitung,* November 22, 1968, cited in Mendershausen, "Germany Go Nuclear?" 426.

32. The SIPRI treatment in the 1972 *Yearbook* is perhaps a start toward more popular re-examination of the all-too-widespread simplistic assumptions on this issue. *SIPRI Yearbook,* 288–98, 375–88.

33. See Uwe Nerlich's reasoning along similar lines in his "Nuclear Weapons and European Politics: Some Structural Interdependencies" in *Security, Order, and the Bomb,* ed. Johan J. Holst (Oslo: Universitetsforlaget, 1972), 47–92.

APPENDIX: SOURCES

1. See the descriptions of the interviewing technique used for this panel that are given at various points throughout Daniel Lerner and Morton Gorden, *Euratlantica* (Cambridge: MIT Press, 1969). The author's involvement in the Lerner project throughout her graduate career contributed immeasurably to her understanding of the foreign policy of European states.

2. The reference is to the project headed by Karl Deutsch and reported on in Karl W. Deutsch, Lewis J. Edinger, Roy C. Macridis, and Richard L. Merritt, *France, Germany and the Western Alliance* (New York: Wiley, 1967).

3. Invaluable advice as well as generous hospitality was offered here by the late Wilhelm Cornides, then director of the Gesellschaft, by Uwe Nerlich, head of the Forschungsinstitut, by Helga Haftendorn, a research associate of the Institute, and by all the Gesellschaft staff.

4. The Institute's final conclusions stemming from a study made under contract with ACDA, were reported in two volumes: William T. R. Fox and Warner R. Schilling (eds.), *European Security and the Atlantic System* (New York: Columbia University Press, 1973) and Warner R. Schilling, William T. R. Fox, Catherine M. Kelleher, and Donald J. Puchala, *American Arms and a Changing Europe* (New York: Columbia University Press, 1973).

5. A person who was most helpful in establishing contacts reported to the author—only half in jest—that the two most frequent questions asked by potential German respondents were: ''Does she work for the CIA? Are you sure she's not working for *Der Spiegel?*'' The outcry which surrounded Project Camelot did make contacts more suspicious, however.

6. Principally this was true of interviews conducted a long distance from Bonn or with retired officials or military men.

7. Some of the common components concerned historical events—EDC, the Radford crisis, the Athens council meeting, the MLF—in an effort to ascertain the information level of the respondent and his political position. Most, however, focused on specific historically defined issues or relationships within the German decision-making process.

INDEX

Wehner, Herbert, 114
Weinstein, Adalbert, 37, 142, 216
Weizsäcker, Carl Friedrich von, 12-13
Welt, Die, 212
Western European Union (WEU): established, 22-23; and arms controls, 27, 105, 181, 221, 229; report of, 84; Strauss addresses, 86, 140; with own deterrent, 146; Schröder addresses, 212; von Hassel addresses, 237

Wilson, Charles, 53
Wilson, Harold: opposes MLF, 246; and British nuclear force, 251; modifies MLF view, 252; discusses MLF with Johnson, 253-54; and ANF, 255; and German MLF participation, 275

Zeit, Die, 239